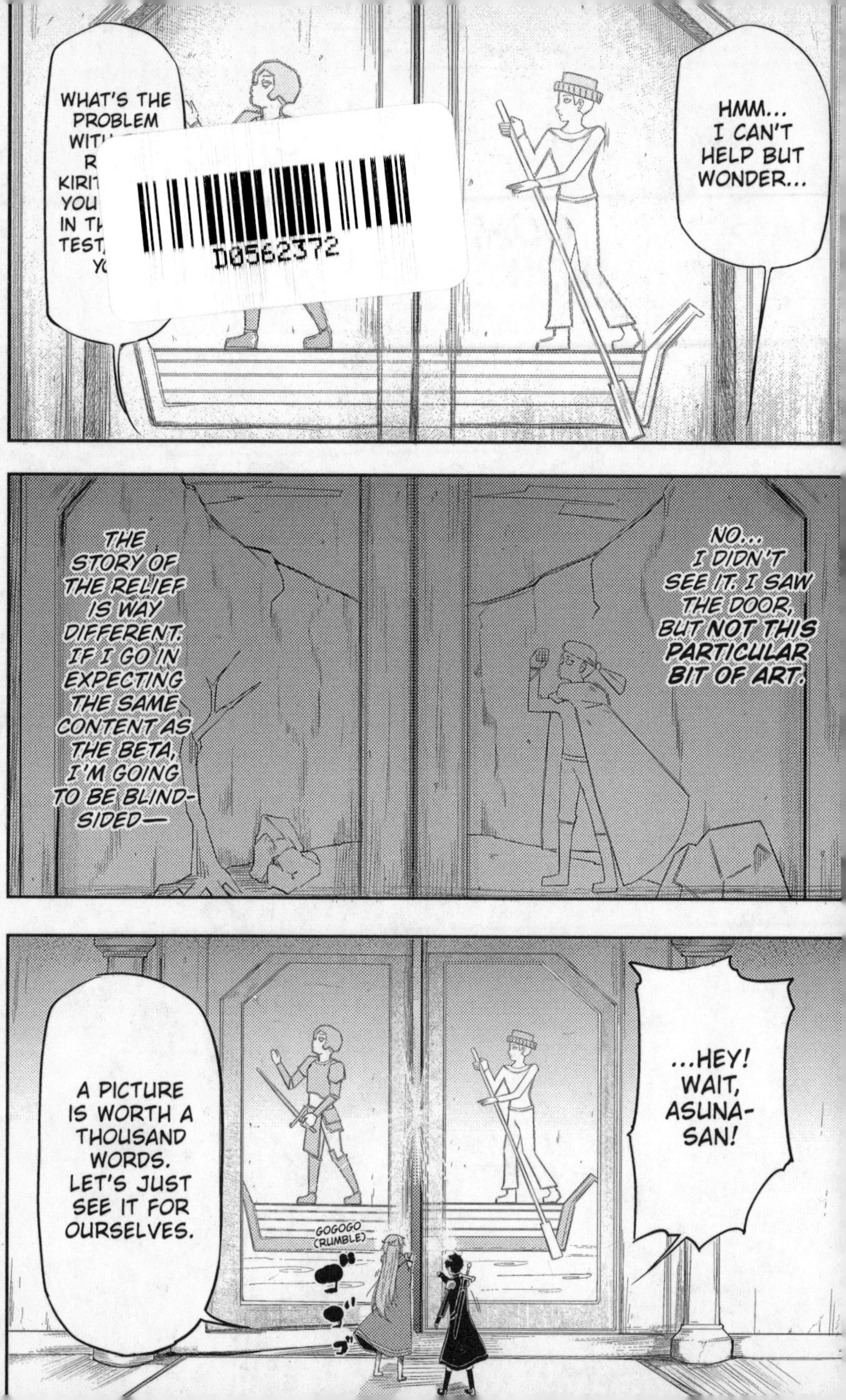
HMM... I CAN'T HELP BUT WONDER...
WHAT'S THE PROBLEM WITH
NO... I DIDN'T SEE IT. I SAW THE DOOR, BUT NOT THIS PARTICULAR BIT OF ART.
THE STORY OF THE RELIEF IS WAY DIFFERENT. IF I GO IN EXPECTING THE SAME CONTENT AS THE BETA, I'M GOING TO BE BLIND-SIDED—
...HEY! WAIT, ASUNA-SAN!
GOGOGO (RUMBLE)
A PICTURE IS WORTH A THOUSAND WORDS. LET'S JUST SEE IT FOR OURSELVES.

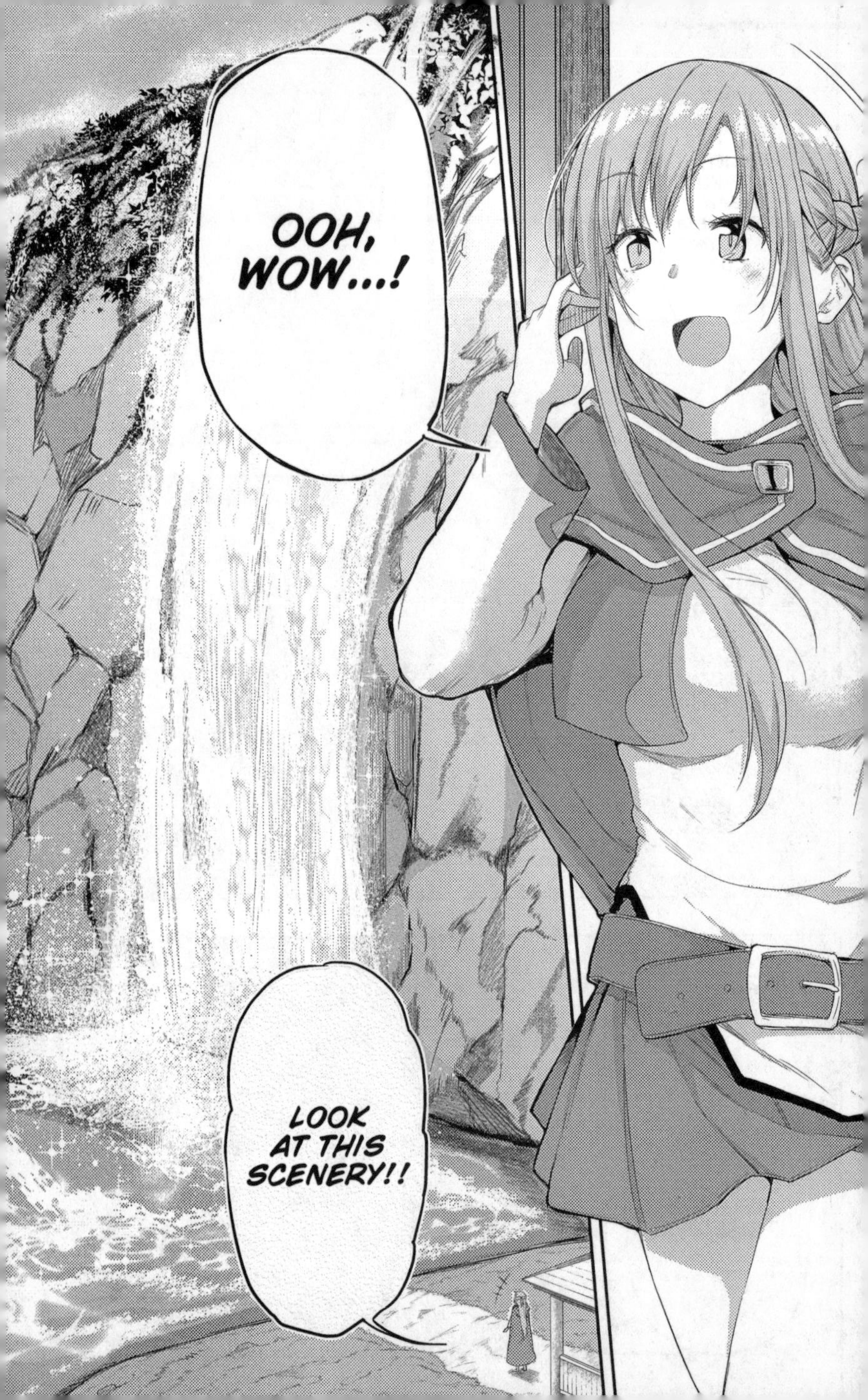
OOH, WOW...!
LOOK AT THIS SCENERY!!

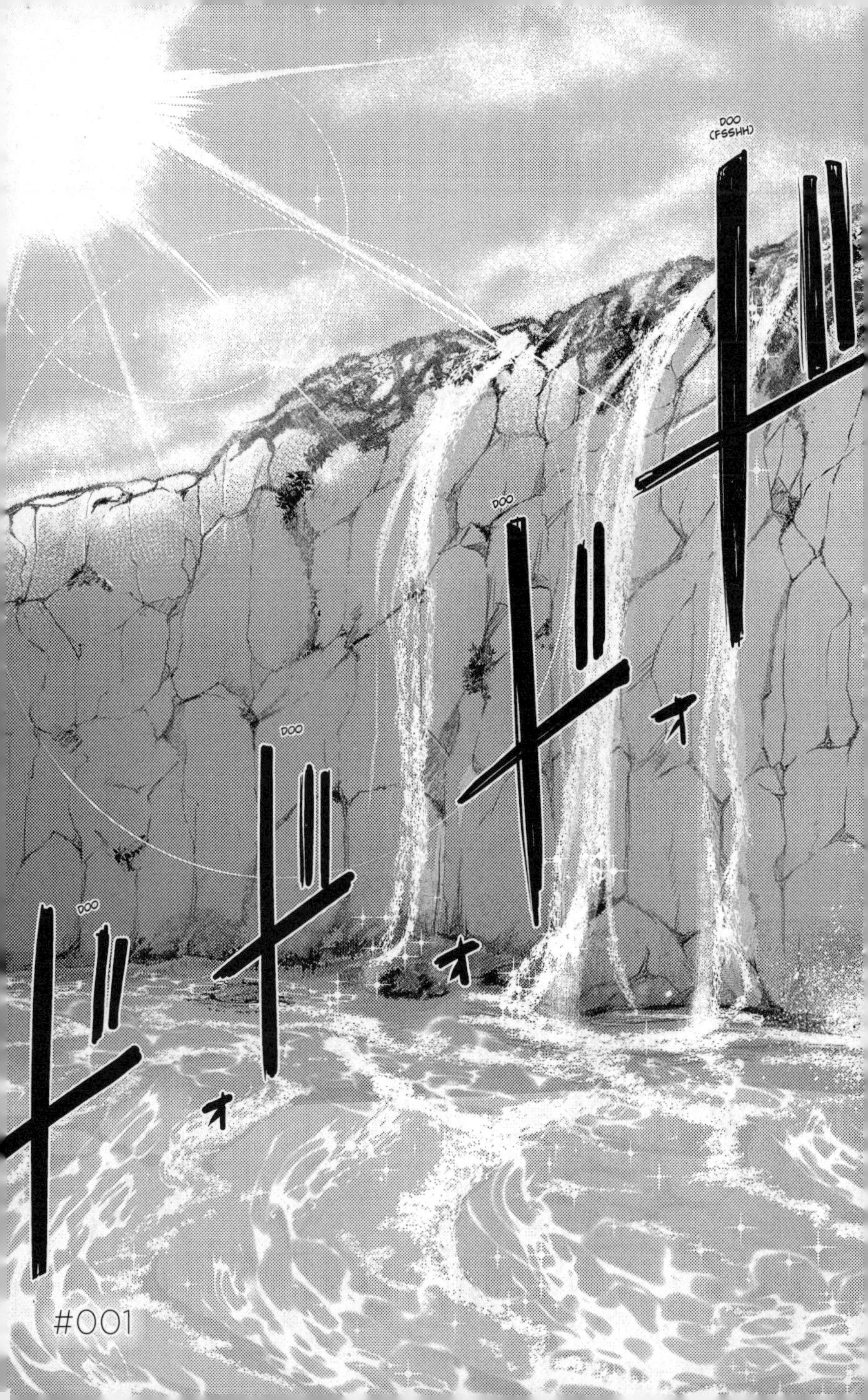
DOO (FSSHH)
ドォ
DOO
ドォ
DOO
ドォ
DOO
ドォ

#001

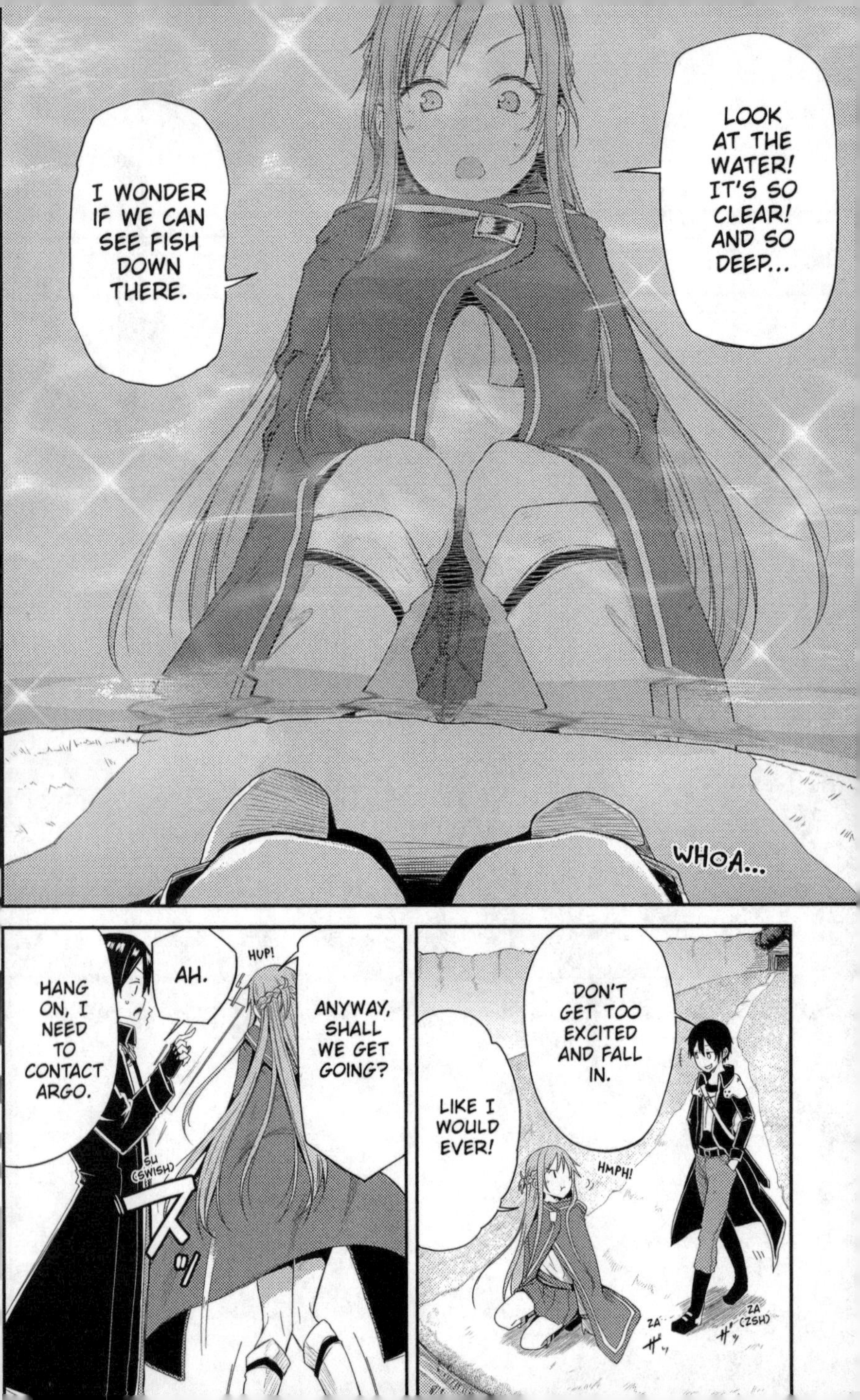
LOOK AT THE WATER! IT'S SO CLEAR! AND SO DEEP...
I WONDER IF WE CAN SEE FISH DOWN THERE.
WHOA...
DON'T GET TOO EXCITED AND FALL IN.
LIKE I WOULD EVER!
HMPH!
ZA (ZSH)
ZA
ANYWAY, SHALL WE GET GOING?
HUP!
AH.
HANG ON, I NEED TO CONTACT ARGO.
SU (SWISH)

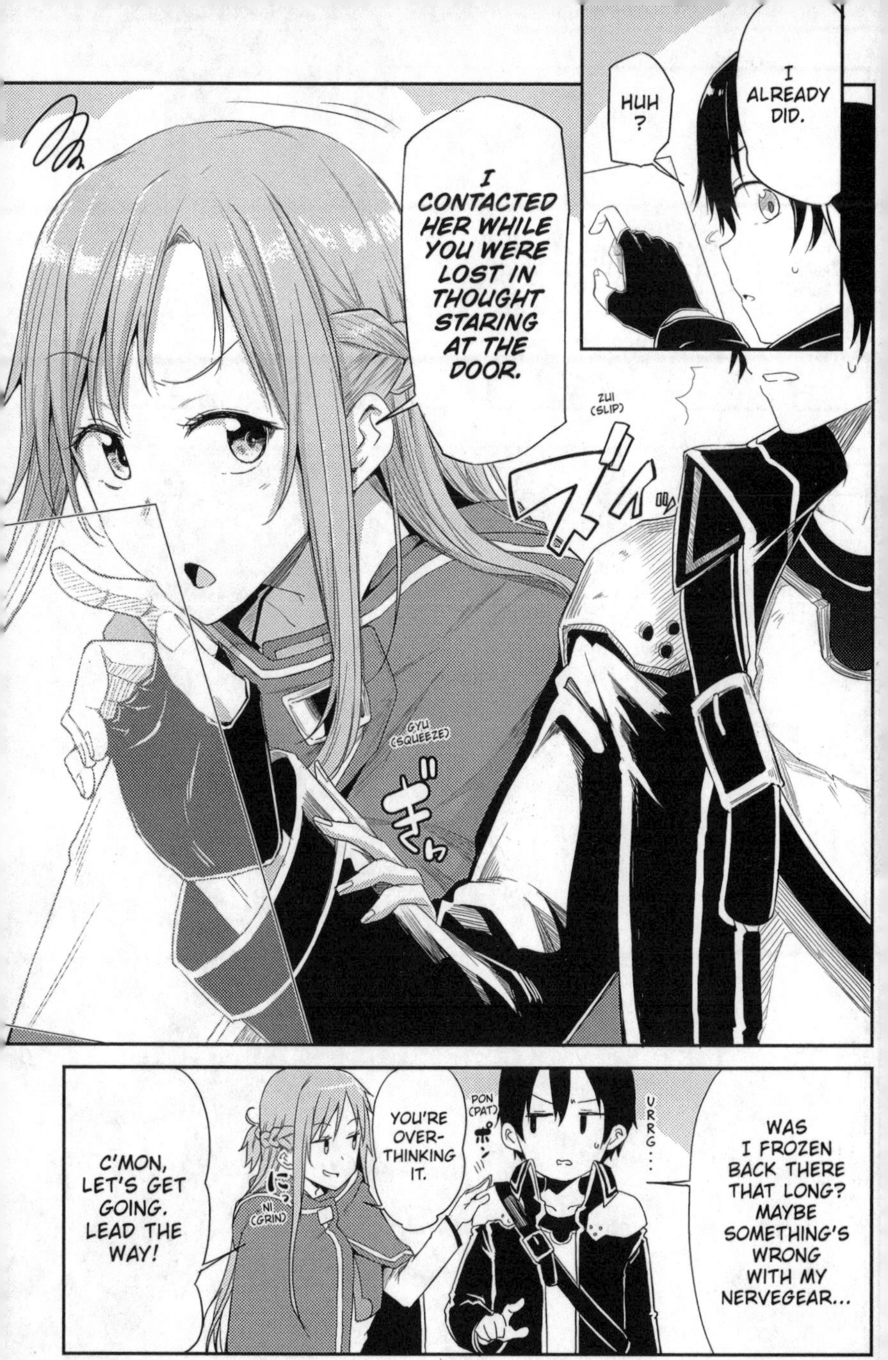
I ALREADY DID.
HUH?
I CONTACTED HER WHILE YOU WERE LOST IN THOUGHT STARING AT THE DOOR.
ZUI (SLIP)
GYU (SQUEEZE)
WAS I FROZEN BACK THERE THAT LONG? MAYBE SOMETHING'S WRONG WITH MY NERVEGEAR...
URRG...
PON (PAT)
YOU'RE OVER-THINKING IT.
NI (GRIN)
C'MON, LET'S GET GOING. LEAD THE WAY!

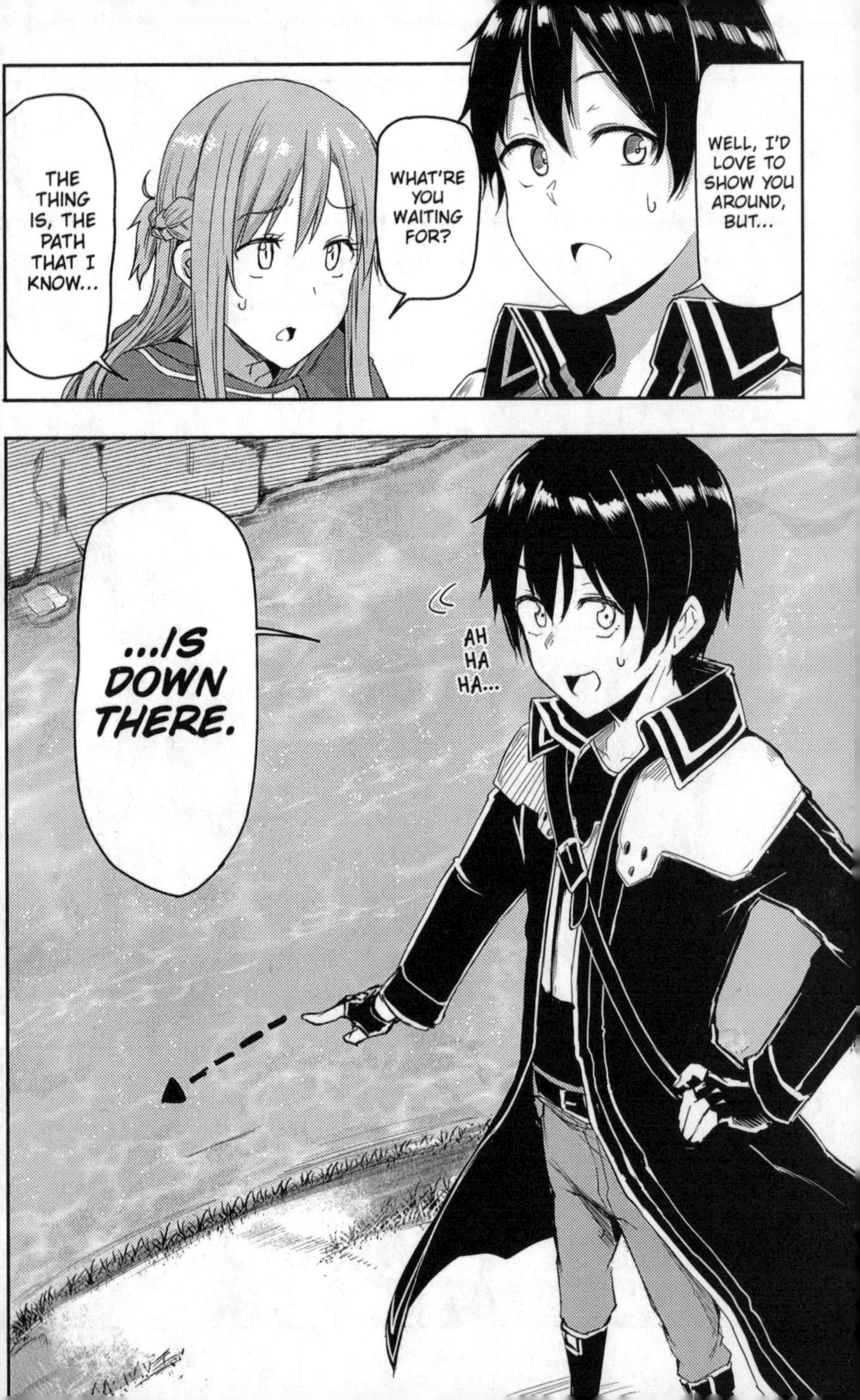
WELL, I'D LOVE TO SHOW YOU AROUND, BUT...
WHAT'RE YOU WAITING FOR?
THE THING IS, THE PATH THAT I KNOW...
...IS DOWN THERE.
AH HA HA...

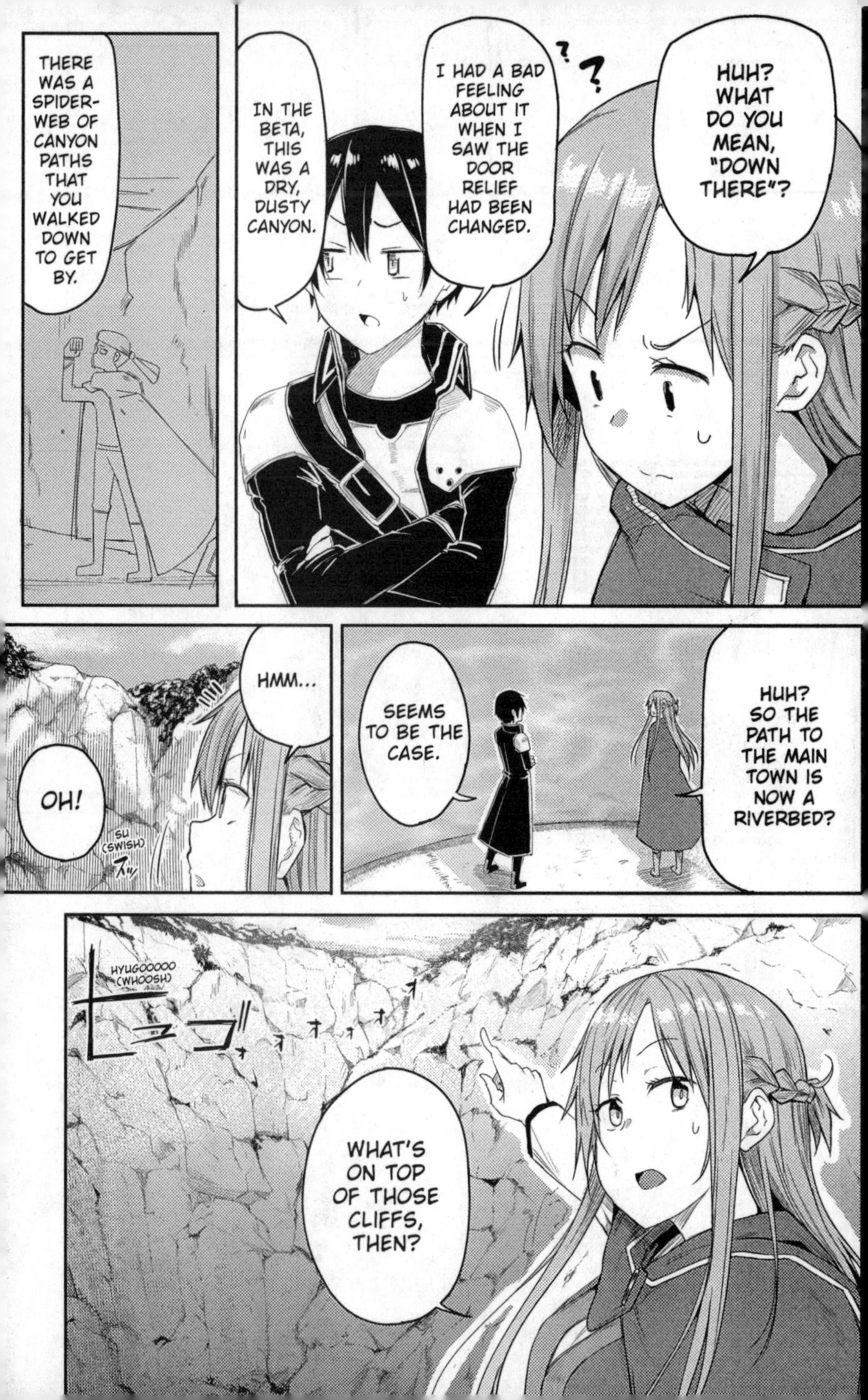

HUH? WHAT DO YOU MEAN, "DOWN THERE"?
??
I HAD A BAD FEELING ABOUT IT WHEN I SAW THE DOOR RELIEF HAD BEEN CHANGED.
IN THE BETA, THIS WAS A DRY, DUSTY CANYON.
THERE WAS A SPIDER-WEB OF CANYON PATHS THAT YOU WALKED DOWN TO GET BY.
HUH? SO THE PATH TO THE MAIN TOWN IS NOW A RIVERBED?
SEEMS TO BE THE CASE.
HMM...
OH!
SU (SWISH)
HYUGOOOOO (WHOOSH)
WHAT'S ON TOP OF THOSE CLIFFS, THEN?

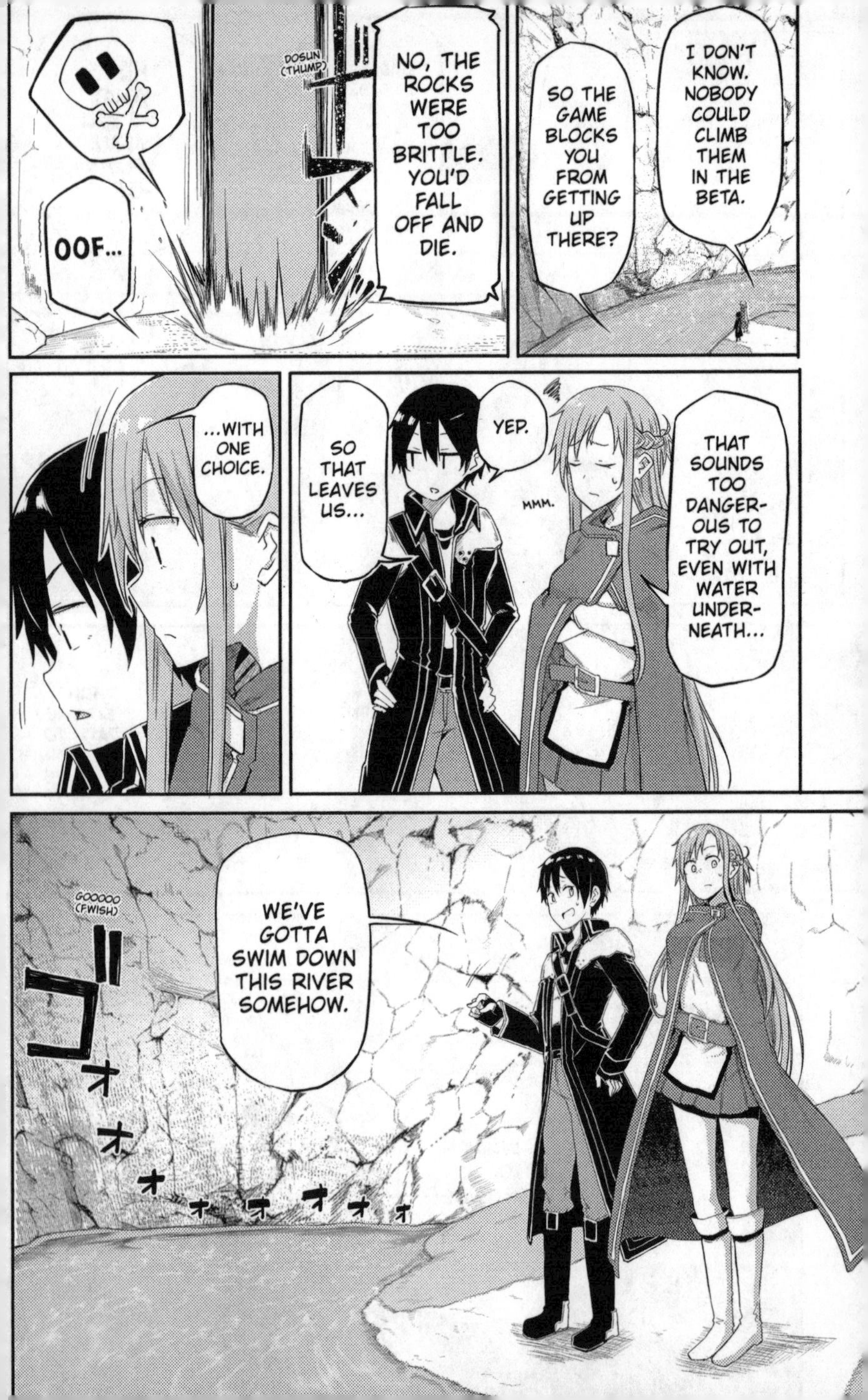
I DON'T KNOW. NOBODY COULD CLIMB THEM IN THE BETA.
SO THE GAME BLOCKS YOU FROM GETTING UP THERE?
NO, THE ROCKS WERE TOO BRITTLE. YOU'D FALL OFF AND DIE.
DOSUN (THUMP)
OOF...
THAT SOUNDS TOO DANGER-OUS TO TRY OUT, EVEN WITH WATER UNDER-NEATH...
MMM.
YEP.
SO THAT LEAVES US...
...WITH ONE CHOICE.
WE'VE GOTTA SWIM DOWN THIS RIVER SOMEHOW.
GOOOOO (FWISH)

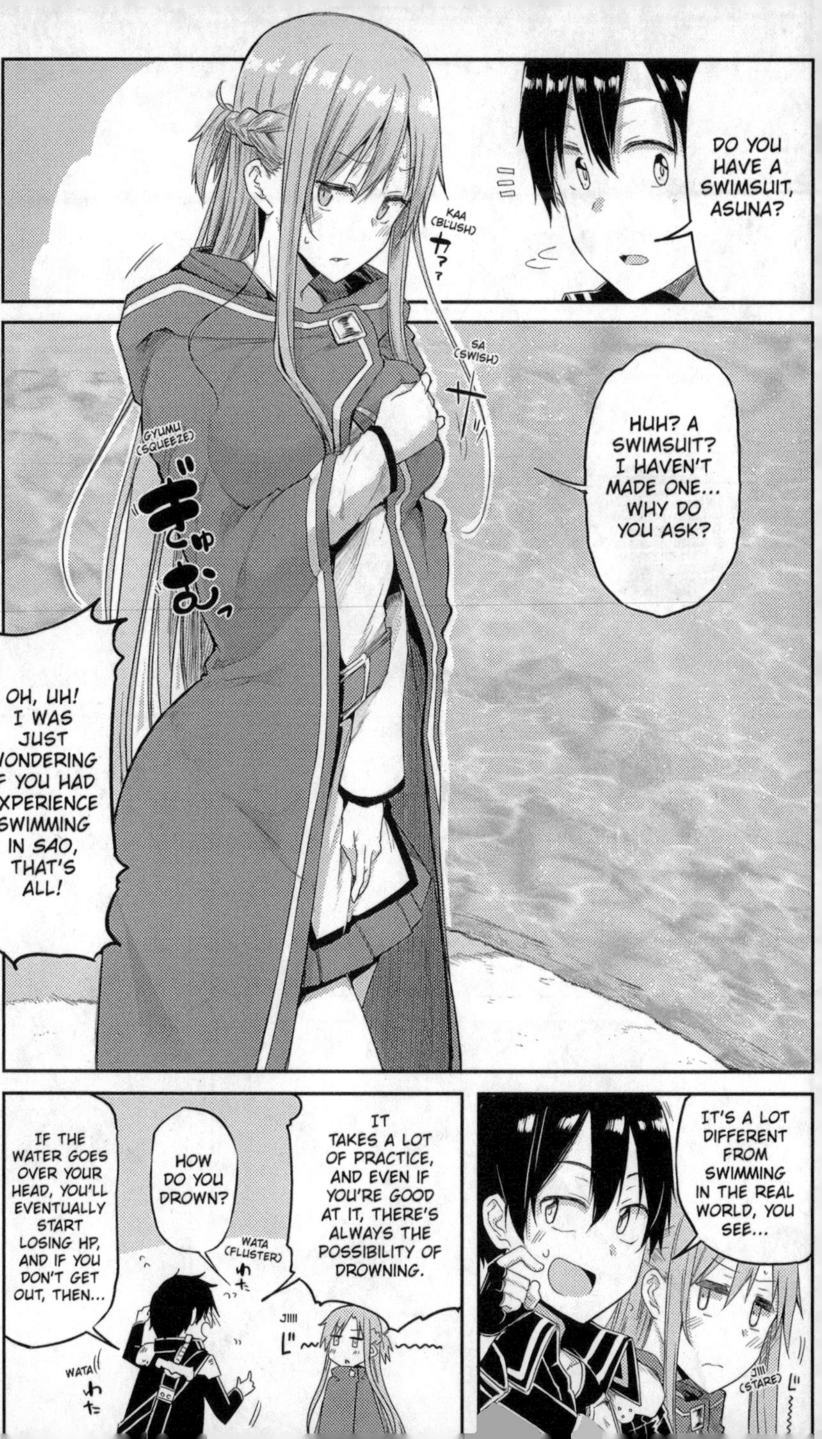
DO YOU HAVE A SWIMSUIT, ASUNA?
KAA (BLUSH)
HUH? A SWIMSUIT? I HAVEN'T MADE ONE... WHY DO YOU ASK?
SA (SWISH)
GYUMU (SQUEEZE)
OH, UH! I WAS JUST WONDERING IF YOU HAD EXPERIENCE SWIMMING IN SAO, THAT'S ALL!
IT'S A LOT DIFFERENT FROM SWIMMING IN THE REAL WORLD, YOU SEE...
JIII (STARE)
IT TAKES A LOT OF PRACTICE, AND EVEN IF YOU'RE GOOD AT IT, THERE'S ALWAYS THE POSSIBILITY OF DROWNING.
HOW DO YOU DROWN?
WATA (FLUSTER)
IF THE WATER GOES OVER YOUR HEAD, YOU'LL EVENTUALLY START LOSING HP, AND IF YOU DON'T GET OUT, THEN...
JIIII
WATA

...YOU DIE.

......

EVERY-BODY KNOWS THAT.

BINGO.

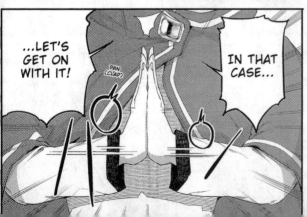

...LET'S GET ON WITH IT!

PAN (CLAP)

IN THAT CASE...

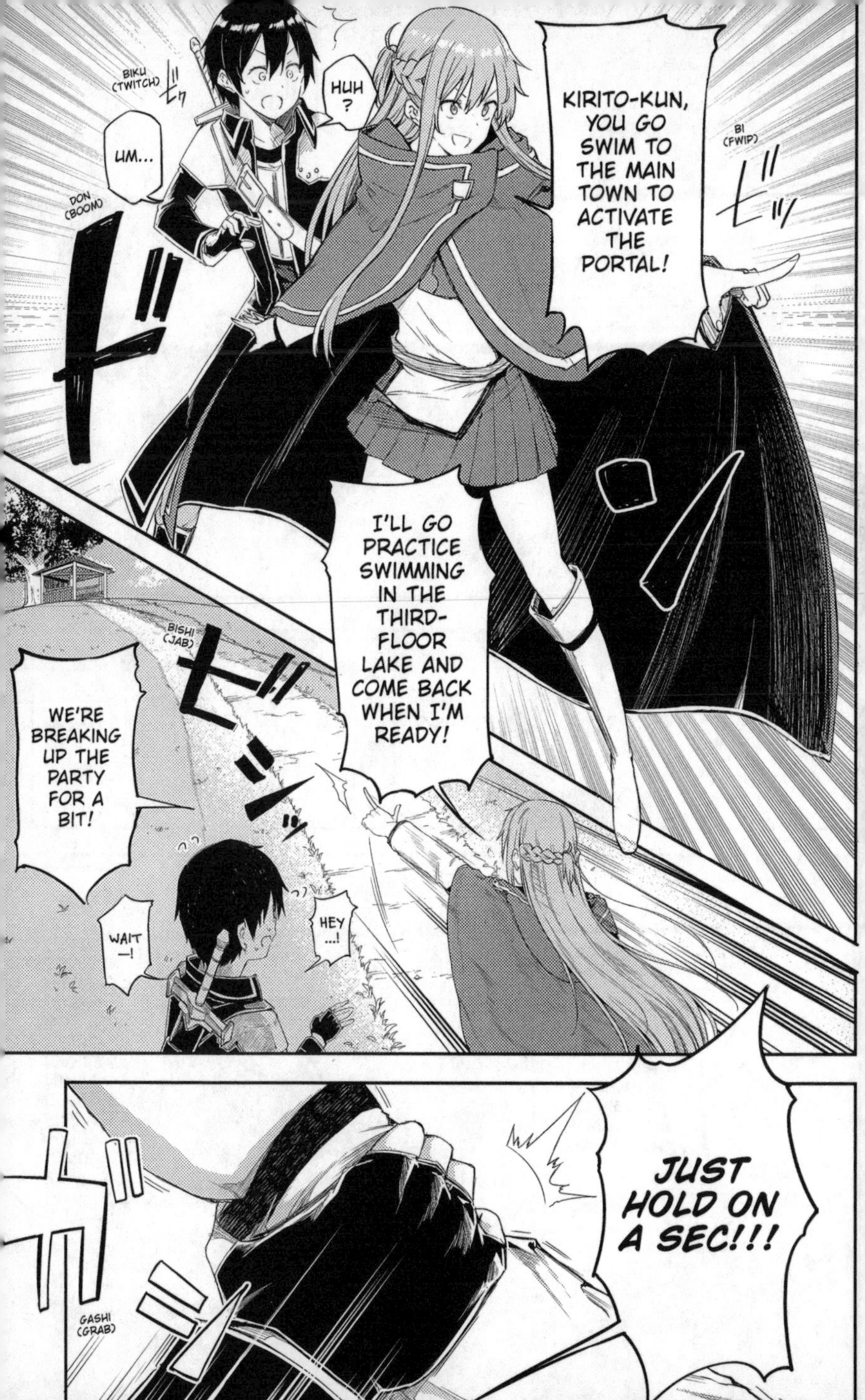
BI (FWIP)
KIRITO-KUN, YOU GO SWIM TO THE MAIN TOWN TO ACTIVATE THE PORTAL!
HUH?
BIKU (TWITCH)
UM...
DON (BOOM)
I'LL GO PRACTICE SWIMMING IN THE THIRD-FLOOR LAKE AND COME BACK WHEN I'M READY!
BISHI (JAB)
WE'RE BREAKING UP THE PARTY FOR A BIT!
HEY ...!
WAIT —!
JUST HOLD ON A SEC!!!
GASHI (GRAB)

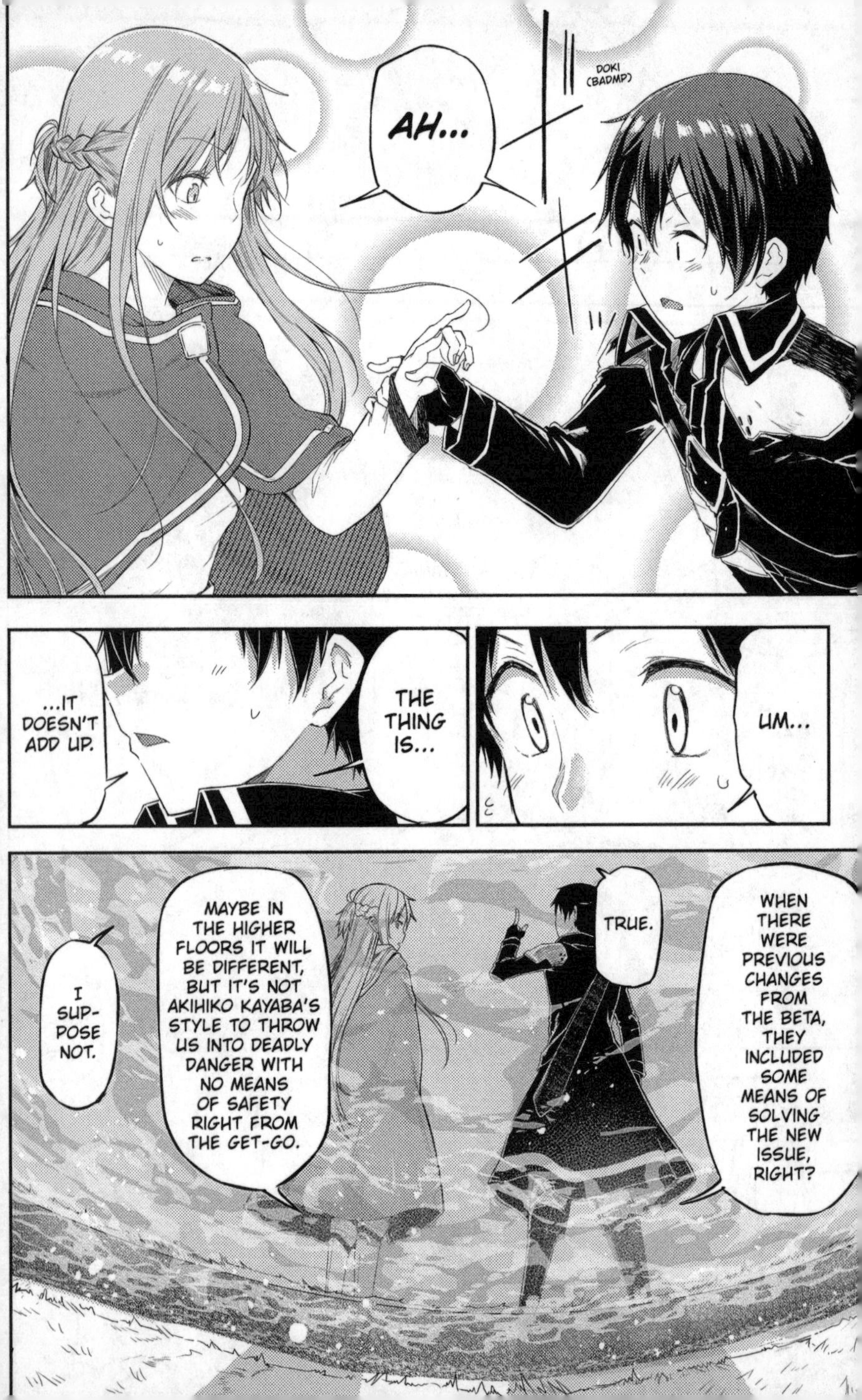
DOKI (BADMP)
AH...
UM...
THE THING IS...
...IT DOESN'T ADD UP.
WHEN THERE WERE PREVIOUS CHANGES FROM THE BETA, THEY INCLUDED SOME MEANS OF SOLVING THE NEW ISSUE, RIGHT?
TRUE.
MAYBE IN THE HIGHER FLOORS IT WILL BE DIFFERENT, BUT IT'S NOT AKIHIKO KAYABA'S STYLE TO THROW US INTO DEADLY DANGER WITH NO MEANS OF SAFETY RIGHT FROM THE GET-GO.
I SUP-POSE NOT.

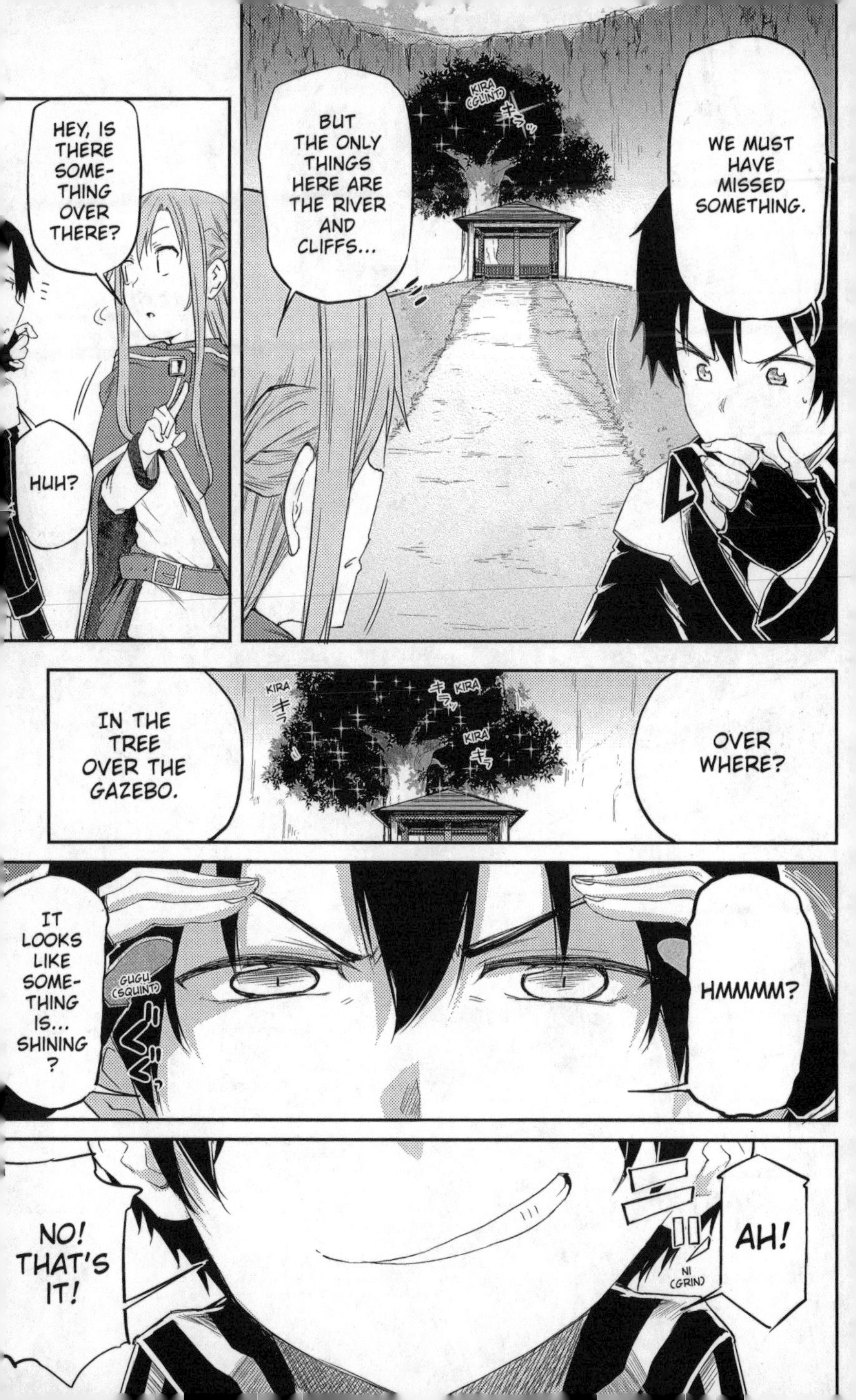
WE MUST HAVE MISSED SOMETHING.
KIRA (GLINT)
BUT THE ONLY THINGS HERE ARE THE RIVER AND CLIFFS...
HEY, IS THERE SOME-THING OVER THERE?
HUH?
OVER WHERE?
KIRA
KIRA
KIRA
IN THE TREE OVER THE GAZEBO.
HMMMM?
GUGU (SQUINT)
IT LOOKS LIKE SOME-THING IS... SHINING?
AH!
NI (GRIN)
NO! THAT'S IT!

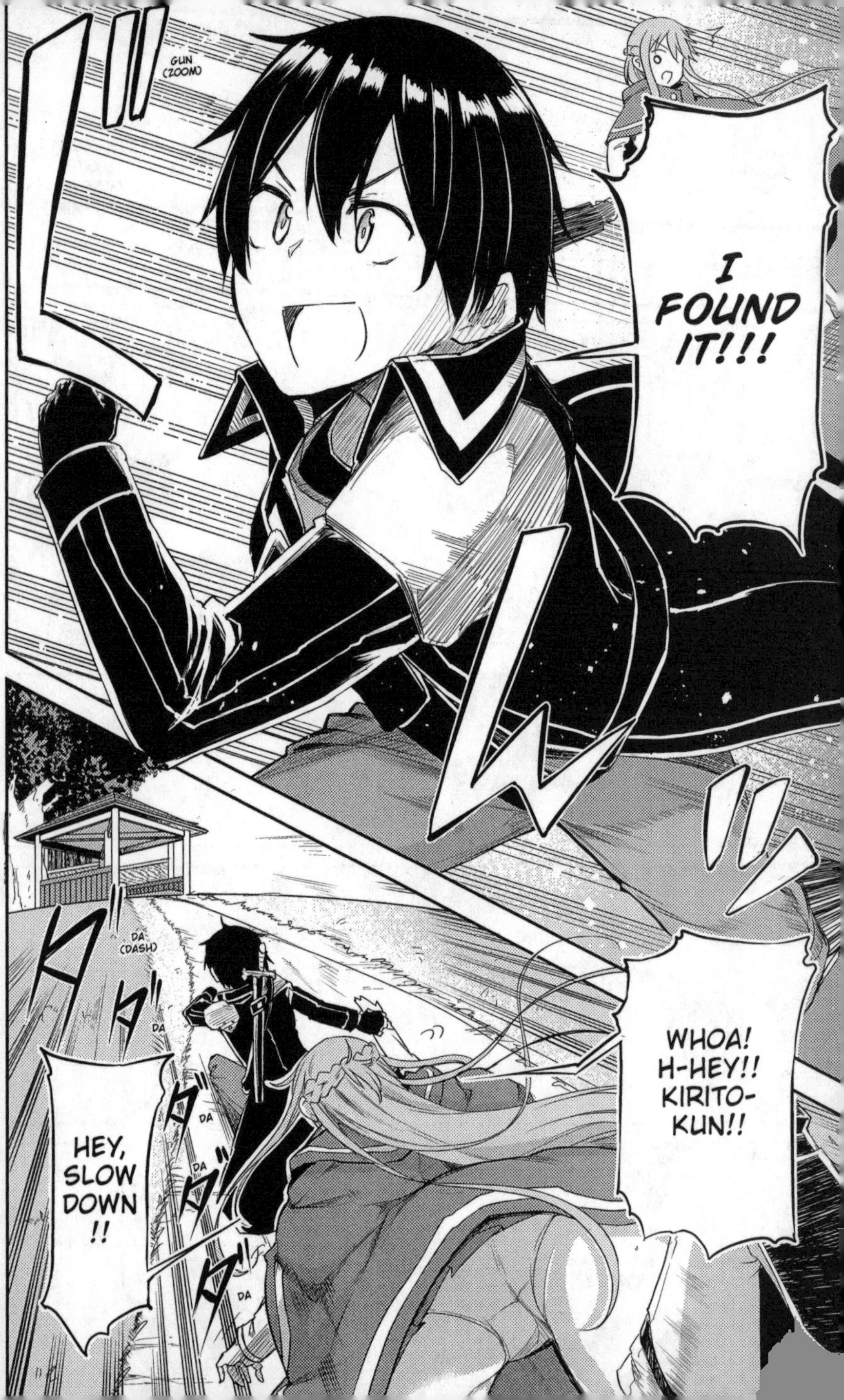
I FOUND IT!!!
GUN (ZOOM)
WHOA! H-HEY!! KIRITO-KUN!!
DA (DASH)
DA
DA
DA
DA
HEY, SLOW DOWN !!

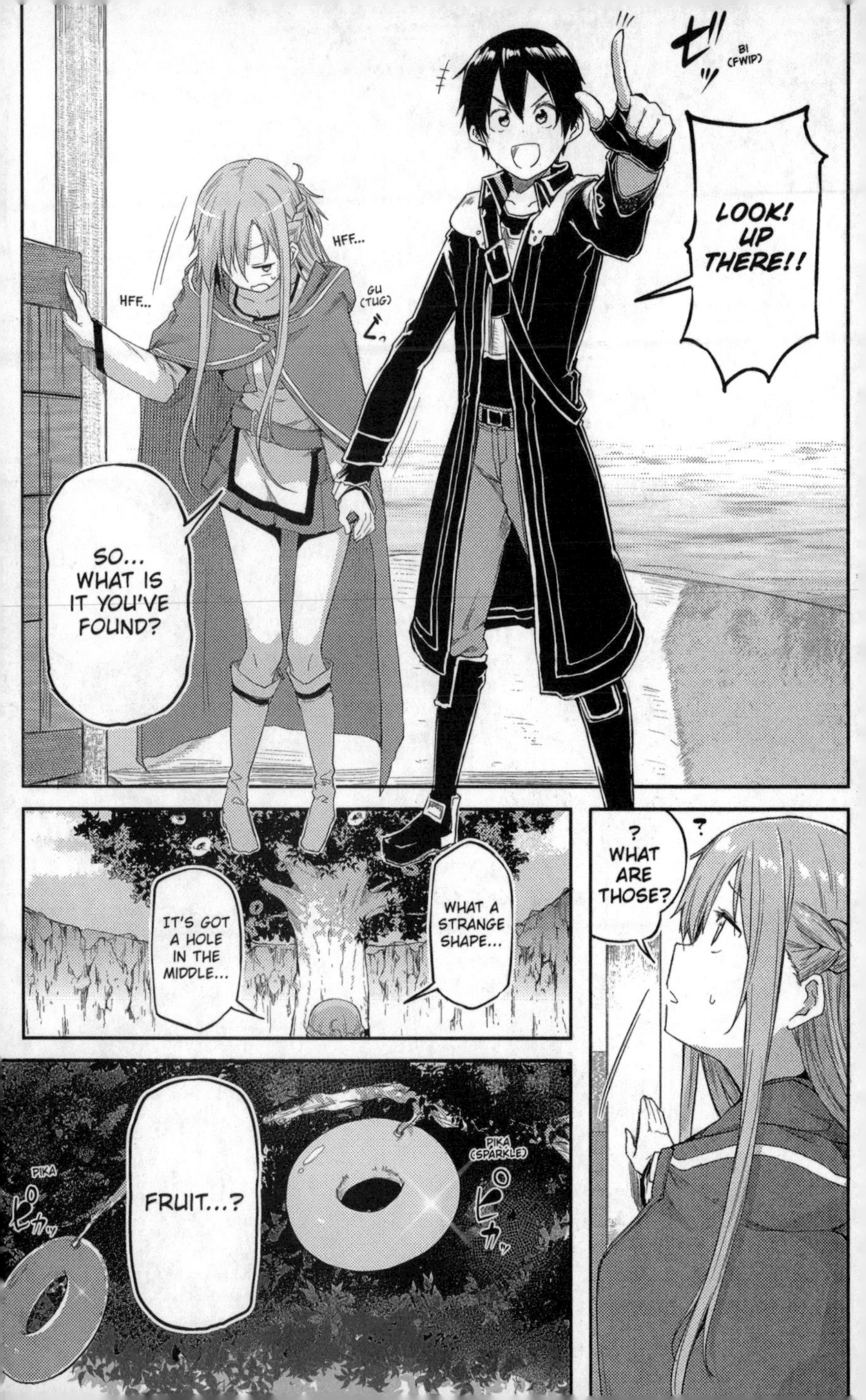
BI (FWIP)
LOOK! UP THERE!!
HFF...
GU (TUG)
HFF...
SO... WHAT IS IT YOU'VE FOUND?
? WHAT ARE THOSE?
WHAT A STRANGE SHAPE...
IT'S GOT A HOLE IN THE MIDDLE...
PIKA (SPARKLE)
FRUIT...?
PIKA

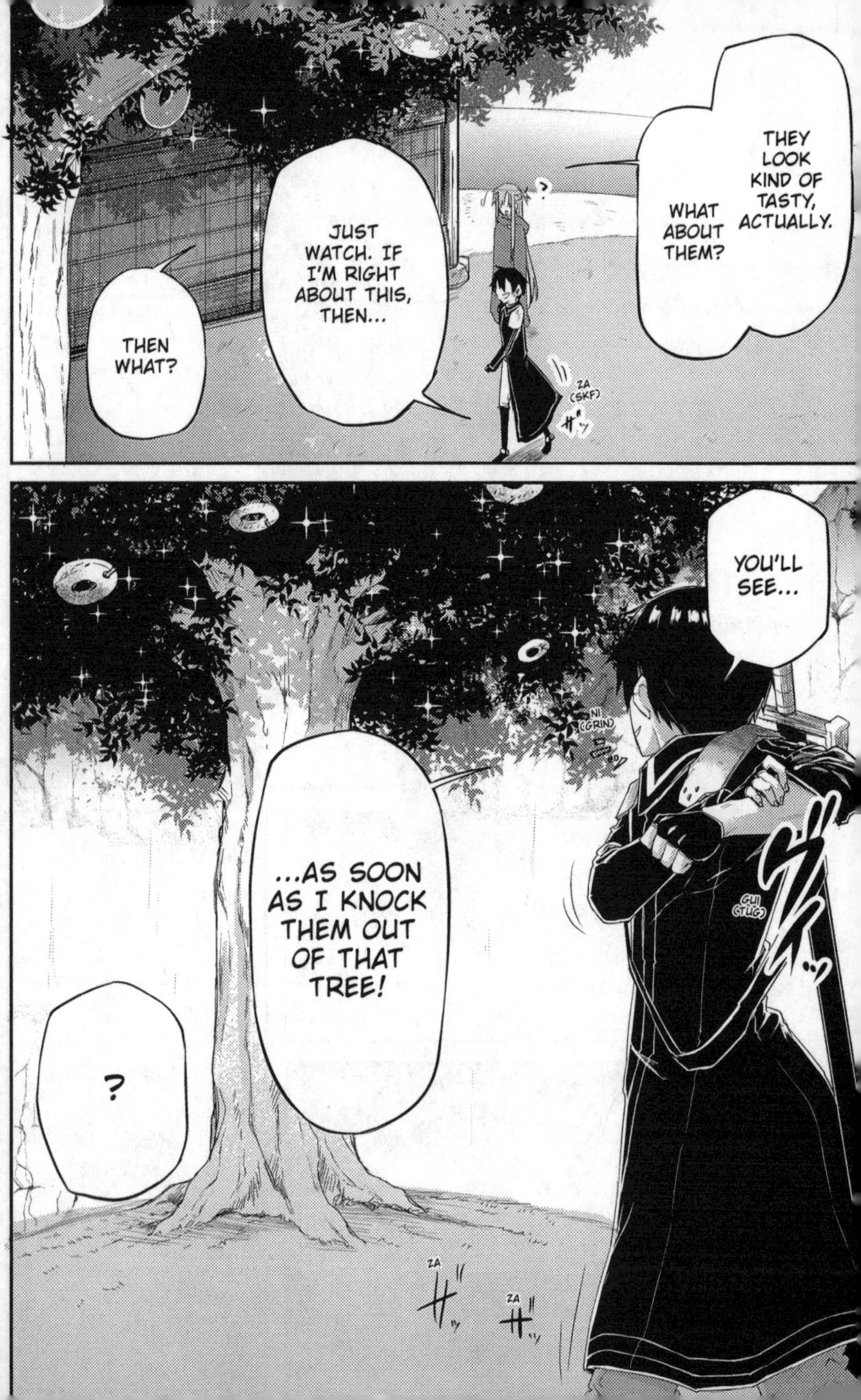
THEY LOOK KIND OF TASTY, ACTUALLY.
WHAT ABOUT THEM?
?
JUST WATCH. IF I'M RIGHT ABOUT THIS, THEN...
ZA (SKF)
THEN WHAT?
YOU'LL SEE...
NI (GRIN)
...AS SOON AS I KNOCK THEM OUT OF THAT TREE!
GUI (TUG)
?
ZA
ZA

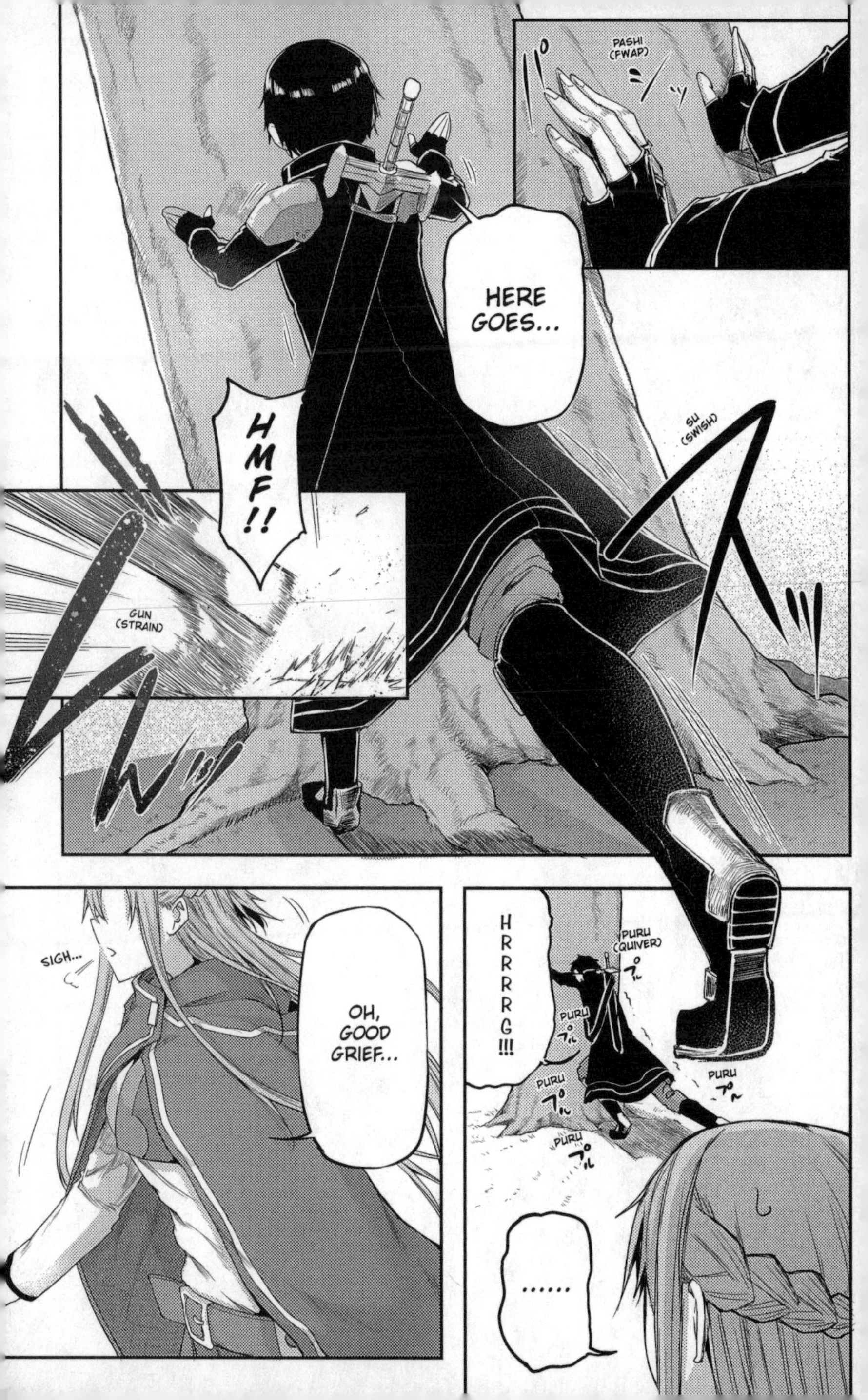
PASHI (FWAP)
HERE GOES...
SU (SWISH)
HMF!!
GUN (STRAIN)
HRRRRG!!!
PURU (QUIVER)
PURU
PURU
PURU
PURU
......
SIGH...
OH, GOOD GRIEF...

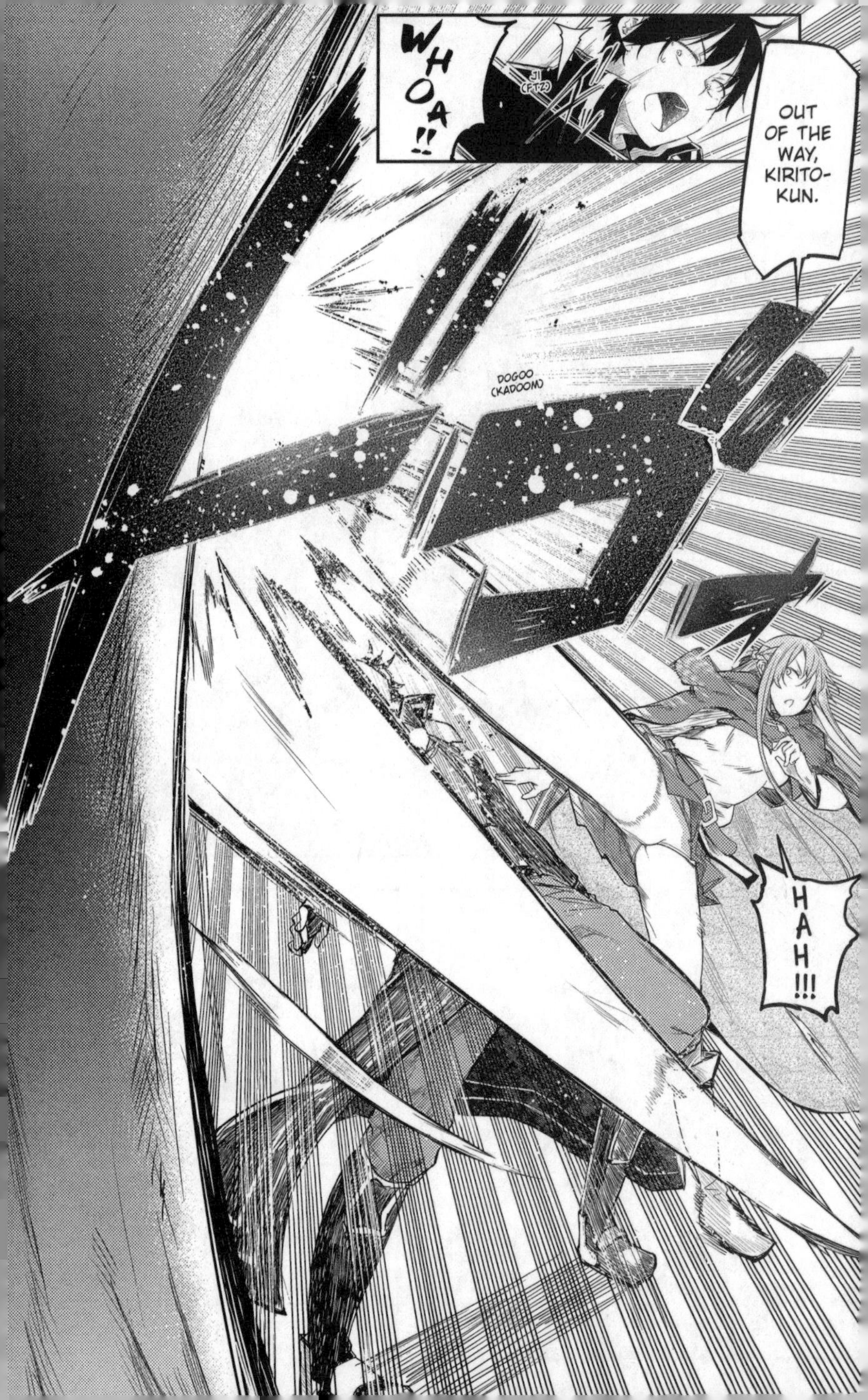
OUT OF THE WAY, KIRITO-KUN.
WHOA!!
JI (FTZ)
DOGOO (KADOOM)
HAH!!!

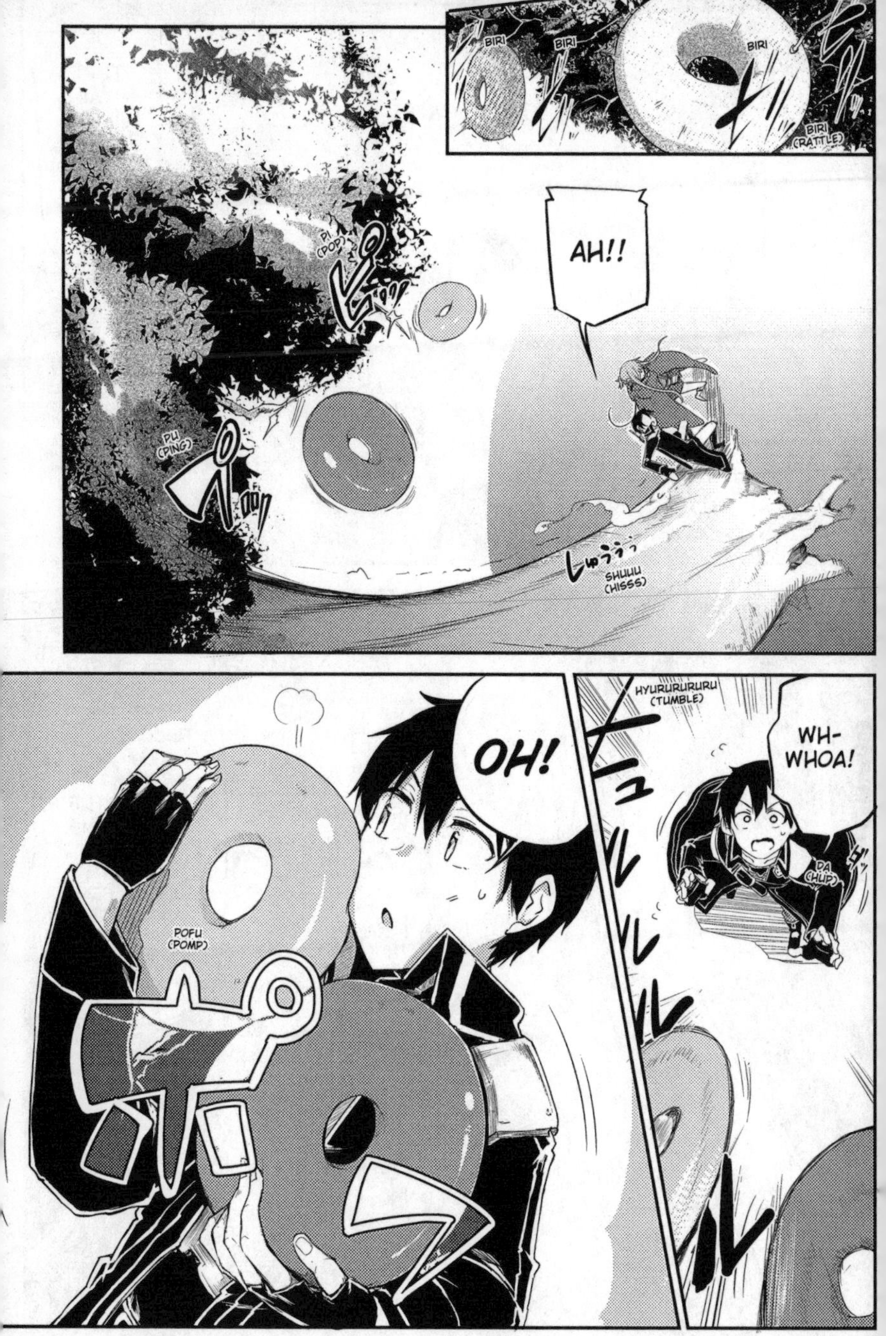
BIRI
BIRI
BIRI
BIRI (RATTLE)
AH!!
PI (POP)
PU (PING)
SHUUU (HISSS)
HYURURURURU (TUMBLE)
WH- WHOA!
DA (HUP)
OH!
POFU (POMP)

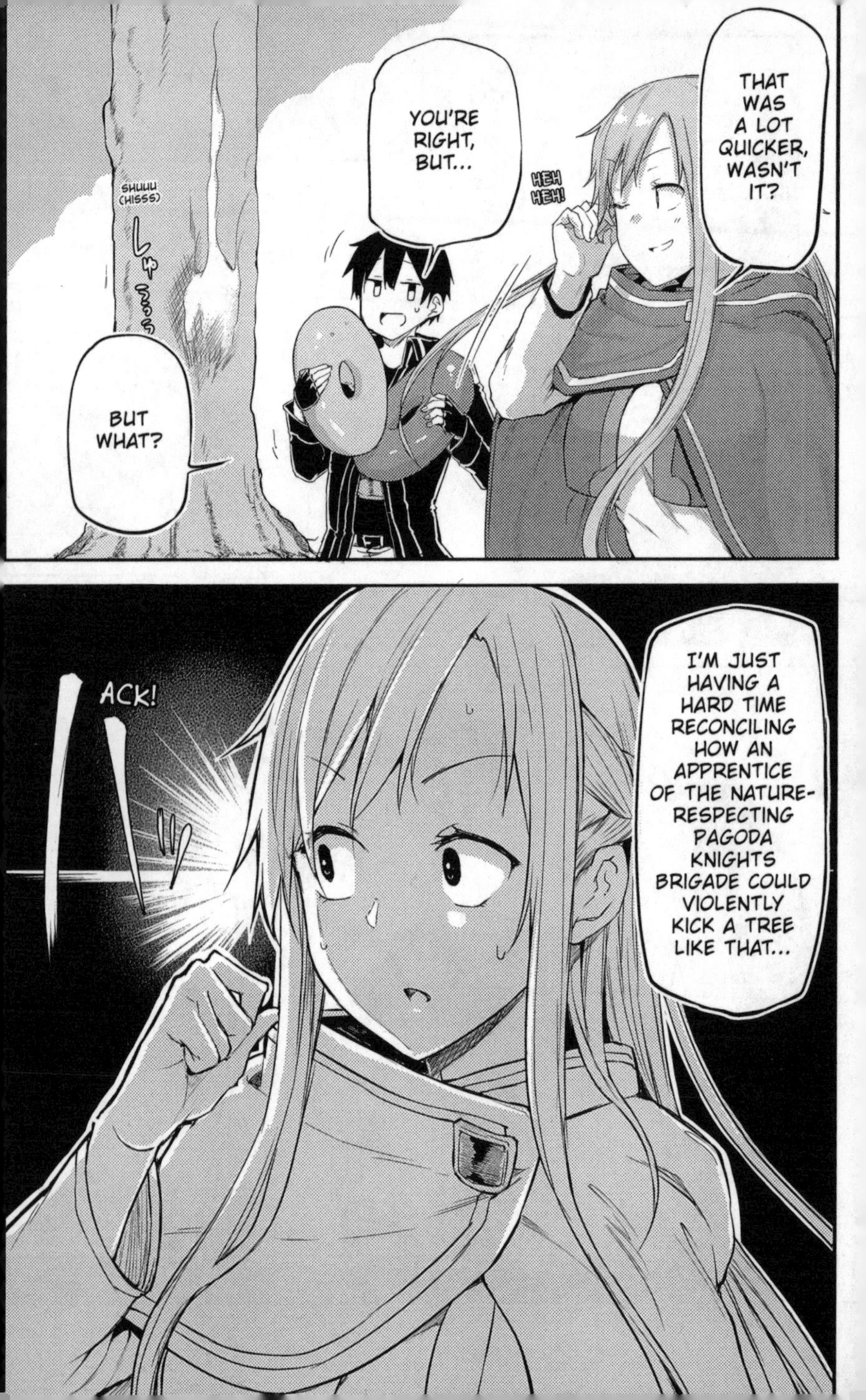
THAT WAS A LOT QUICKER, WASN'T IT?
HEH HEH!
YOU'RE RIGHT, BUT...
SHUUU (HISSS)
BUT WHAT?
I'M JUST HAVING A HARD TIME RECONCILING HOW AN APPRENTICE OF THE NATURE-RESPECTING PAGODA KNIGHTS BRIGADE COULD VIOLENTLY KICK A TREE LIKE THAT...
ACK!

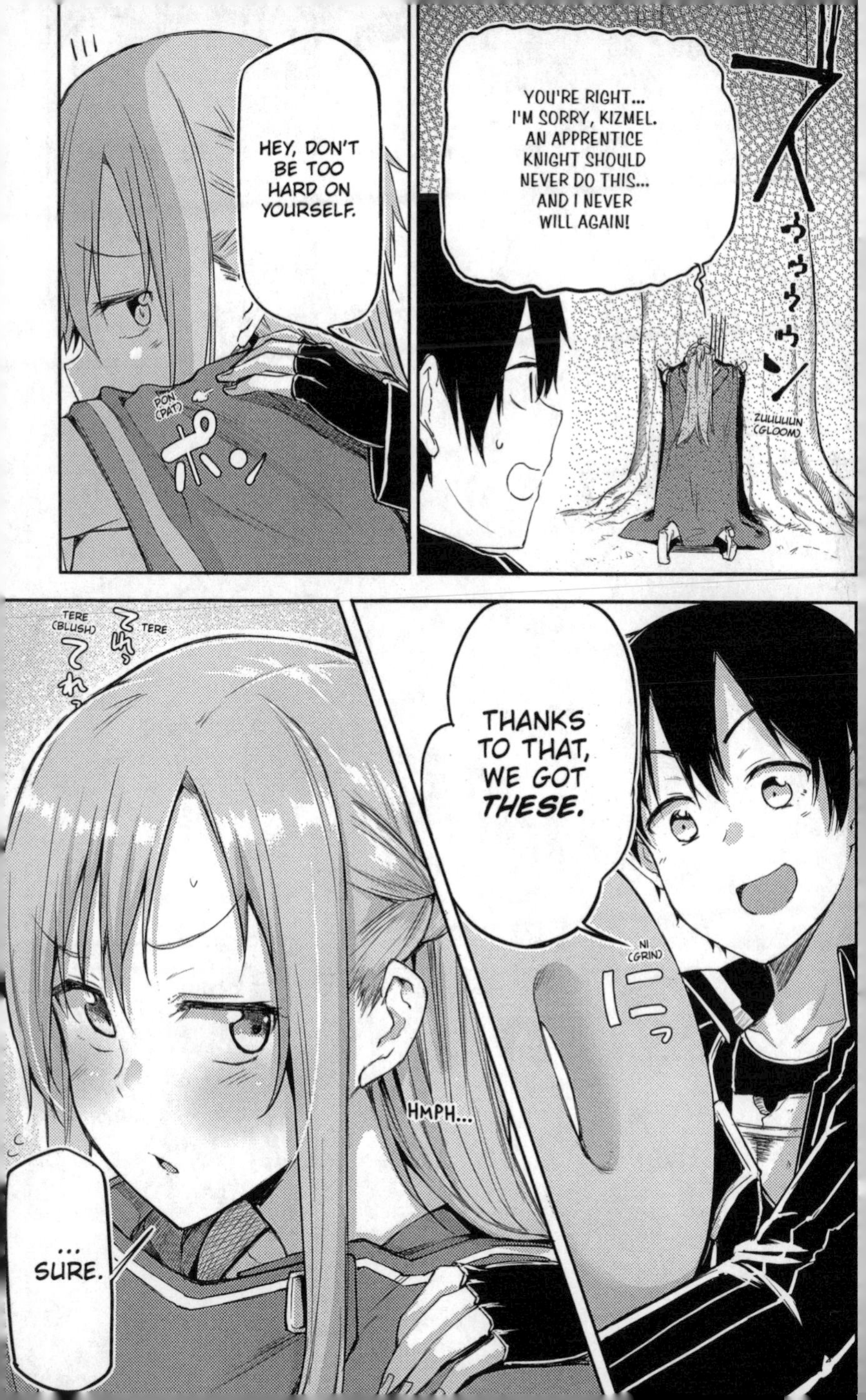
YOU'RE RIGHT... I'M SORRY, KIZMEL. AN APPRENTICE KNIGHT SHOULD NEVER DO THIS... AND I NEVER WILL AGAIN!
ZUUUUUN (GLOOM)
HEY, DON'T BE TOO HARD ON YOURSELF.
PON (PAT)
THANKS TO THAT, WE GOT *THESE.*
NI (GRIN)
TERE (BLUSH) TERE
HMPH...
... SURE.

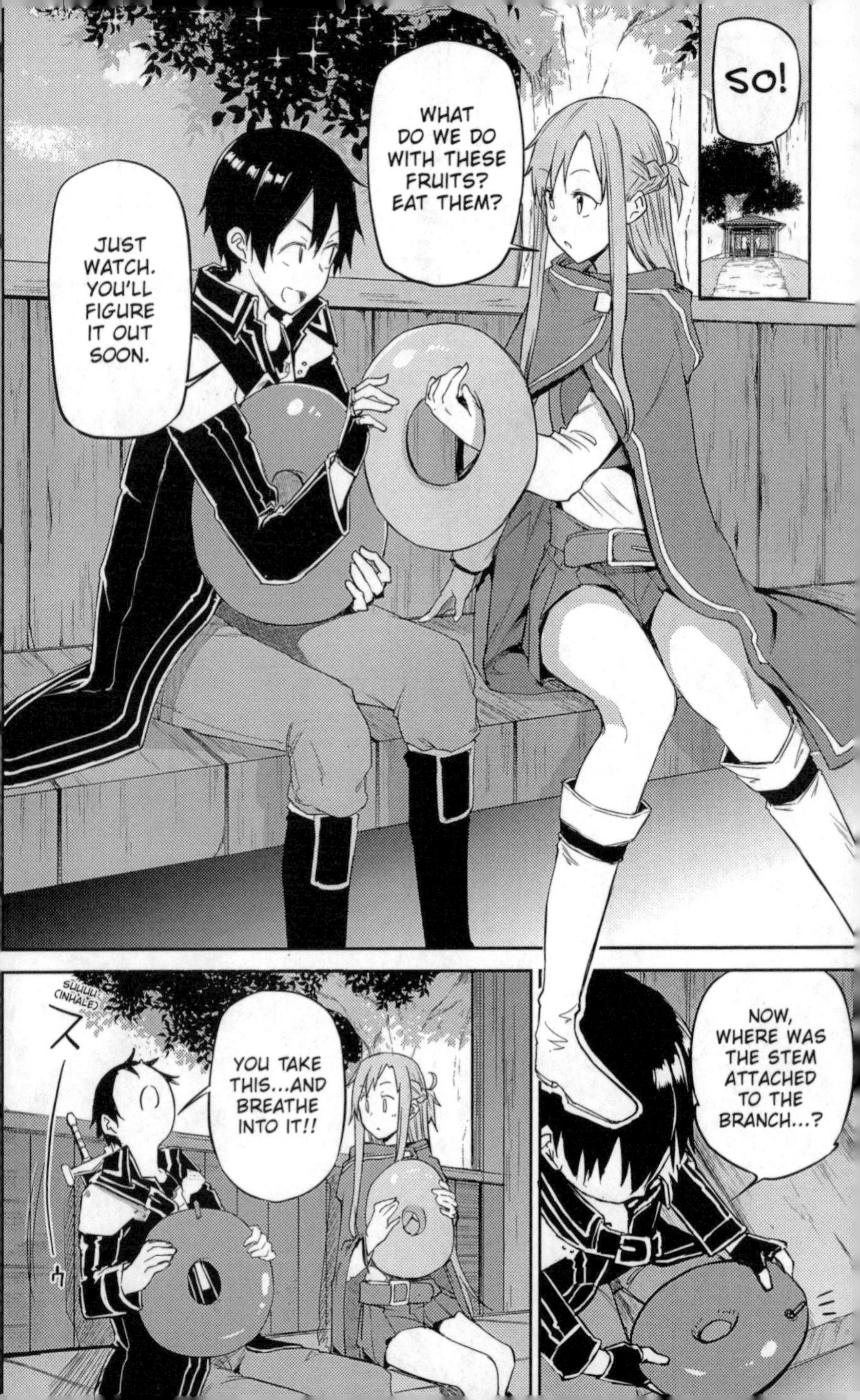
SO!
WHAT DO WE DO WITH THESE FRUITS? EAT THEM?
JUST WATCH. YOU'LL FIGURE IT OUT SOON.
NOW, WHERE WAS THE STEM ATTACHED TO THE BRANCH...?
YOU TAKE THIS...AND BREATHE INTO IT!!
SUUUUU (INHALE)
ス
ウ

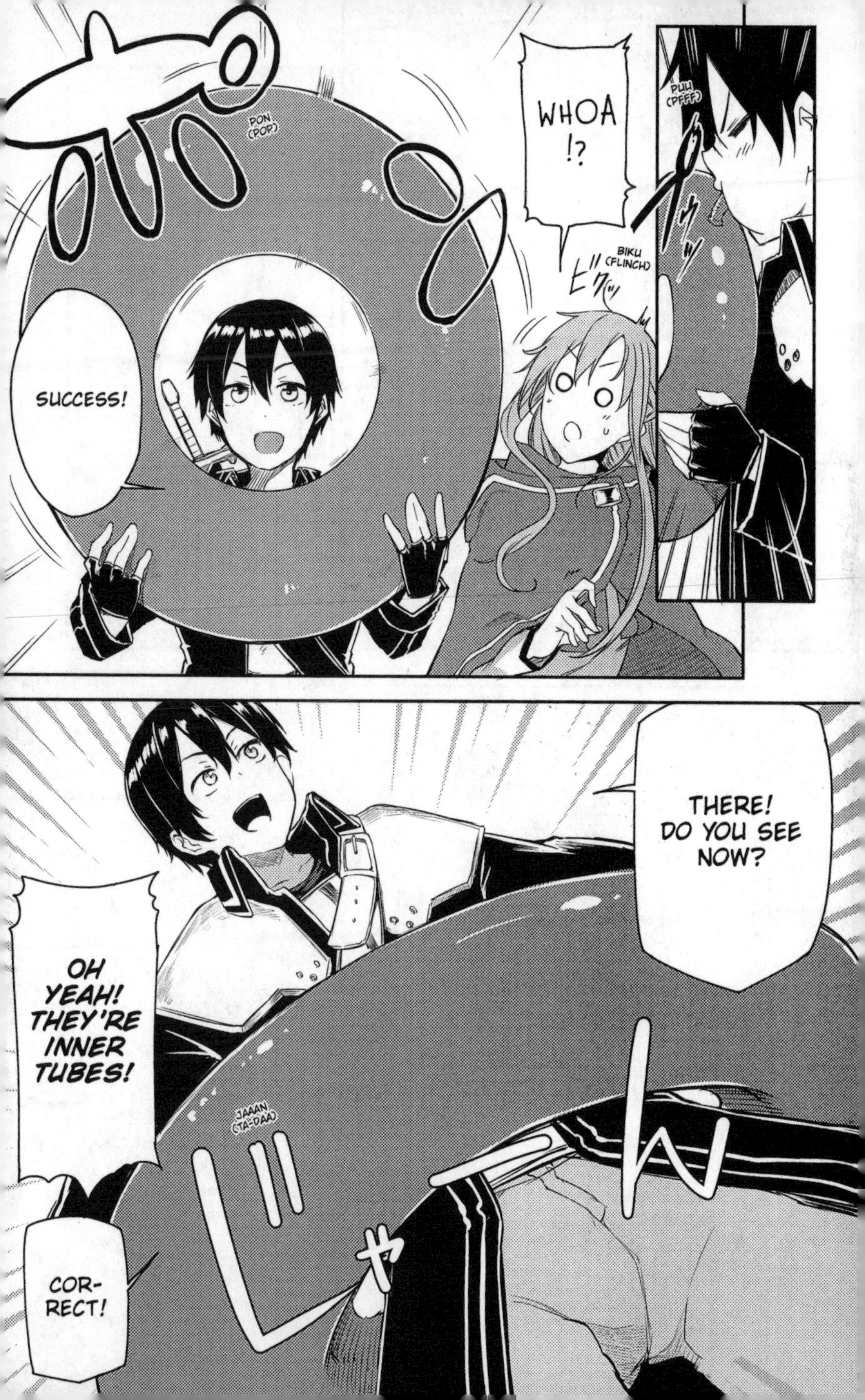
PUU (PFFFF)
WHOA !?
PON (POP)
BIKU (FLINCH)
SUCCESS!
THERE! DO YOU SEE NOW?
JAAAN (TA-DAA)
OH YEAH! THEY'RE INNER TUBES!
COR- RECT!

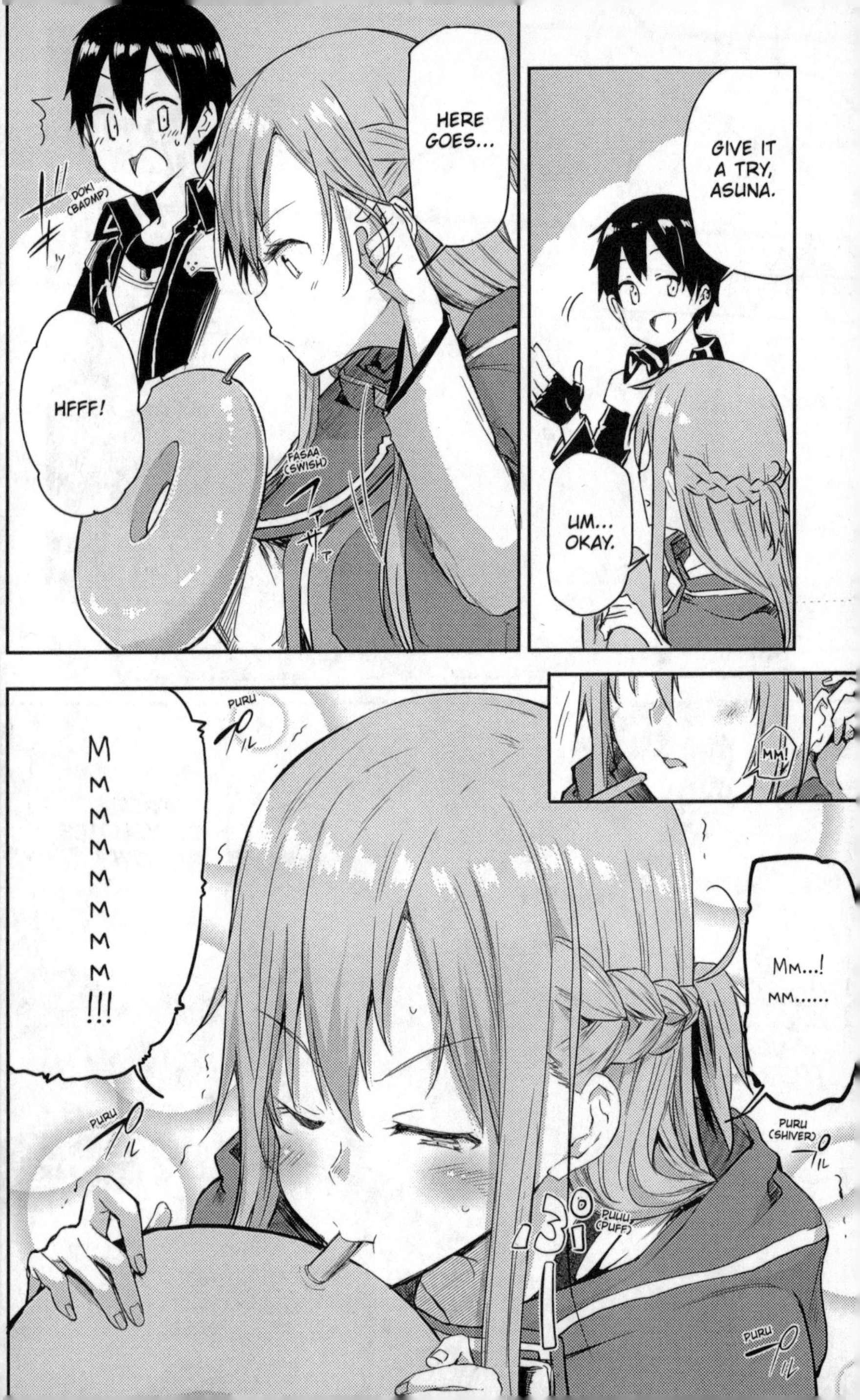
GIVE IT A TRY, ASUNA.
UM... OKAY.
HERE GOES...
DOKI (BADMP)
FASAA (SWISH)
HFFF!
MM!
Mm...! mm......
PURU (SHIVER)
PUUU (PUFF)
PURU
PURU
MMMMMMMMM!!!
PURU

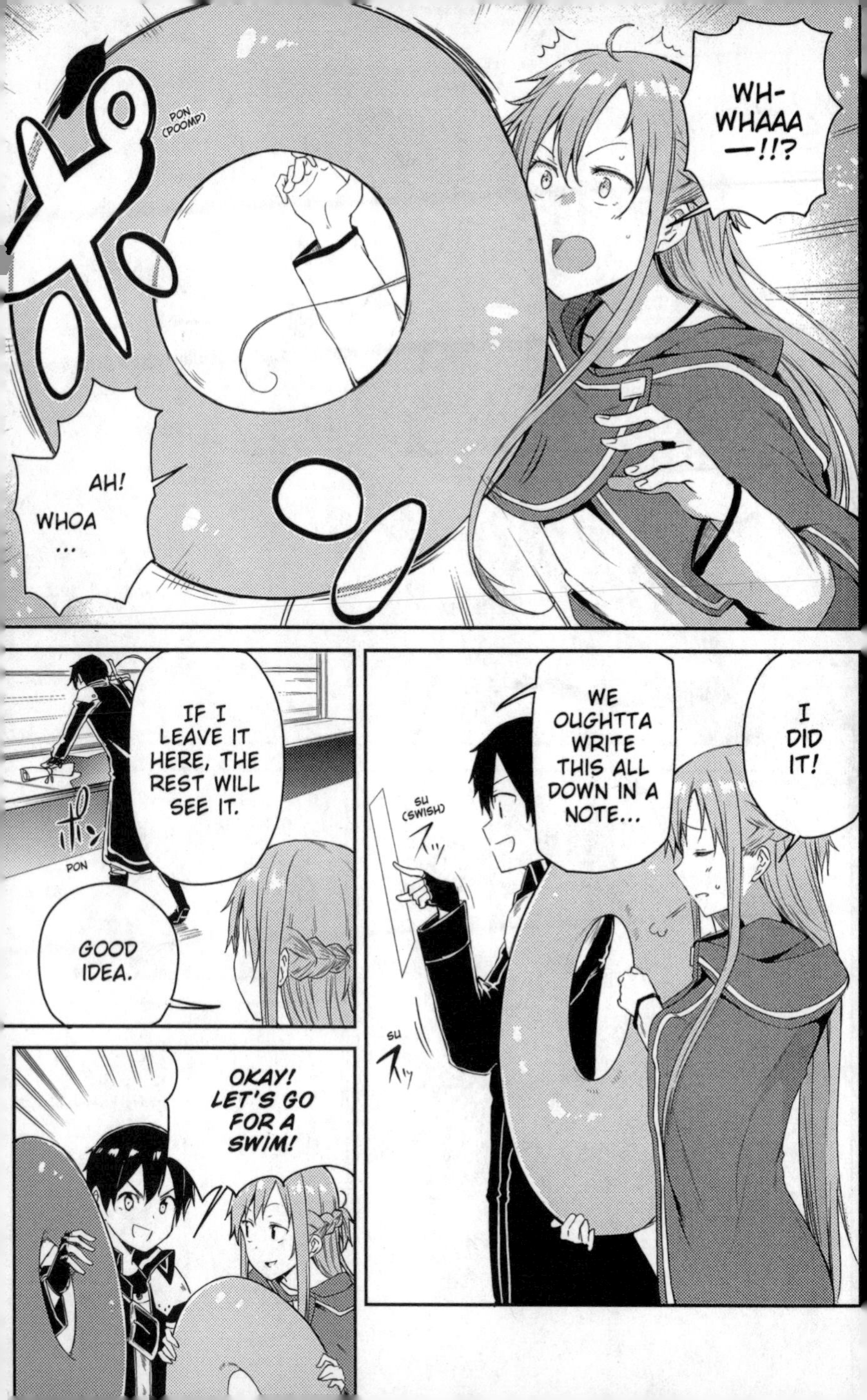

WH-WHAAA—!!?
PON (POOMP)
AH! WHOA...
I DID IT!
WE OUGHTTA WRITE THIS ALL DOWN IN A NOTE...
SU (SWISH)
SU
IF I LEAVE IT HERE, THE REST WILL SEE IT.
PON
GOOD IDEA.
OKAY! LET'S GO FOR A SWIM!

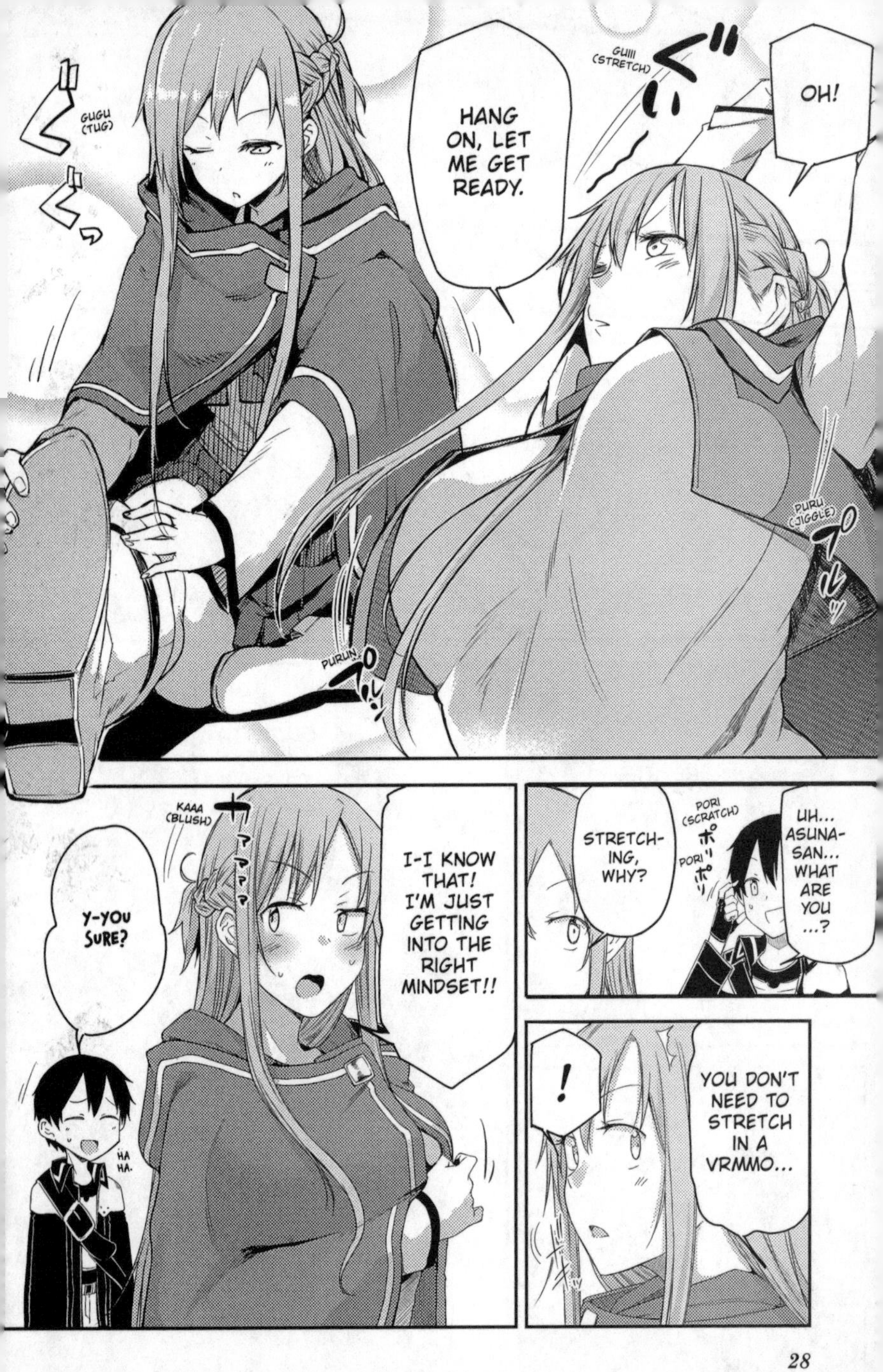
OH!
GUIII (STRETCH)
HANG ON, LET ME GET READY.
GUGU (TUG)
PURU (JIGGLE)
PURUN
UH... ASUNA-SAN... WHAT ARE YOU ...?
PORI (SCRATCH)
PORI
STRETCH-ING, WHY?
YOU DON'T NEED TO STRETCH IN A VRMMO...
!
I-I KNOW THAT! I'M JUST GETTING INTO THE RIGHT MINDSET!!
KAAA (BLUSH)
Y-YOU SURE?
HA HA.

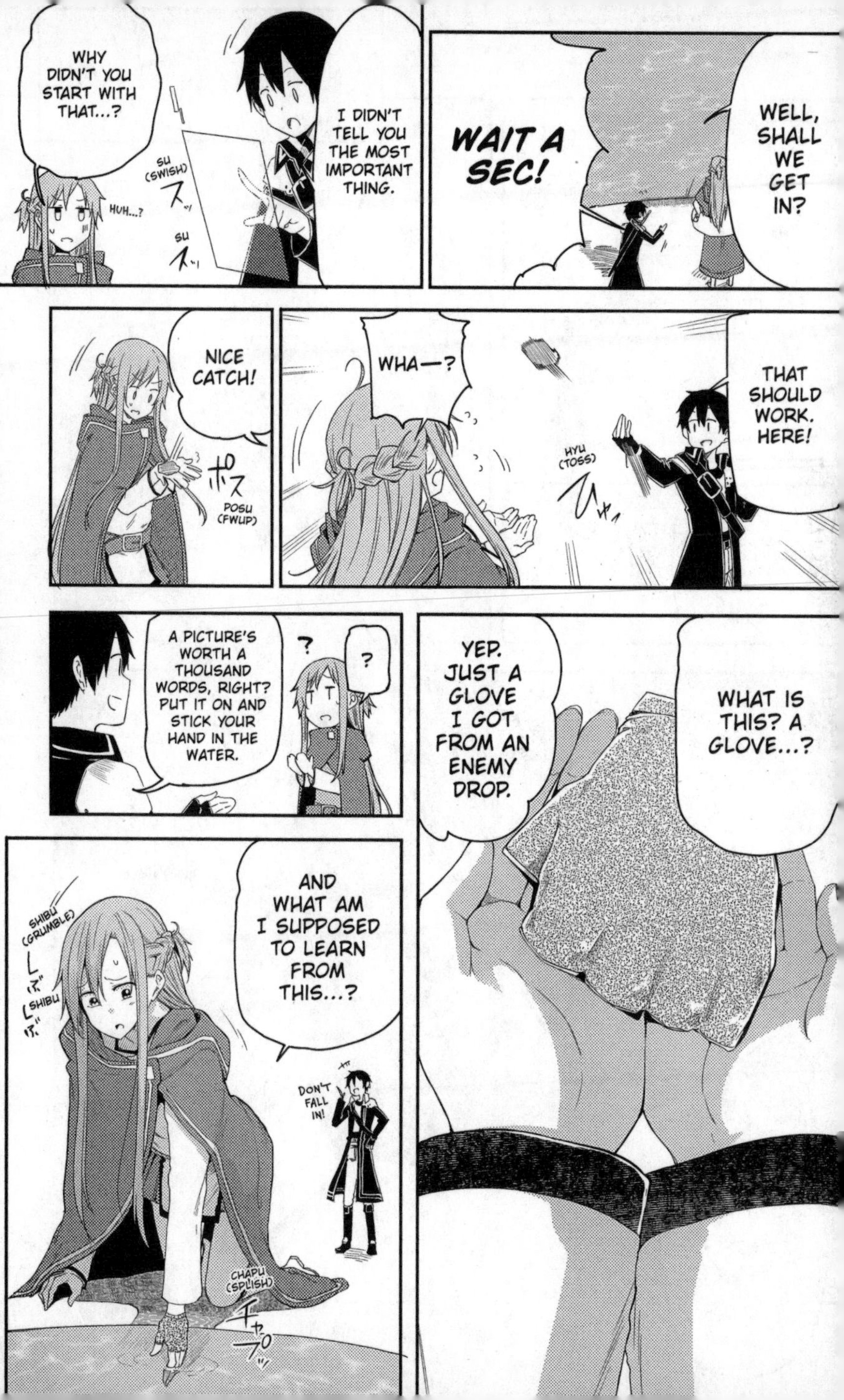
WELL, SHALL WE GET IN?
WAIT A SEC!
I DIDN'T TELL YOU THE MOST IMPORTANT THING.
SU (SWISH)
SU
HUH...?
WHY DIDN'T YOU START WITH THAT...?
THAT SHOULD WORK. HERE!
HYU (TOSS)
ひゅ
WHA—?
NICE CATCH!
ポス
POSU (FWUP)
WHAT IS THIS? A GLOVE...?
YEP. JUST A GLOVE I GOT FROM AN ENEMY DROP.
?
?
A PICTURE'S WORTH A THOUSAND WORDS, RIGHT? PUT IT ON AND STICK YOUR HAND IN THE WATER.
AND WHAT AM I SUPPOSED TO LEARN FROM THIS...?
SHIBU (GRUMBLE)
SHIBU
DON'T FALL IN!
CHAPU (SPLISH)

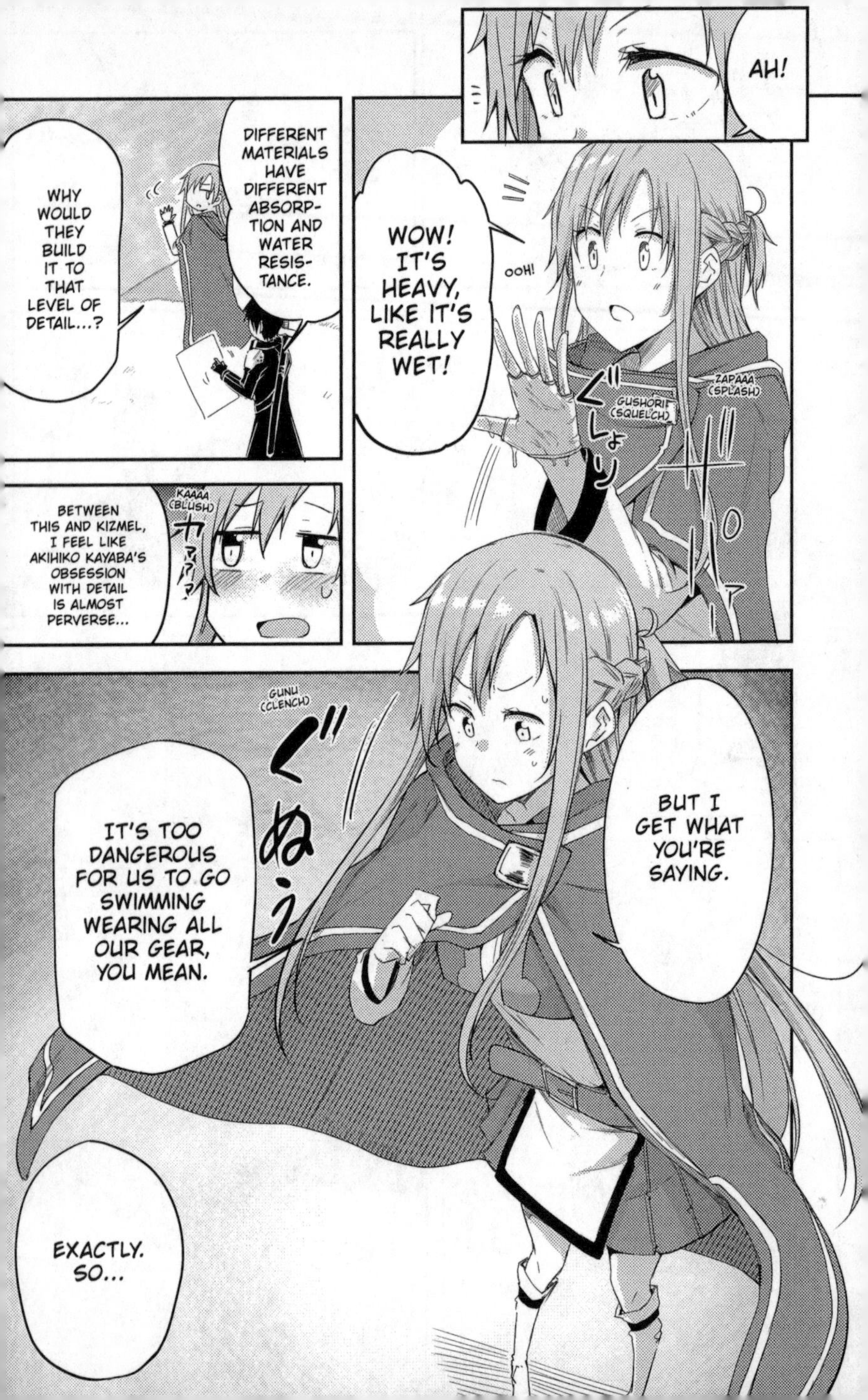
AH!
WOW! IT'S HEAVY, LIKE IT'S REALLY WET!
OOH!
ZAPAAA (SPLASH)
GUSHORI (SQUELCH)
DIFFERENT MATERIALS HAVE DIFFERENT ABSORPTION AND WATER RESISTANCE.
WHY WOULD THEY BUILD IT TO THAT LEVEL OF DETAIL...?
KAAAA (BLUSH)
BETWEEN THIS AND KIZMEL, I FEEL LIKE AKIHIKO KAYABA'S OBSESSION WITH DETAIL IS ALMOST PERVERSE...
BUT I GET WHAT YOU'RE SAYING.
GUNU (CLENCH)
IT'S TOO DANGEROUS FOR US TO GO SWIMMING WEARING ALL OUR GEAR, YOU MEAN.
EXACTLY. SO...

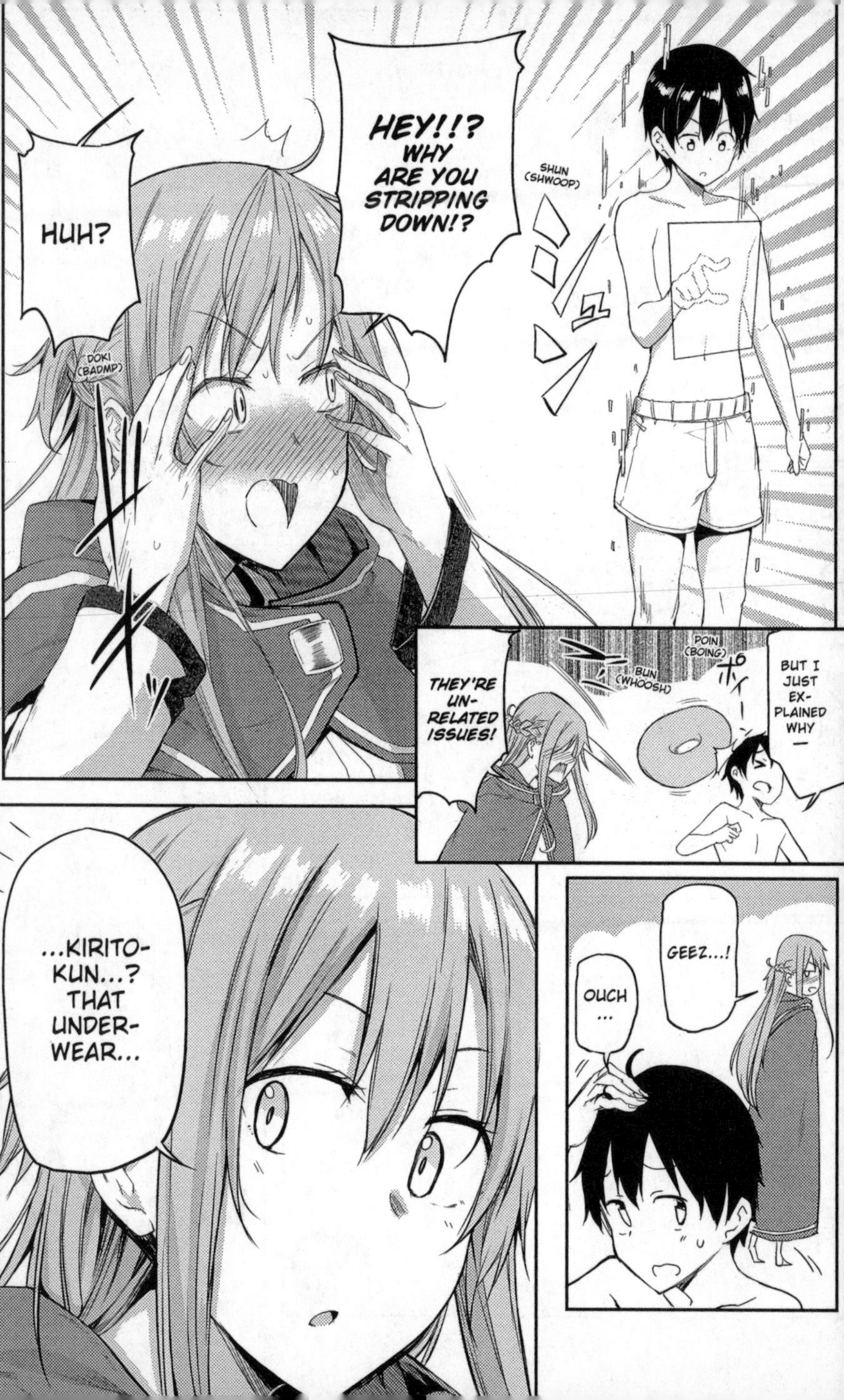
SHUN (SHWOOP)
HEY!!? WHY ARE YOU STRIPPING DOWN!?
HUH?
DOKI (BADMP)
BUT I JUST EXPLAINED WHY —
POIN (BOING)
BUN (WHOOSH)
THEY'RE UNRELATED ISSUES!
GEEZ...!
OUCH ...
...KIRITO-KUN...? THAT UNDERWEAR...

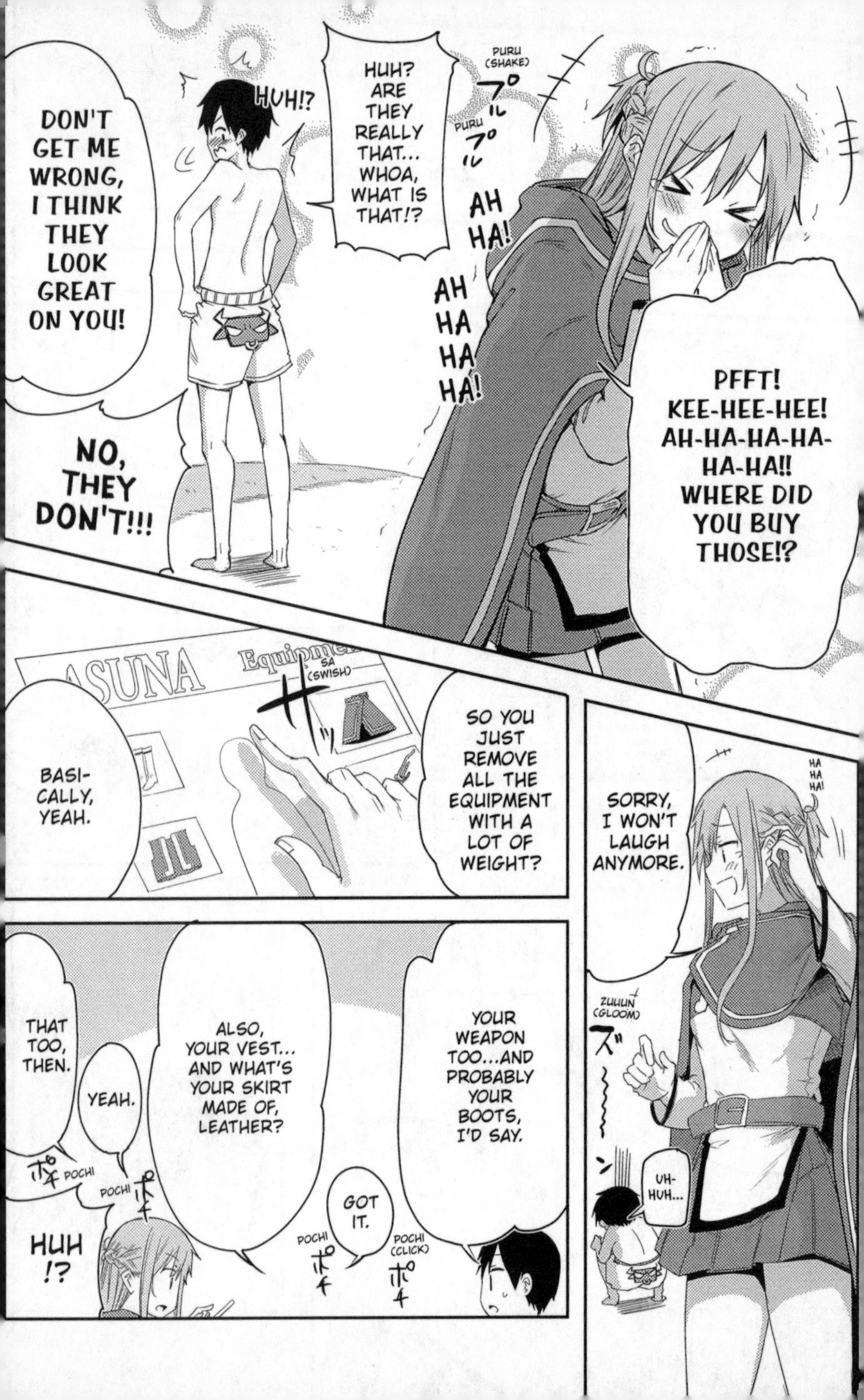
PFFT! KEE-HEE-HEE! AH-HA-HA-HA-HA-HA!! WHERE DID YOU BUY THOSE!?
AH HA!
AH HA HA HA!
PURU (SHAKE)
PURU
HUH? ARE THEY REALLY THAT... WHOA, WHAT IS THAT!?
HUH!?
DON'T GET ME WRONG, I THINK THEY LOOK GREAT ON YOU!
NO, THEY DON'T!!!
HA HA HA!
SORRY, I WON'T LAUGH ANYMORE.
ZUUUN (GLOOM)
UH-HUH...
ASUNA
SA (SWISH)
SO YOU JUST REMOVE ALL THE EQUIPMENT WITH A LOT OF WEIGHT?
BASI-CALLY, YEAH.
YOUR WEAPON TOO...AND PROBABLY YOUR BOOTS, I'D SAY.
POCHI (CLICK)
GOT IT.
POCHI
ALSO, YOUR VEST... AND WHAT'S YOUR SKIRT MADE OF, LEATHER?
YEAH.
POCHI
THAT TOO, THEN.
POCHI
HUH !?

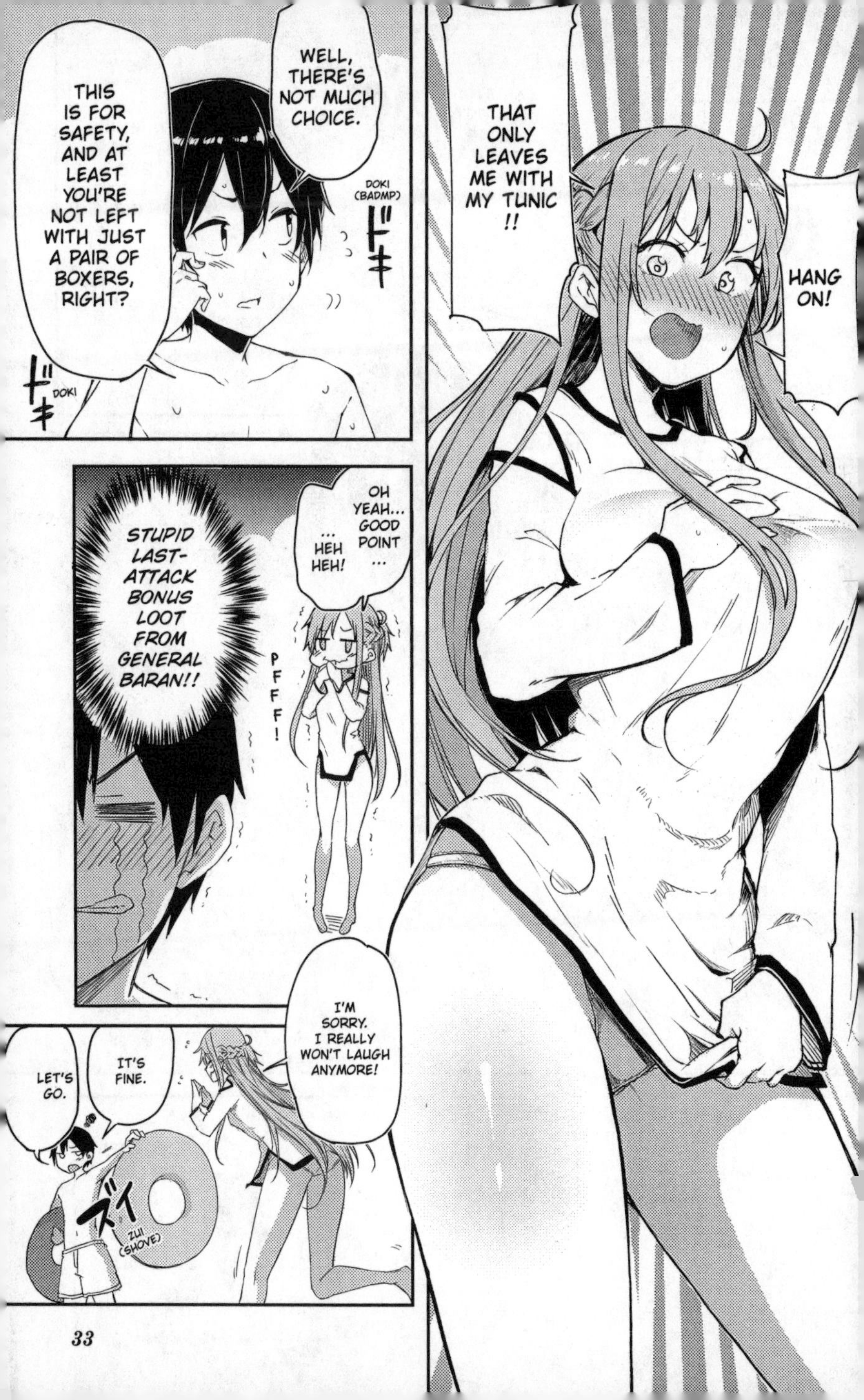
HANG ON!
THAT ONLY LEAVES ME WITH MY TUNIC!!
WELL, THERE'S NOT MUCH CHOICE.
DOKI (BADMP)
ドキ
THIS IS FOR SAFETY, AND AT LEAST YOU'RE NOT LEFT WITH JUST A PAIR OF BOXERS, RIGHT?
ドキ
DOKI
OH YEAH... GOOD POINT...
... HEH HEH!
PFFF!
STUPID LAST-ATTACK BONUS LOOT FROM GENERAL BARAN!!
I'M SORRY. I REALLY WON'T LAUGH ANYMORE!
IT'S FINE.
LET'S GO.
ズイ
ZUI (SHOVE)

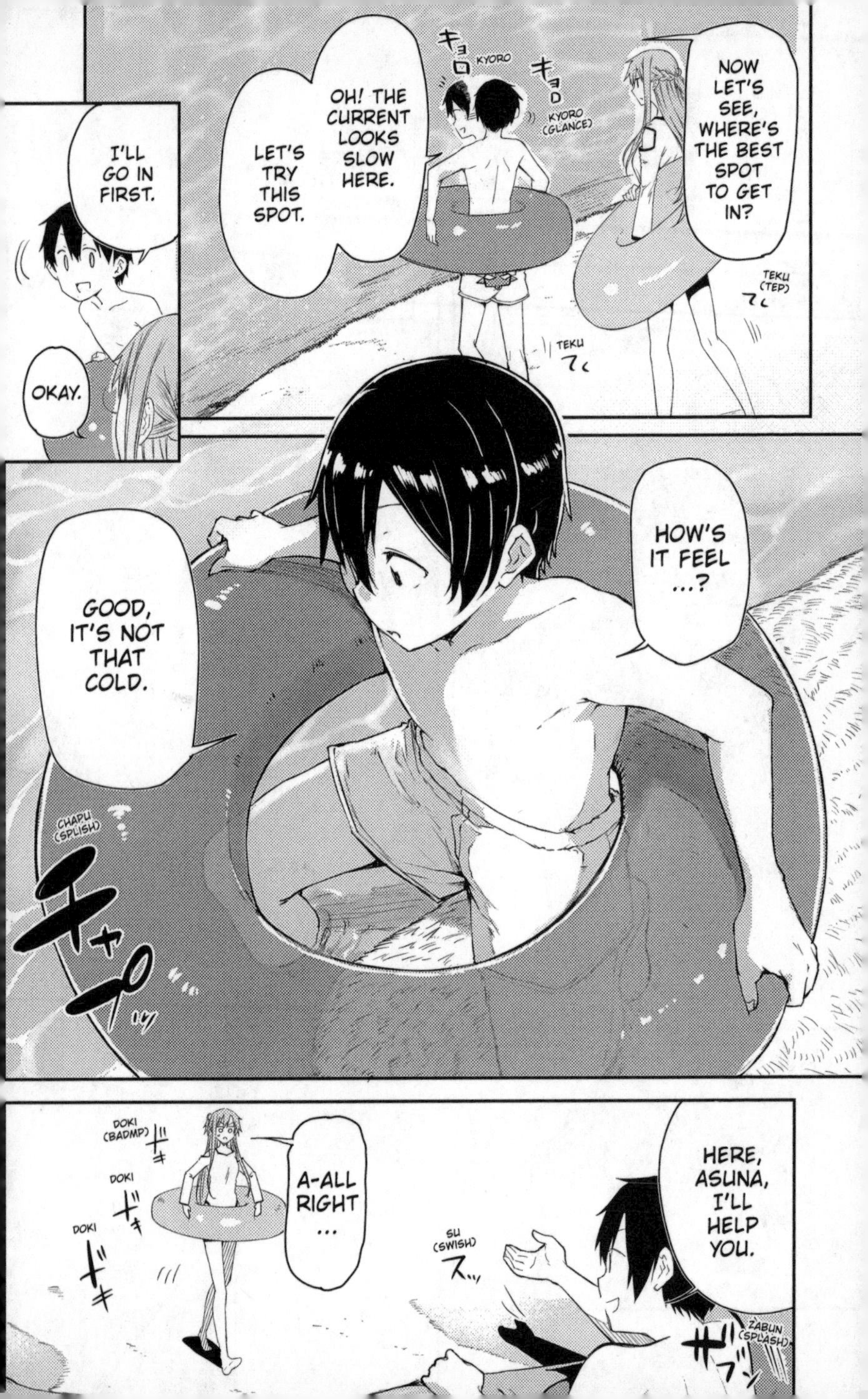
NOW LET'S SEE, WHERE'S THE BEST SPOT TO GET IN?
TEKU (TEP)
KYORO
KYORO (GLANCE)
OH! THE CURRENT LOOKS SLOW HERE.
LET'S TRY THIS SPOT.
TEKU
I'LL GO IN FIRST.
OKAY.
HOW'S IT FEEL ...?
GOOD, IT'S NOT THAT COLD.
CHAPU (SPLISH)
HERE, ASUNA, I'LL HELP YOU.
ZABUN (SPLASH)
SU (SWISH)
A-ALL RIGHT ...
DOKI (BADMP)
DOKI
DOKI

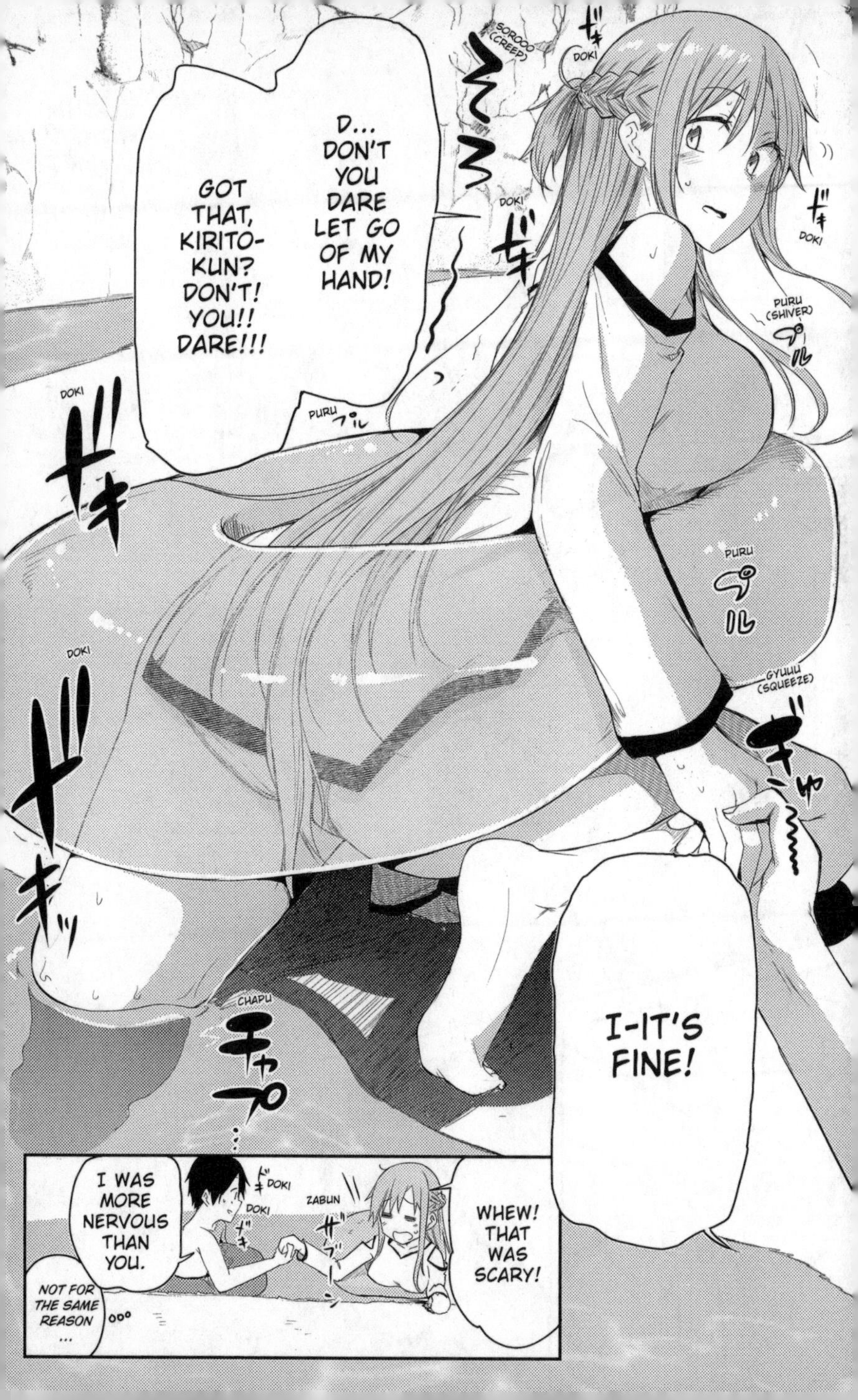

DOKI
SOROOO (CREEP)
D... DON'T YOU DARE LET GO OF MY HAND!
GOT THAT, KIRITO-KUN? DON'T! YOU!! DARE!!!
DOKI
DOKI
PURU (SHIVER)
PURU
DOKI
PURU
DOKI
GYUUU (SQUEEZE)
I-IT'S FINE!
CHAPU
WHEW! THAT WAS SCARY!
ZABUN
DOKI
DOKI
I WAS MORE NERVOUS THAN YOU.
NOT FOR THE SAME REASON ...

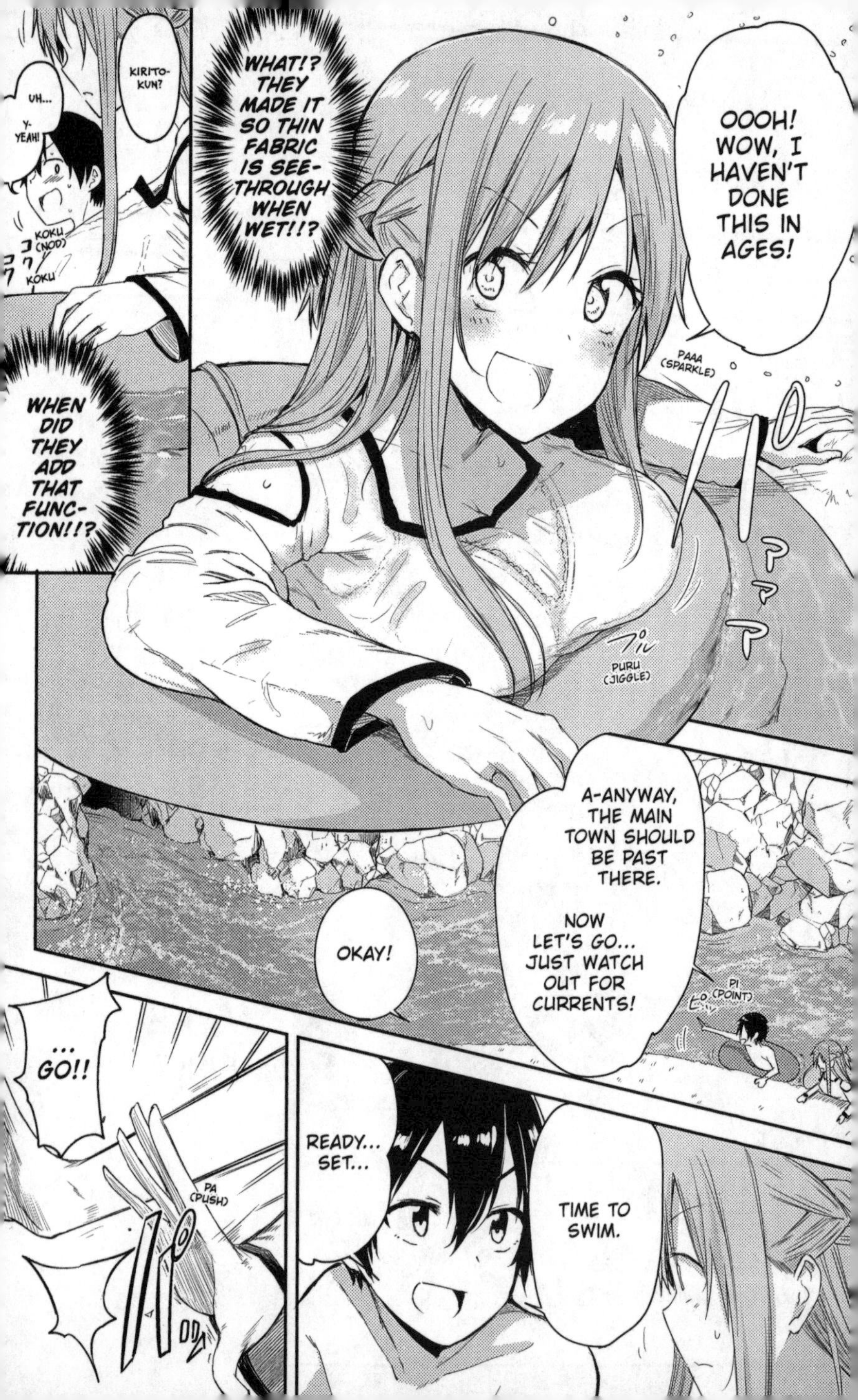
OOOH! WOW, I HAVEN'T DONE THIS IN AGES!
PAAA (SPARKLE)
PURU (JIGGLE)
WHAT!? THEY MADE IT SO THIN FABRIC IS SEE-THROUGH WHEN WET!!?
KIRITO-KUN?
UH...
Y-YEAH!
KOKU (NOD)
KOKU
WHEN DID THEY ADD THAT FUNCTION!!?
A-ANYWAY, THE MAIN TOWN SHOULD BE PAST THERE.
NOW LET'S GO... JUST WATCH OUT FOR CURRENTS!
PI (POINT)
OKAY!
TIME TO SWIM.
READY... SET...
... GO!!
PA (PUSH)

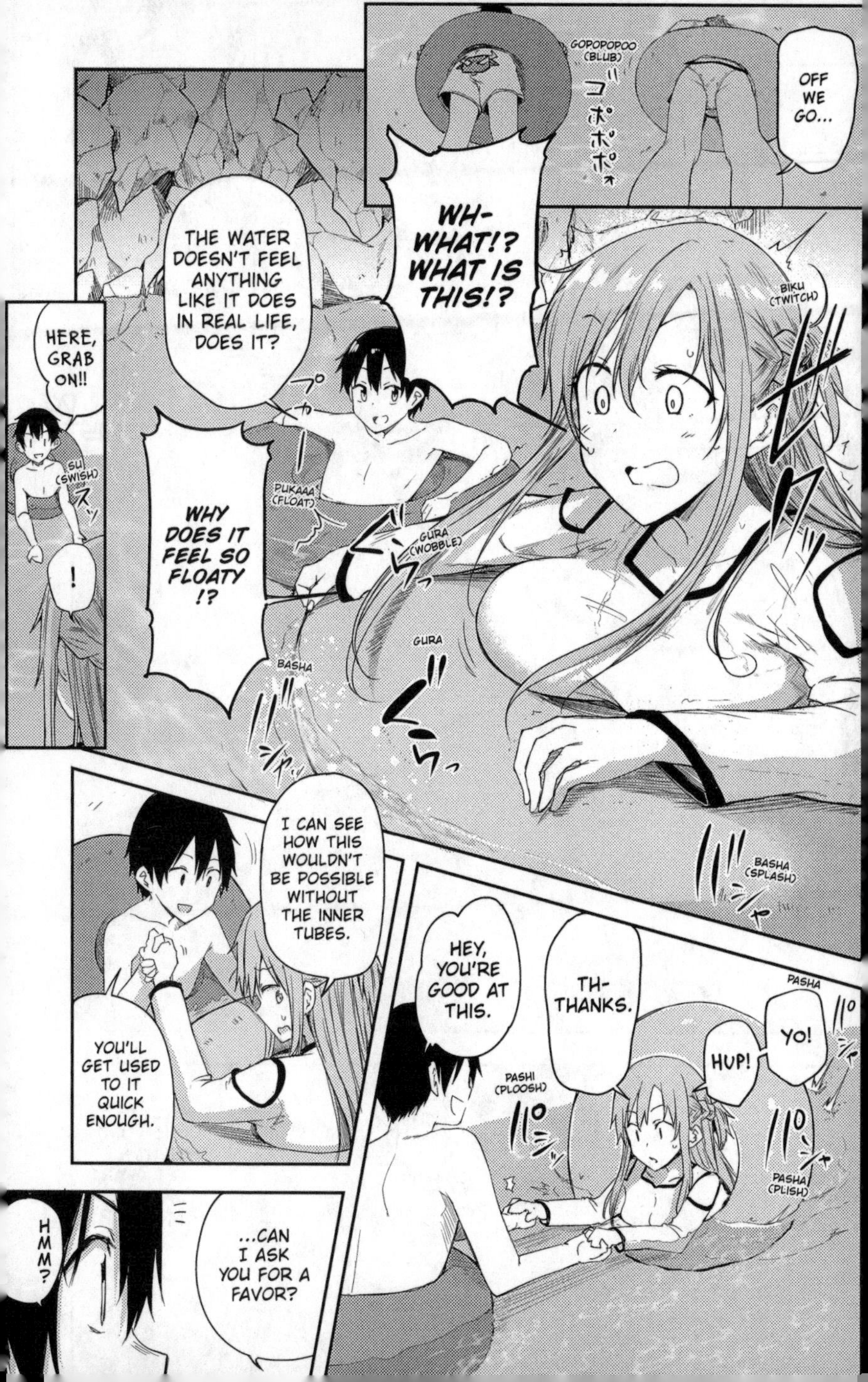
OFF WE GO...
GOPOPOPOO (BLUB)
ゴポポポ
BIKU (TWITCH)
WH- WHAT!? WHAT IS THIS!?
THE WATER DOESN'T FEEL ANYTHING LIKE IT DOES IN REAL LIFE, DOES IT?
WHY DOES IT FEEL SO FLOATY !?
PUKAAA (FLOAT)
GURA (WOBBLE)
GURA
BASHA
HERE, GRAB ON!!
SU (SWISH)
!
BASHA (SPLASH)
PASHA
YO!
HUP!
TH- THANKS.
HEY, YOU'RE GOOD AT THIS.
PASHI (PLOOSH)
PASHA (PLISH)
I CAN SEE HOW THIS WOULDN'T BE POSSIBLE WITHOUT THE INNER TUBES.
YOU'LL GET USED TO IT QUICK ENOUGH.
...CAN I ASK YOU FOR A FAVOR?
HMM?

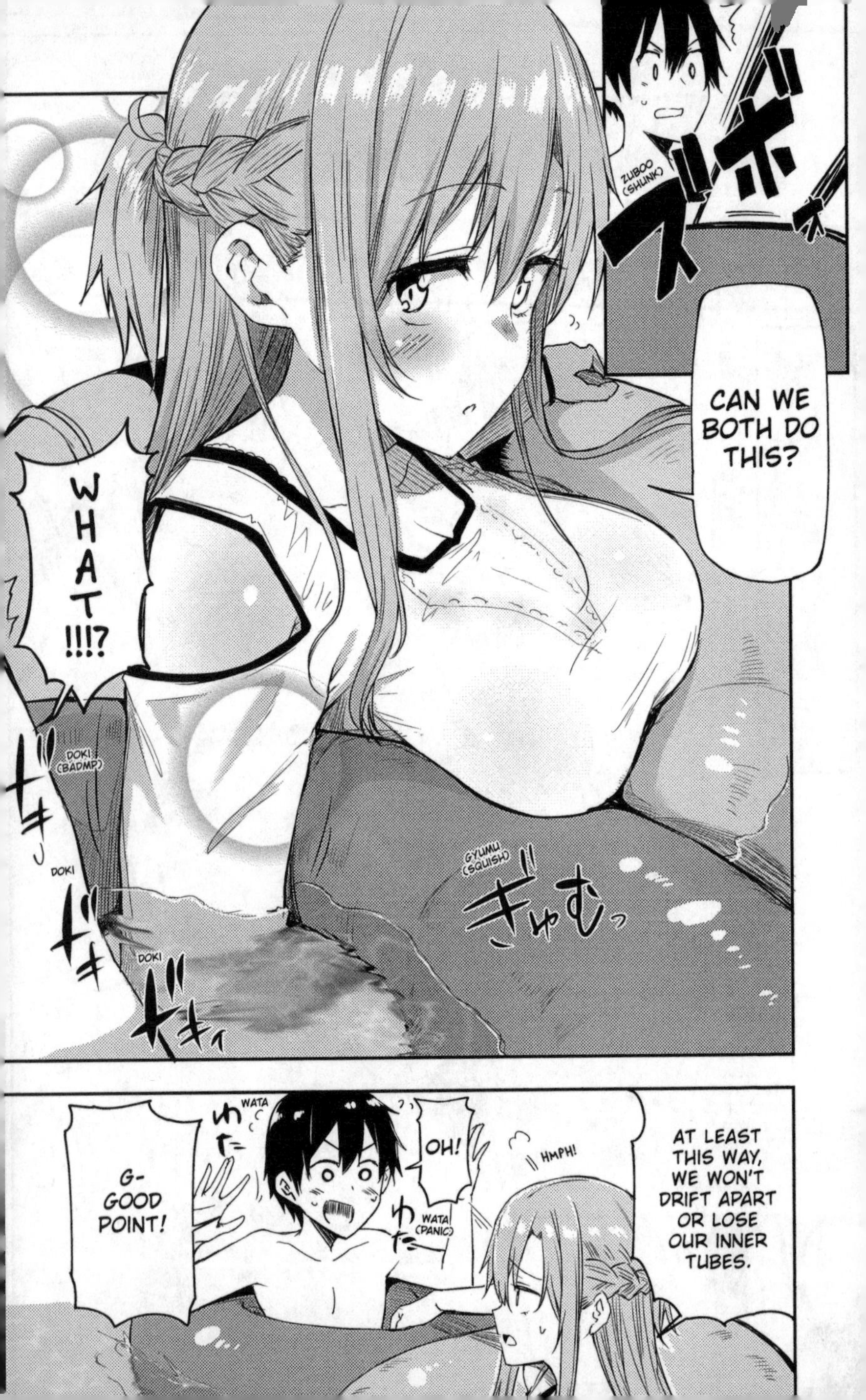

ZUBOO (SHUNK)
CAN WE BOTH DO THIS?
WHAT !!!?
GYUMU (SQUISH)
ぎゅむっ
DOKI (BADMP)
DOKI
DOKI
AT LEAST THIS WAY, WE WON'T DRIFT APART OR LOSE OUR INNER TUBES.
HMPH!
OH!
WATA (PANIC)
WATA
G-GOOD POINT!

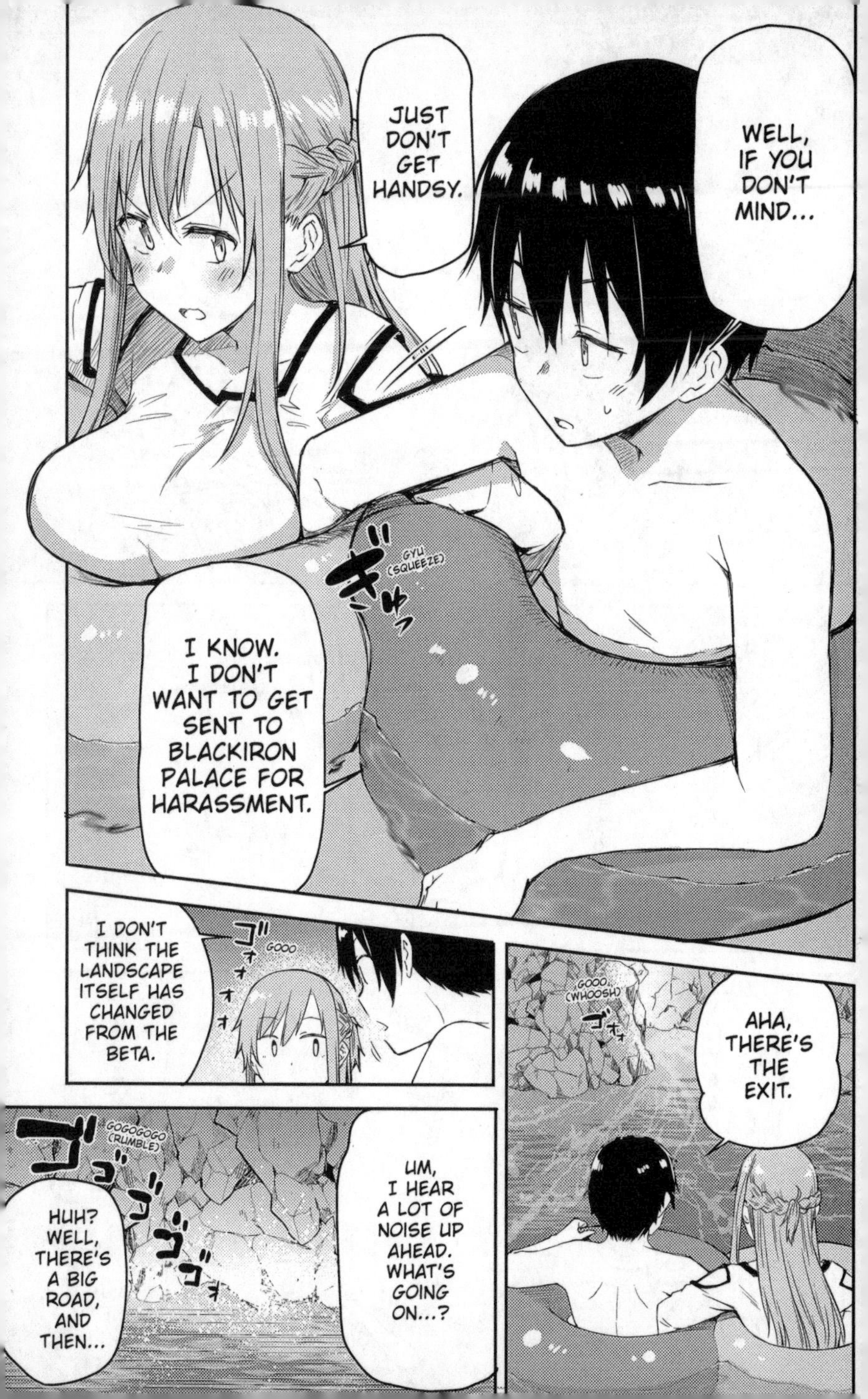
WELL, IF YOU DON'T MIND...
JUST DON'T GET HANDSY.
GYU (SQUEEZE)
I KNOW. I DON'T WANT TO GET SENT TO BLACKIRON PALACE FOR HARASSMENT.
GOOO (WHOOSH)
AHA, THERE'S THE EXIT.
I DON'T THINK THE LANDSCAPE ITSELF HAS CHANGED FROM THE BETA.
GOOO
UM, I HEAR A LOT OF NOISE UP AHEAD. WHAT'S GOING ON...?
GOGOGOGO (RUMBLE)
HUH? WELL, THERE'S A BIG ROAD, AND THEN...

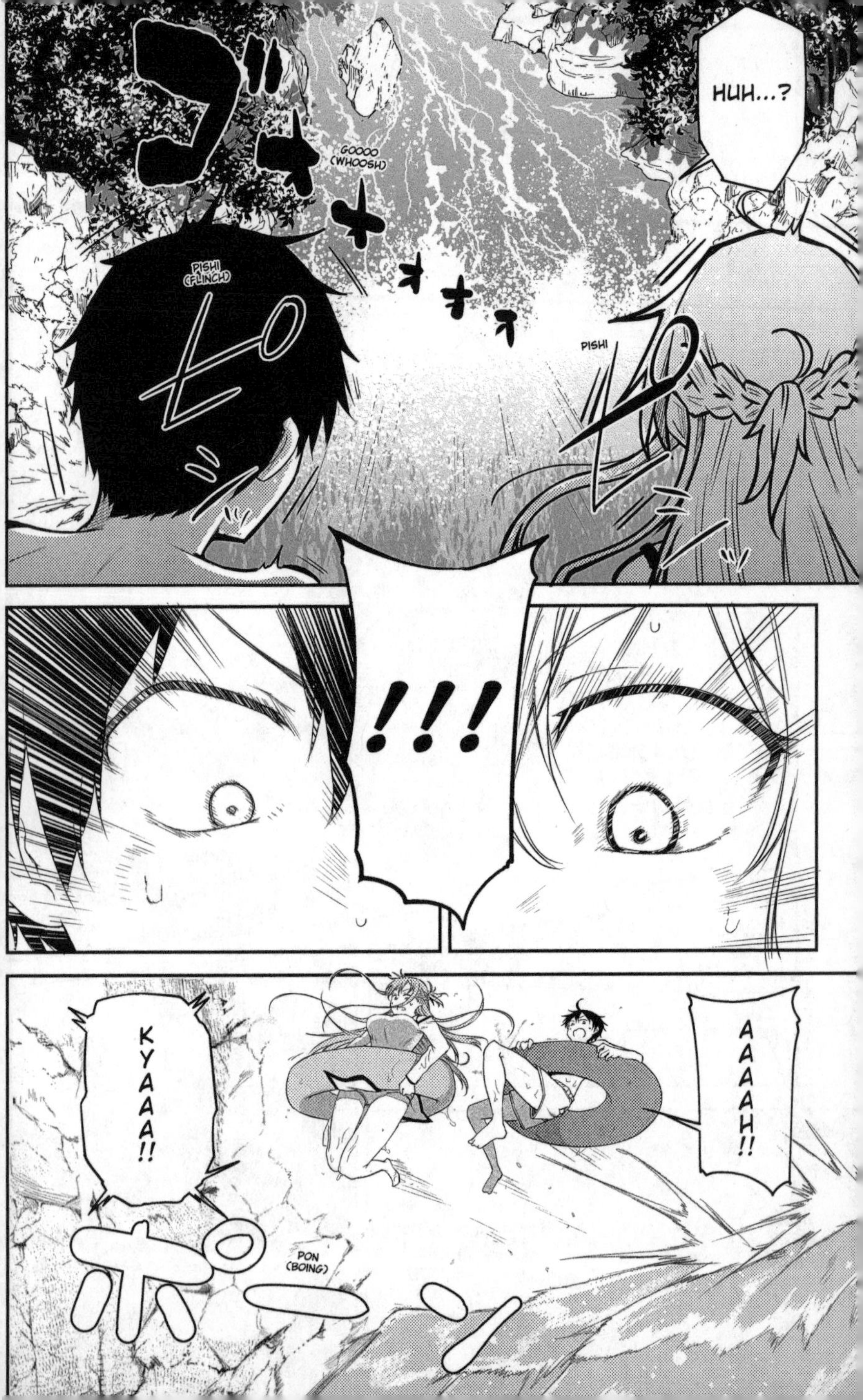
HUH...?
GOOOO (WHOOSH)
PISHI
PISHI (FLINCH)
!!!
AAAAAH!!
KYAAAA!!
PON (BOING)

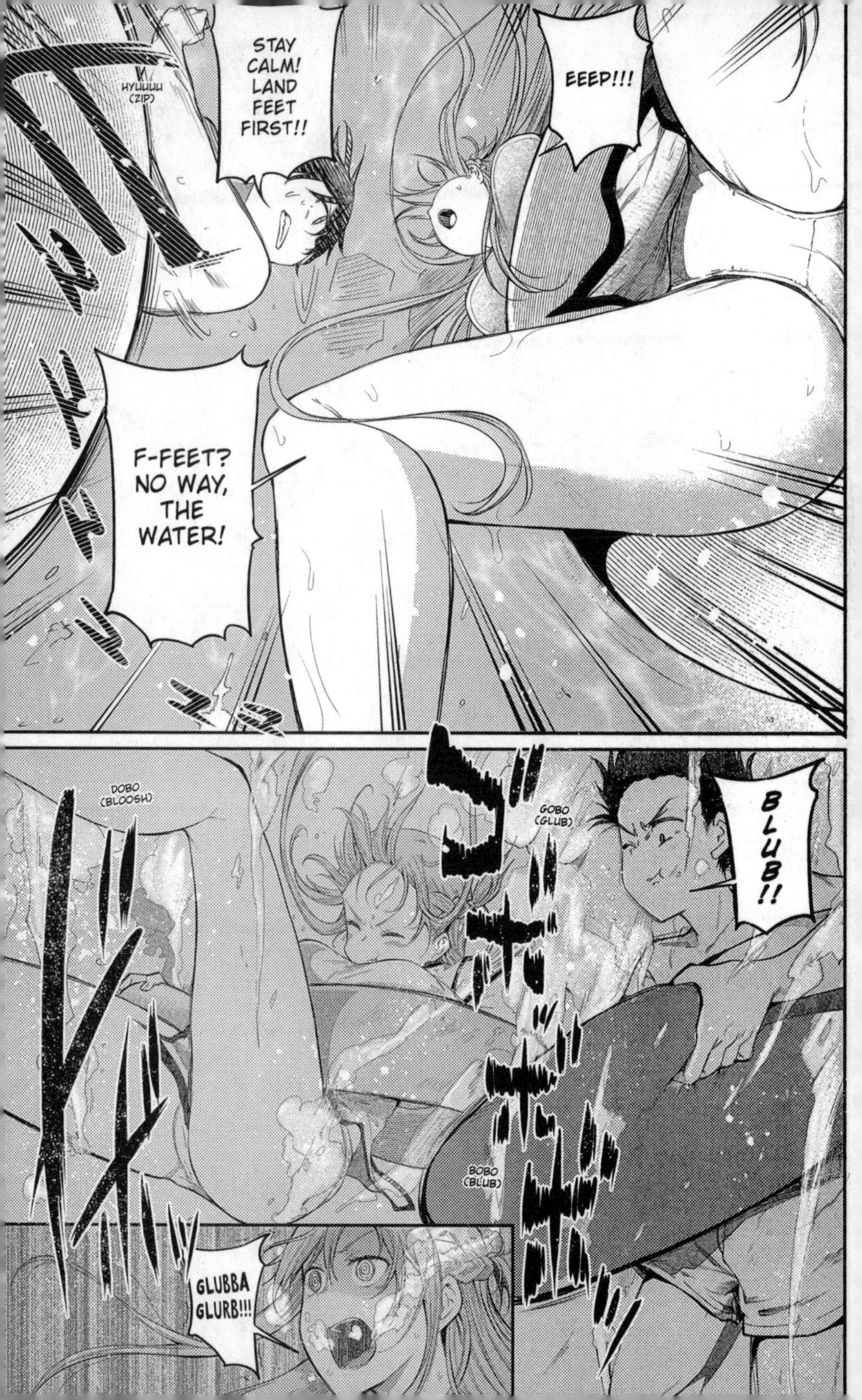
EEEP!!!
STAY CALM! LAND FEET FIRST!!
HYUUUU (ZIP)
F-FEET? NO WAY, THE WATER!
BLUB!!
GOBO (GLUB)
DOBO (BLOOSH)
BOBO (BLUB)
GLUBBA GLURB!!!

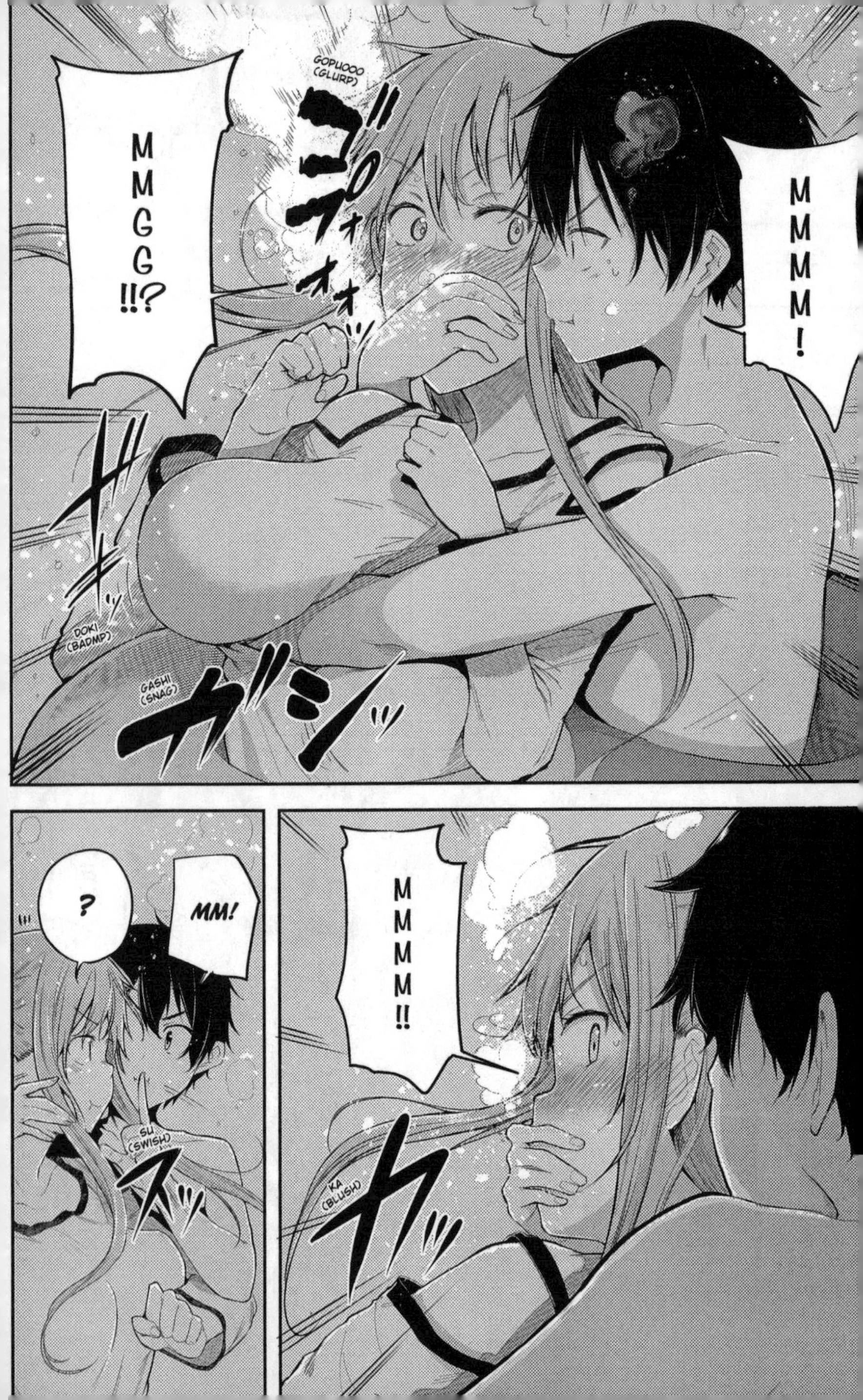
MMMM!
GOPUOOO (GLURP)
MMGG!!?
DOKI (BADMP)
GASHI (SNAG)
MMMM!!
KA (BLUSH)
MM!
?
SU (SWISH)

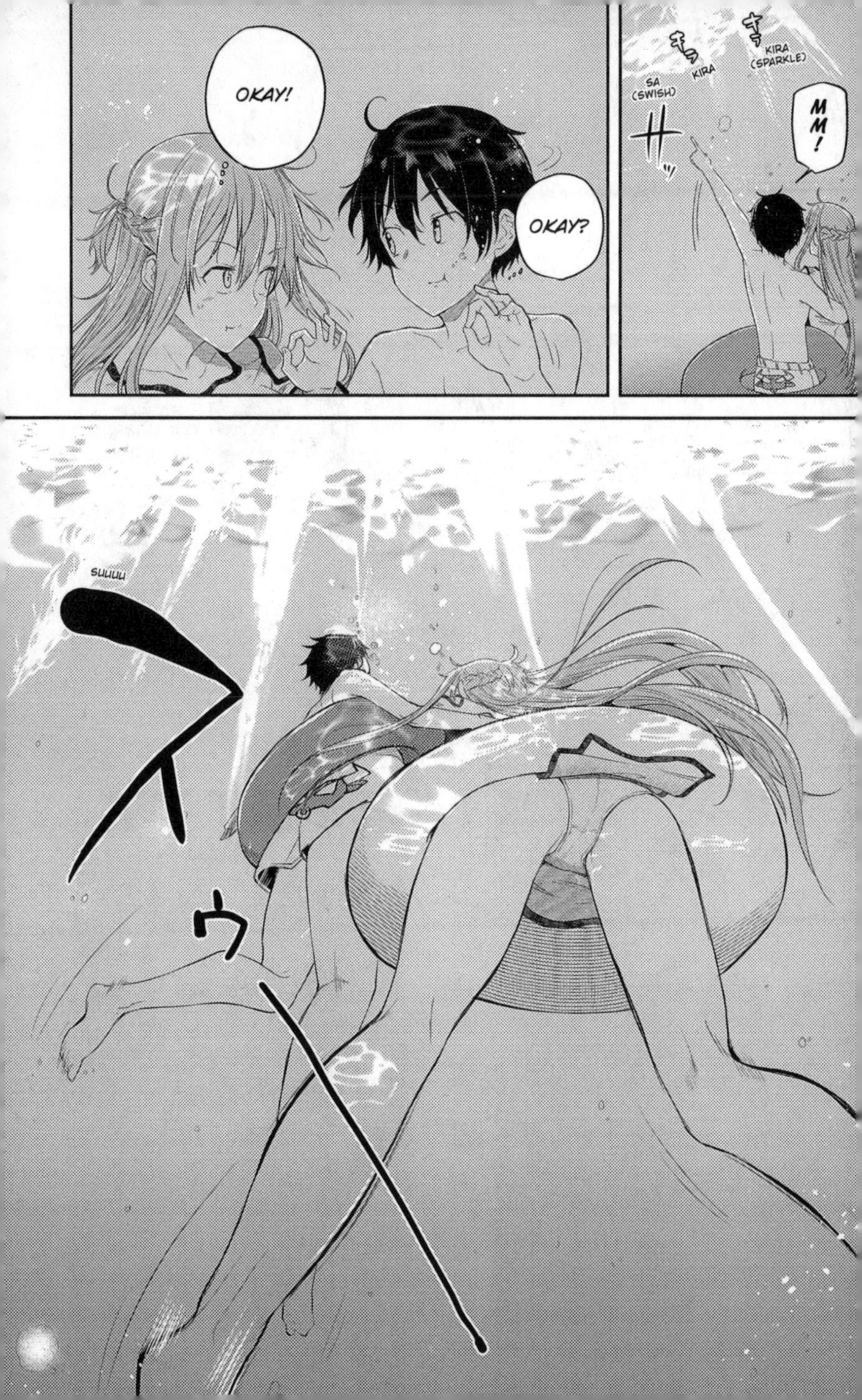
KIRA (SPARKLE)
KIRA
SA (SWISH)
MM!
OKAY?
OKAY!
SUUUU

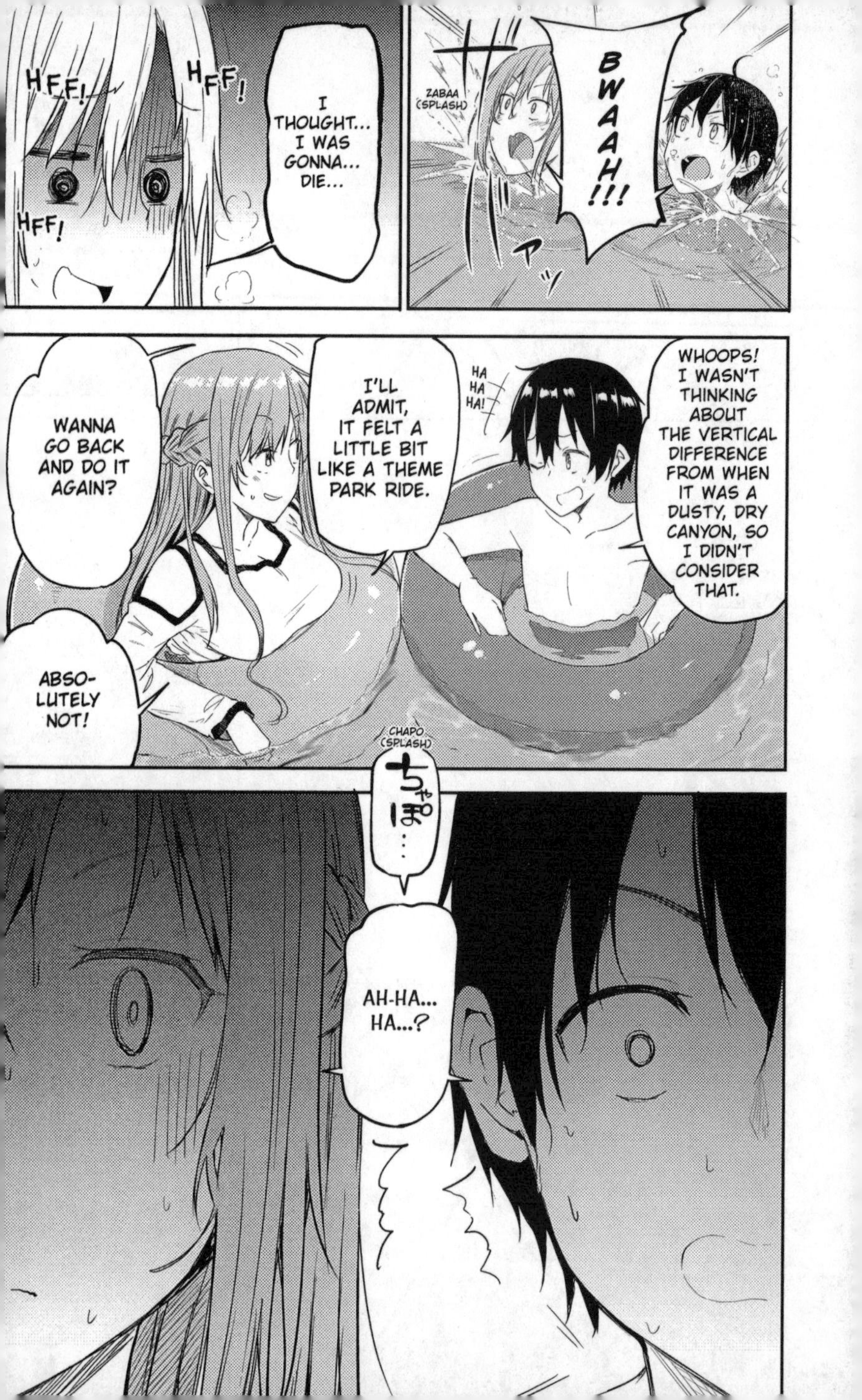
BWAAAH!!!
ZABAA (SPLASH)
I THOUGHT... I WAS GONNA... DIE...
HFF!
HFF!
HFF!
WHOOPS! I WASN'T THINKING ABOUT THE VERTICAL DIFFERENCE FROM WHEN IT WAS A DUSTY, DRY CANYON, SO I DIDN'T CONSIDER THAT.
HA HA HA!
I'LL ADMIT, IT FELT A LITTLE BIT LIKE A THEME PARK RIDE.
WANNA GO BACK AND DO IT AGAIN?
ABSO-LUTELY NOT!
CHAPO (SPLASH)
ちゃぽ…
AH-HA... HA...?

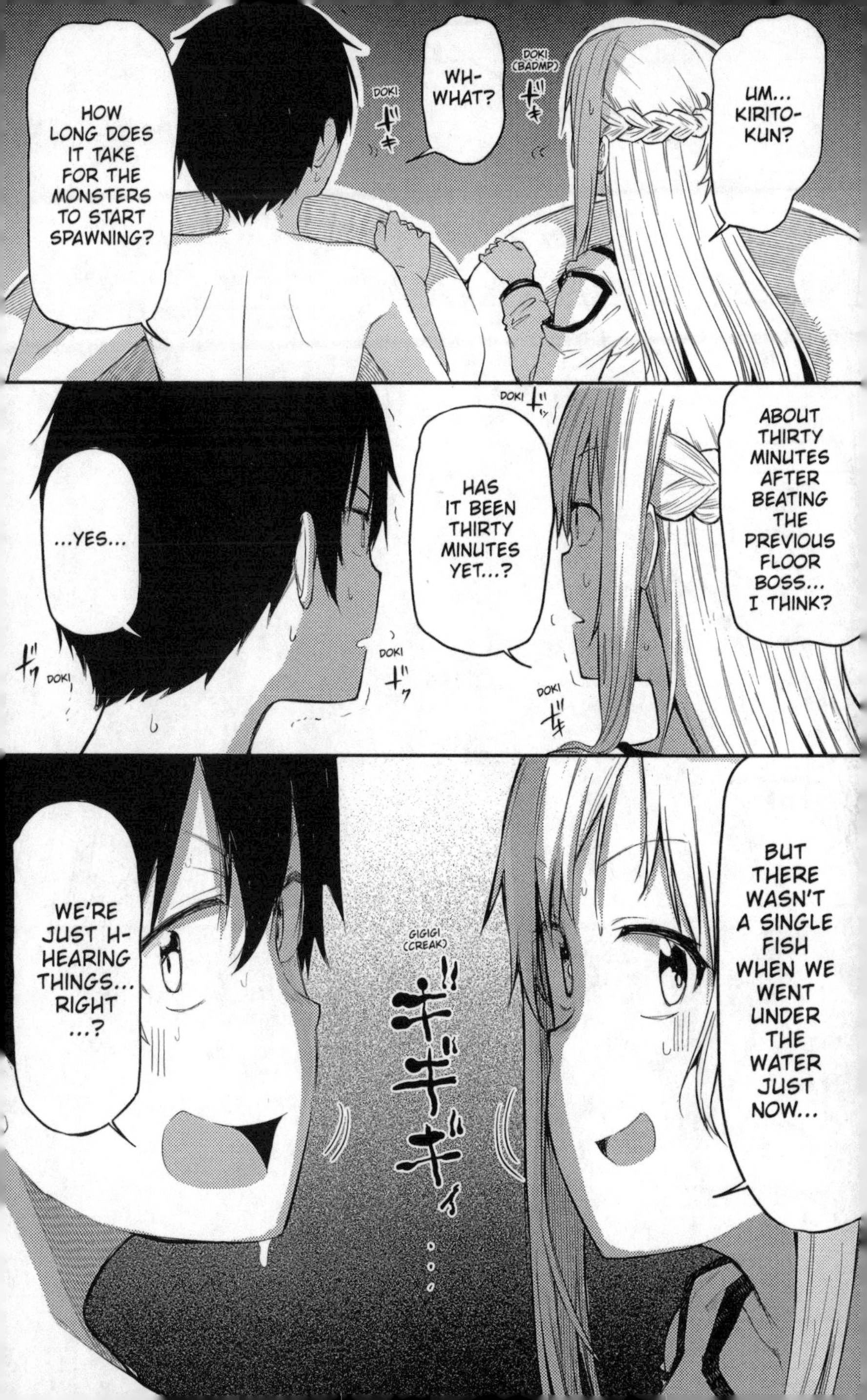
UM... KIRITO-KUN?
DOKI (BADMP)
WH- WHAT?
DOKI
HOW LONG DOES IT TAKE FOR THE MONSTERS TO START SPAWNING?
ABOUT THIRTY MINUTES AFTER BEATING THE PREVIOUS FLOOR BOSS... I THINK?
DOKI
HAS IT BEEN THIRTY MINUTES YET...?
DOKI
DOKI
...YES...
DOKI
BUT THERE WASN'T A SINGLE FISH WHEN WE WENT UNDER THE WATER JUST NOW...
GIGIGI (CREAK)
WE'RE JUST H-HEARING THINGS... RIGHT ...?

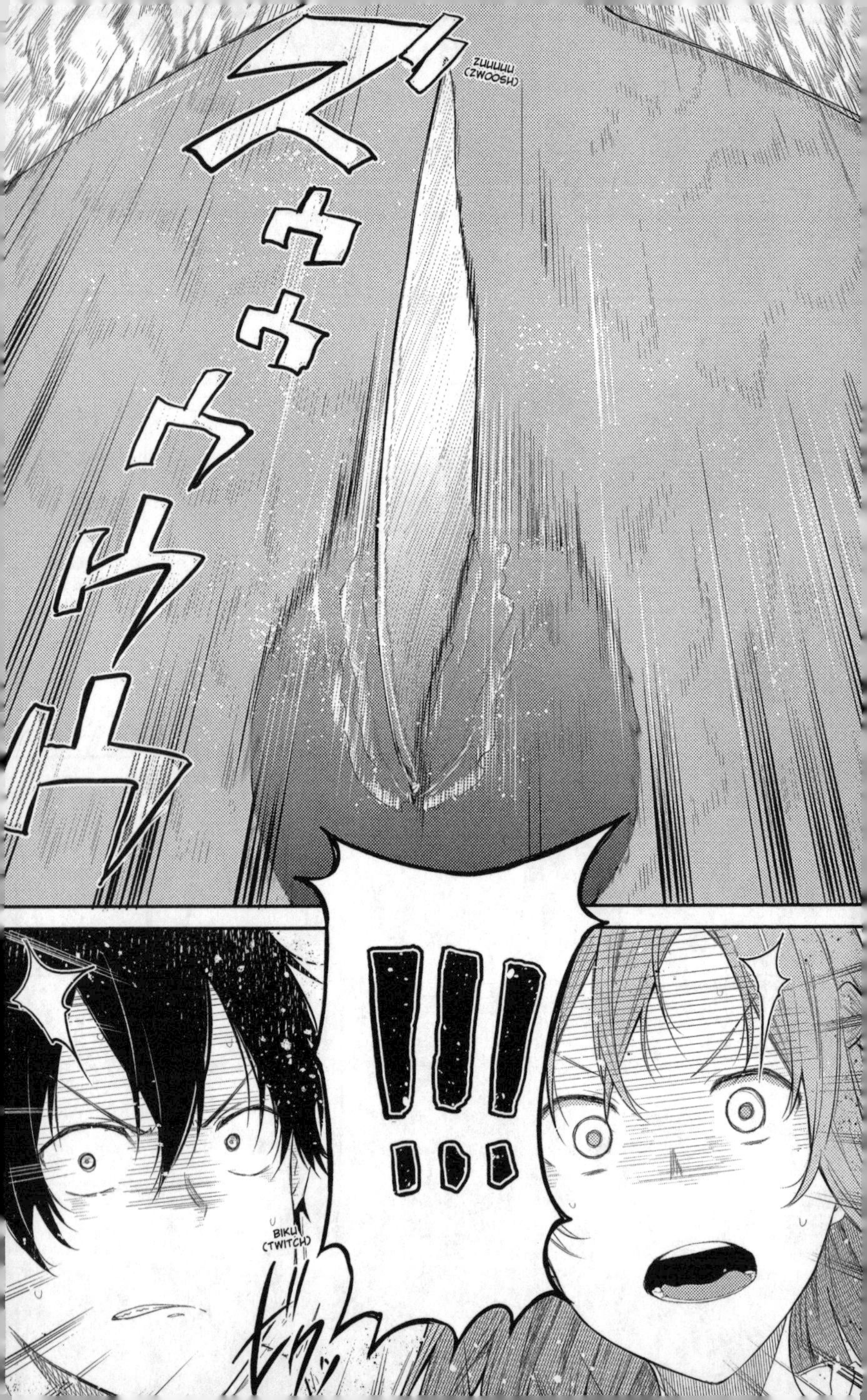
ZUUUUU
(ZWOOSH)
!!!
BIKU
(TWITCH)

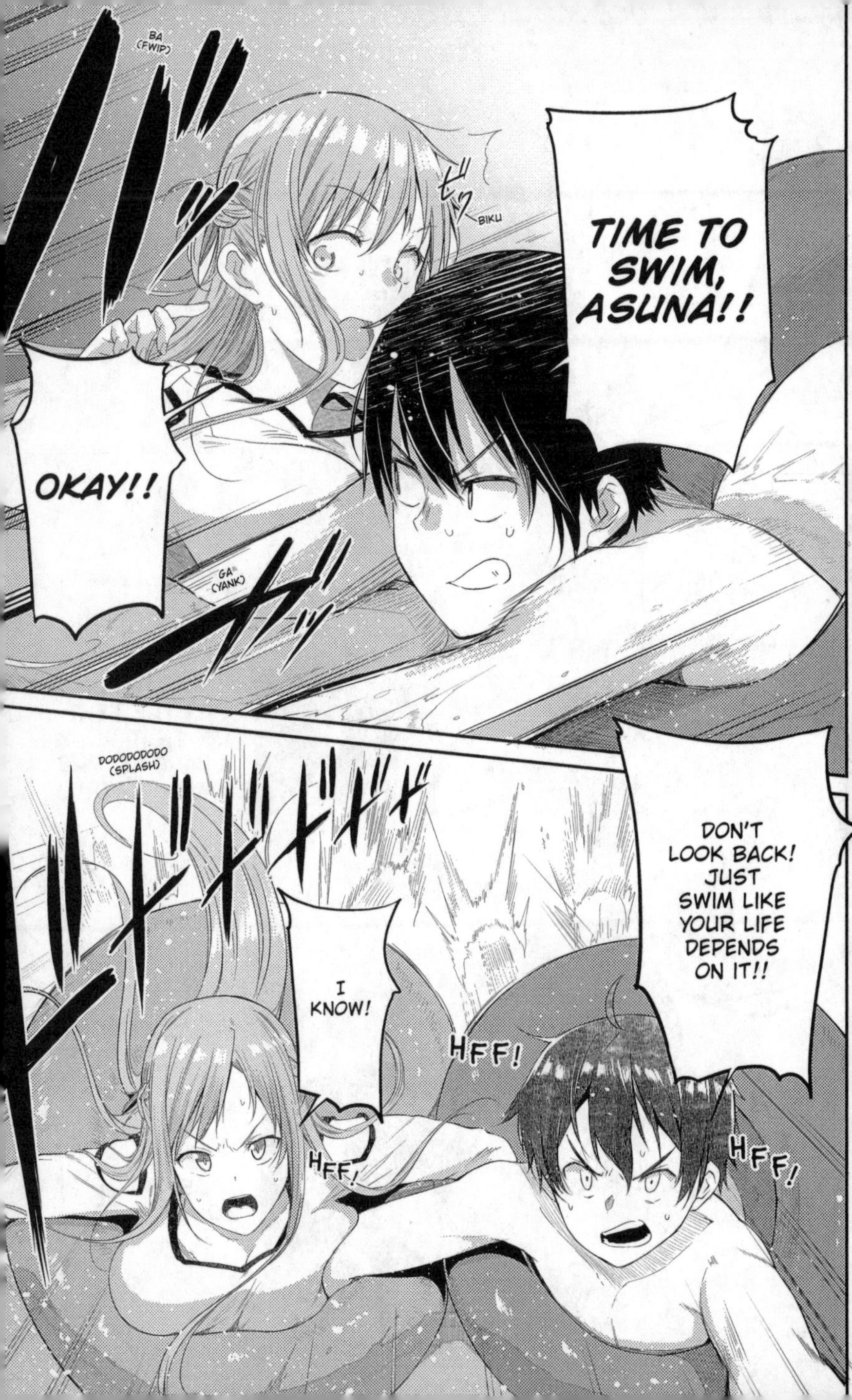
TIME TO SWIM, ASUNA!!
BIKU
BA (FWIP)
OKAY!!
GA (YANK)
DON'T LOOK BACK! JUST SWIM LIKE YOUR LIFE DEPENDS ON IT!!
I KNOW!
DODODODODO (SPLASH)
HFF!
HFF!
HFF!

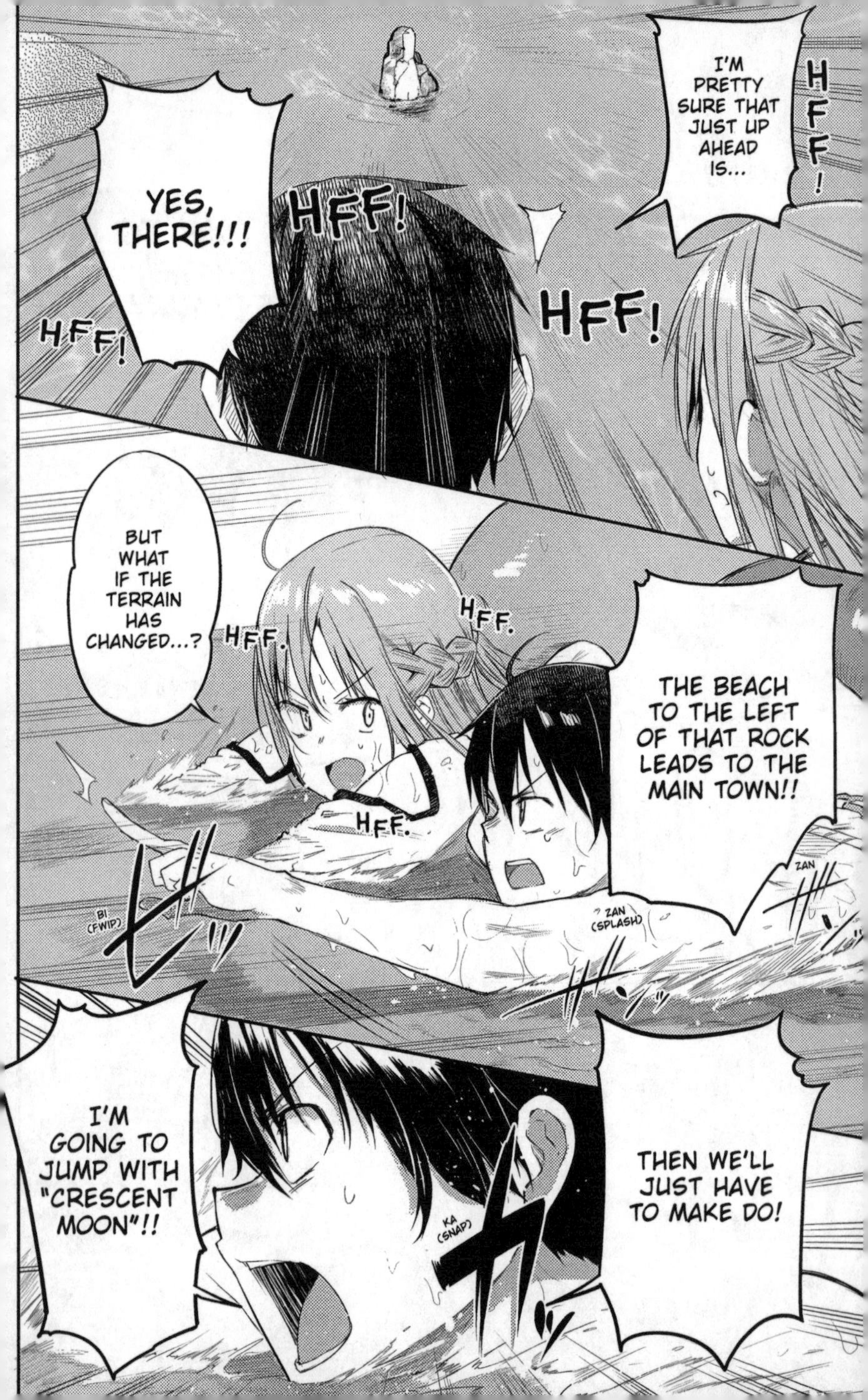
I'M PRETTY SURE THAT JUST UP AHEAD IS...
HFF!
HFF!
HFF!
YES, THERE!!!
HFF!
THE BEACH TO THE LEFT OF THAT ROCK LEADS TO THE MAIN TOWN!!
HFF.
BUT WHAT IF THE TERRAIN HAS CHANGED...?
HFF.
HFF.
ZAN
ZAN (SPLASH)
BI (FWIP)
THEN WE'LL JUST HAVE TO MAKE DO!
KA (SNAP)
I'M GOING TO JUMP WITH "CRESCENT MOON"!!

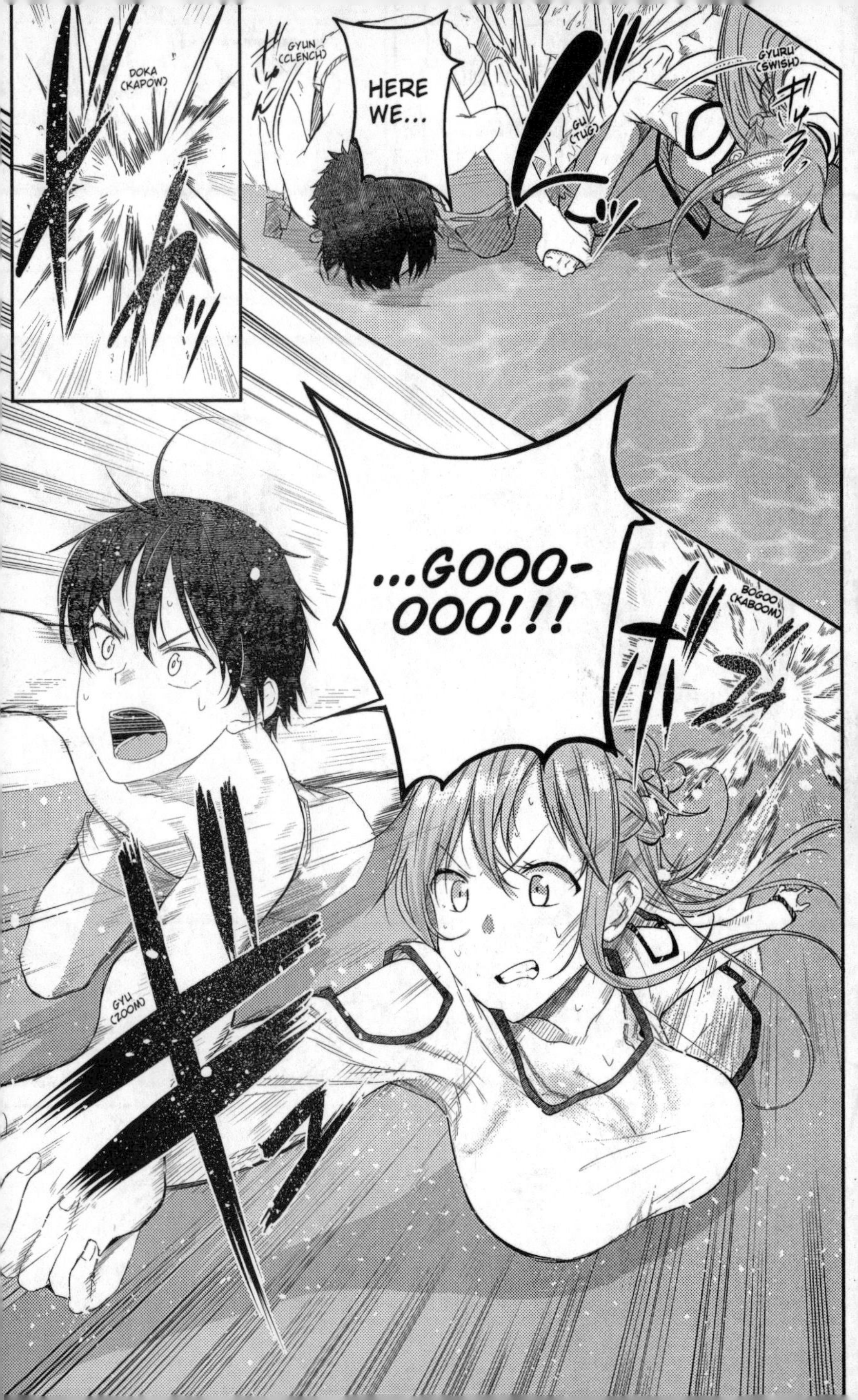
GYURU (SWISH)
GU (TUG)
HERE WE...
GYUN (CLENCH)
DOKA (KAPOW)
BOGOO (KABOOM)
...GOOO-OOO!!!
GYU (ZOOM)

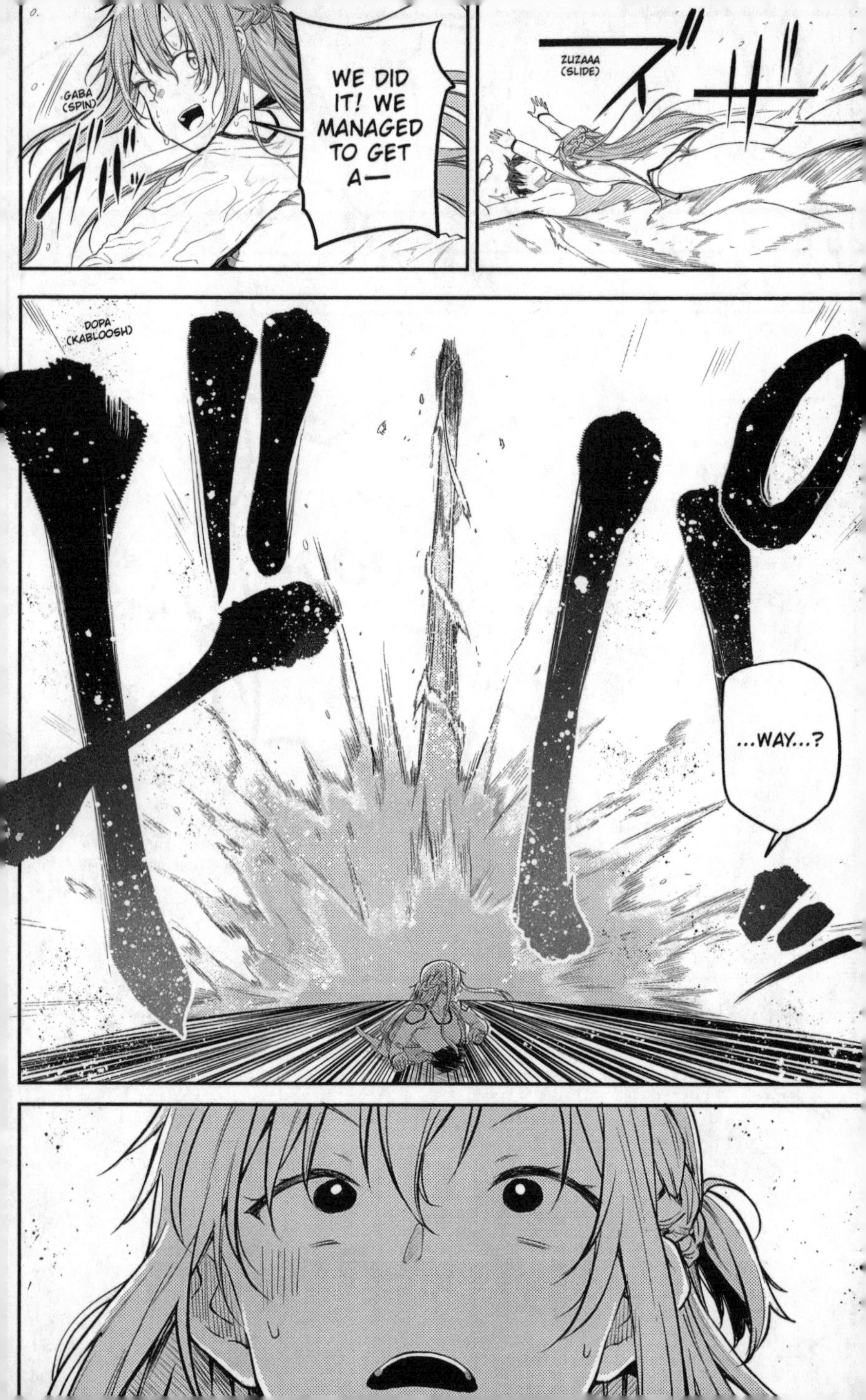
ZUZAAA (SLIDE)
GABA (SPIN)
WE DID IT! WE MANAGED TO GET A—
DOPA (KABLOOSH)
...WAY...?

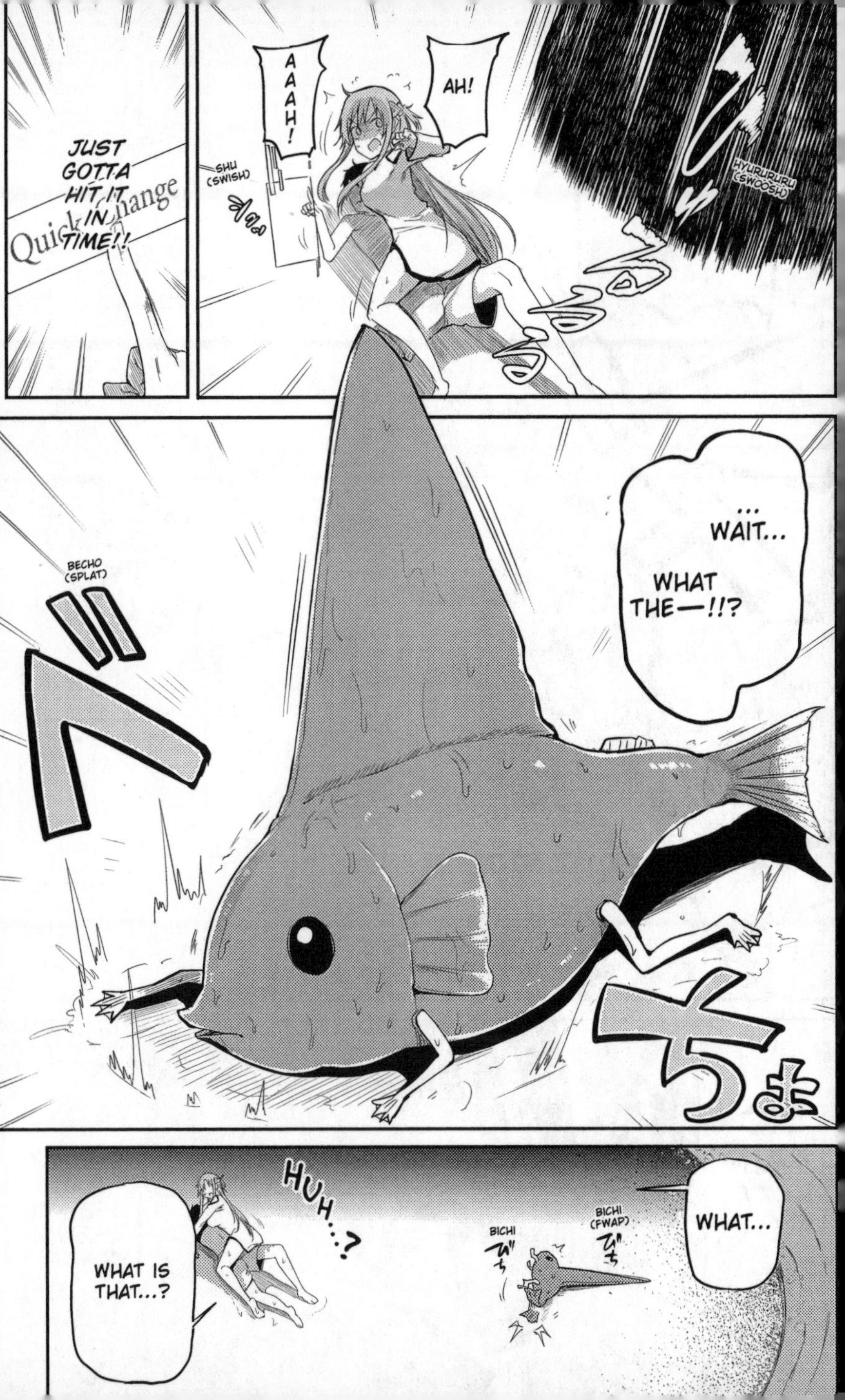
HYURURURU (SWOOSH)
AH!
AAAAH!
SHU (SWISH)
JUST GOTTA HIT IT IN TIME!!
Quick Change
... WAIT...
WHAT THE—!!?
BECHO (SPLAT)
WHAT...
BICHI (FWAP)
BICHI
HUH...?
WHAT IS THAT...?

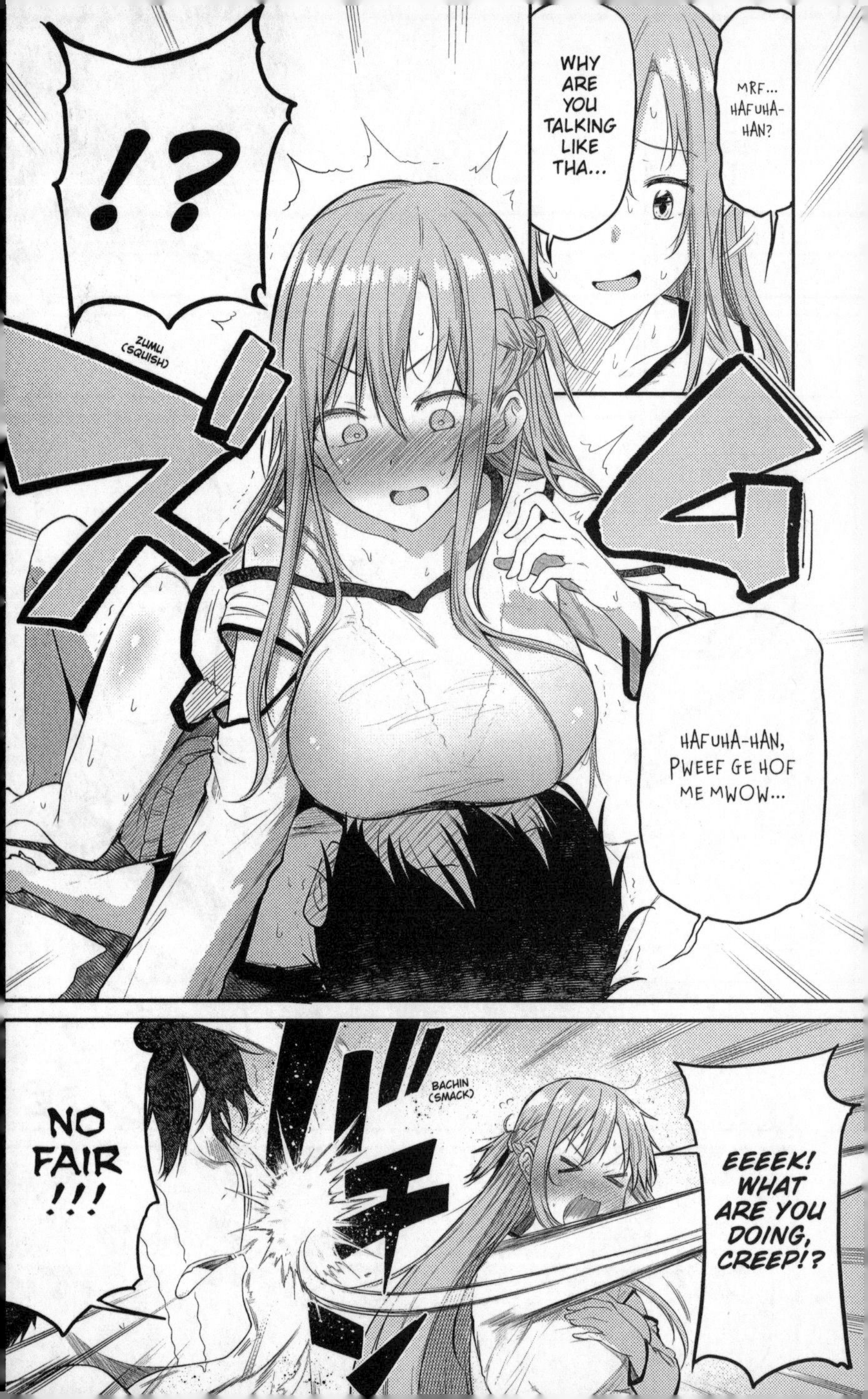
MRF... HAFUHA-HAN?
WHY ARE YOU TALKING LIKE THA...
!?
ZUMU (SQUISH)
HAFUHA-HAN, PWEEF GE HOF ME MWOW...
EEEEK! WHAT ARE YOU DOING, CREEP!?
BACHIN (SMACK)
NO FAIR!!!

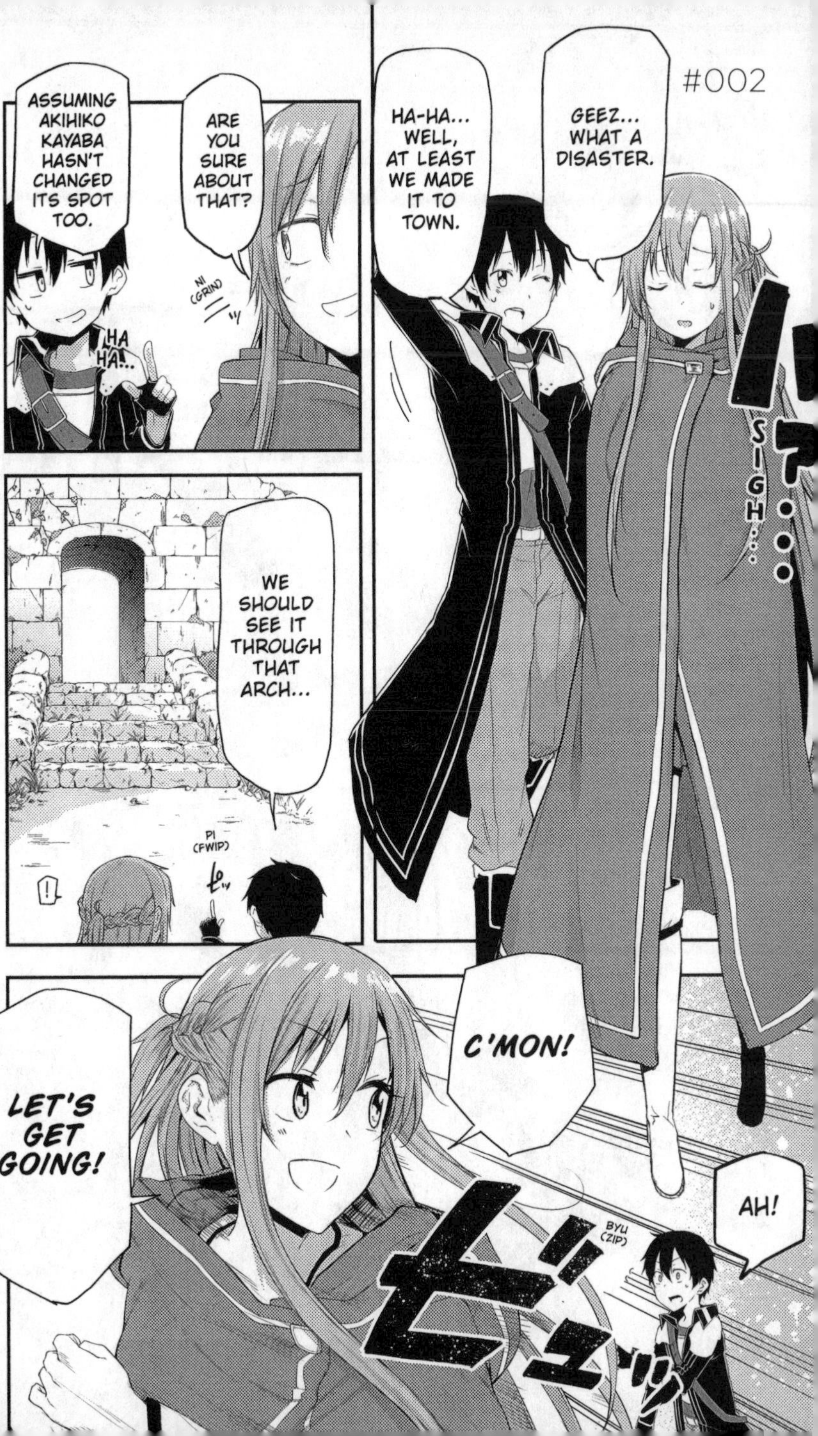
#002
GEEZ... WHAT A DISASTER.
HA-HA... WELL, AT LEAST WE MADE IT TO TOWN.
SIGH...
ARE YOU SURE ABOUT THAT?
ASSUMING AKIHIKO KAYABA HASN'T CHANGED ITS SPOT TOO.
NI (GRIN)
HA HA...
WE SHOULD SEE IT THROUGH THAT ARCH...
PI (FWIP)
!
C'MON!
LET'S GET GOING!
AH!
BYU (ZIP)

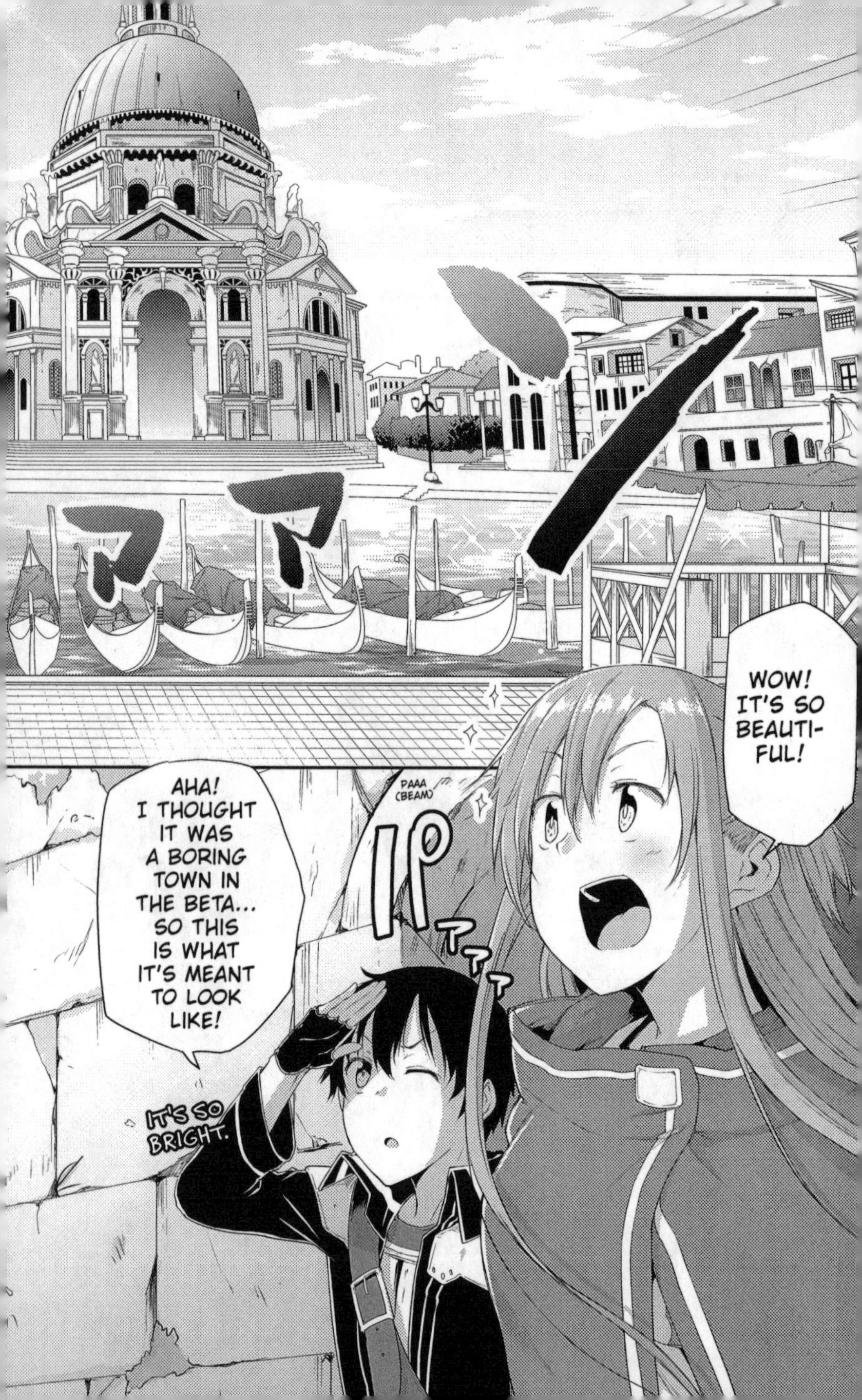

マアー
WOW! IT'S SO BEAUTIFUL!
PAAA (BEAM)
AHA! I THOUGHT IT WAS A BORING TOWN IN THE BETA... SO THIS IS WHAT IT'S MEANT TO LOOK LIKE!
IT'S SO BRIGHT.

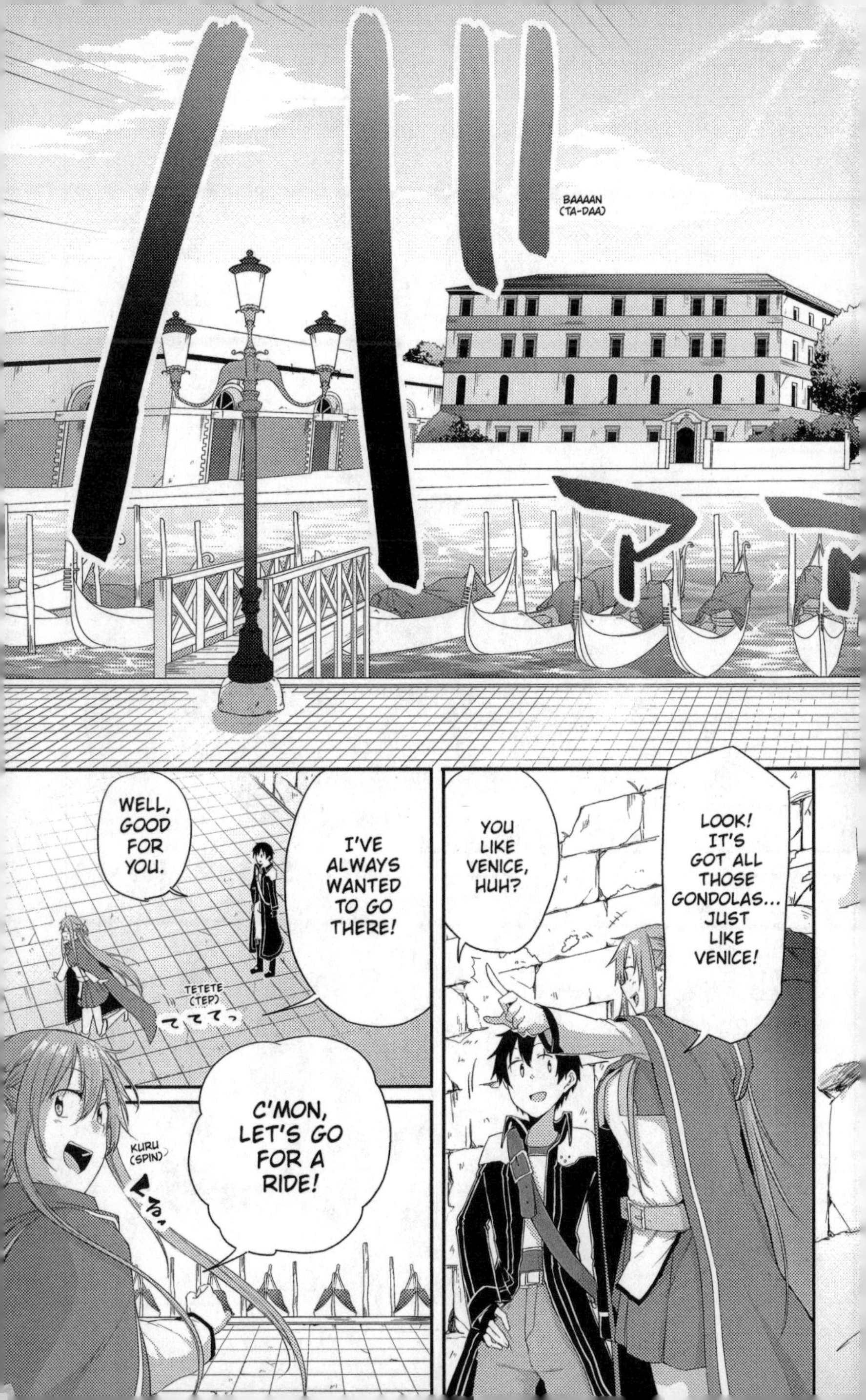
BAAAAN (TA-DAA)
LOOK! IT'S GOT ALL THOSE GONDOLAS... JUST LIKE VENICE!
YOU LIKE VENICE, HUH?
I'VE ALWAYS WANTED TO GO THERE!
WELL, GOOD FOR YOU.
TETETE (TEP)
てててっ
KURU (SPIN)
C'MON, LET'S GO FOR A RIDE!

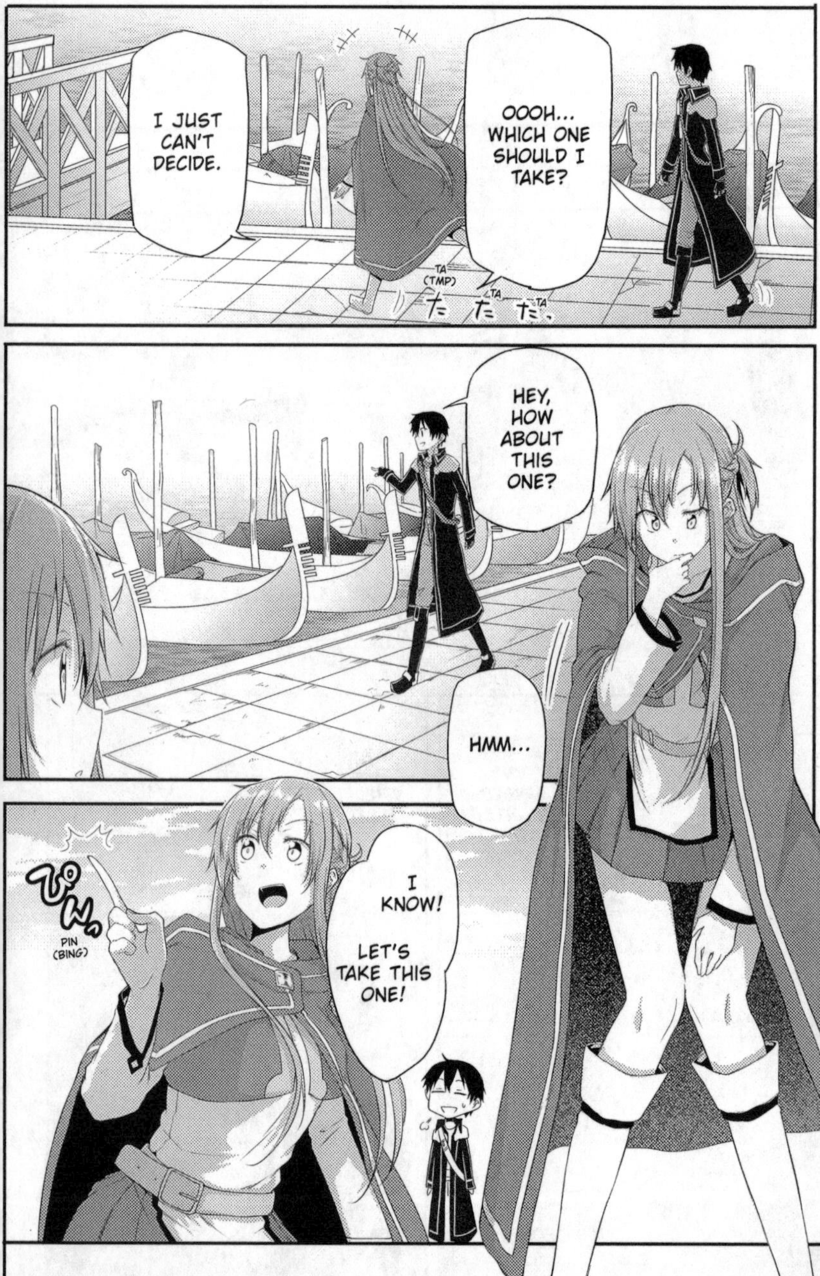
OOOH... WHICH ONE SHOULD I TAKE?
I JUST CAN'T DECIDE.
た TA (TMP) た TA た TA
HEY, HOW ABOUT THIS ONE?
HMM...
I KNOW!
LET'S TAKE THIS ONE!
ぴんっ PIN (BING)

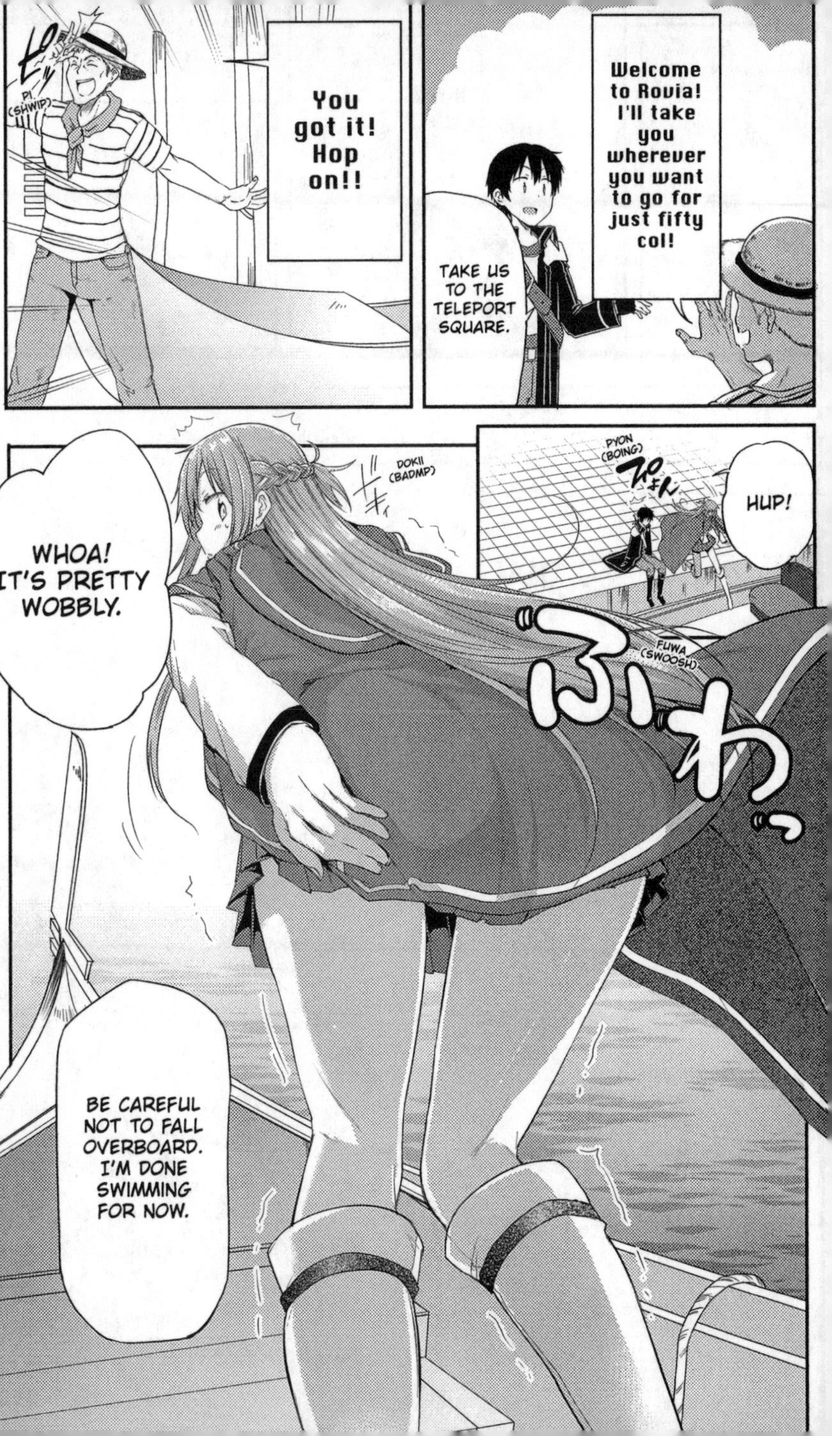
Welcome to Rovia! I'll take you wherever you want to go for just fifty col!
TAKE US TO THE TELEPORT SQUARE.
PI (SHWIP)
You got it! Hop on!!
PYON (BOING)
HUP!
WHOA! IT'S PRETTY WOBBLY.
DOKI! (BADMP)
ふわっ
FUWA (SWOOSH)
BE CAREFUL NOT TO FALL OVERBOARD. I'M DONE SWIMMING FOR NOW.

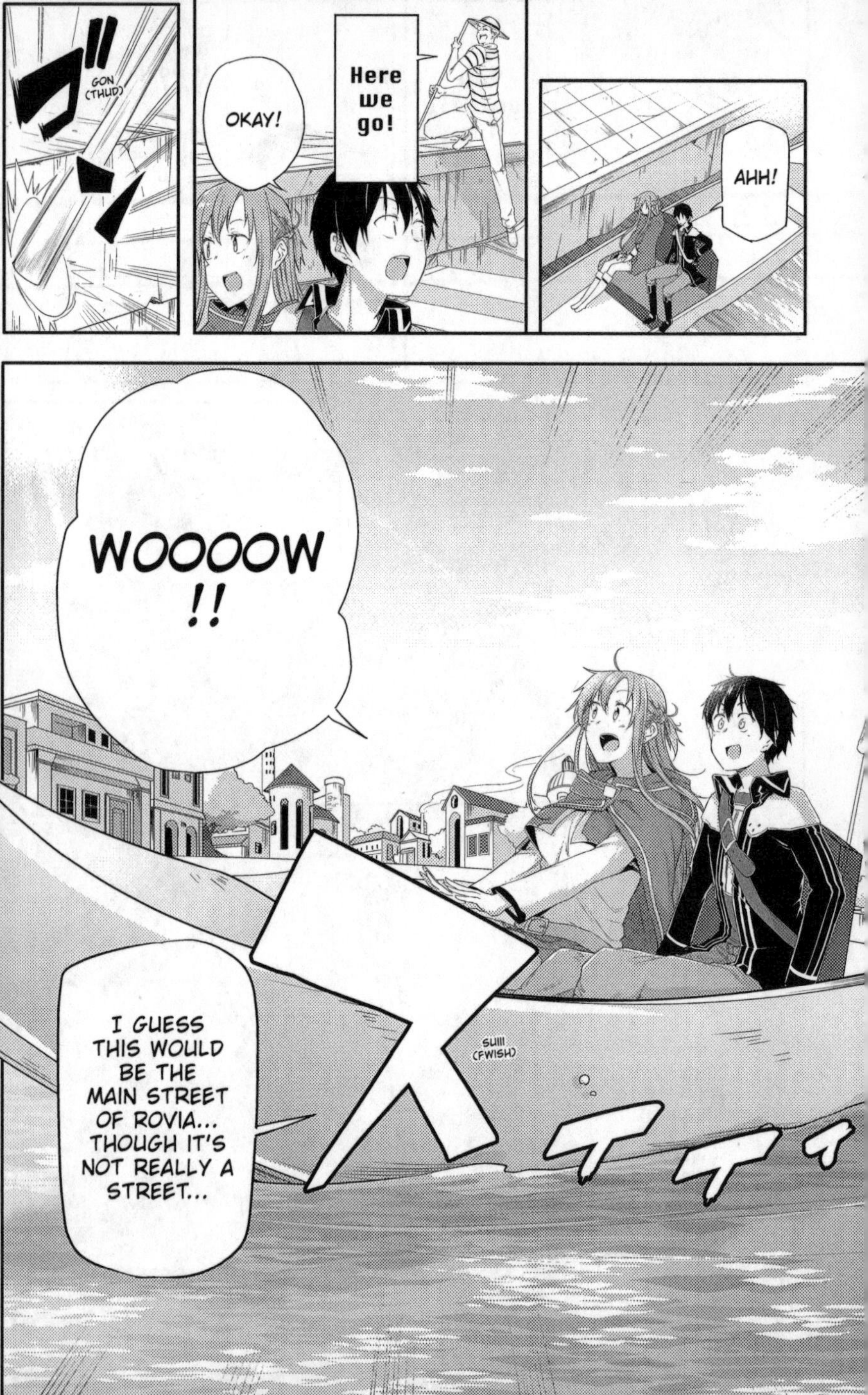
AHH!
Here we go!
OKAY!
GON (THUD)
WOOOOW!!
SUIII (FWISH)
I GUESS THIS WOULD BE THE MAIN STREET OF ROVIA... THOUGH IT'S NOT REALLY A STREET...

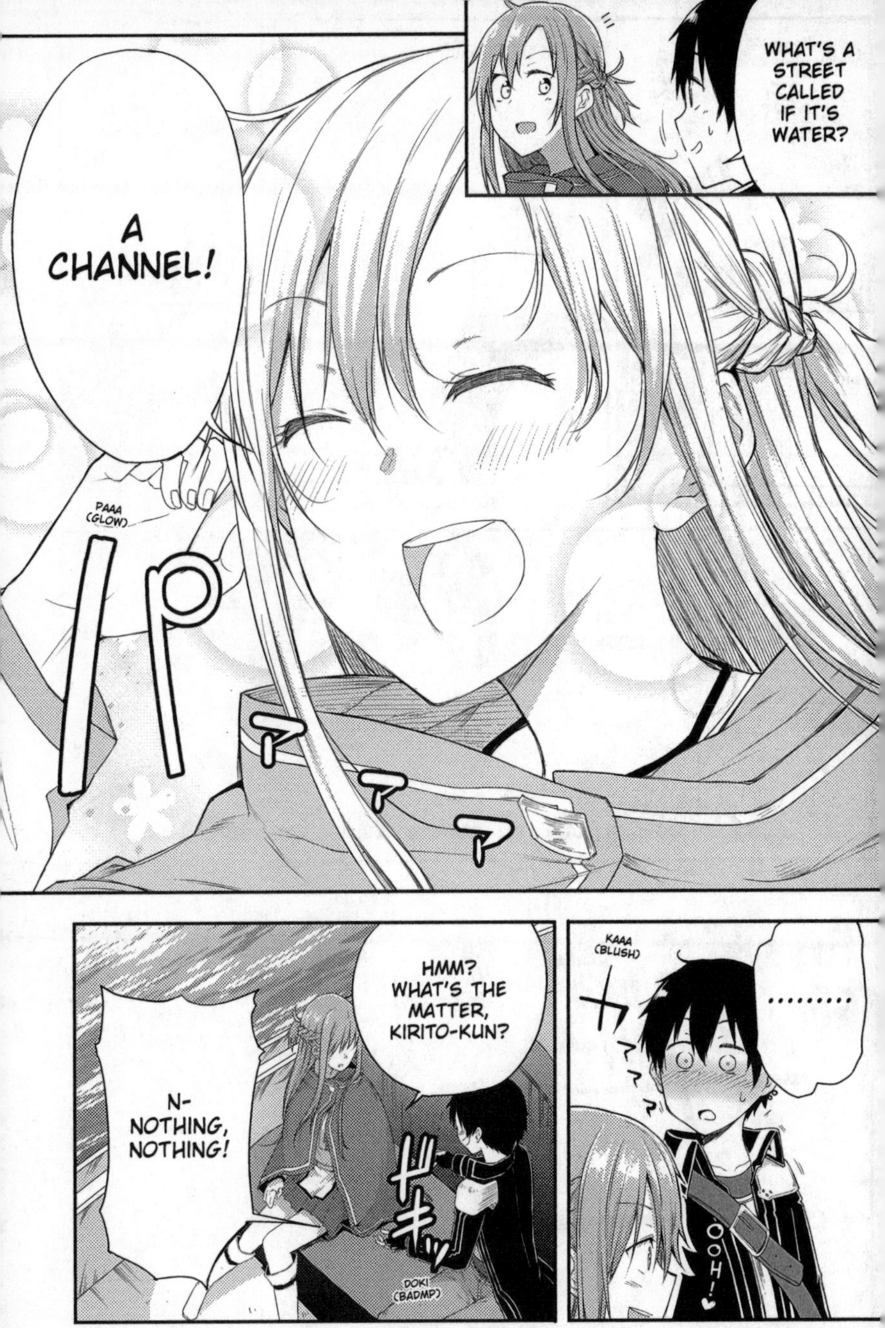
WHAT'S A STREET CALLED IF IT'S WATER?
A CHANNEL!
PAAA (GLOW)
KAAA (BLUSH)
....
OOH!
HMM? WHAT'S THE MATTER, KIRITO-KUN?
N- NOTHING, NOTHING!
DOKI (BADMP)

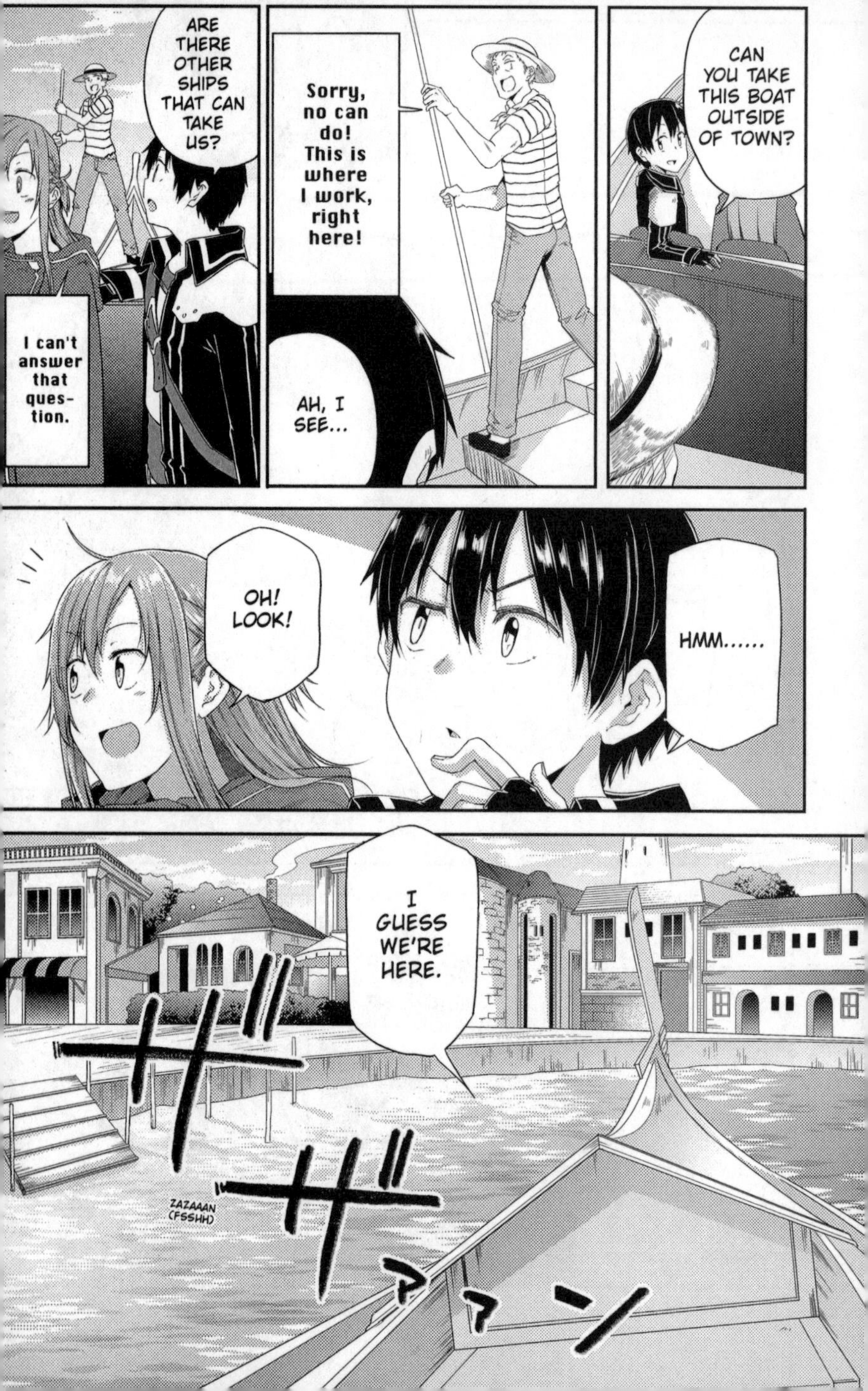
CAN YOU TAKE THIS BOAT OUTSIDE OF TOWN?
Sorry, no can do! This is where I work, right here!
AH, I SEE...
ARE THERE OTHER SHIPS THAT CAN TAKE US?
I can't answer that ques-tion.
HMM......
OH! LOOK!
I GUESS WE'RE HERE.
ZAZAAAN (FSSHH)

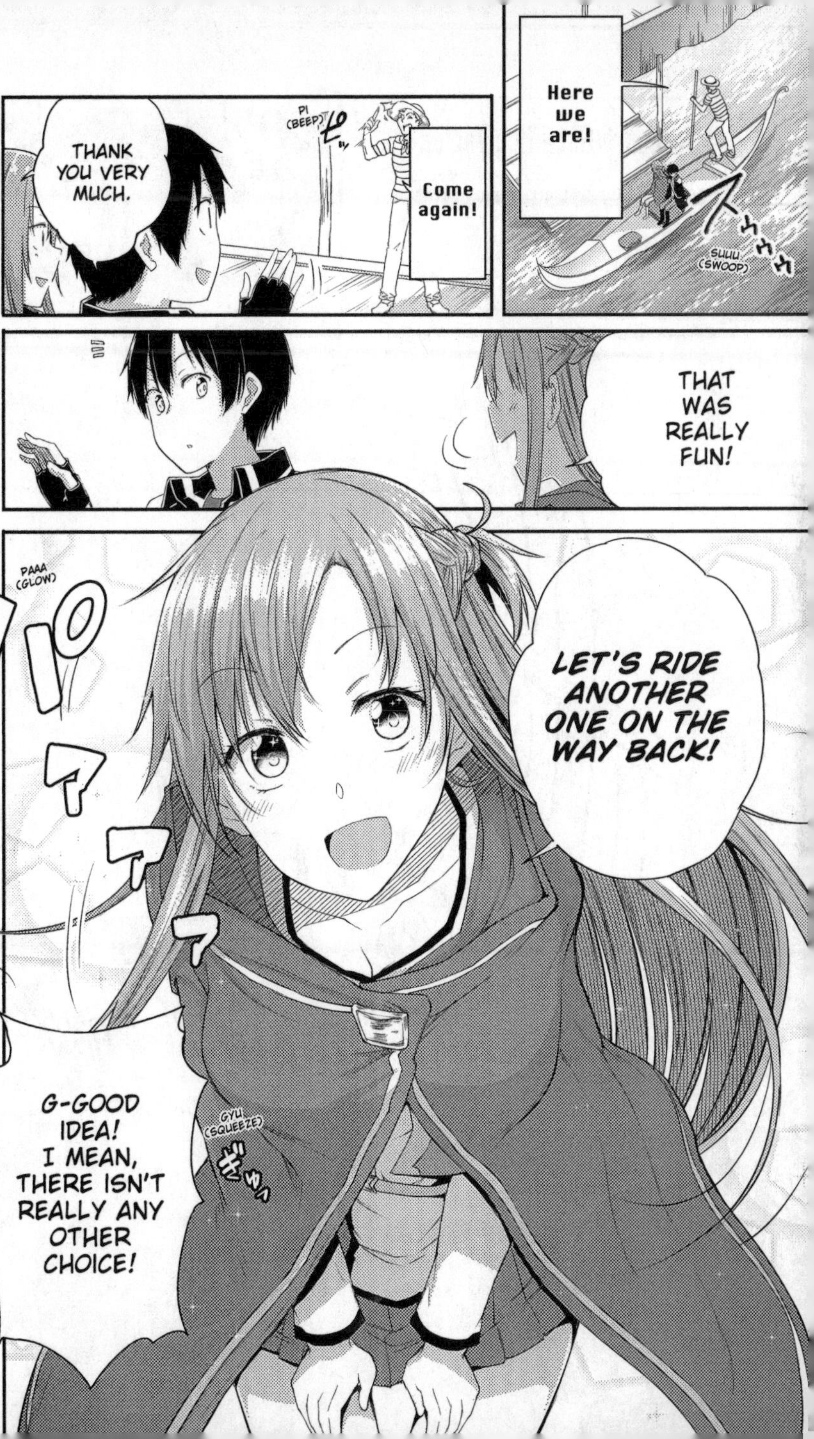
Here we are!
SUUU (SWOOP)
PI (BEEP)
Come again!
THANK YOU VERY MUCH.
THAT WAS REALLY FUN!
LET'S RIDE ANOTHER ONE ON THE WAY BACK!
PAAA (GLOW)
GYU (SQUEEZE)
G-GOOD IDEA! I MEAN, THERE ISN'T REALLY ANY OTHER CHOICE!

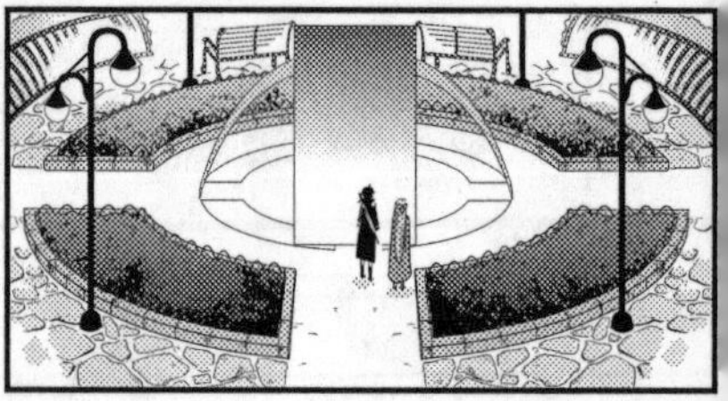

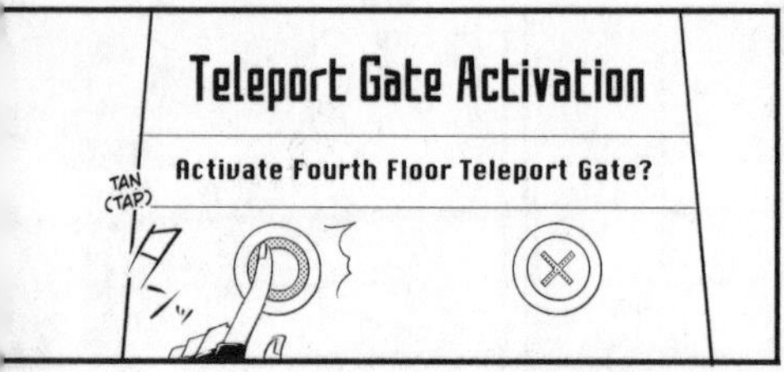
Teleport Gate Activation
Activate Fourth Floor Teleport Gate?
TAN (TAP)

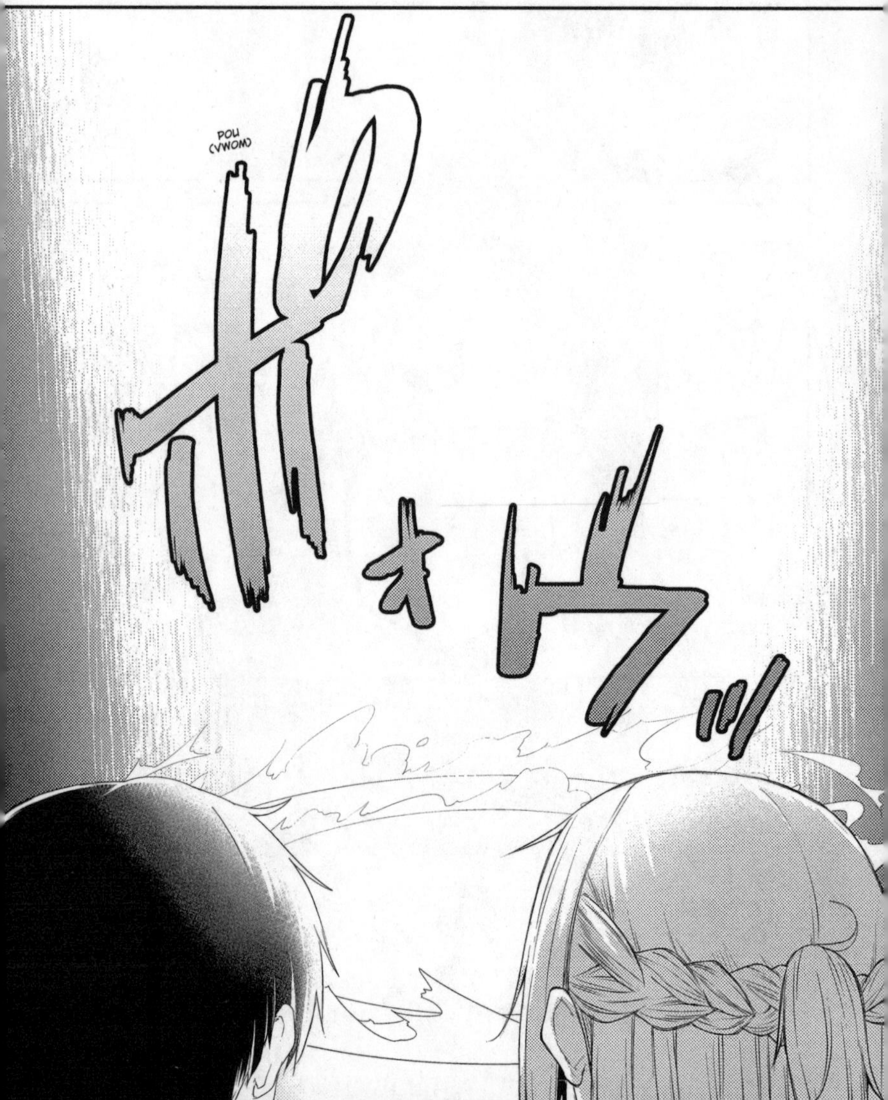
POU (VWOM)

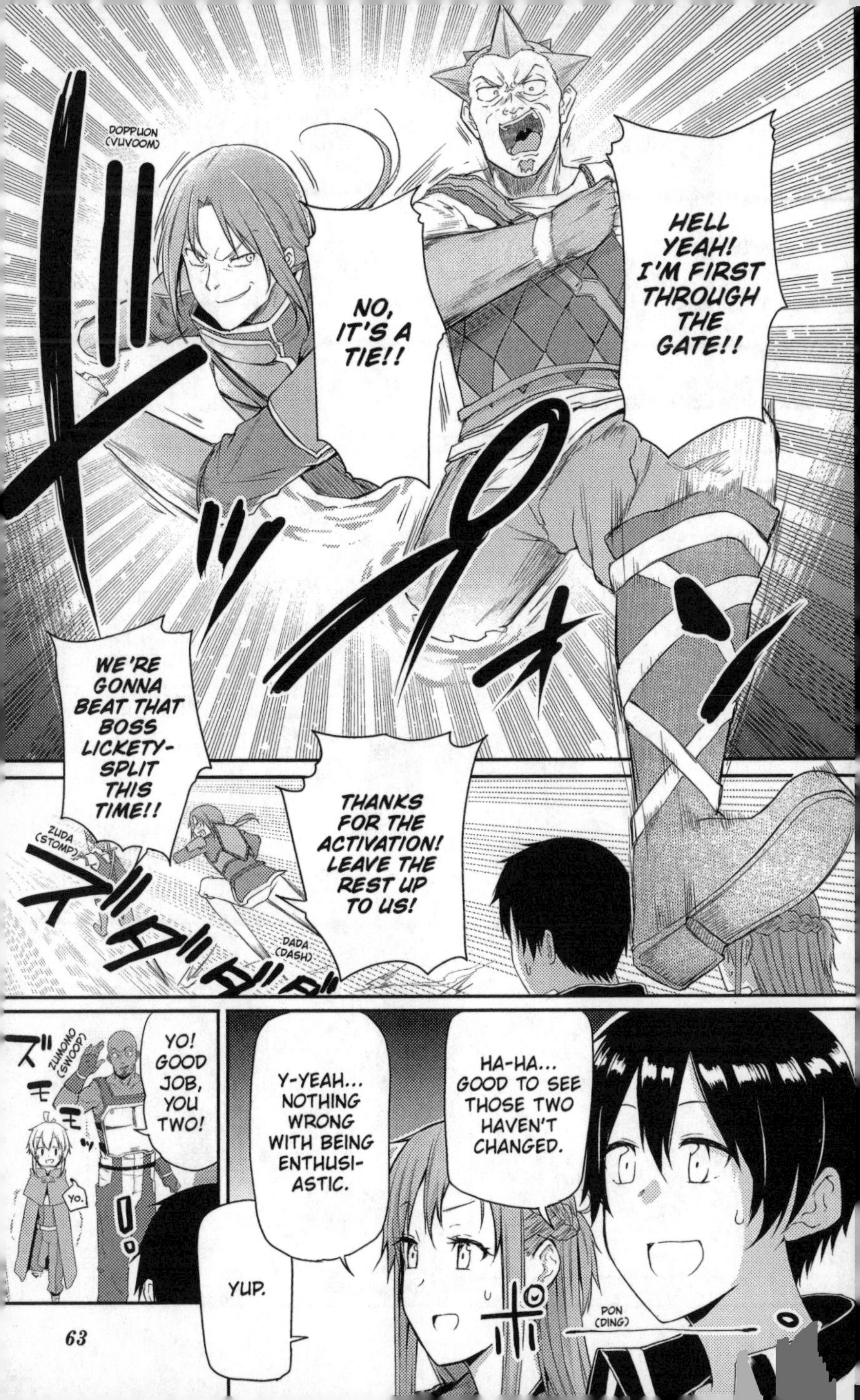
DOPPUON (VUVOOM)
HELL YEAH! I'M FIRST THROUGH THE GATE!!
NO, IT'S A TIE!!
THANKS FOR THE ACTIVATION! LEAVE THE REST UP TO US!
WE'RE GONNA BEAT THAT BOSS LICKETY-SPLIT THIS TIME!!
ZUDA (STOMP)
DADA (DASH)
HA-HA... GOOD TO SEE THOSE TWO HAVEN'T CHANGED.
Y-YEAH... NOTHING WRONG WITH BEING ENTHUSI-ASTIC.
YUP.
PON (DING)
YO! GOOD JOB, YOU TWO!
ZUMOMO (SWOOP)
YO.

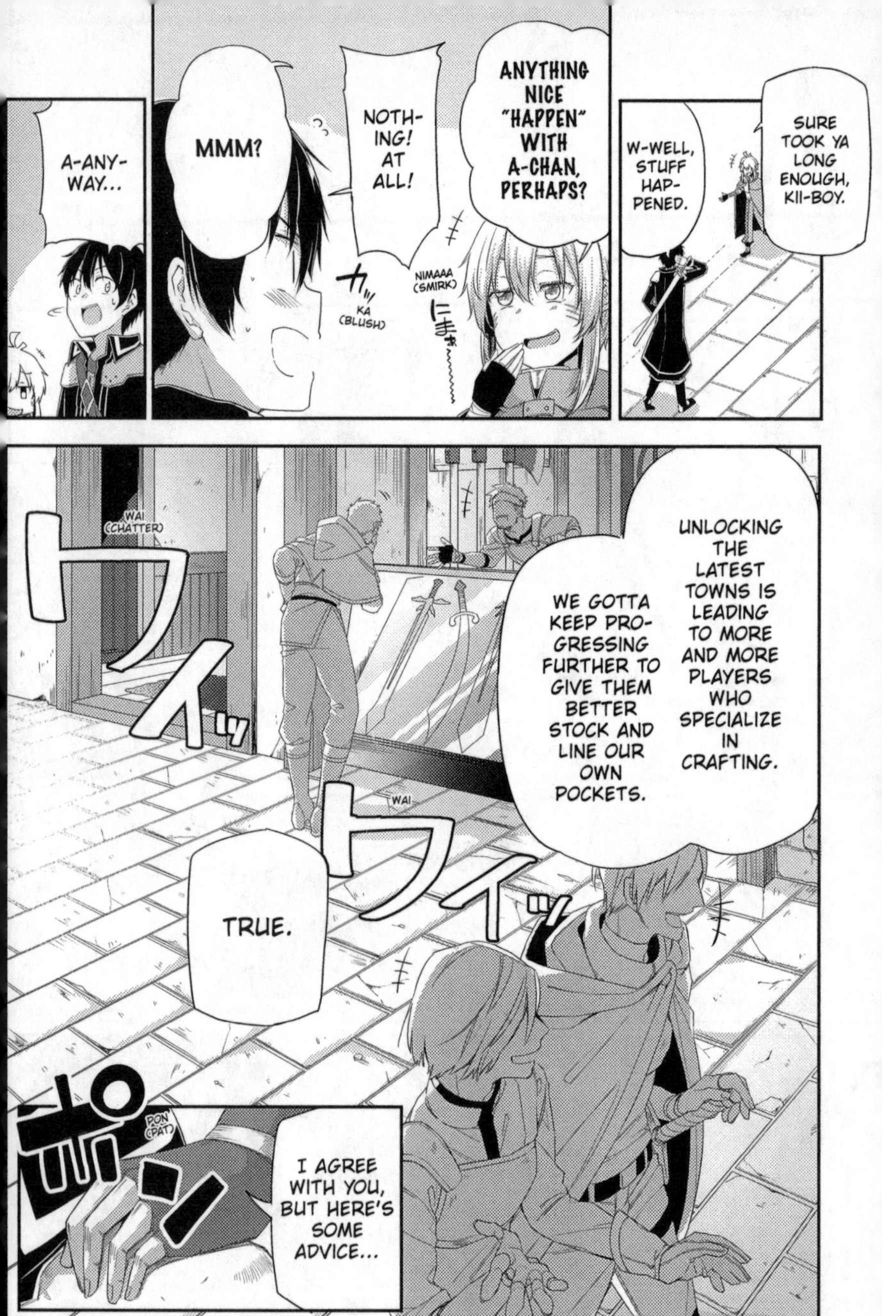
SURE TOOK YA LONG ENOUGH, KII-BOY.
W-WELL, STUFF HAP-PENED.
ANYTHING NICE "HAPPEN" WITH A-CHAN, PERHAPS?
NIMAAA (SMIRK)
NOTH-ING! AT ALL!
KA (BLUSH)
MMM?
A-ANY-WAY...
UNLOCKING THE LATEST TOWNS IS LEADING TO MORE AND MORE PLAYERS WHO SPECIALIZE IN CRAFTING.
WE GOTTA KEEP PRO-GRESSING FURTHER TO GIVE THEM BETTER STOCK AND LINE OUR OWN POCKETS.
WAI (CHATTER)
WAI
TRUE.
I AGREE WITH YOU, BUT HERE'S SOME ADVICE...
PON (PAT)

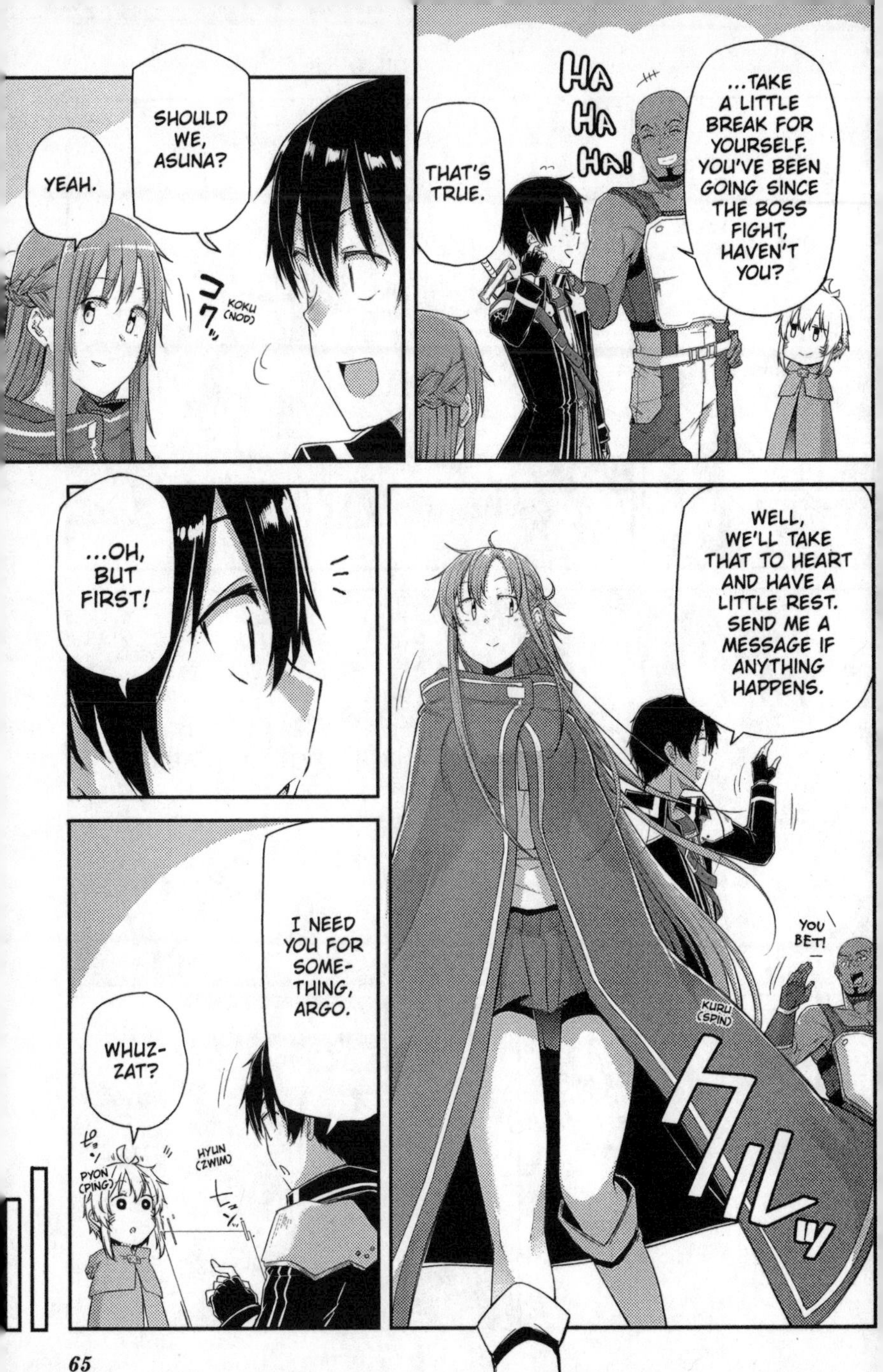
...TAKE A LITTLE BREAK FOR YOURSELF. YOU'VE BEEN GOING SINCE THE BOSS FIGHT, HAVEN'T YOU?
HA HA HA!
THAT'S TRUE.
SHOULD WE, ASUNA?
KOKU (NOD)
YEAH.
WELL, WE'LL TAKE THAT TO HEART AND HAVE A LITTLE REST. SEND ME A MESSAGE IF ANYTHING HAPPENS.
YOU BET!
KURU (SPIN)
...OH, BUT FIRST!
I NEED YOU FOR SOME-THING, ARGO.
WHUZ-ZAT?
HYUN (ZWIM)
PYON (PING)

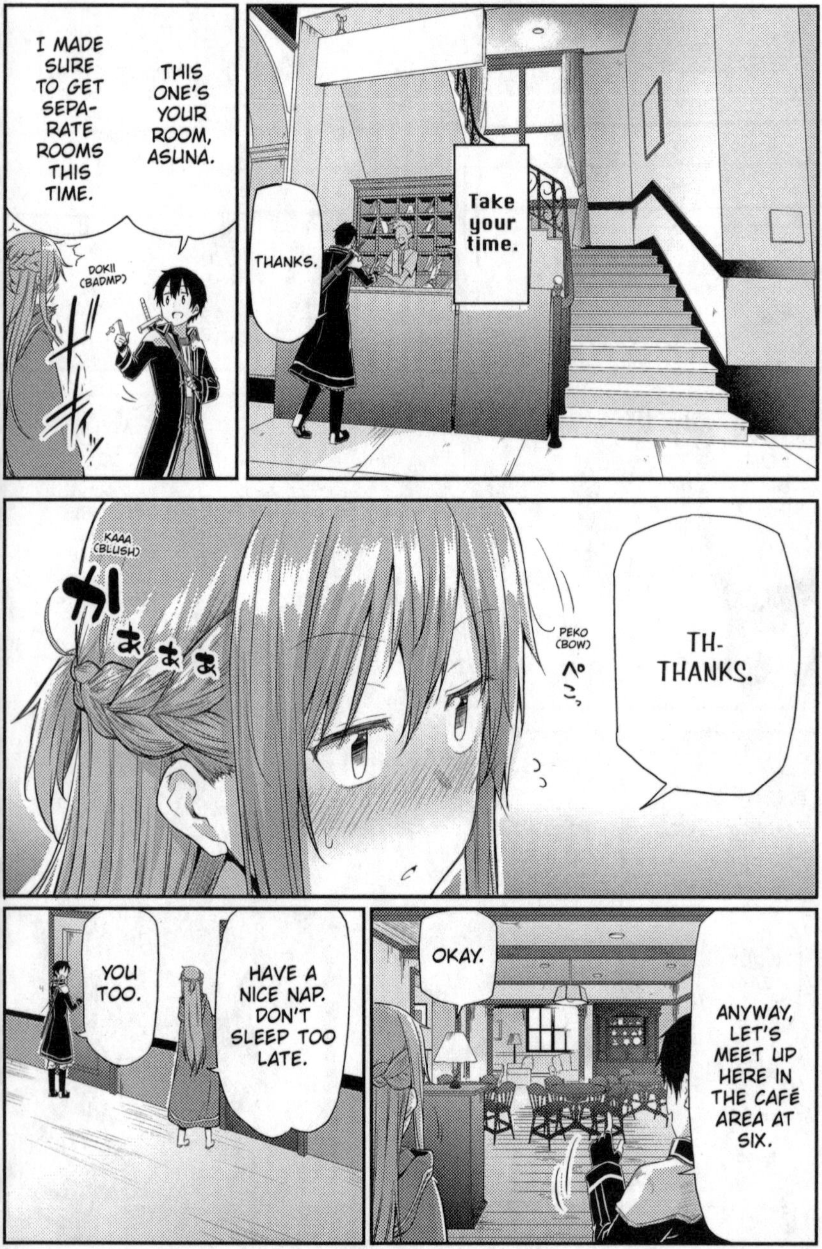
Take your time.
THANKS.
THIS ONE'S YOUR ROOM, ASUNA.
I MADE SURE TO GET SEPA-RATE ROOMS THIS TIME.
DOKII (BADMP)
TH-THANKS.
PEKO (BOW)
KAAA (BLUSH)
ANYWAY, LET'S MEET UP HERE IN THE CAFÉ AREA AT SIX.
OKAY.
HAVE A NICE NAP. DON'T SLEEP TOO LATE.
YOU TOO.

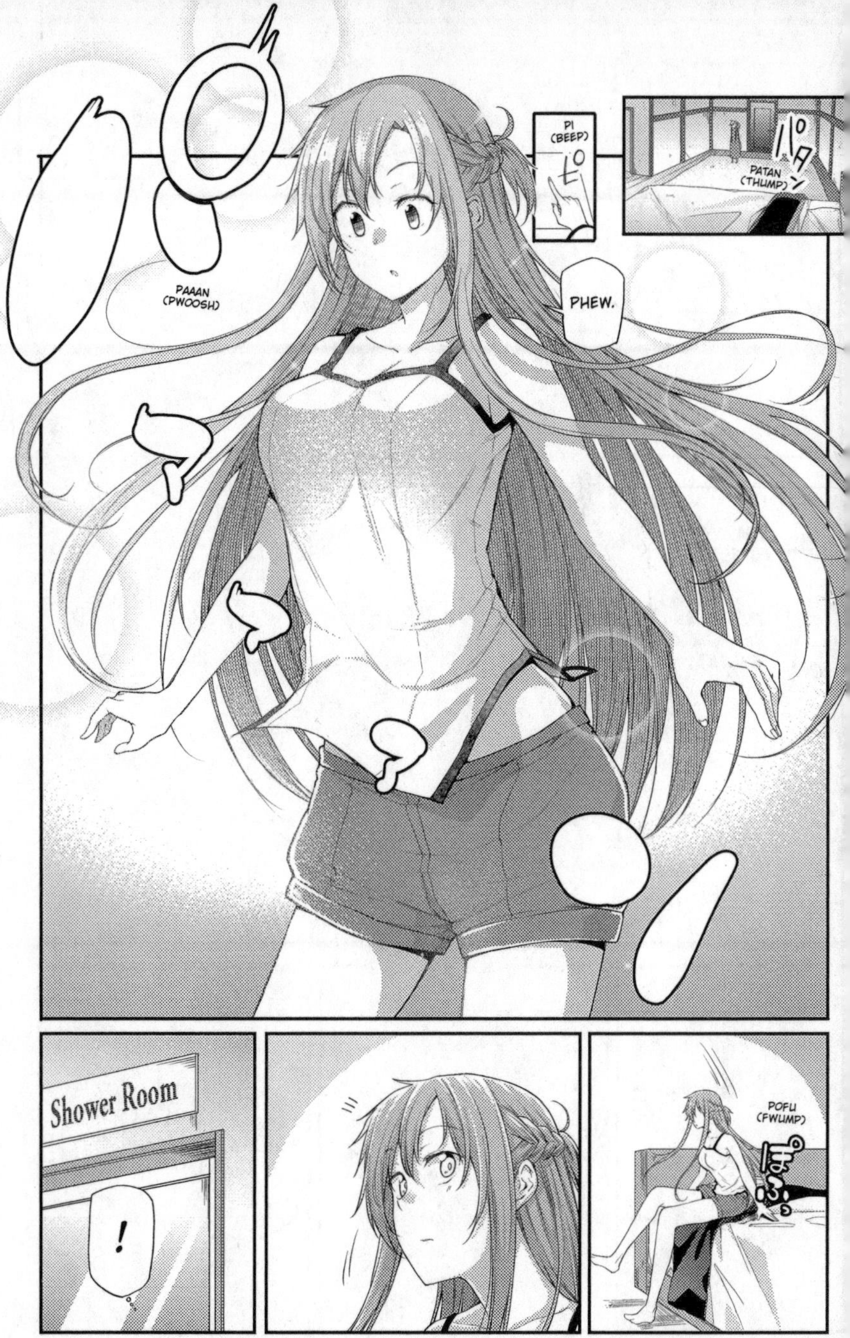
PATAN (THUMP)
PI (BEEP)
PHEW.
PAAAN (PWOOSH)
POFU (FWUMP)
Shower Room
!

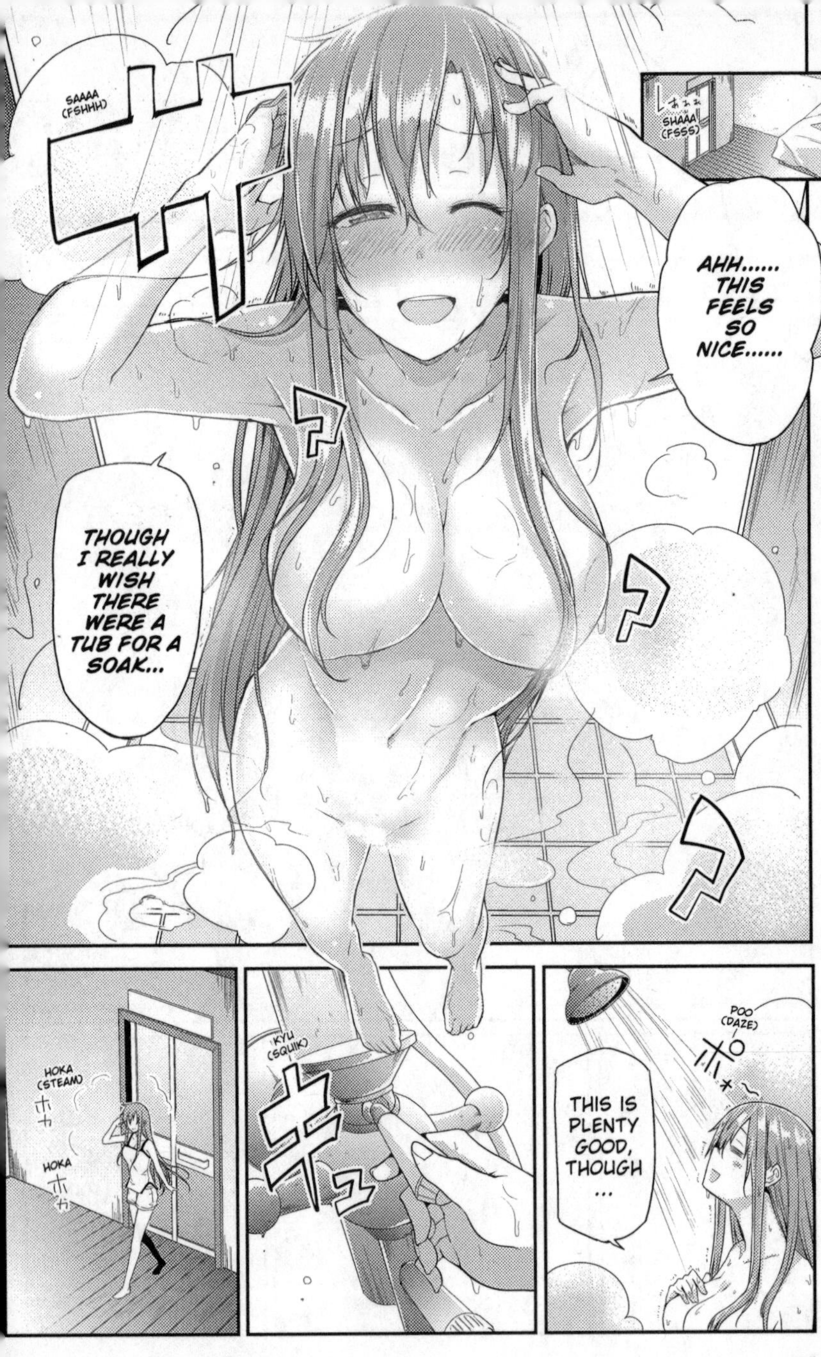
SHAAA (FSSS)
AHH...... THIS FEELS SO NICE......
SAAAA (FSHHH)
THOUGH I REALLY WISH THERE WERE A TUB FOR A SOAK...
POO (DAZE)
THIS IS PLENTY GOOD, THOUGH ...
KYU (SQUIIK)
HOKA (STEAM)
HOKA

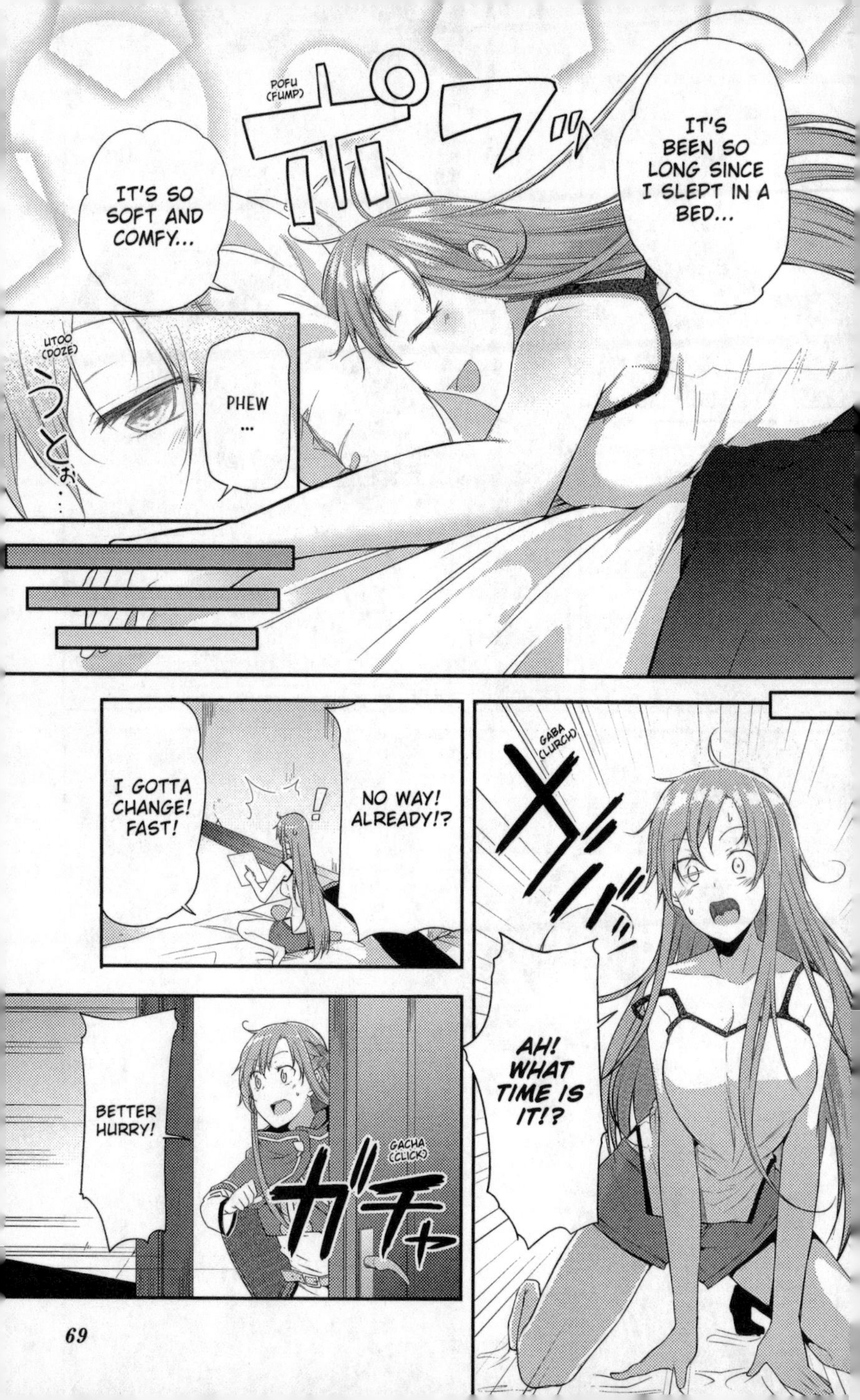
IT'S BEEN SO LONG SINCE I SLEPT IN A BED...
POFU (FUMP)
IT'S SO SOFT AND COMFY...
PHEW ...
UTOO (DOZE)
GABA (LURCH)
AH! WHAT TIME IS IT!?
NO WAY! ALREADY!?
I GOTTA CHANGE! FAST!
GACHA (CLICK)
BETTER HURRY!

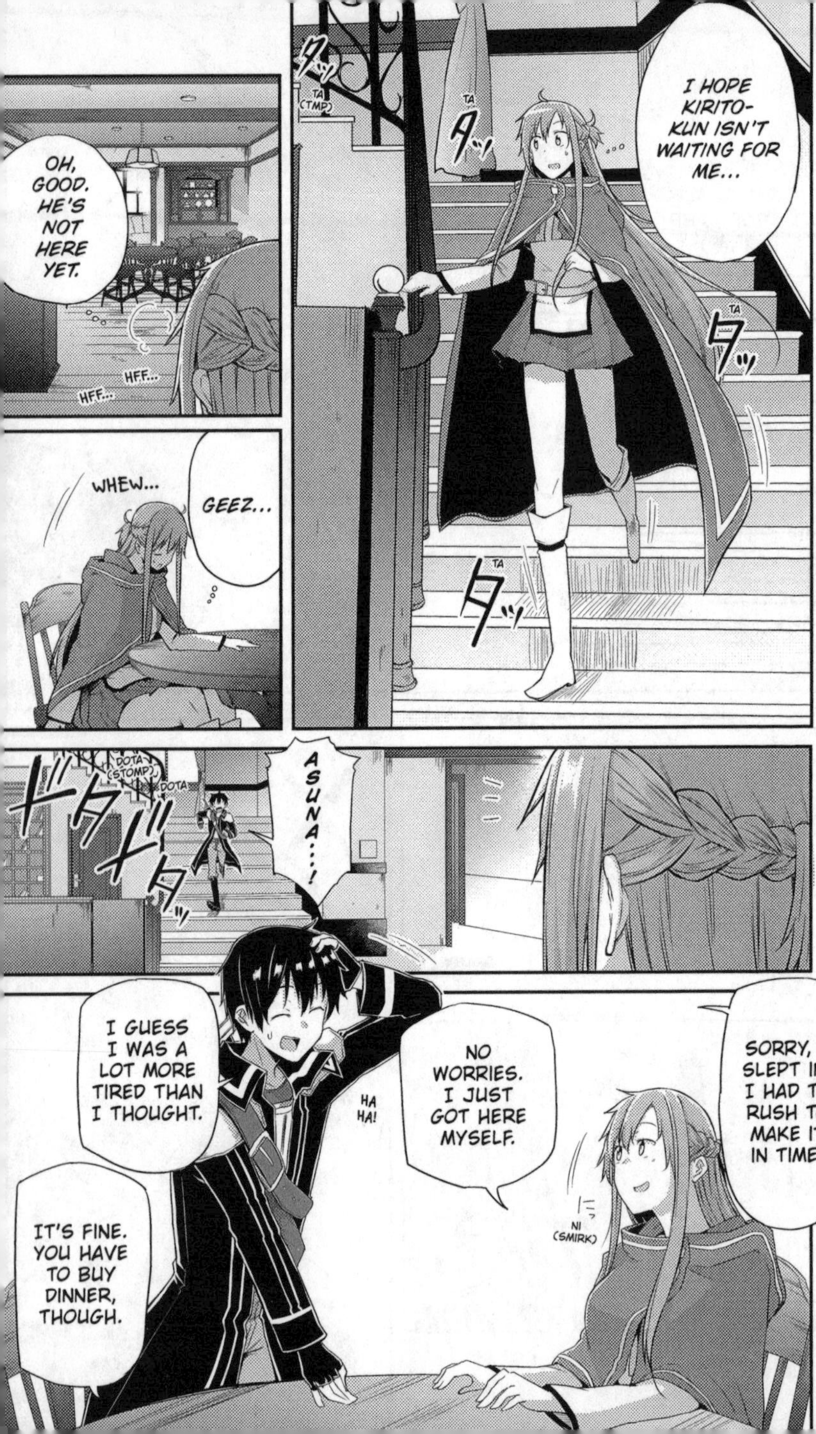
I HOPE KIRITO-KUN ISN'T WAITING FOR ME...
TA (TMP)
TA
TA
TA
OH, GOOD. HE'S NOT HERE YET.
HFF... HFF...
GEEZ...
WHEW...
ASUNA...!
DOTA (STOMP) DOTA
SORRY, I SLEPT IN! I HAD TO RUSH TO MAKE IT IN TIME.
NI (SMIRK)
NO WORRIES. I JUST GOT HERE MYSELF.
HA HA!
I GUESS I WAS A LOT MORE TIRED THAN I THOUGHT.
IT'S FINE. YOU HAVE TO BUY DINNER, THOUGH.

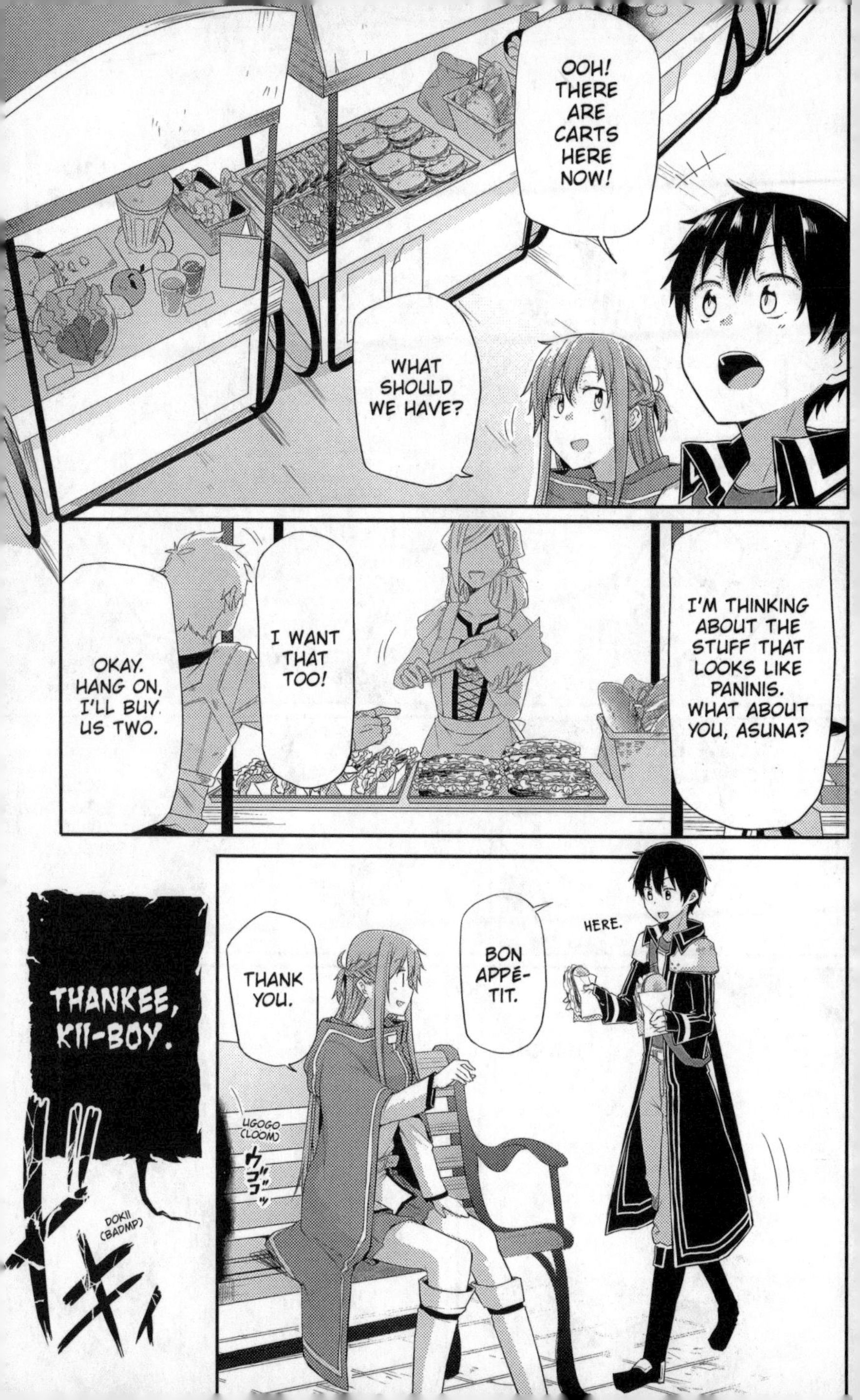
OOH! THERE ARE CARTS HERE NOW!
WHAT SHOULD WE HAVE?
I'M THINKING ABOUT THE STUFF THAT LOOKS LIKE PANINIS. WHAT ABOUT YOU, ASUNA?
I WANT THAT TOO!
OKAY. HANG ON, I'LL BUY US TWO.
HERE.
BON APPÉ-TIT.
THANK YOU.
ウゴゴッ
UGOGO (LOOM)
THANKEE, KII-BOY.
ドキィ
DOKII (BADMP)

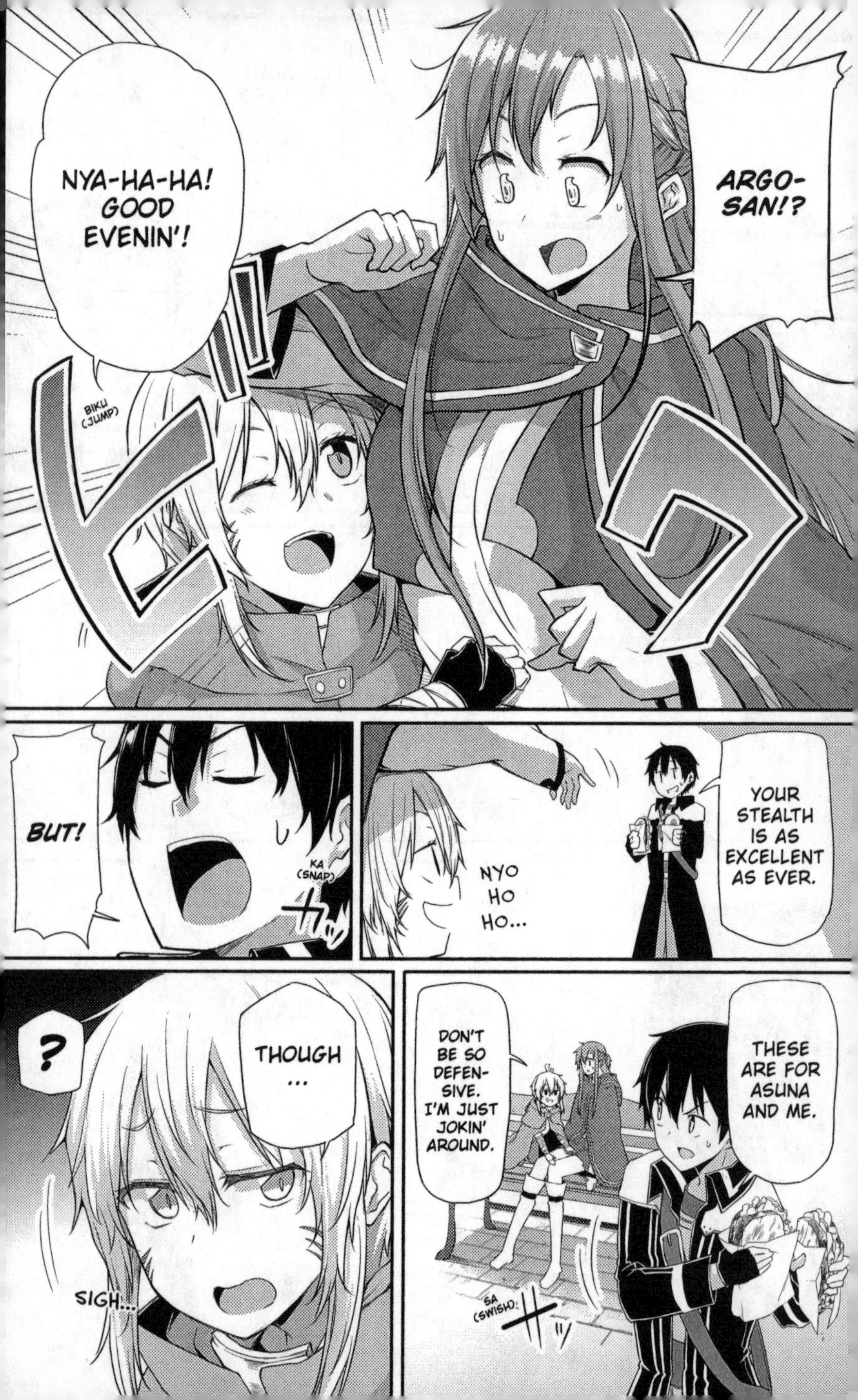
ARGO-SAN!?
NYA-HA-HA! GOOD EVENIN'!
BIKU (JUMP)
YOUR STEALTH IS AS EXCELLENT AS EVER.
NYO HO HO...
KA (SNAP)
BUT!
THESE ARE FOR ASUNA AND ME.
DON'T BE SO DEFENSIVE. I'M JUST JOKIN' AROUND.
SA (SWISH)
THOUGH ...
?
SIGH...

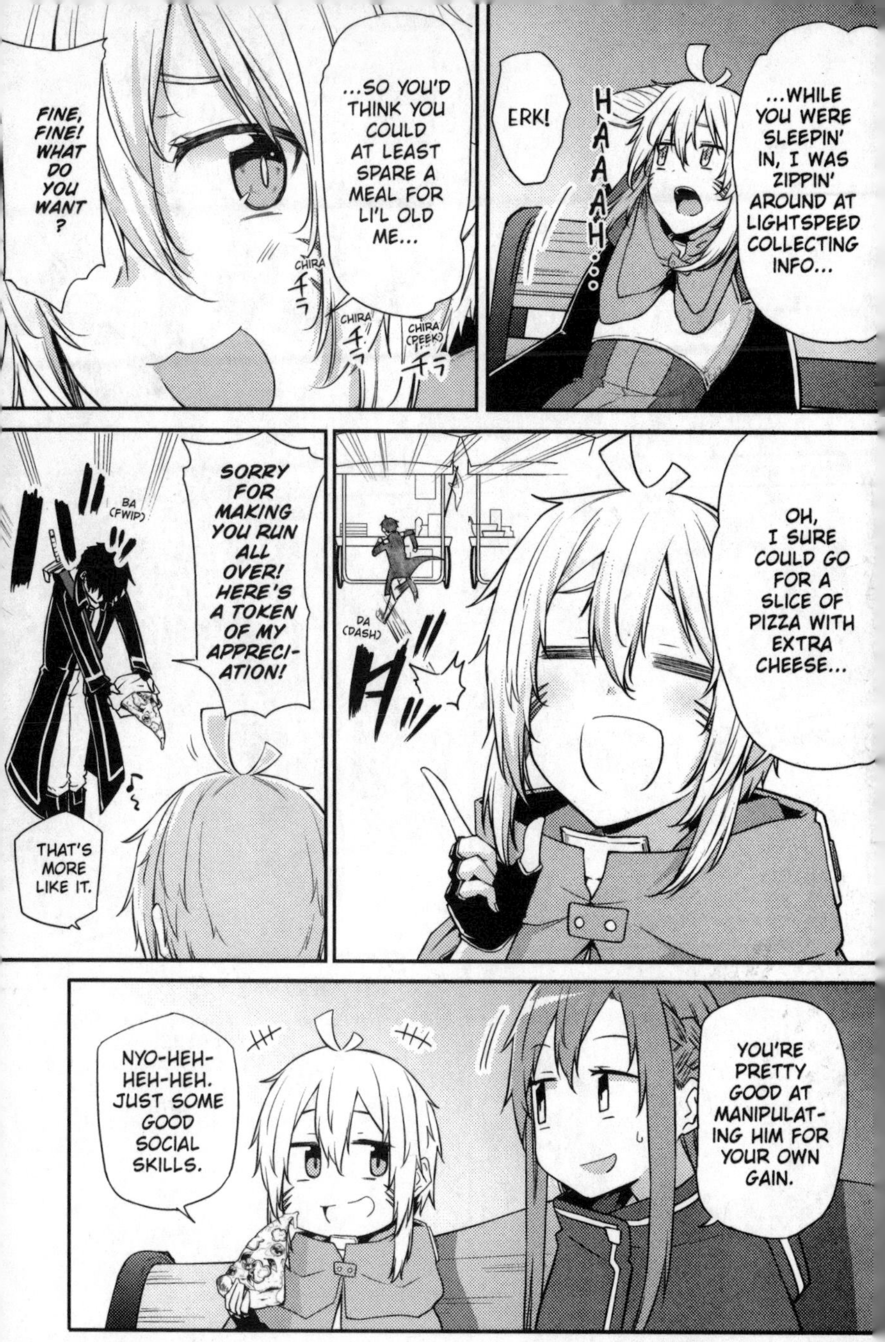
...WHILE YOU WERE SLEEPIN' IN, I WAS ZIPPIN' AROUND AT LIGHTSPEED COLLECTING INFO...
HAAAAH...
ERK!
...SO YOU'D THINK YOU COULD AT LEAST SPARE A MEAL FOR LI'L OLD ME...
CHIRA
CHIRA
CHIRA (PEEK)
FINE, FINE! WHAT DO YOU WANT?
OH, I SURE COULD GO FOR A SLICE OF PIZZA WITH EXTRA CHEESE...
DA (DASH)
BA (FWIP)
SORRY FOR MAKING YOU RUN ALL OVER! HERE'S A TOKEN OF MY APPRECIATION!
THAT'S MORE LIKE IT.
YOU'RE PRETTY GOOD AT MANIPULATING HIM FOR YOUR OWN GAIN.
NYO-HEH-HEH-HEH. JUST SOME GOOD SOCIAL SKILLS.

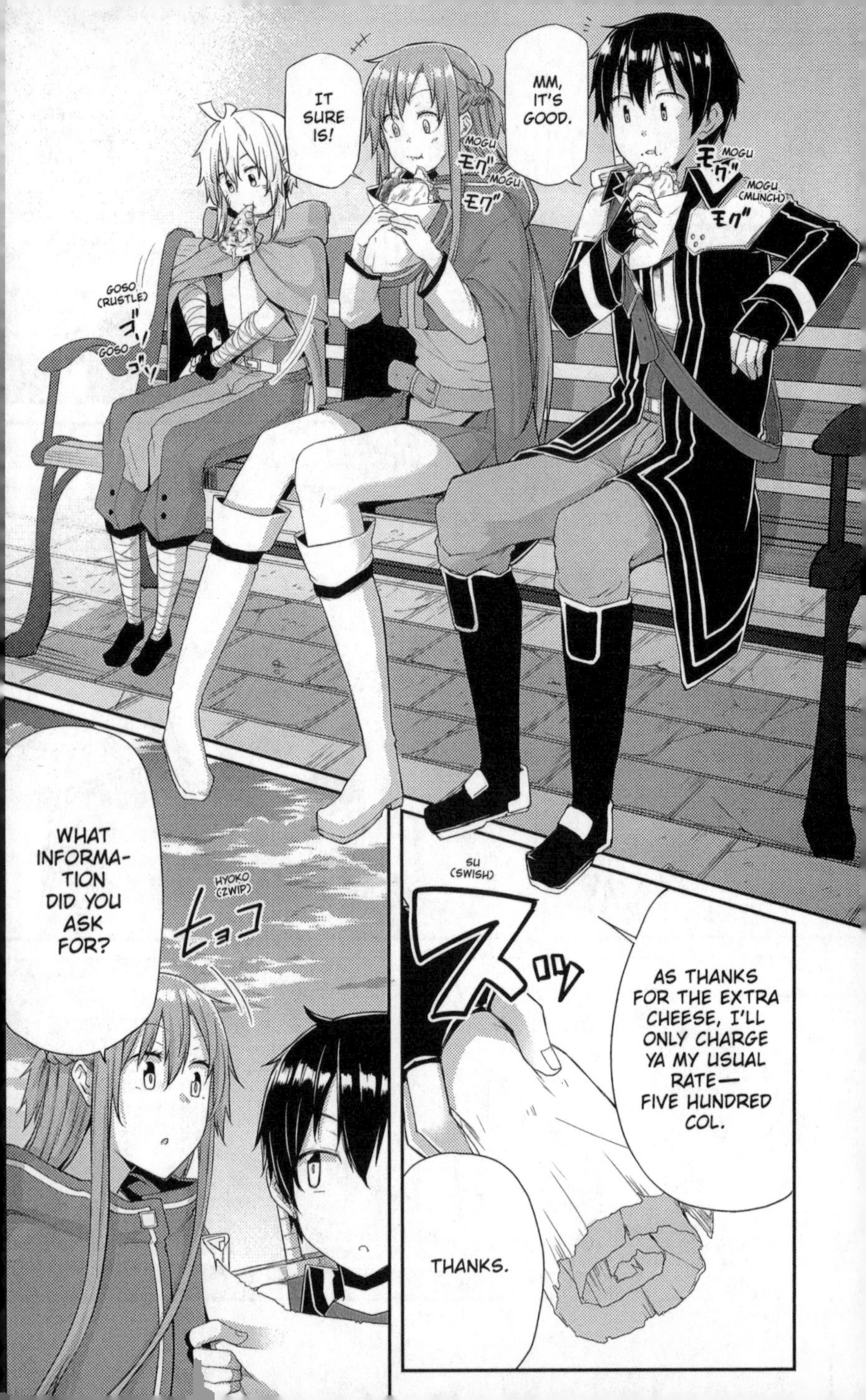

MM, IT'S GOOD.
MOGU
モグ
MOGU (MUNCH)
モグ
IT SURE IS!
MOGU
モグ
MOGU
モグ
GOSO (RUSTLE)
ゴソ
GOSO
ゴソ
AS THANKS FOR THE EXTRA CHEESE, I'LL ONLY CHARGE YA MY USUAL RATE— FIVE HUNDRED COL.
SU (SWISH)
スッ
THANKS.
WHAT INFORMATION DID YOU ASK FOR?
HYOKO (ZWIP)
ヒョコ

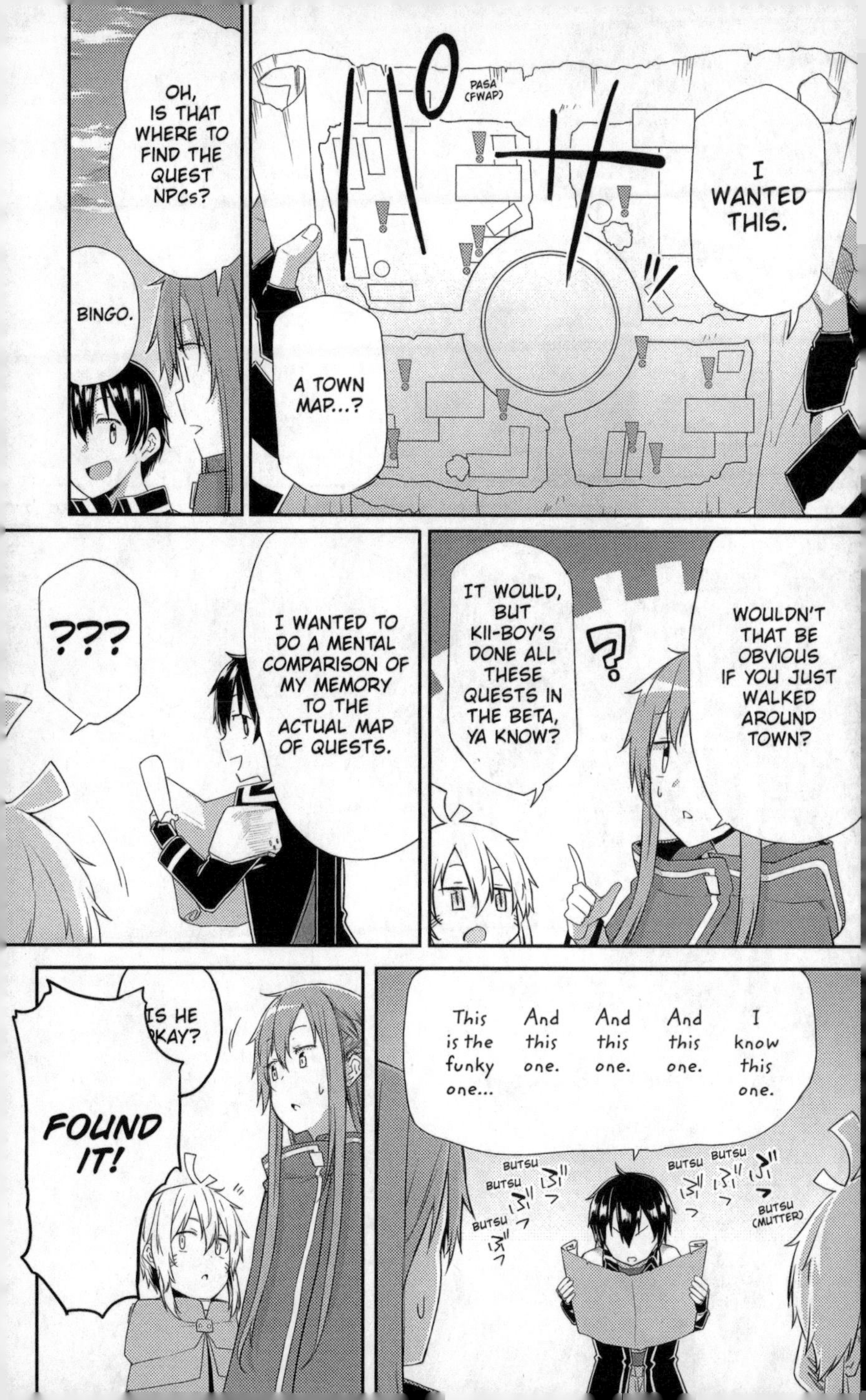
PASA (FWAP)
I WANTED THIS.
A TOWN MAP...?
OH, IS THAT WHERE TO FIND THE QUEST NPCs?
BINGO.
WOULDN'T THAT BE OBVIOUS IF YOU JUST WALKED AROUND TOWN?
IT WOULD, BUT KII-BOY'S DONE ALL THESE QUESTS IN THE BETA, YA KNOW?
I WANTED TO DO A MENTAL COMPARISON OF MY MEMORY TO THE ACTUAL MAP OF QUESTS.
???
I know this one.
And this one.
And this one.
And this one.
This is the funky one...
BUTSU (MUTTER)
BUTSU
BUTSU
BUTSU
BUTSU
BUTSU
IS HE OKAY?
FOUND IT!

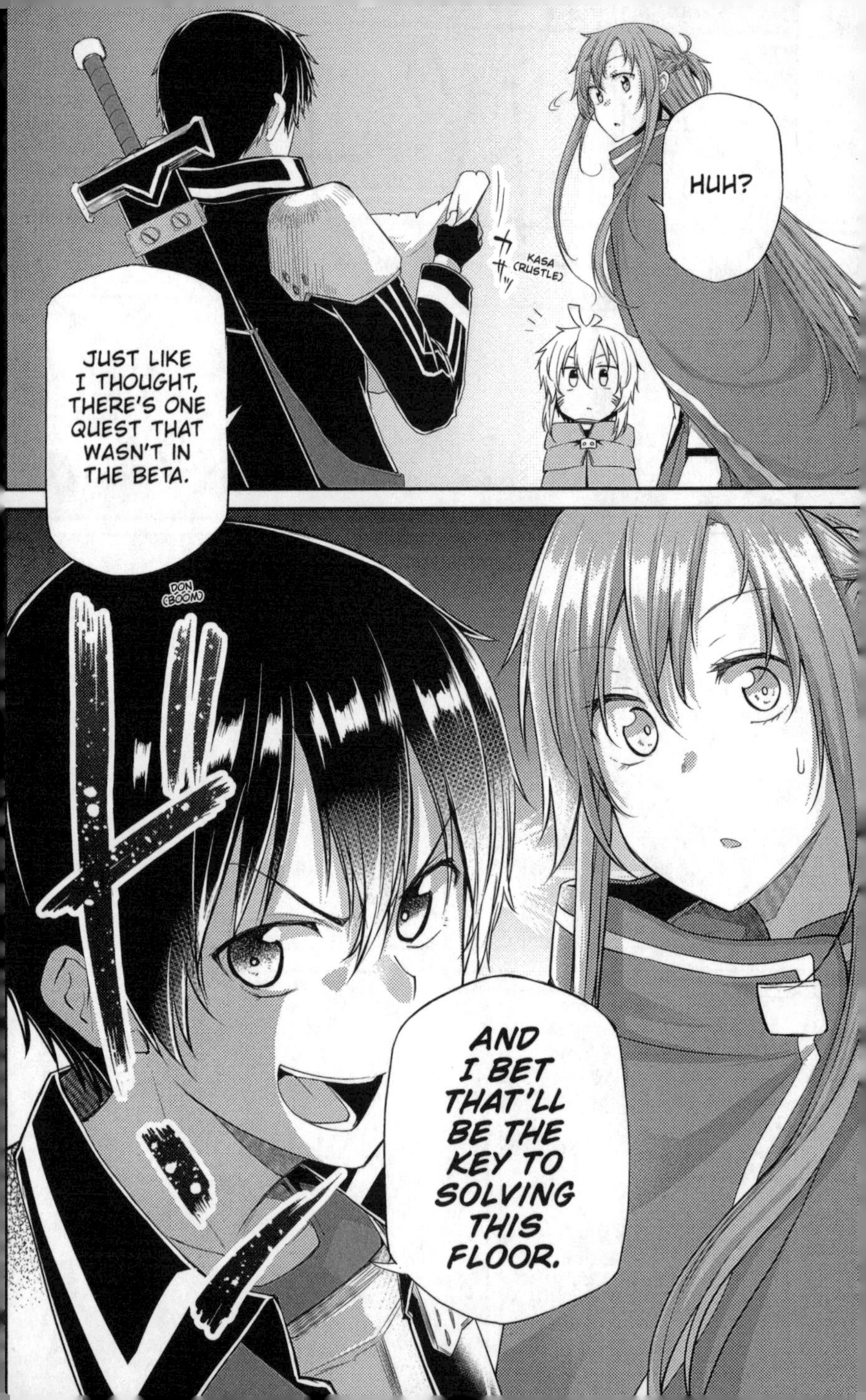
HUH?
KASA (RUSTLE)
JUST LIKE I THOUGHT, THERE'S ONE QUEST THAT WASN'T IN THE BETA.
DON (BOOM)
AND I BET THAT'LL BE THE KEY TO SOLVING THIS FLOOR.

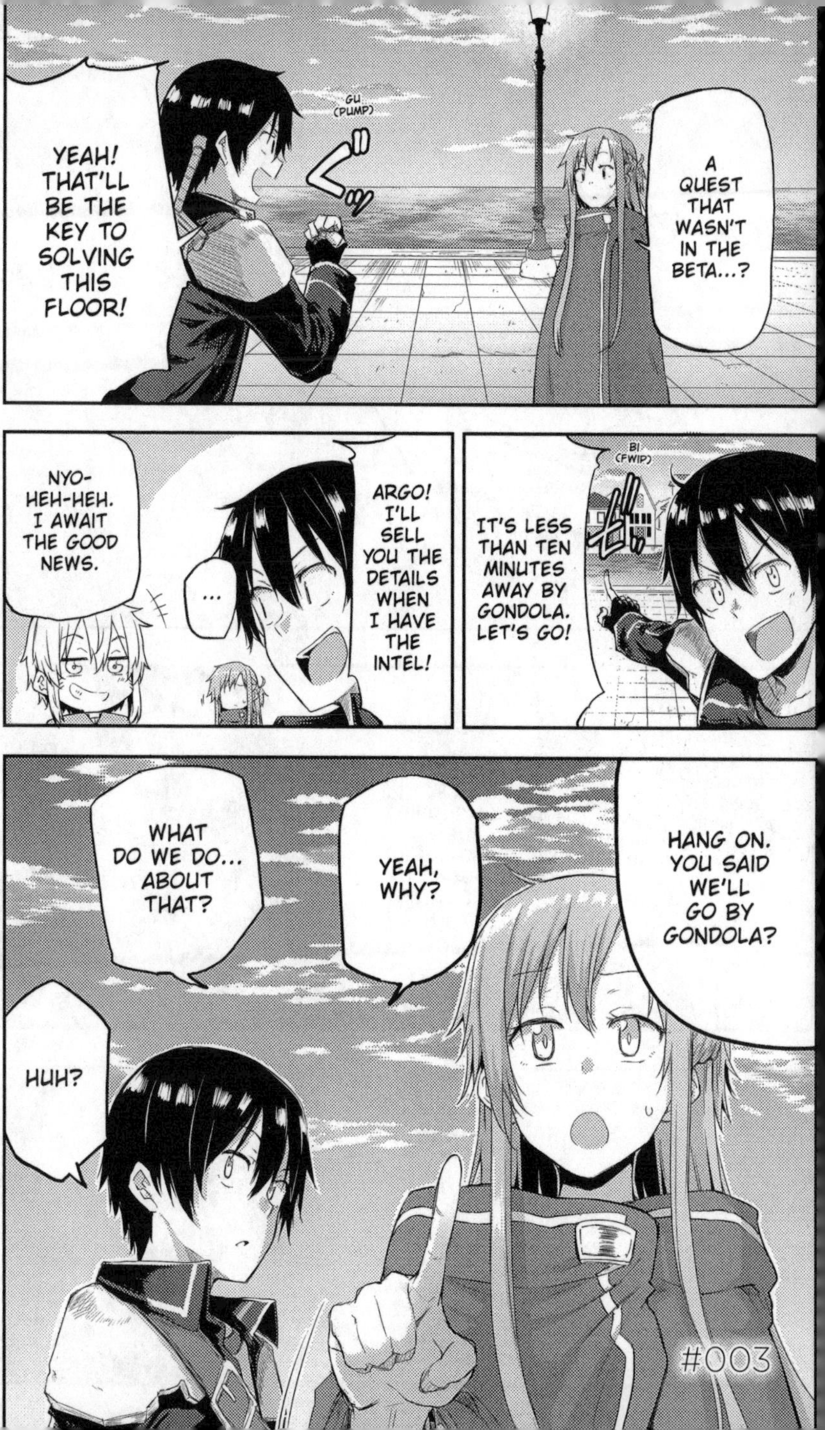
A QUEST THAT WASN'T IN THE BETA...?
GU (PUMP)
YEAH! THAT'LL BE THE KEY TO SOLVING THIS FLOOR!
BI (FWIP)
IT'S LESS THAN TEN MINUTES AWAY BY GONDOLA. LET'S GO!
ARGO! I'LL SELL YOU THE DETAILS WHEN I HAVE THE INTEL!
...
NYO-HEH-HEH. I AWAIT THE GOOD NEWS.
HANG ON. YOU SAID WE'LL GO BY GONDOLA?
YEAH, WHY?
WHAT DO WE DO... ABOUT THAT?
HUH?
#003

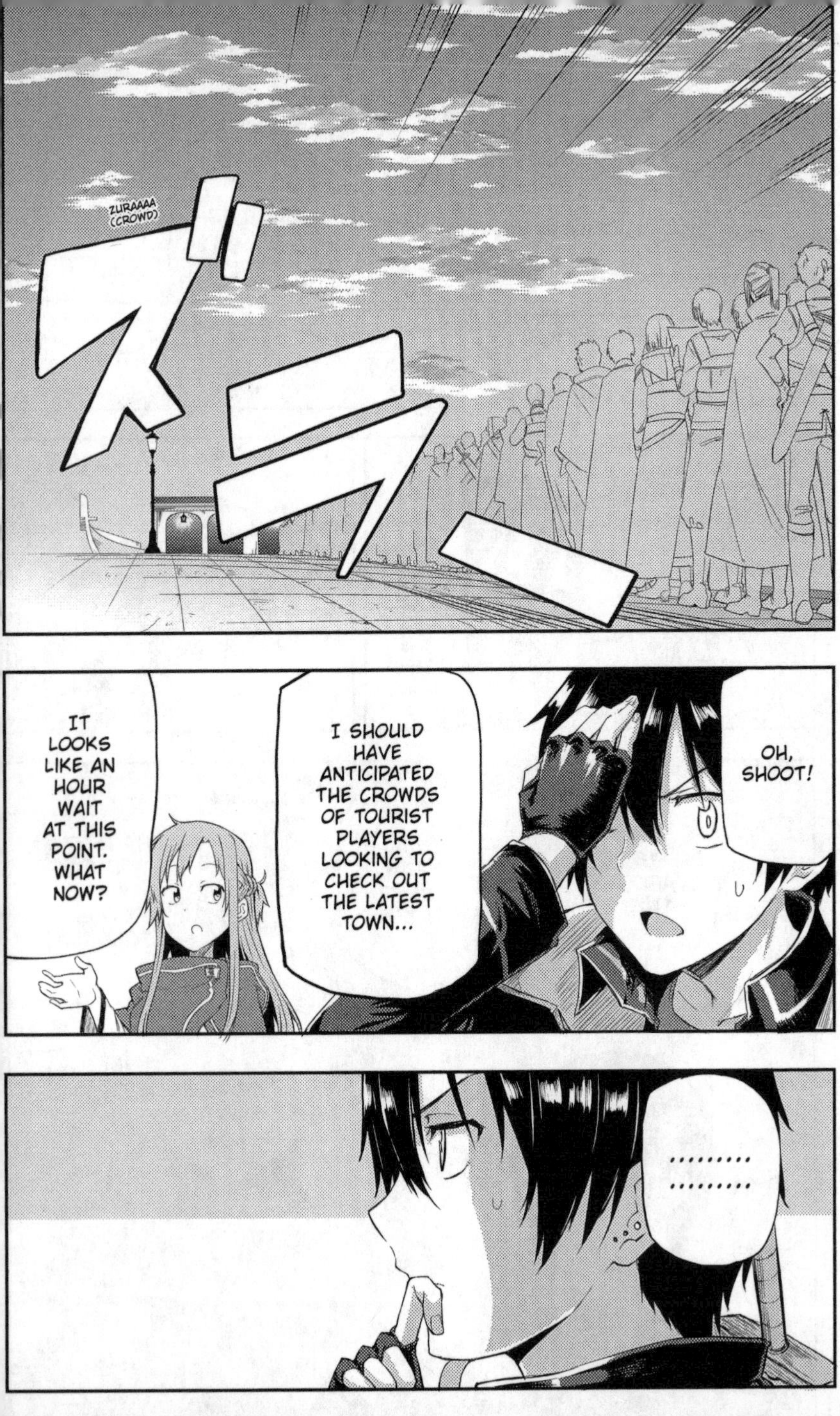
ZURAAAA (CROWD)
ズラ
OH, SHOOT!
I SHOULD HAVE ANTICIPATED THE CROWDS OF TOURIST PLAYERS LOOKING TO CHECK OUT THE LATEST TOWN...
IT LOOKS LIKE AN HOUR WAIT AT THIS POINT. WHAT NOW?
....
....

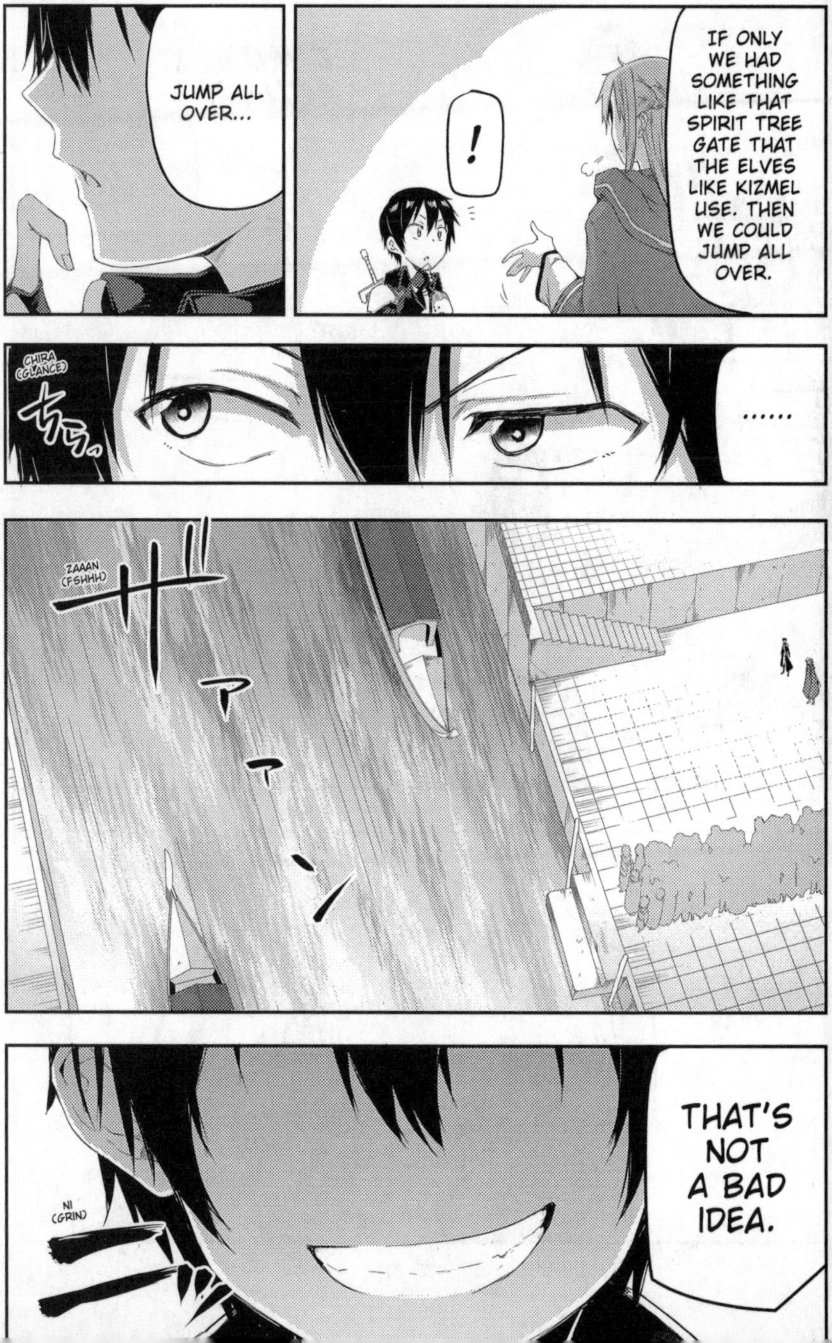
IF ONLY WE HAD SOMETHING LIKE THAT SPIRIT TREE GATE THAT THE ELVES LIKE KIZMEL USE. THEN WE COULD JUMP ALL OVER.
!
JUMP ALL OVER...
......
CHIRA (GLANCE)
ZAAAN (FSHHH)
THAT'S NOT A BAD IDEA.
NI (GRIN)

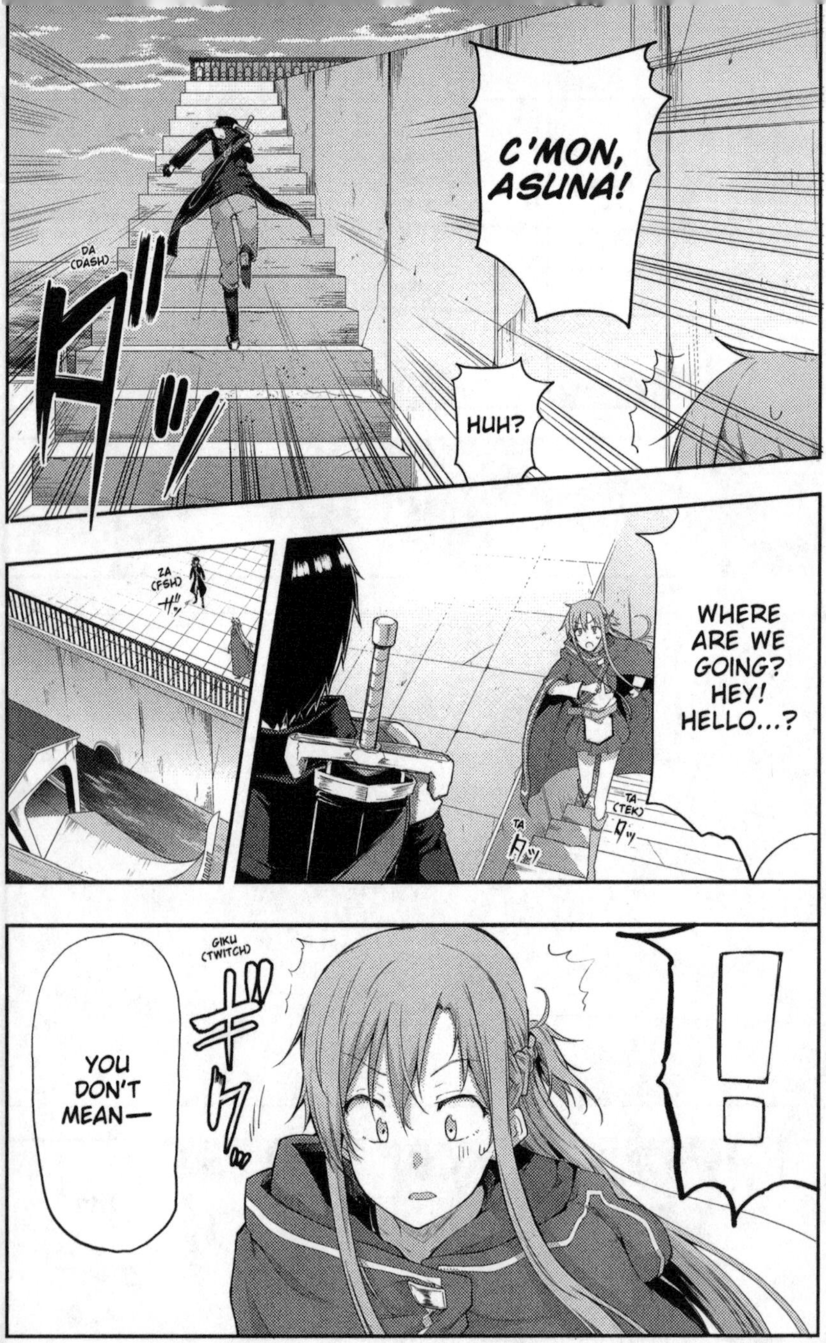
C'MON, ASUNA!
HUH?
DA (DASH)
WHERE ARE WE GOING? HEY! HELLO...?
TA (TEK)
TA
ZA (FSH)
!
GIKU (TWITCH)
YOU DON'T MEAN—

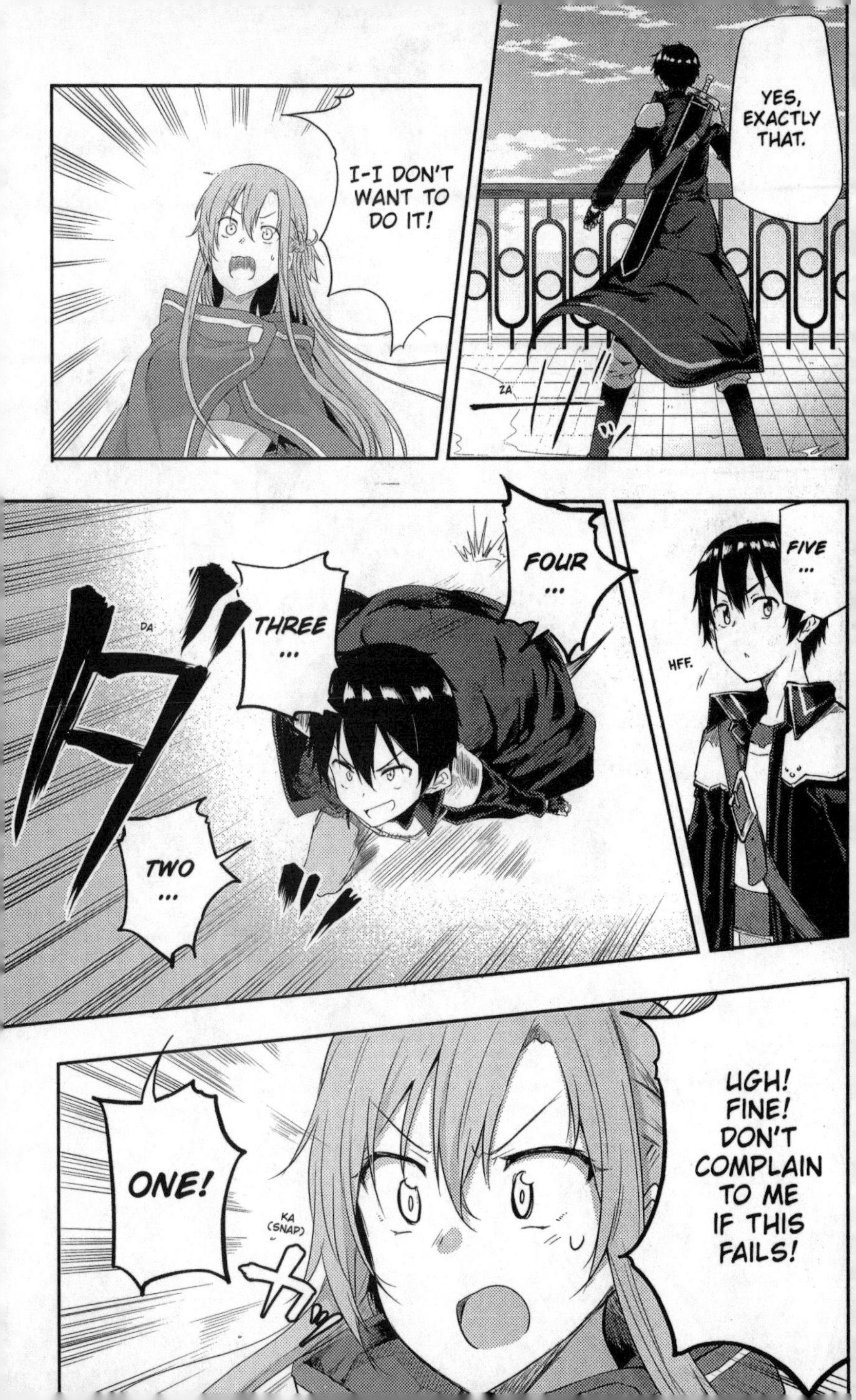
YES, EXACTLY THAT.
ZA
I-I DON'T WANT TO DO IT!
FIVE ...
HFF.
FOUR ...
THREE ...
DA
TWO ...
ONE!
KA (SNAP)
UGH! FINE! DON'T COMPLAIN TO ME IF THIS FAILS!

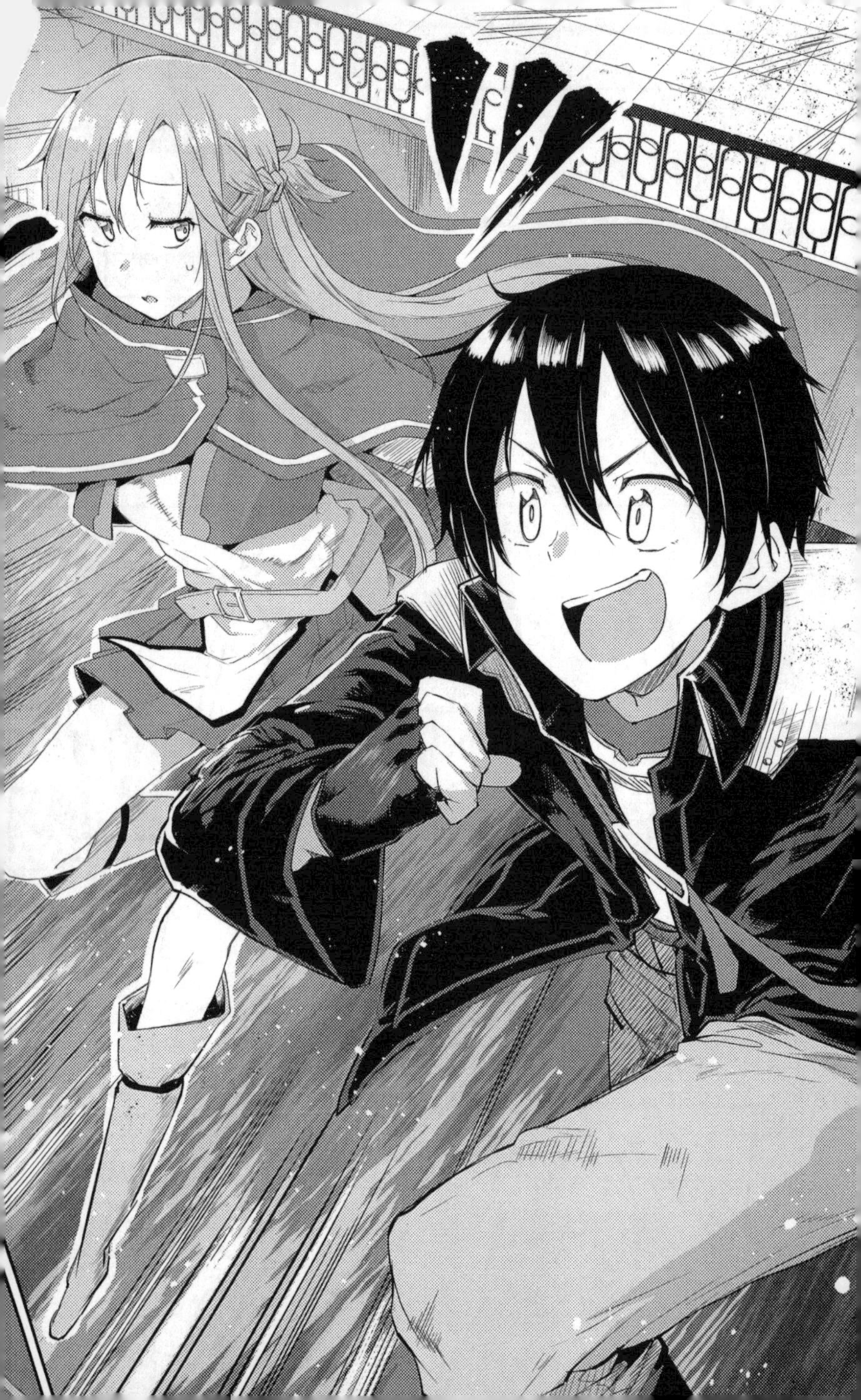

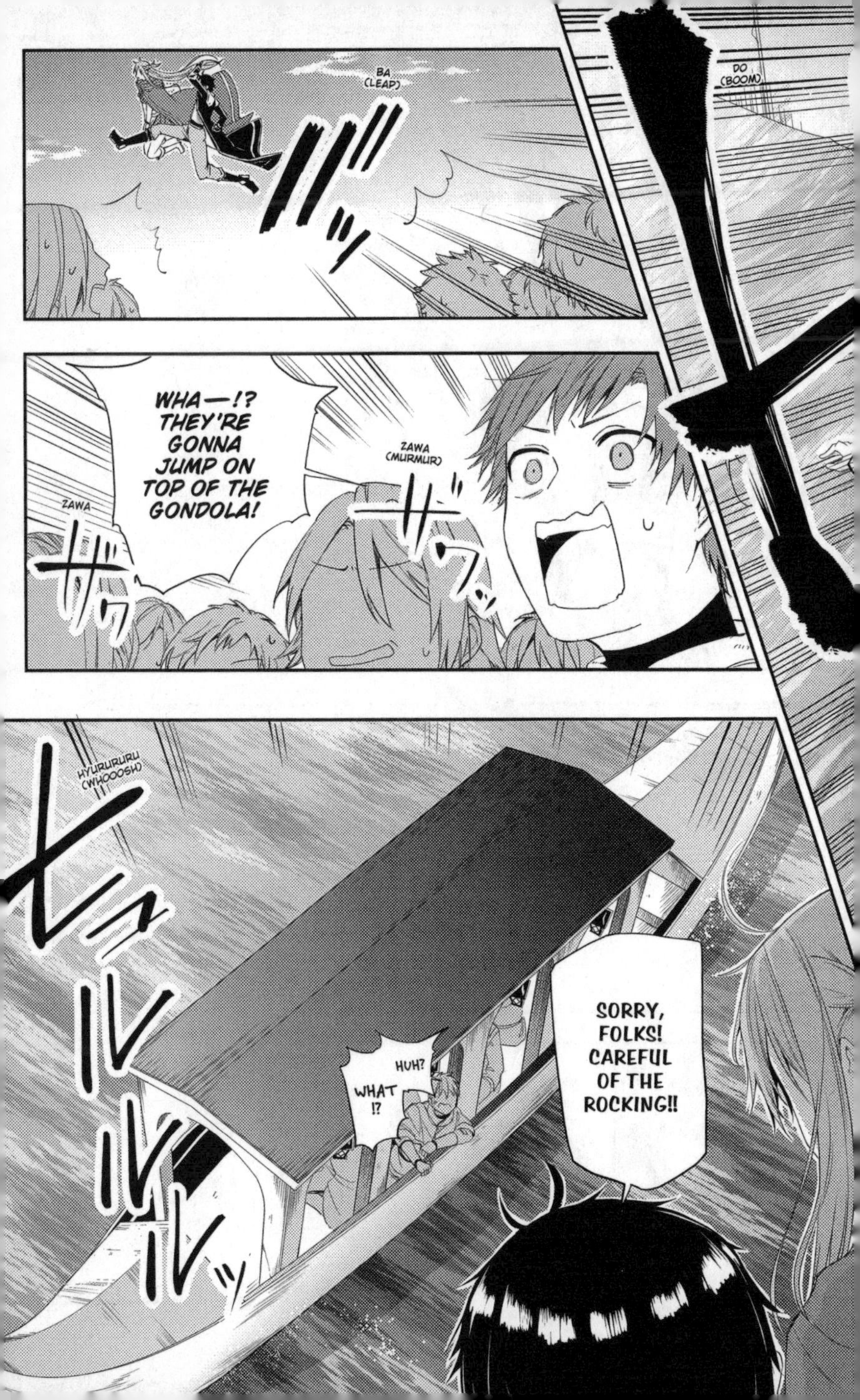
DO (BOOM)
BA (LEAP)
WHA—!? THEY'RE GONNA JUMP ON TOP OF THE GONDOLA!
ZAWA (MURMUR)
ZAWA
SORRY, FOLKS! CAREFUL OF THE ROCKING!!
HUH?
WHAT !?
HYURURURU (WHOOOSH)

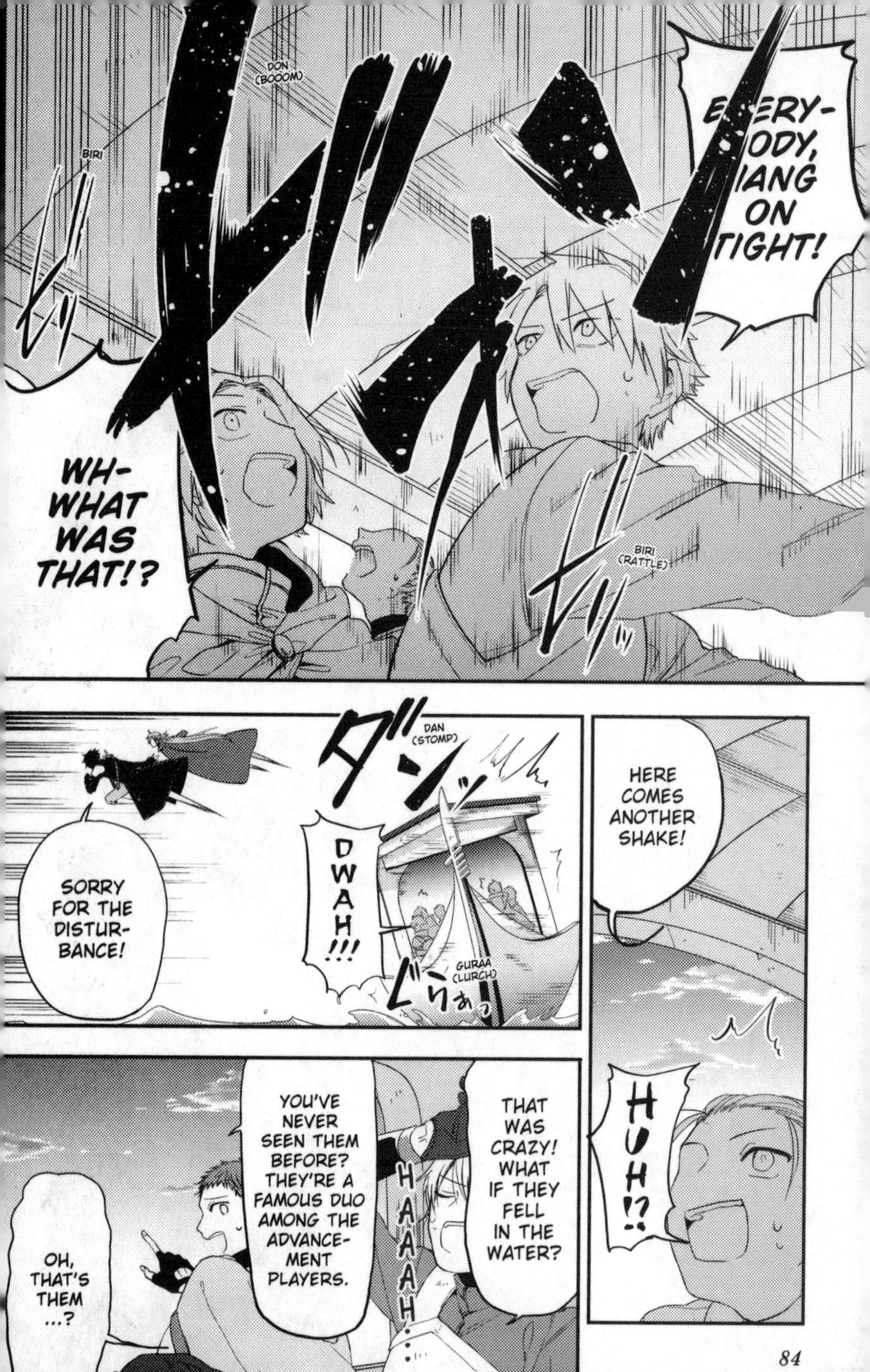
DON (BOOOM)
BIRI
EVERY-BODY, HANG ON TIGHT!
WH-WHAT WAS THAT!?
BIRI (RATTLE)
HERE COMES ANOTHER SHAKE!
DAN (STOMP)
DWAH!!!
GURAA (LURCH)
SORRY FOR THE DISTURBANCE!
HUH!?
THAT WAS CRAZY! WHAT IF THEY FELL IN THE WATER?
HAAAAH
YOU'VE NEVER SEEN THEM BEFORE? THEY'RE A FAMOUS DUO AMONG THE ADVANCEMENT PLAYERS.
OH, THAT'S THEM ...?

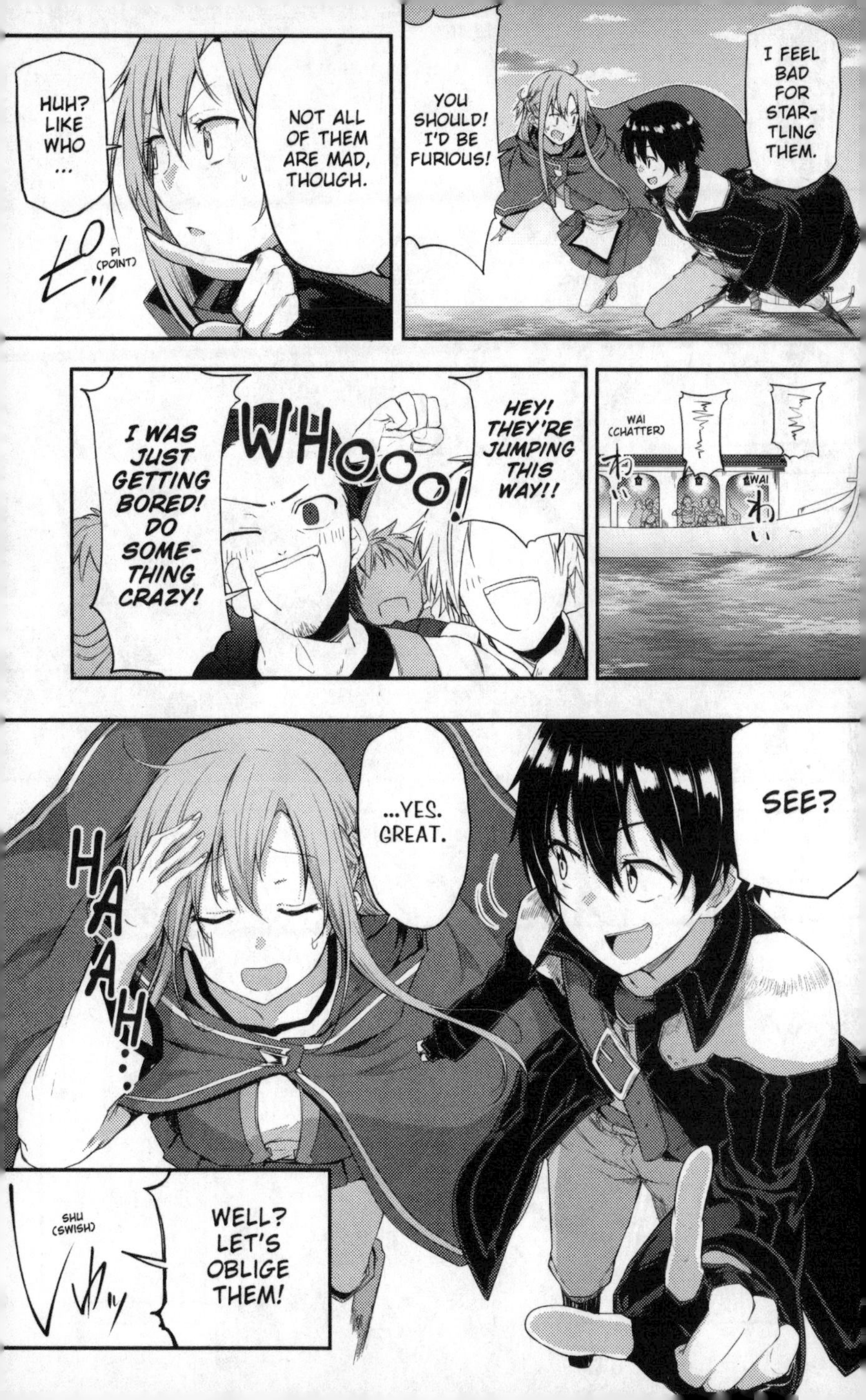

I FEEL BAD FOR STARTLING THEM.
YOU SHOULD! I'D BE FURIOUS!
NOT ALL OF THEM ARE MAD, THOUGH.
HUH? LIKE WHO ...
PI (POINT)
WAI (CHATTER)
WAI
HEY! THEY'RE JUMPING THIS WAY!!
WHOOOO!
I WAS JUST GETTING BORED! DO SOMETHING CRAZY!
SEE?
...YES. GREAT.
HAAAH...
WELL? LET'S OBLIGE THEM!
SHU (SWISH)

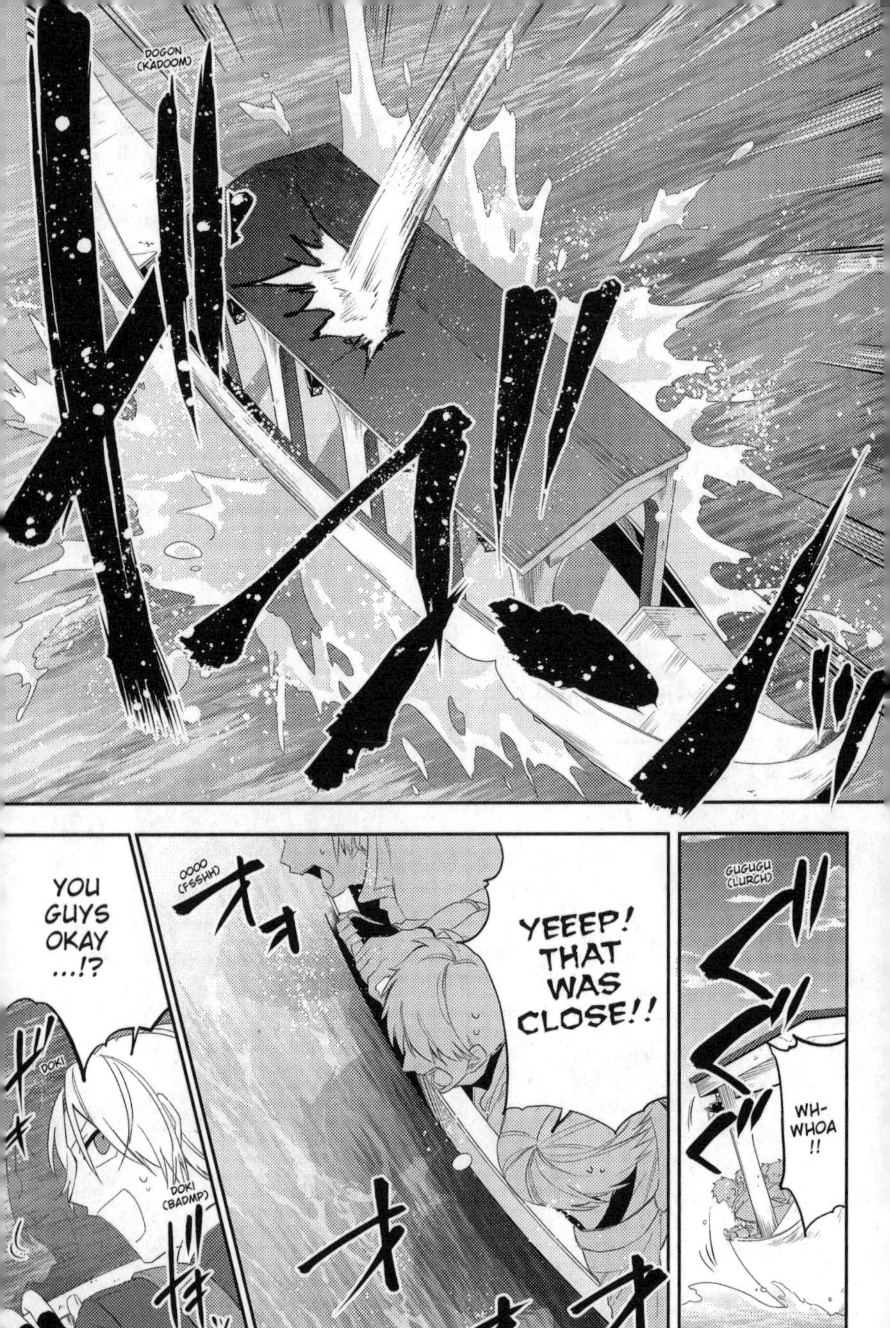
DOGON (KADOOM)
GUGUGU (LURCH)
WH-WHOA!!
OOOO (FSSHH)
YEEEP! THAT WAS CLOSE!!
YOU GUYS OKAY...!?
DOKI
DOKI (BADMP)

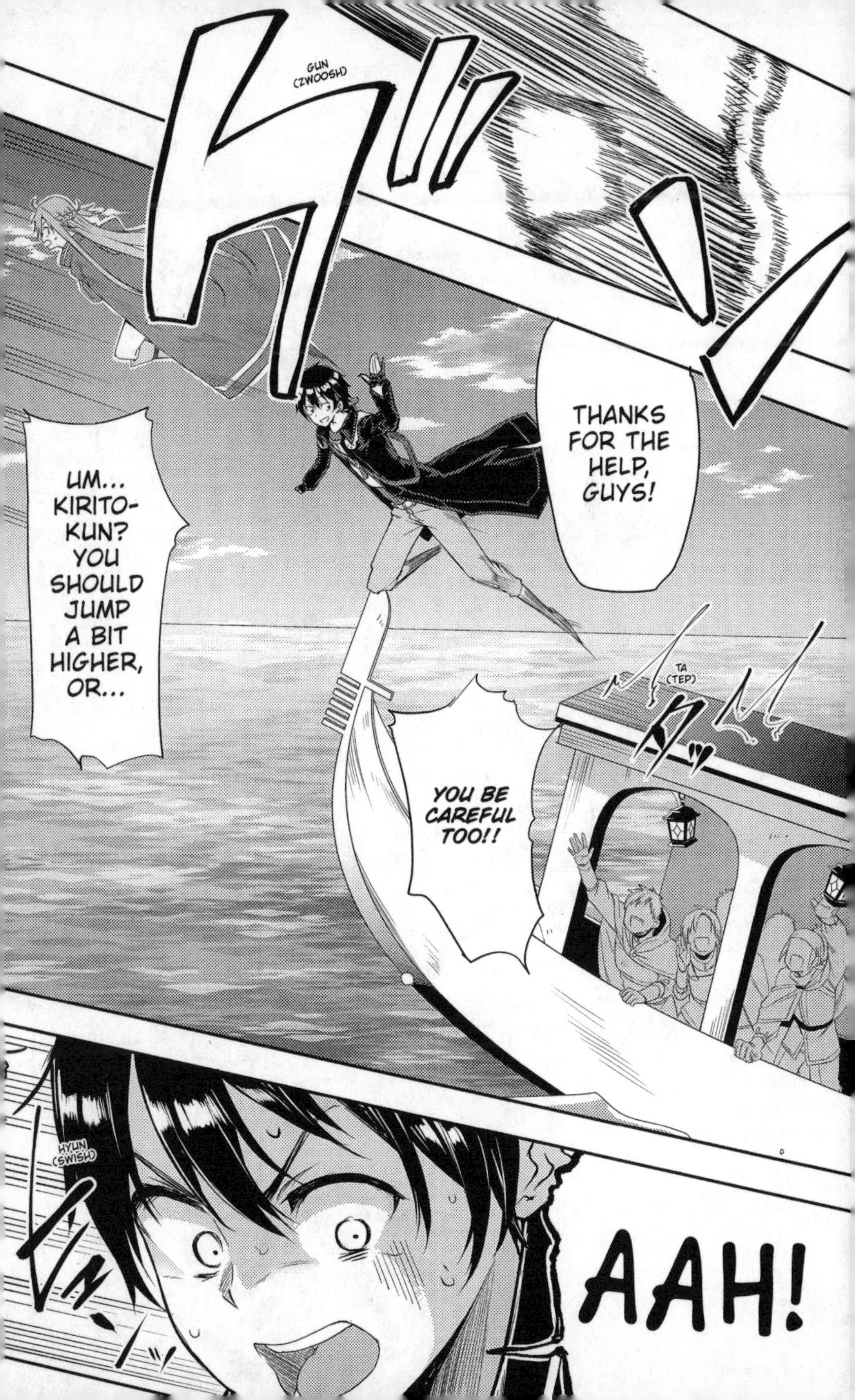
GUN (ZWOOSH)
THANKS FOR THE HELP, GUYS!
TA (TEP)
YOU BE CAREFUL TOO!!
UM... KIRITO-KUN? YOU SHOULD JUMP A BIT HIGHER, OR...
AAH!
HYUN (SWISH)

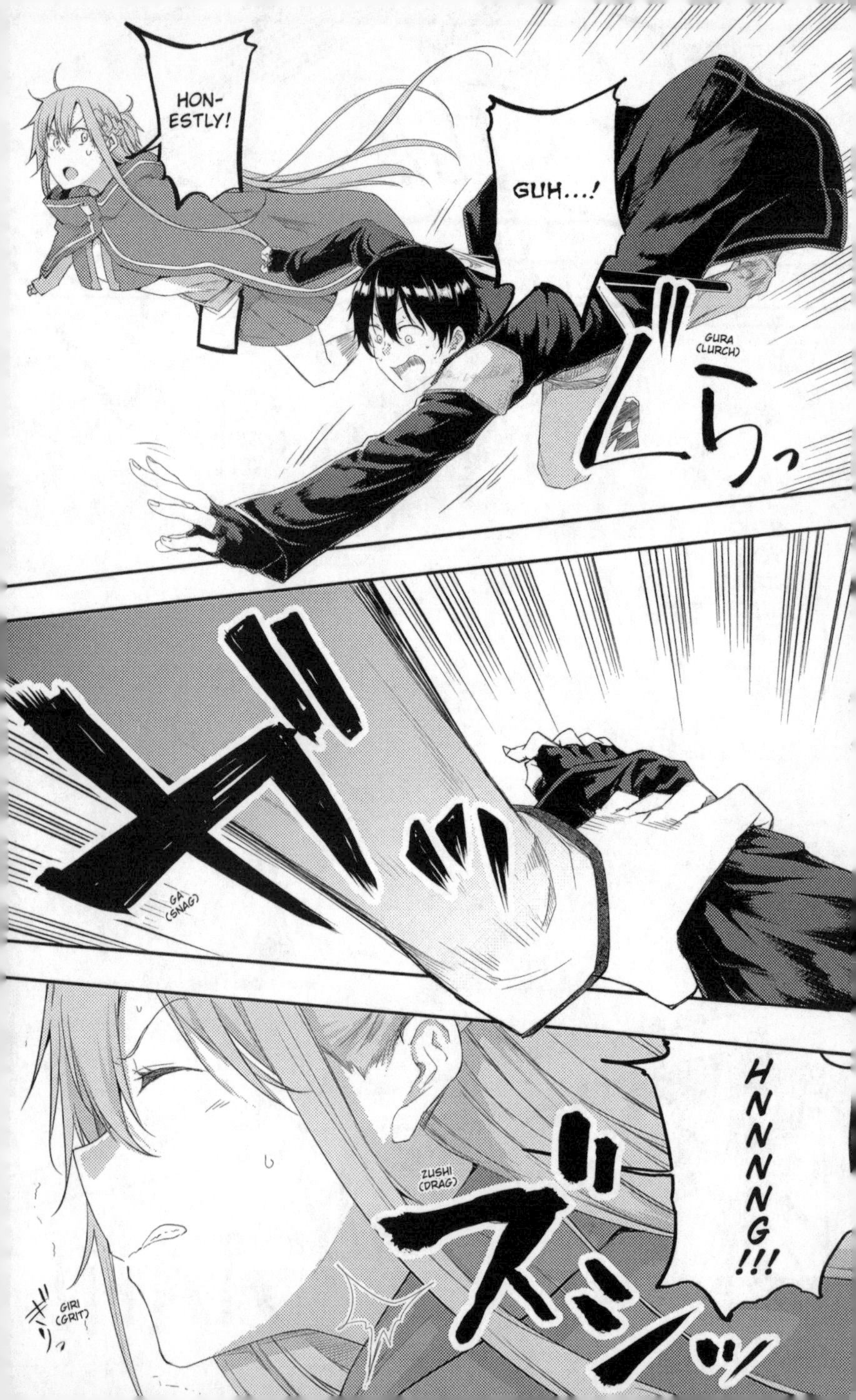
GUH...!
HON-
ESTLY!
GURA
(LURCH)
GA
(SNAG)
HNNNNG!!!
ZUSHI
(DRAG)
GIRI
(GRIT)

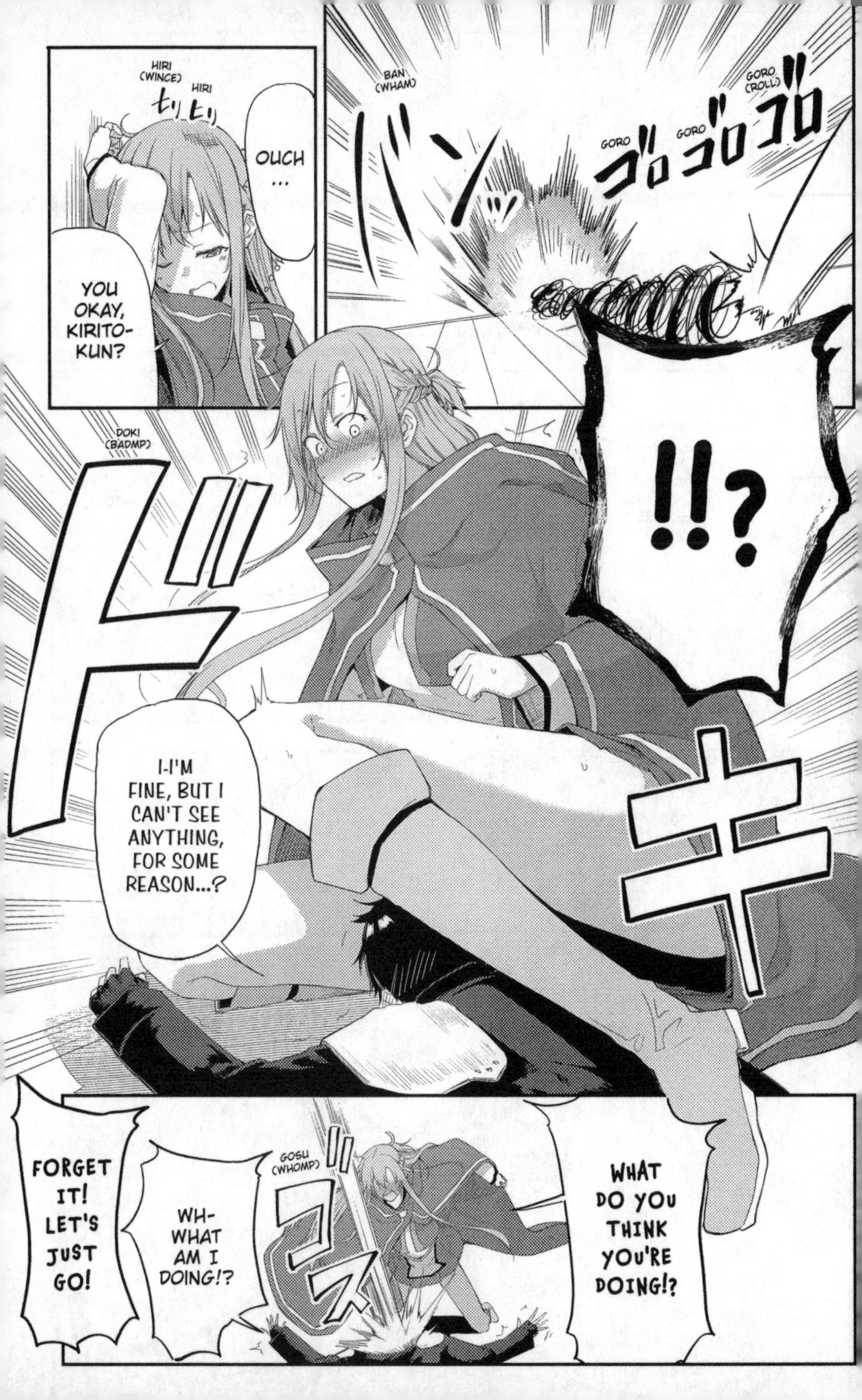
GORO (ROLL)
GORO
GORO
BAN (WHAM)
HIRI (WINCE) HIRI
OUCH ...
YOU OKAY, KIRITO-KUN?
!!?
DOKI (BADMP)
I-I'M FINE, BUT I CAN'T SEE ANYTHING, FOR SOME REASON...?
WHAT DO YOU THINK YOU'RE DOING!?
GOSU (WHOMP)
WH-WHAT AM I DOING!?
FORGET IT! LET'S JUST GO!

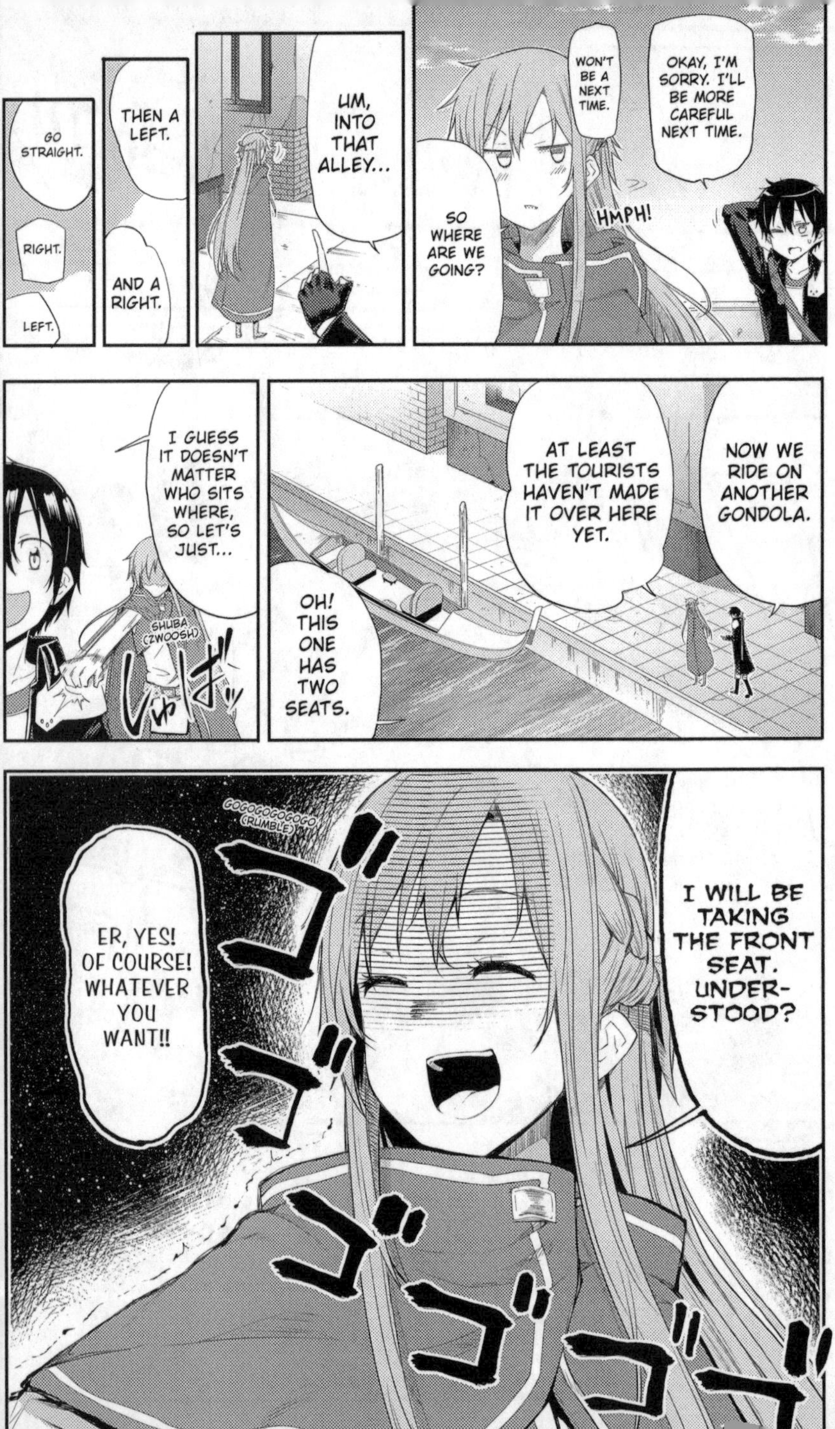
OKAY, I'M SORRY. I'LL BE MORE CAREFUL NEXT TIME.
WON'T BE A NEXT TIME.
HMPH!
SO WHERE ARE WE GOING?
UM, INTO THAT ALLEY...
THEN A LEFT.
AND A RIGHT.
GO STRAIGHT.
RIGHT.
LEFT.
NOW WE RIDE ON ANOTHER GONDOLA.
AT LEAST THE TOURISTS HAVEN'T MADE IT OVER HERE YET.
OH! THIS ONE HAS TWO SEATS.
I GUESS IT DOESN'T MATTER WHO SITS WHERE, SO LET'S JUST...
SHUBA (ZWOOSH)
I WILL BE TAKING THE FRONT SEAT. UNDER-STOOD?
GOGOGOGOGOGO (RUMBLE)
ER, YES! OF COURSE! WHATEVER YOU WANT!!

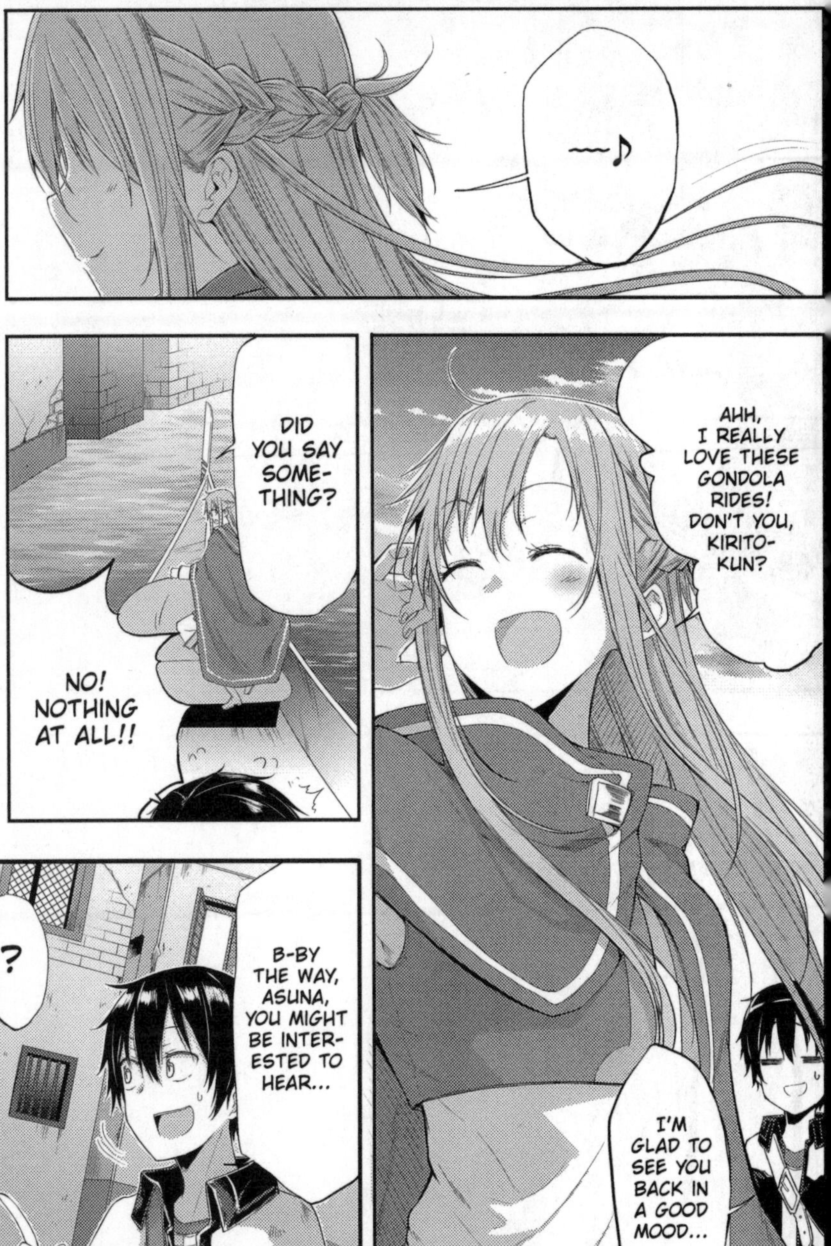

~♪
AHH, I REALLY LOVE THESE GONDOLA RIDES! DON'T YOU, KIRITO-KUN?
I'M GLAD TO SEE YOU BACK IN A GOOD MOOD...
DID YOU SAY SOME-THING?
NO! NOTHING AT ALL!!
B-BY THE WAY, ASUNA, YOU MIGHT BE INTER-ESTED TO HEAR...
?

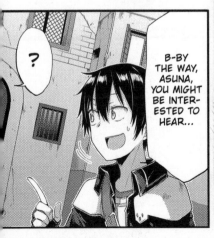

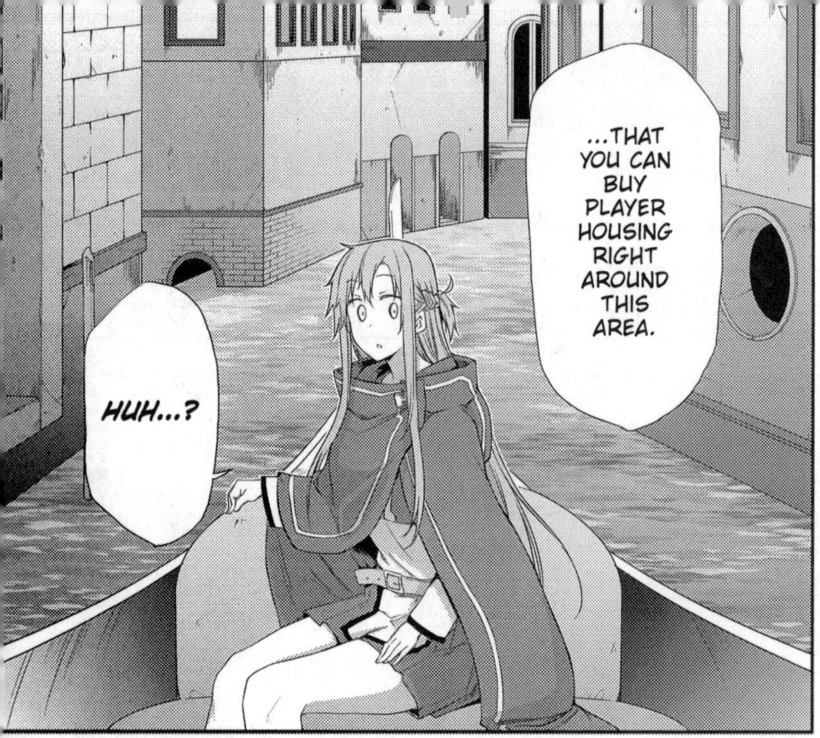
...THAT YOU CAN BUY PLAYER HOUSING RIGHT AROUND THIS AREA.
HUH...?
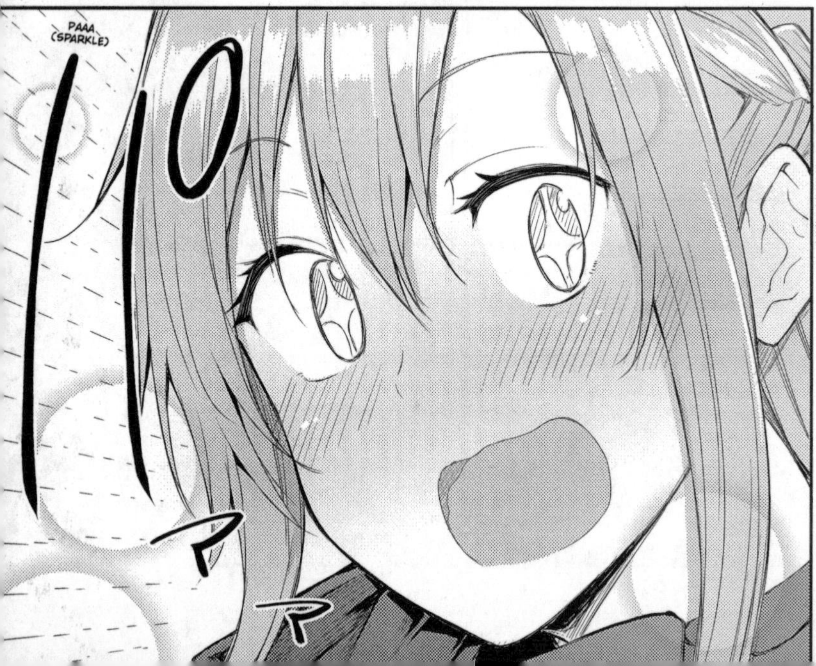
PAAA (SPARKLE)

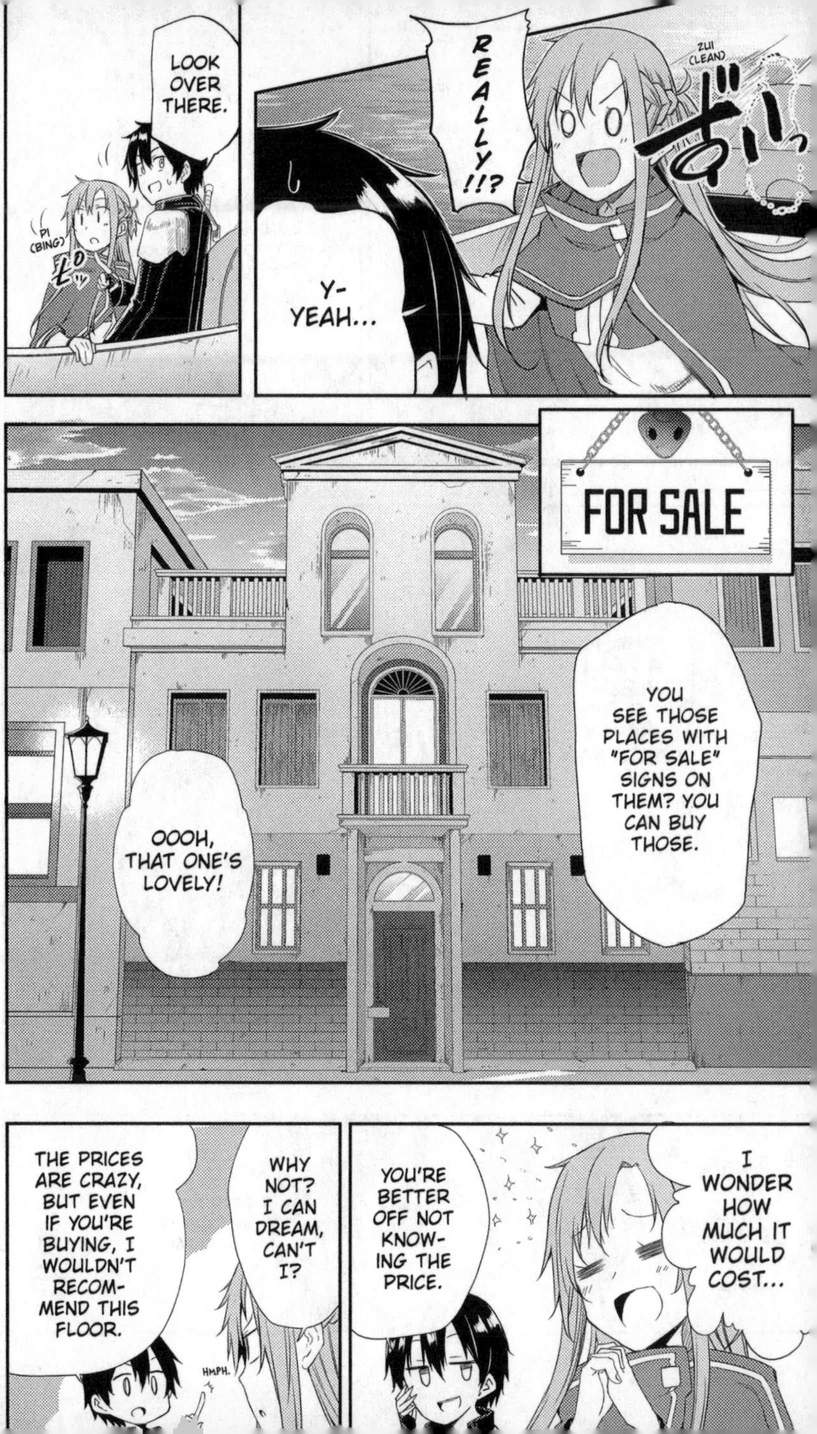
ZUI (LEAN)
REALLY!!?
Y-YEAH...
LOOK OVER THERE.
PI (BING)
FOR SALE
YOU SEE THOSE PLACES WITH "FOR SALE" SIGNS ON THEM? YOU CAN BUY THOSE.
OOOH, THAT ONE'S LOVELY!
I WONDER HOW MUCH IT WOULD COST...
YOU'RE BETTER OFF NOT KNOWING THE PRICE.
WHY NOT? I CAN DREAM, CAN'T I?
HMPH.
THE PRICES ARE CRAZY, BUT EVEN IF YOU'RE BUYING, I WOULDN'T RECOMMEND THIS FLOOR.

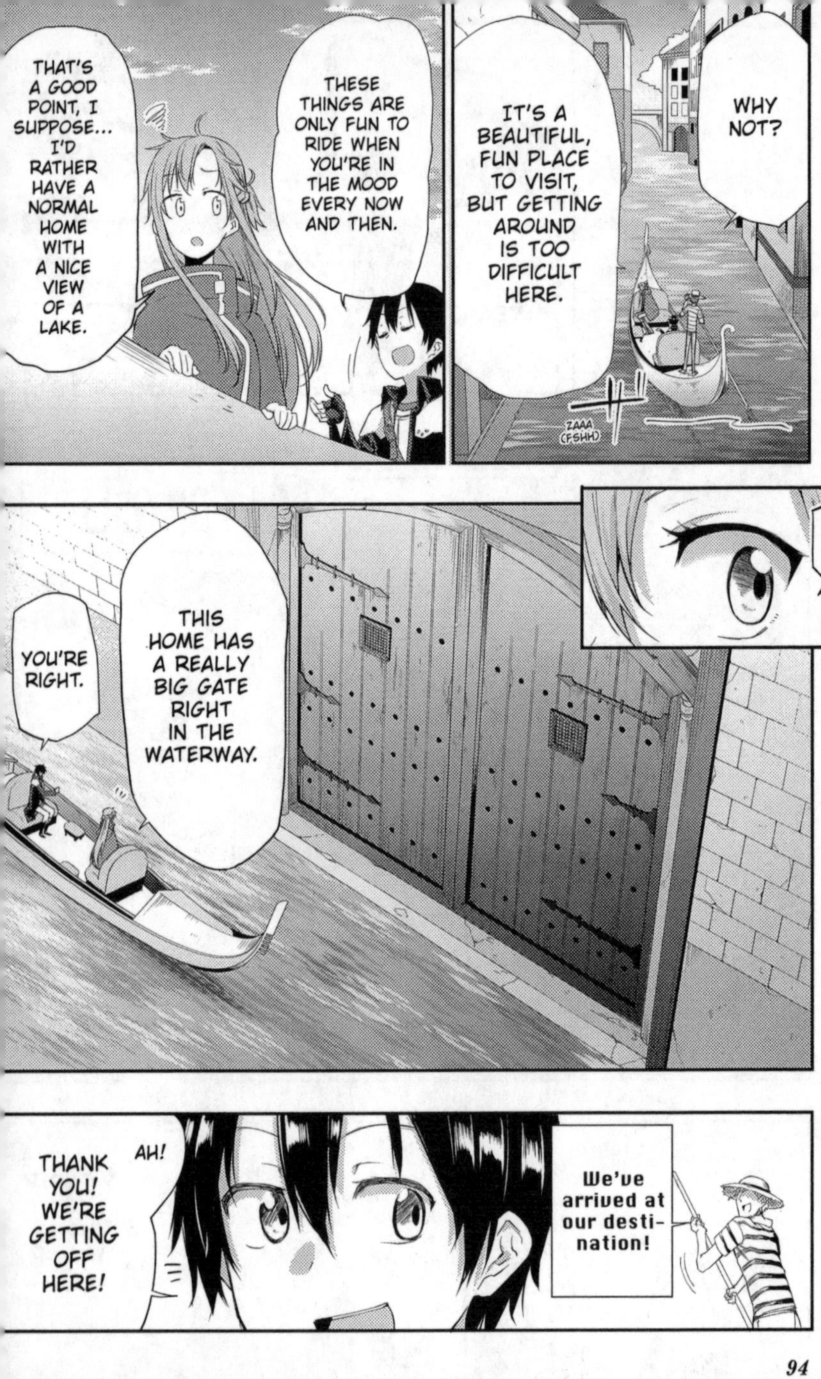
WHY NOT?
IT'S A BEAUTIFUL, FUN PLACE TO VISIT, BUT GETTING AROUND IS TOO DIFFICULT HERE.
ZAAA (FSHH)
THESE THINGS ARE ONLY FUN TO RIDE WHEN YOU'RE IN THE MOOD EVERY NOW AND THEN.
THAT'S A GOOD POINT, I SUPPOSE... I'D RATHER HAVE A NORMAL HOME WITH A NICE VIEW OF A LAKE.
!
THIS HOME HAS A REALLY BIG GATE RIGHT IN THE WATERWAY.
YOU'RE RIGHT.
We've arrived at our desti-nation!
AH!
THANK YOU! WE'RE GETTING OFF HERE!

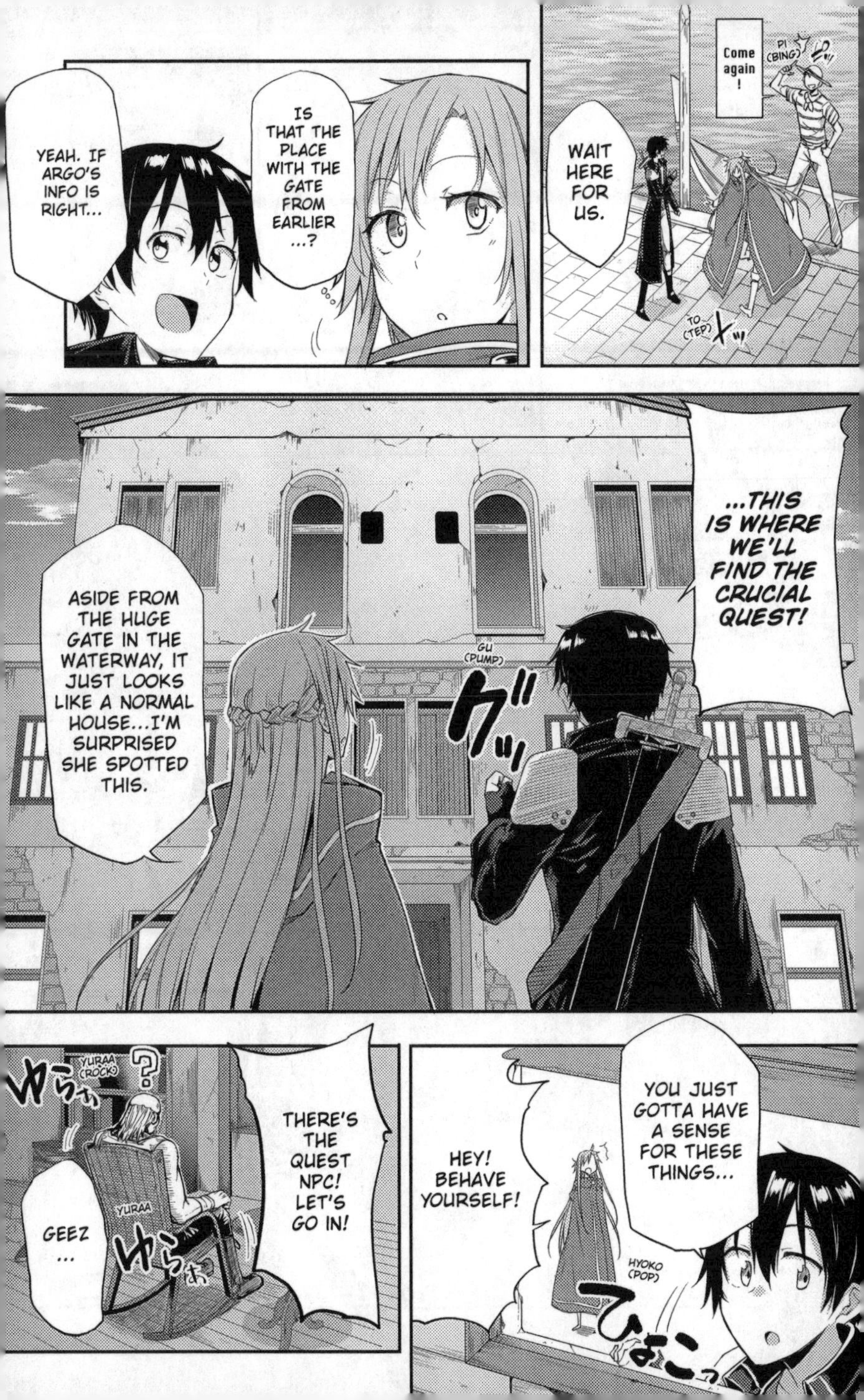
PI (BING)
Come again!
WAIT HERE FOR US.
TO (TEP)
IS THAT THE PLACE WITH THE GATE FROM EARLIER...?
YEAH. IF ARGO'S INFO IS RIGHT...
...THIS IS WHERE WE'LL FIND THE CRUCIAL QUEST!
GU (PUMP)
ASIDE FROM THE HUGE GATE IN THE WATERWAY, IT JUST LOOKS LIKE A NORMAL HOUSE...I'M SURPRISED SHE SPOTTED THIS.
YOU JUST GOTTA HAVE A SENSE FOR THESE THINGS...
HEY! BEHAVE YOURSELF!
HYOKO (POP)
THERE'S THE QUEST NPC! LET'S GO IN!
YURAA (ROCK)
?
GEEZ...
YURAA

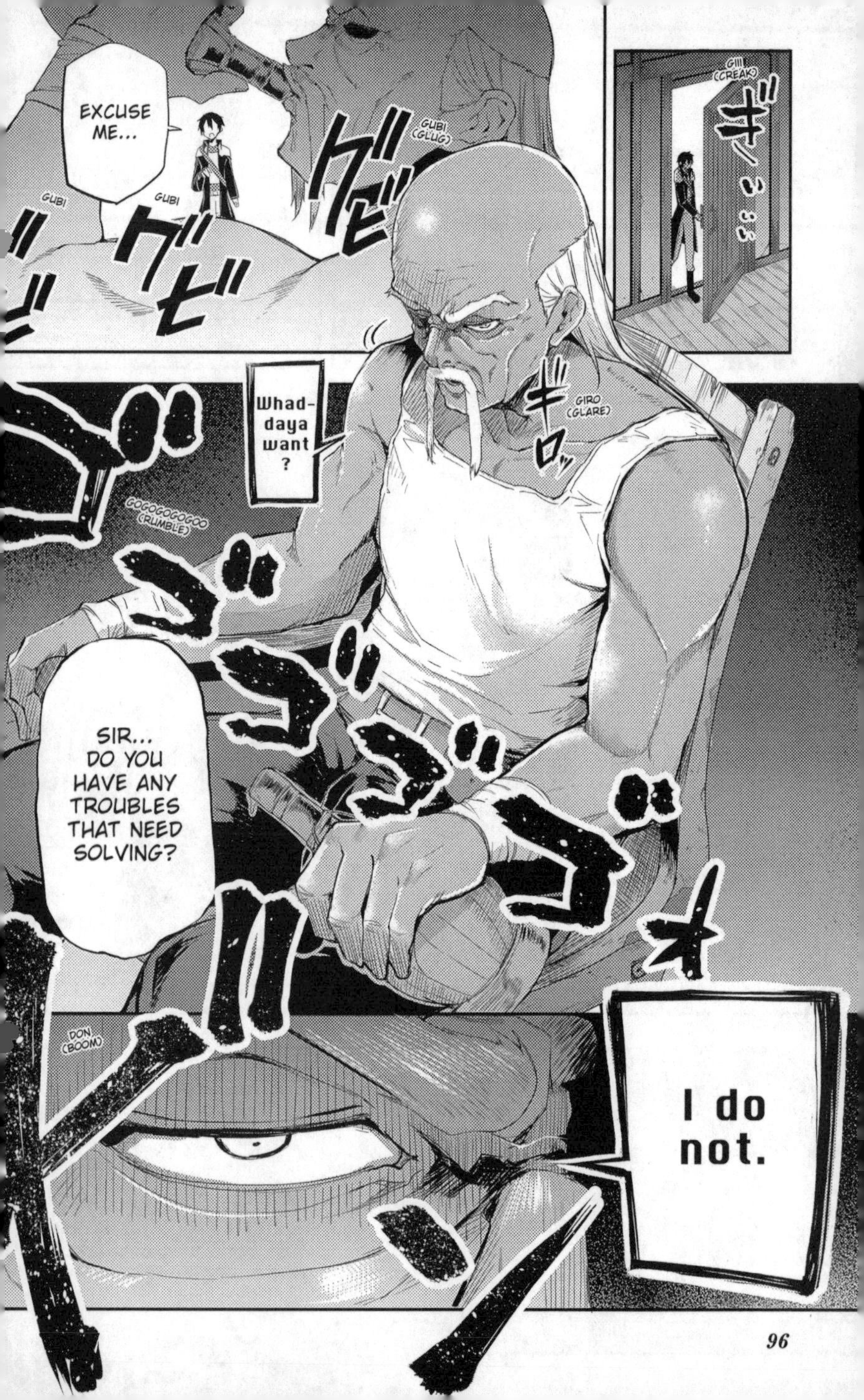
GIII (CREAK)
GUBI (GLUG)
EXCUSE ME...
GUBI
GUBI
GIRO (GLARE)
Whaddaya want?
GOGOGOGOGOO (RUMBLE)
SIR... DO YOU HAVE ANY TROUBLES THAT NEED SOLVING?
I do not.
DON (BOOM)

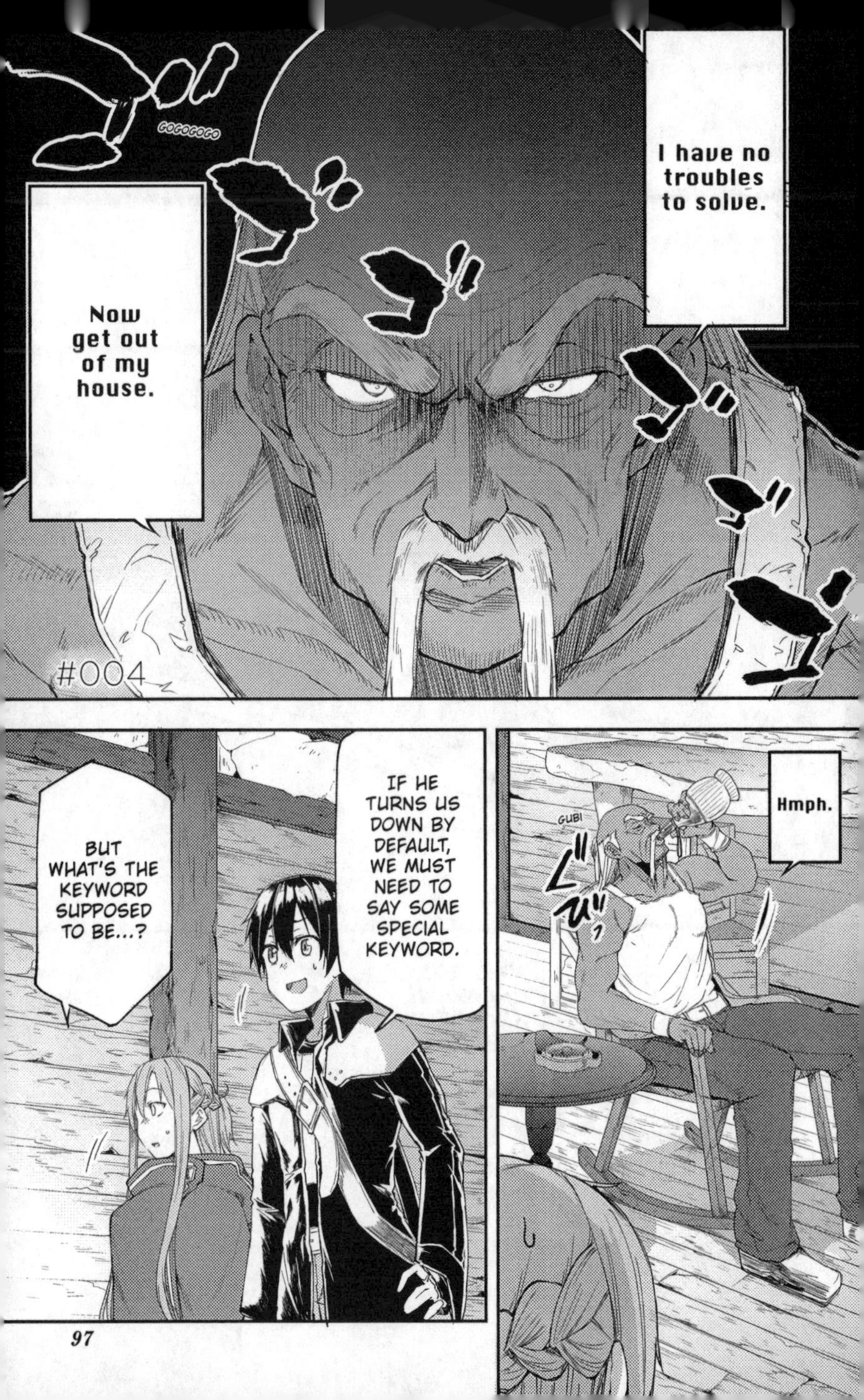
GOGOGOGO
I have no troubles to solve.
Now get out of my house.
#004
GUBI
Hmph.
IF HE TURNS US DOWN BY DEFAULT, WE MUST NEED TO SAY SOME SPECIAL KEYWORD.
BUT WHAT'S THE KEYWORD SUPPOSED TO BE...?

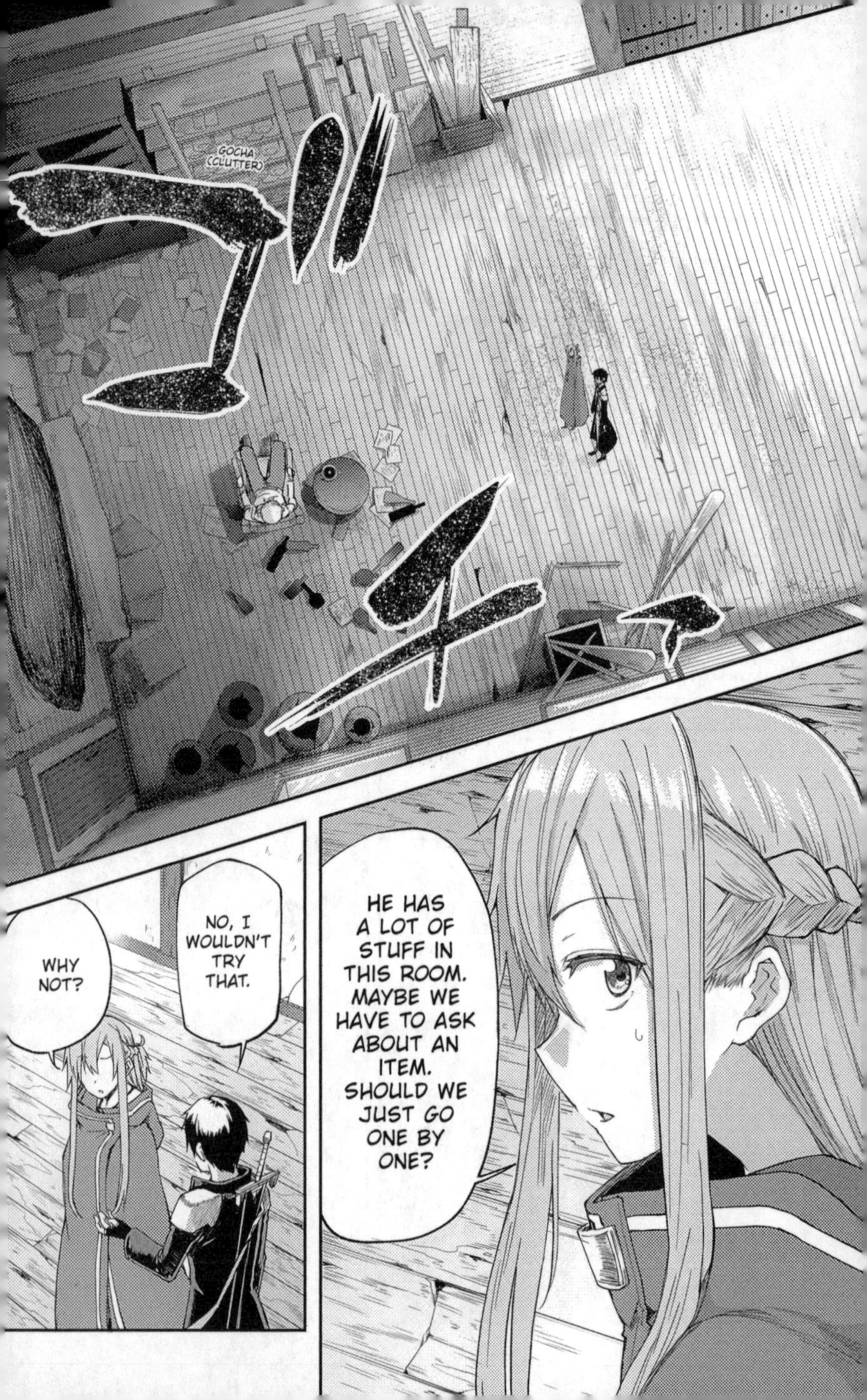
GOCHA (CLUTTER)
HE HAS A LOT OF STUFF IN THIS ROOM. MAYBE WE HAVE TO ASK ABOUT AN ITEM. SHOULD WE JUST GO ONE BY ONE?
NO, I WOULDN'T TRY THAT.
WHY NOT?

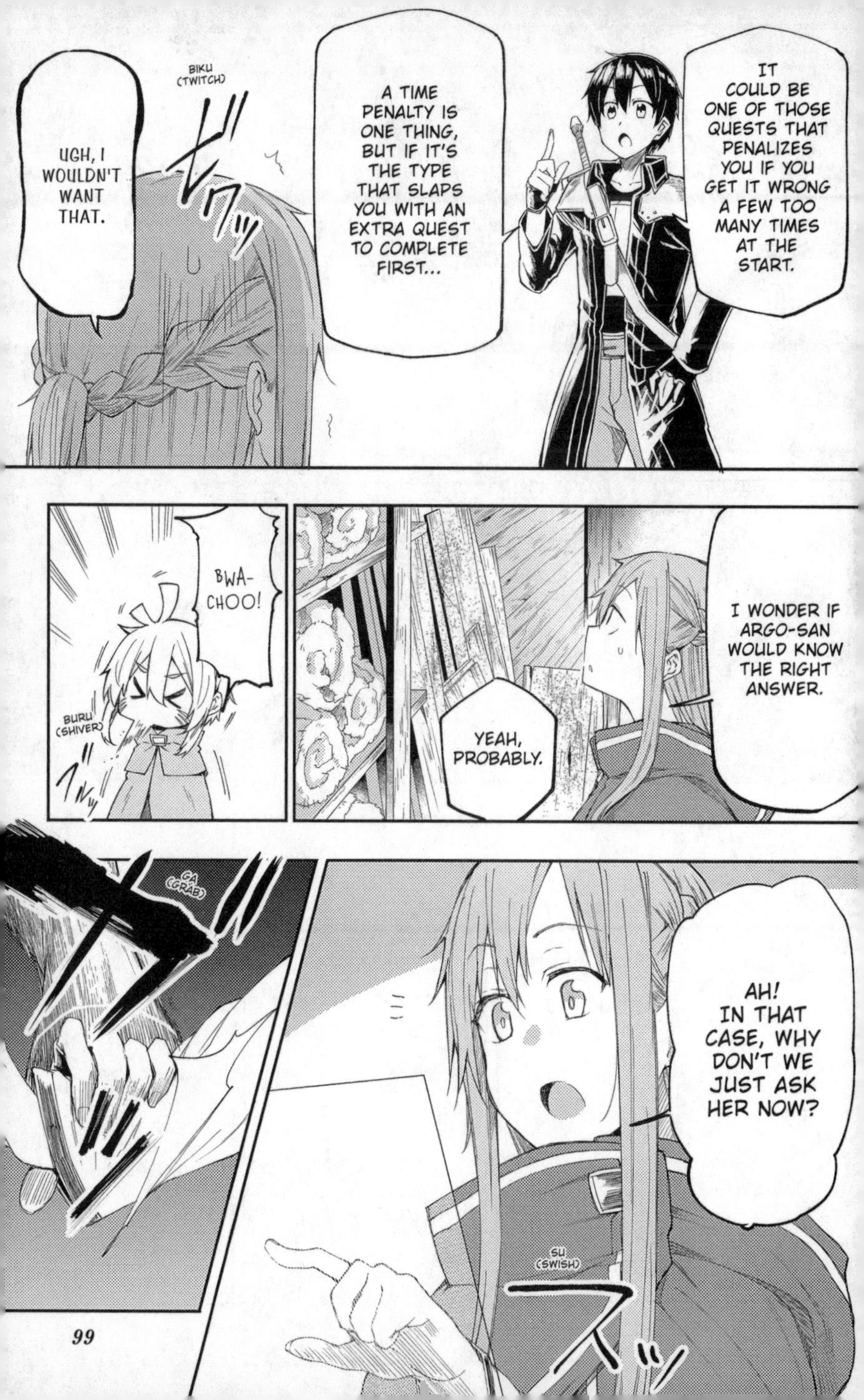
IT COULD BE ONE OF THOSE QUESTS THAT PENALIZES YOU IF YOU GET IT WRONG A FEW TOO MANY TIMES AT THE START.
A TIME PENALTY IS ONE THING, BUT IF IT'S THE TYPE THAT SLAPS YOU WITH AN EXTRA QUEST TO COMPLETE FIRST...
BIKU (TWITCH)
UGH, I WOULDN'T WANT THAT.
I WONDER IF ARGO-SAN WOULD KNOW THE RIGHT ANSWER.
YEAH, PROBABLY.
BWA-CHOO!
BURU (SHIVER)
AH! IN THAT CASE, WHY DON'T WE JUST ASK HER NOW?
SU (SWISH)
GA (GRAB)

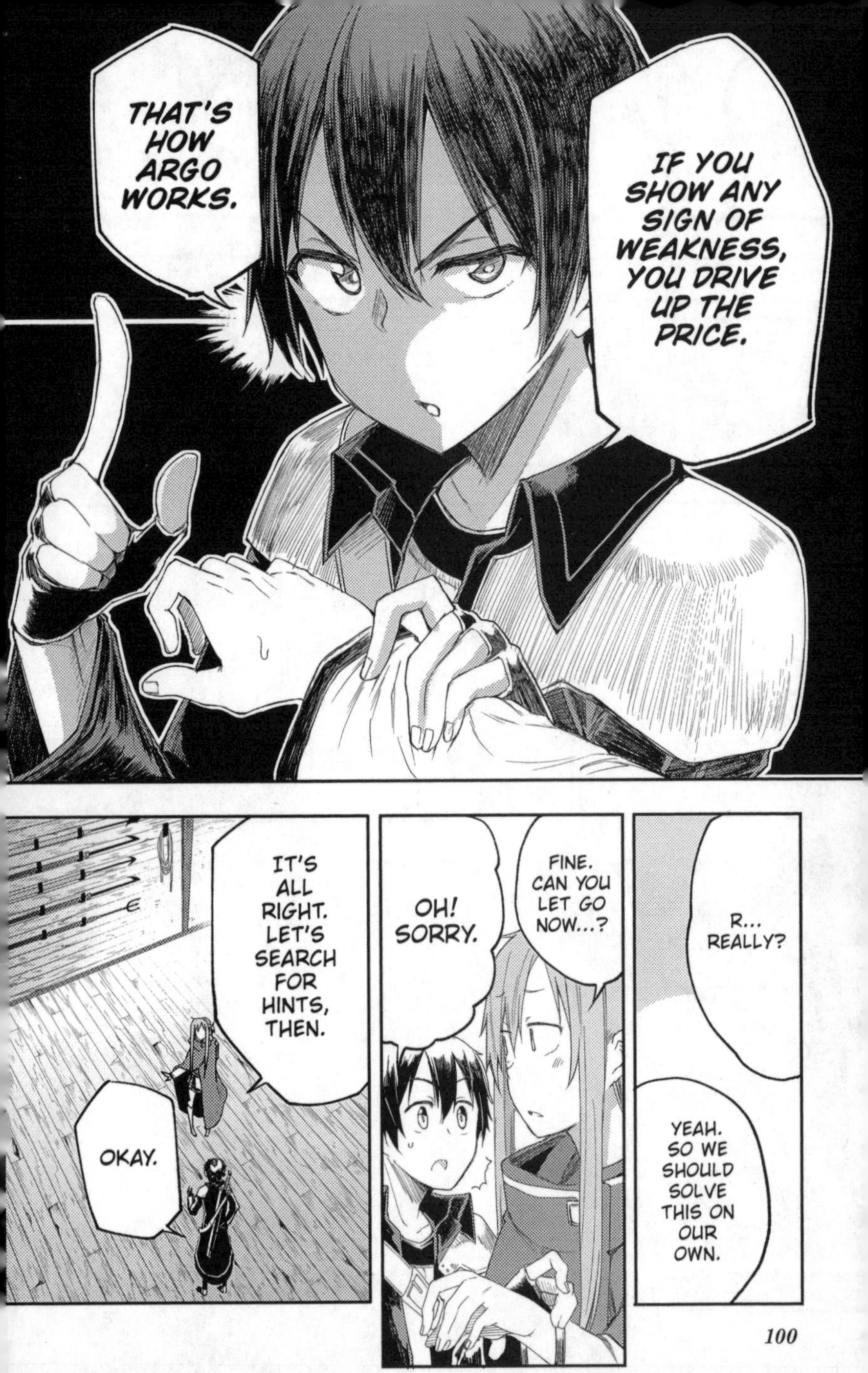
IF YOU SHOW ANY SIGN OF WEAKNESS, YOU DRIVE UP THE PRICE.
THAT'S HOW ARGO WORKS.
R... REALLY?
YEAH. SO WE SHOULD SOLVE THIS ON OUR OWN.
FINE. CAN YOU LET GO NOW...?
OH! SORRY.
IT'S ALL RIGHT. LET'S SEARCH FOR HINTS, THEN.
OKAY.

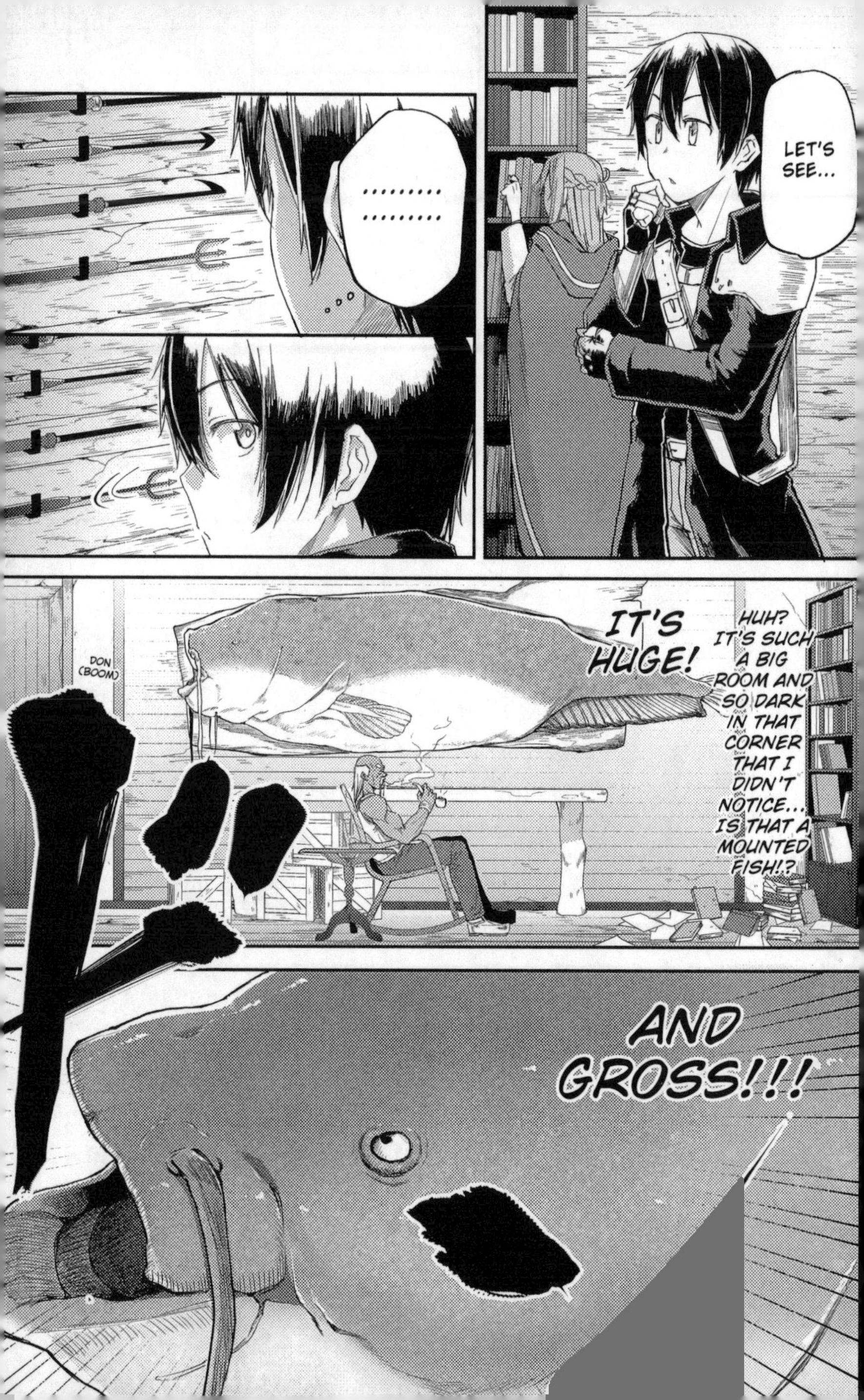
LET'S SEE...
....
....
HUH? IT'S SUCH A BIG ROOM AND SO DARK IN THAT CORNER THAT I DIDN'T NOTICE... IS THAT A MOUNTED FISH!?
IT'S HUGE!
DON (BOOM)
AND GROSS!!!

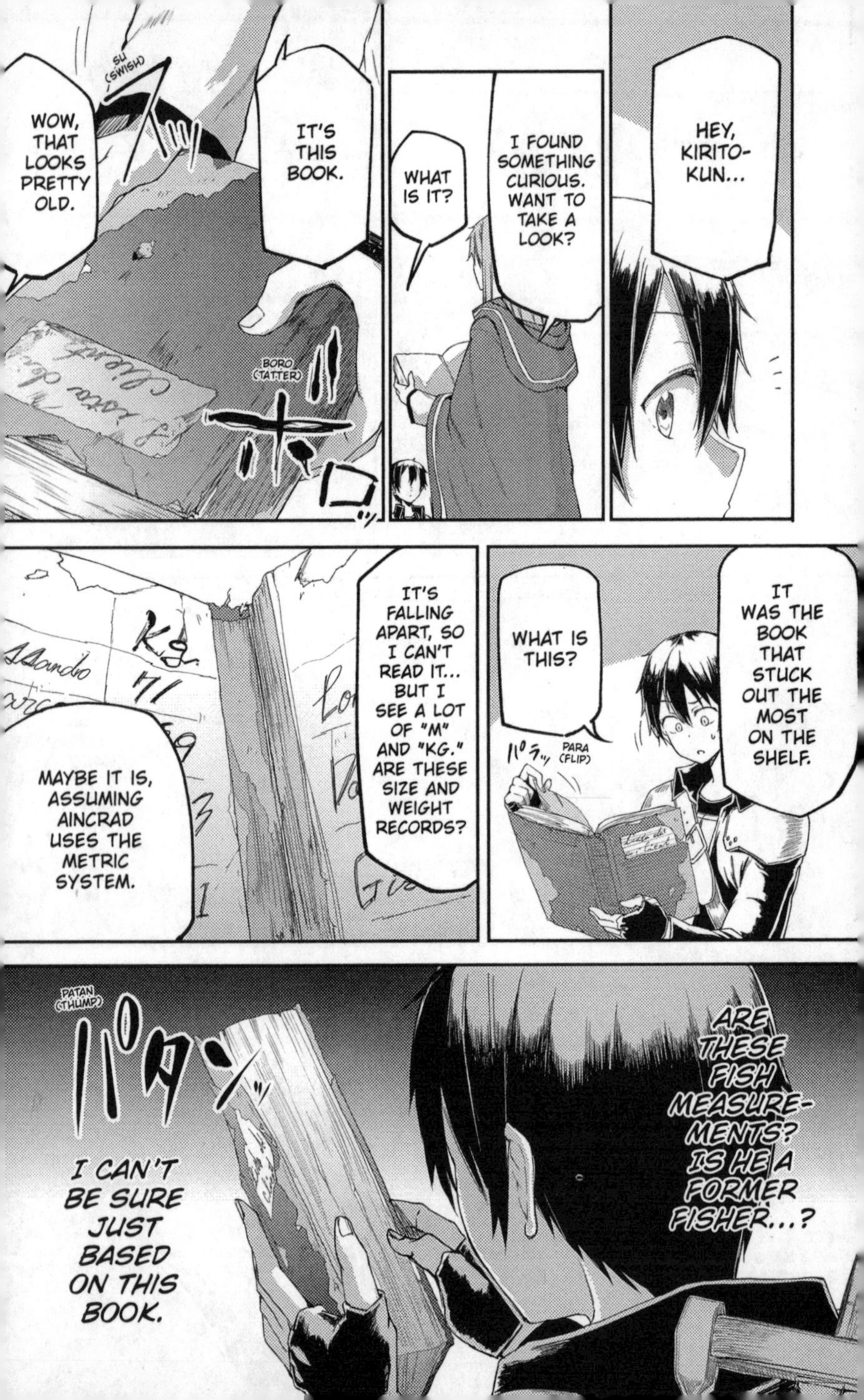
HEY, KIRITO-KUN...
I FOUND SOMETHING CURIOUS. WANT TO TAKE A LOOK?
WHAT IS IT?
IT'S THIS BOOK.
SU (SWISH)
WOW, THAT LOOKS PRETTY OLD.
BORO (TATTER)
IT WAS THE BOOK THAT STUCK OUT THE MOST ON THE SHELF.
WHAT IS THIS?
PARA (FLIP)
IT'S FALLING APART, SO I CAN'T READ IT... BUT I SEE A LOT OF "M" AND "KG." ARE THESE SIZE AND WEIGHT RECORDS?
MAYBE IT IS, ASSUMING AINCRAD USES THE METRIC SYSTEM.
ARE THESE FISH MEASUREMENTS? IS HE A FORMER FISHER...?
PATAN (THUMP)
I CAN'T BE SURE JUST BASED ON THIS BOOK.

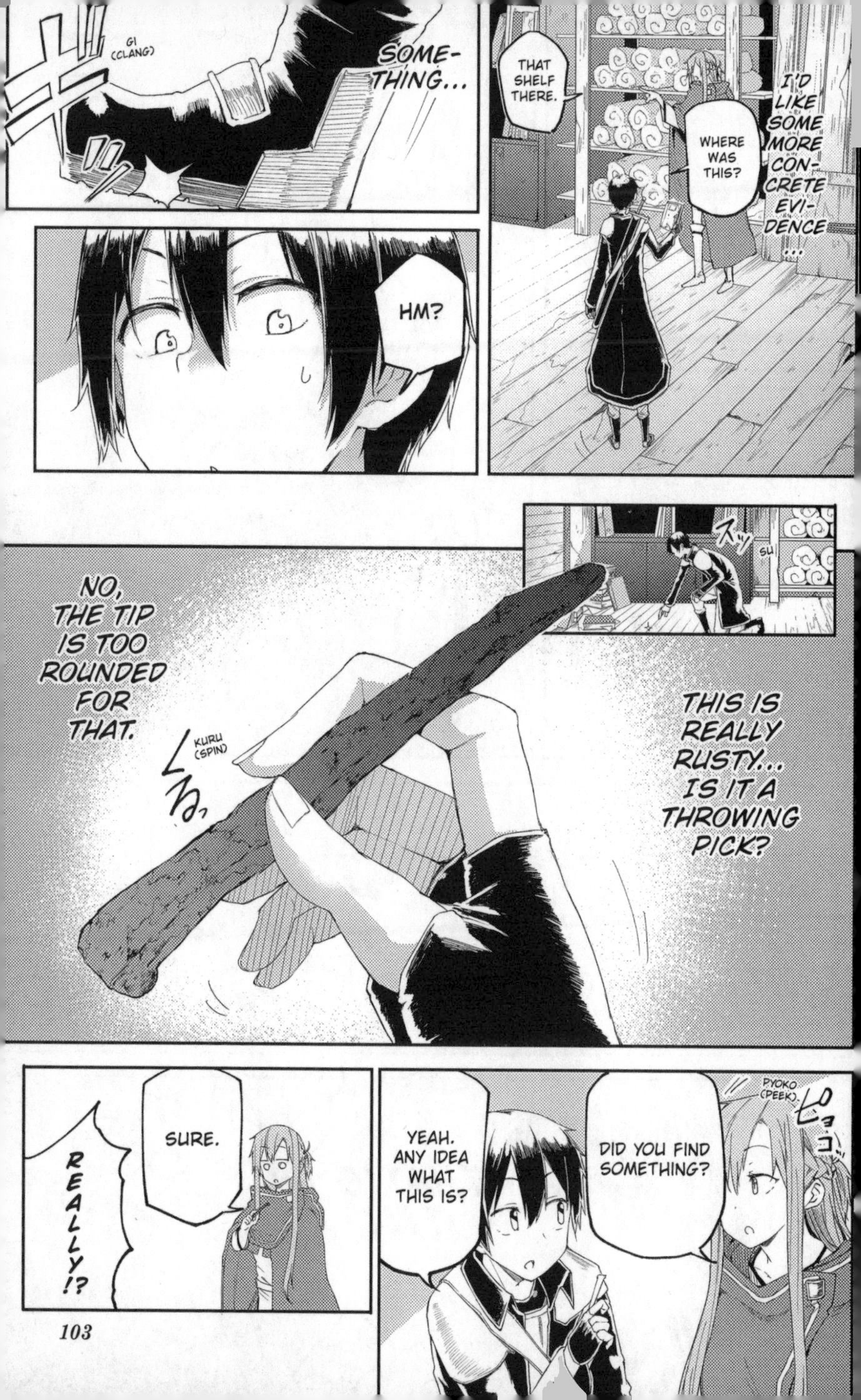
I'D LIKE SOME MORE CON-CRETE EVI-DENCE...
WHERE WAS THIS?
THAT SHELF THERE.
GI (CLANG)
SOME-THING...
HM?
SU
THIS IS REALLY RUSTY... IS IT A THROWING PICK?
KURU (SPIN)
NO, THE TIP IS TOO ROUNDED FOR THAT.
PYOKO (PEEK)
DID YOU FIND SOMETHING?
YEAH. ANY IDEA WHAT THIS IS?
SURE.
REALLY!?

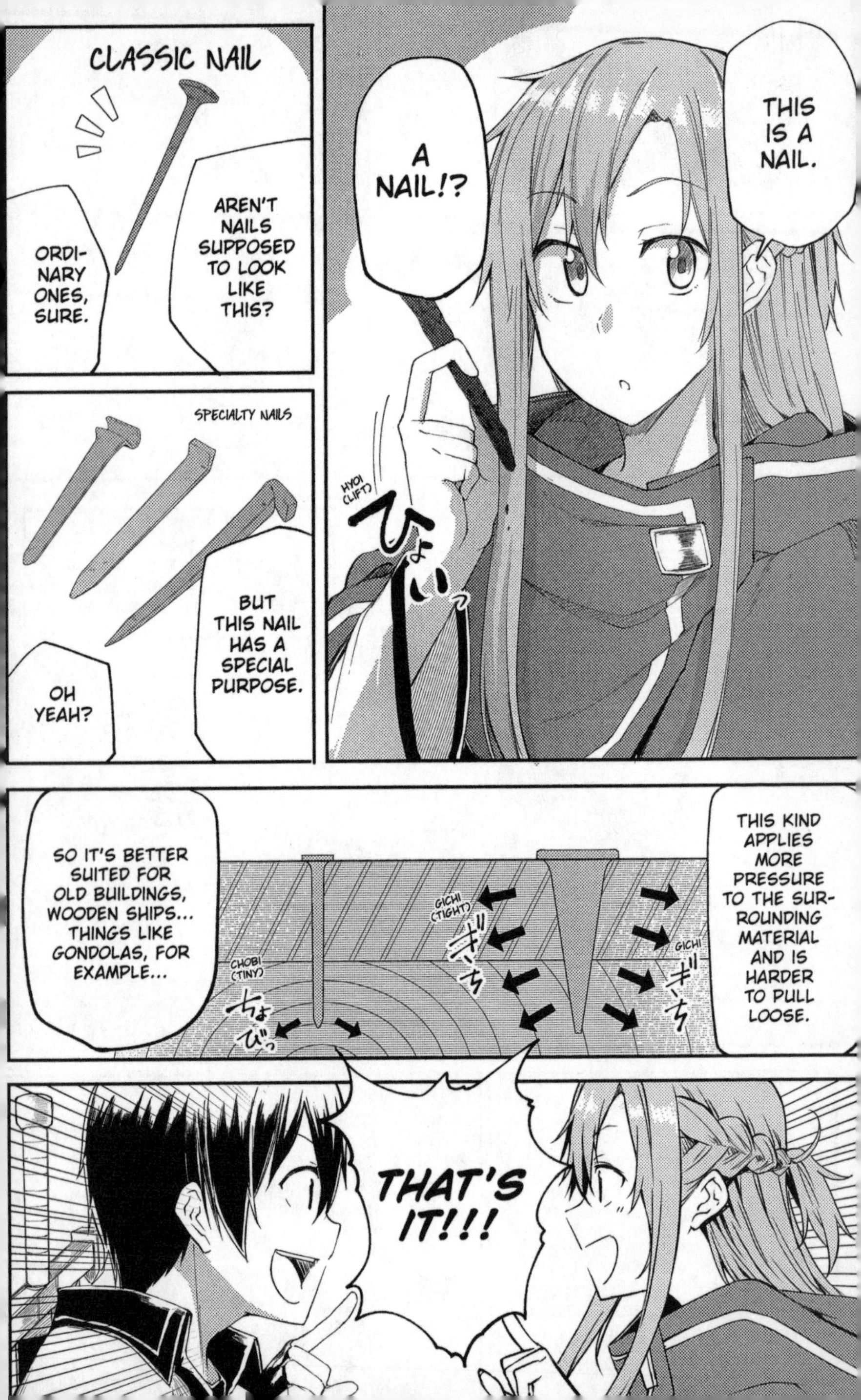

THIS IS A NAIL.
A NAIL!?
HYOI (LIFT)
ひょいっ
CLASSIC NAIL
AREN'T NAILS SUPPOSED TO LOOK LIKE THIS?
ORDI- NARY ONES, SURE.
SPECIALTY NAILS
BUT THIS NAIL HAS A SPECIAL PURPOSE.
OH YEAH?
THIS KIND APPLIES MORE PRESSURE TO THE SUR- ROUNDING MATERIAL AND IS HARDER TO PULL LOOSE.
GICHI
GICHI (TIGHT)
CHOBI (TINY)
ちょびっ
SO IT'S BETTER SUITED FOR OLD BUILDINGS, WOODEN SHIPS... THINGS LIKE GONDOLAS, FOR EXAMPLE...
THAT'S IT!!!

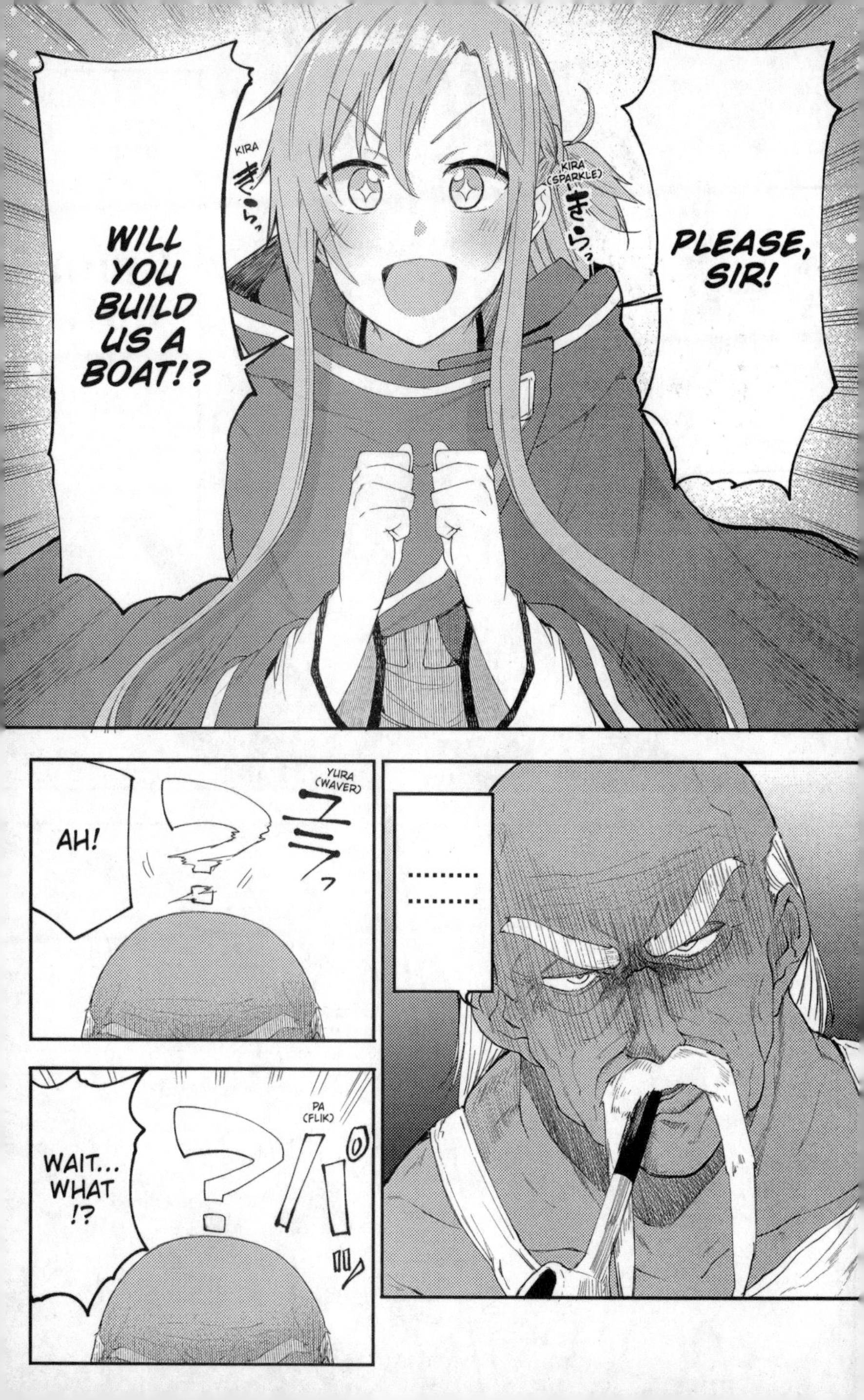
PLEASE, SIR!
KIRA (SPARKLE)
きらっ
KIRA
きらっ
WILL YOU BUILD US A BOAT!?
....
....
YURA (WAVER)
ユラッ
AH!
PA (FLIK)
パッ
WAIT... WHAT !?

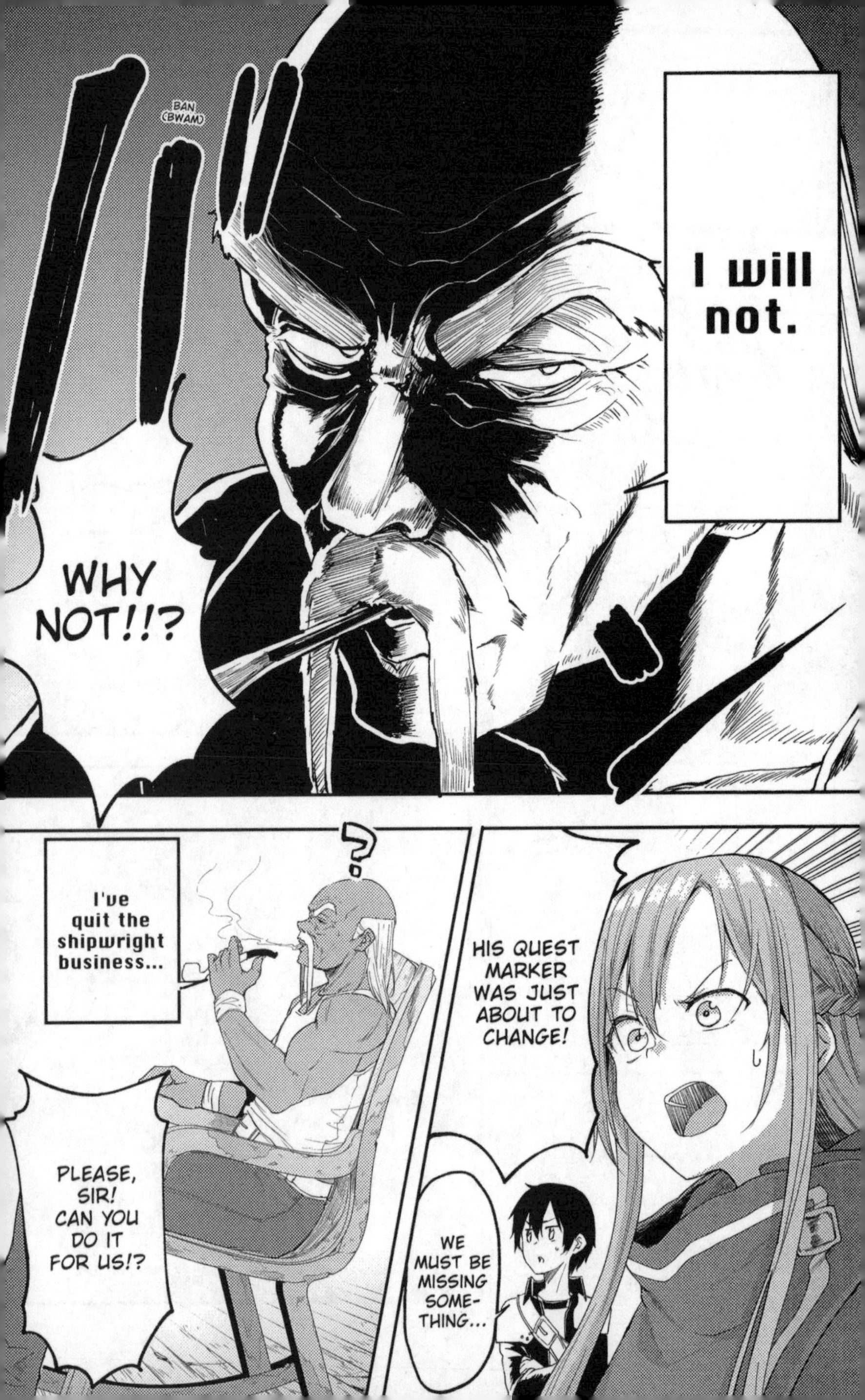
I will not.
BAN (BWAM)
WHY NOT!!?
HIS QUEST MARKER WAS JUST ABOUT TO CHANGE!
WE MUST BE MISSING SOME-THING...
?
I've quit the shipwright business...
PLEASE, SIR! CAN YOU DO IT FOR US!?

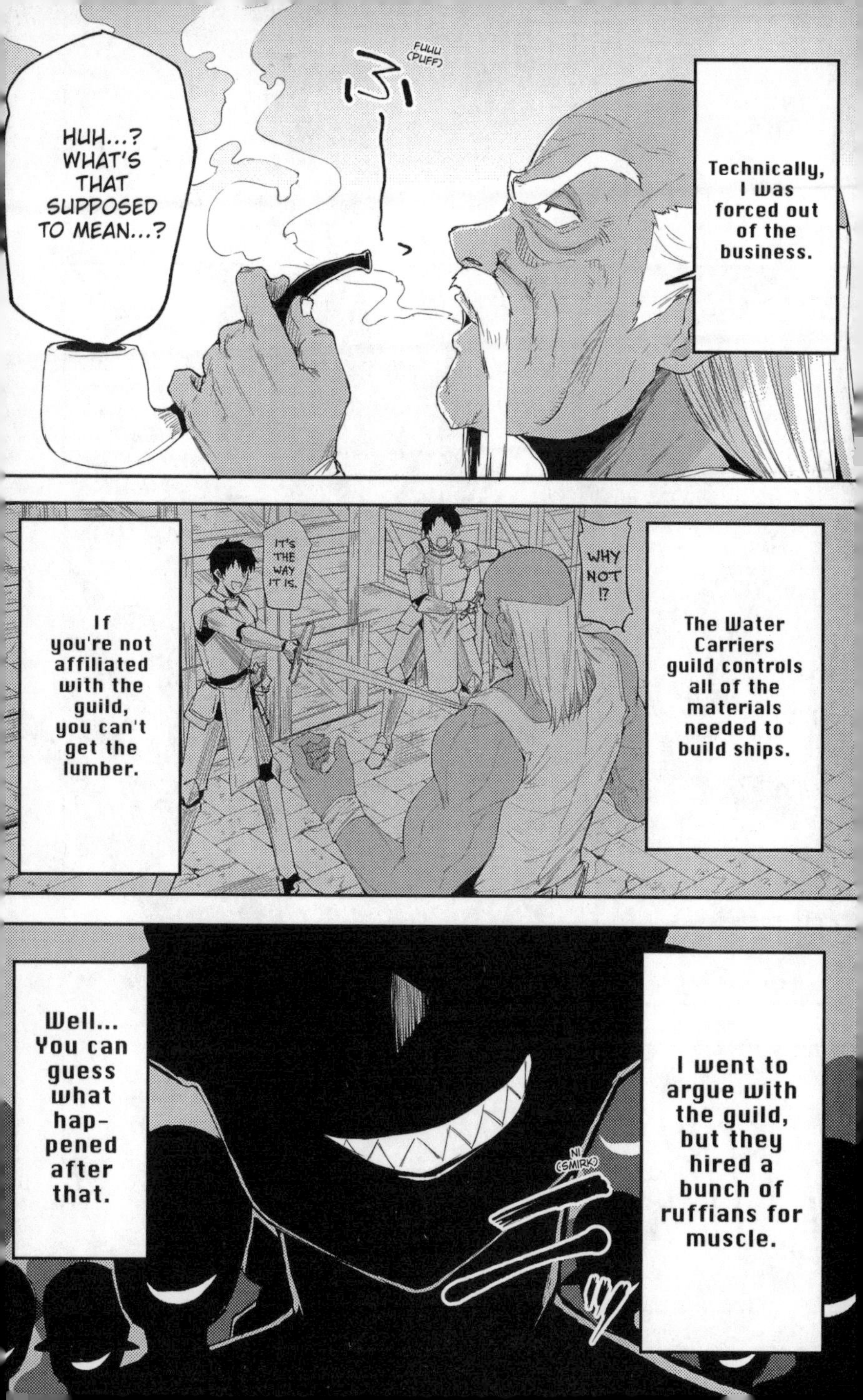
Technically, I was forced out of the business.
FUUU (PUFF)
HUH...? WHAT'S THAT SUPPOSED TO MEAN...?
The Water Carriers guild controls all of the materials needed to build ships.
WHY NOT !?
IT'S THE WAY IT IS.
If you're not affiliated with the guild, you can't get the lumber.
I went to argue with the guild, but they hired a bunch of ruffians for muscle.
NI (SMIRK)
Well... You can guess what hap-pened after that.

IN THAT CASE...

....

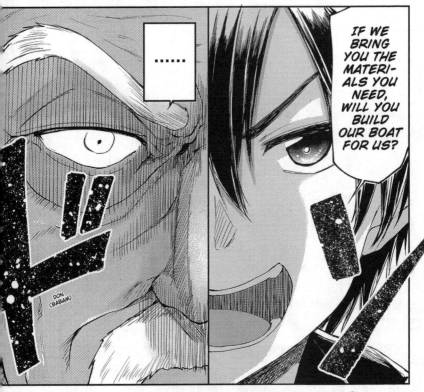

......

IF WE BRING YOU THE MATERIALS YOU NEED, WILL YOU BUILD OUR BOAT FOR US?

DON
(BABAM)

PAAA
(GLOW)

!

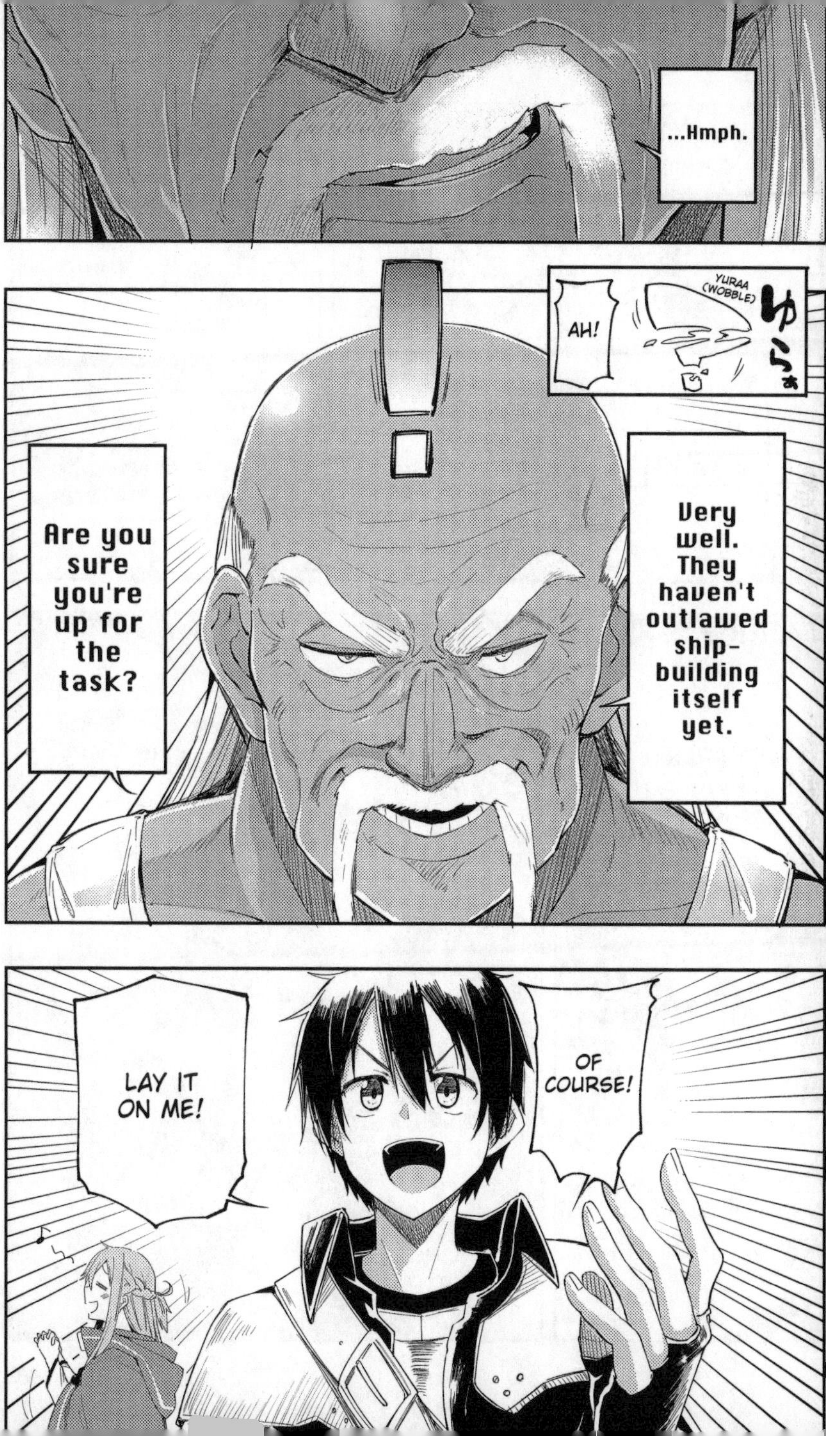
...Hmph.
ゆらぁ
YURAA (WOBBLE)
AH!
Very well. They haven't outlawed ship-building itself yet.
Are you sure you're up for the task?
OF COURSE!
LAY IT ON ME!

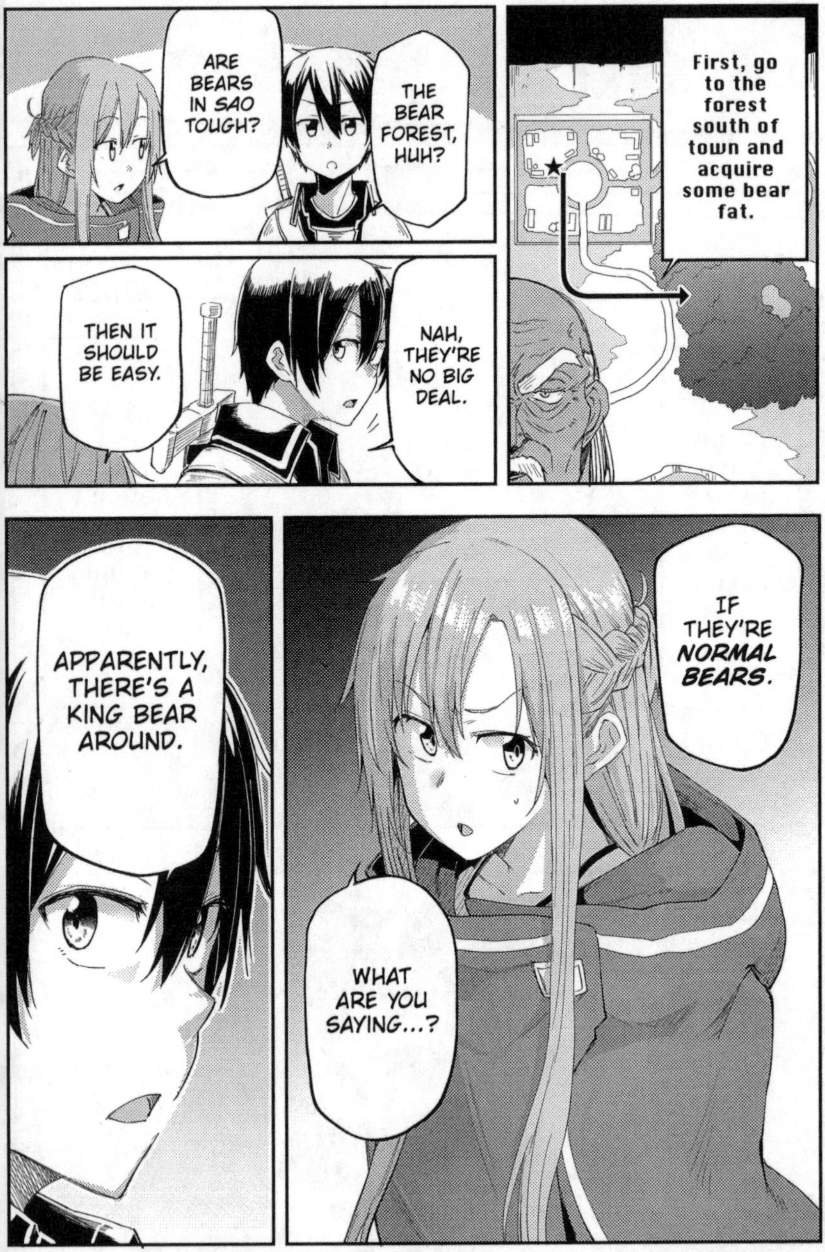
First, go to the forest south of town and acquire some bear fat.
THE BEAR FOREST, HUH?
ARE BEARS IN SAO TOUGH?
NAH, THEY'RE NO BIG DEAL.
THEN IT SHOULD BE EASY.
IF THEY'RE NORMAL BEARS.
WHAT ARE YOU SAYING...?
APPARENTLY, THERE'S A KING BEAR AROUND.

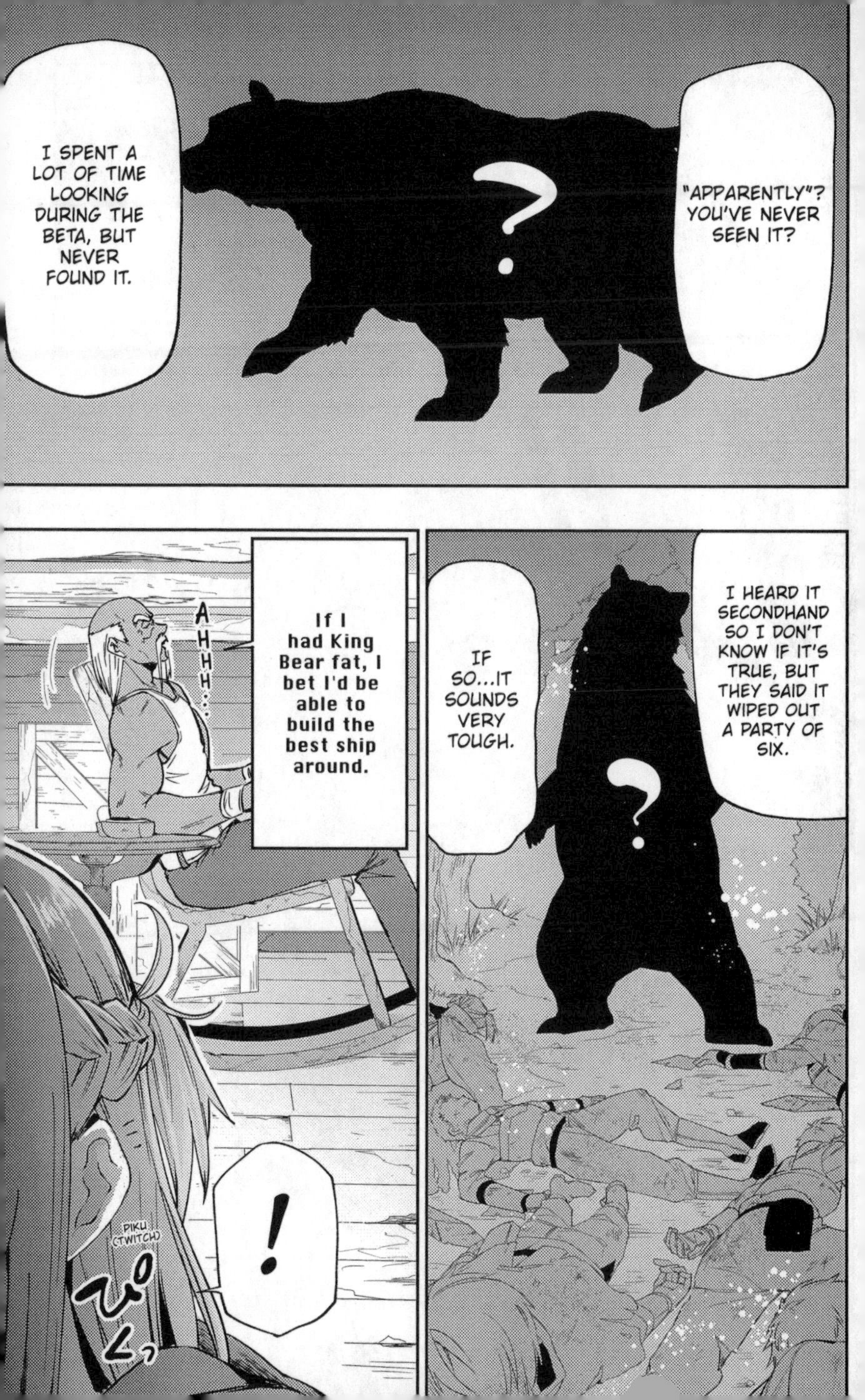
"APPARENTLY"? YOU'VE NEVER SEEN IT?
I SPENT A LOT OF TIME LOOKING DURING THE BETA, BUT NEVER FOUND IT.
I HEARD IT SECONDHAND SO I DON'T KNOW IF IT'S TRUE, BUT THEY SAID IT WIPED OUT A PARTY OF SIX.
IF SO...IT SOUNDS VERY TOUGH.
If I had King Bear fat, I bet I'd be able to build the best ship around.
AHHH...
!
PIKU (TWITCH)

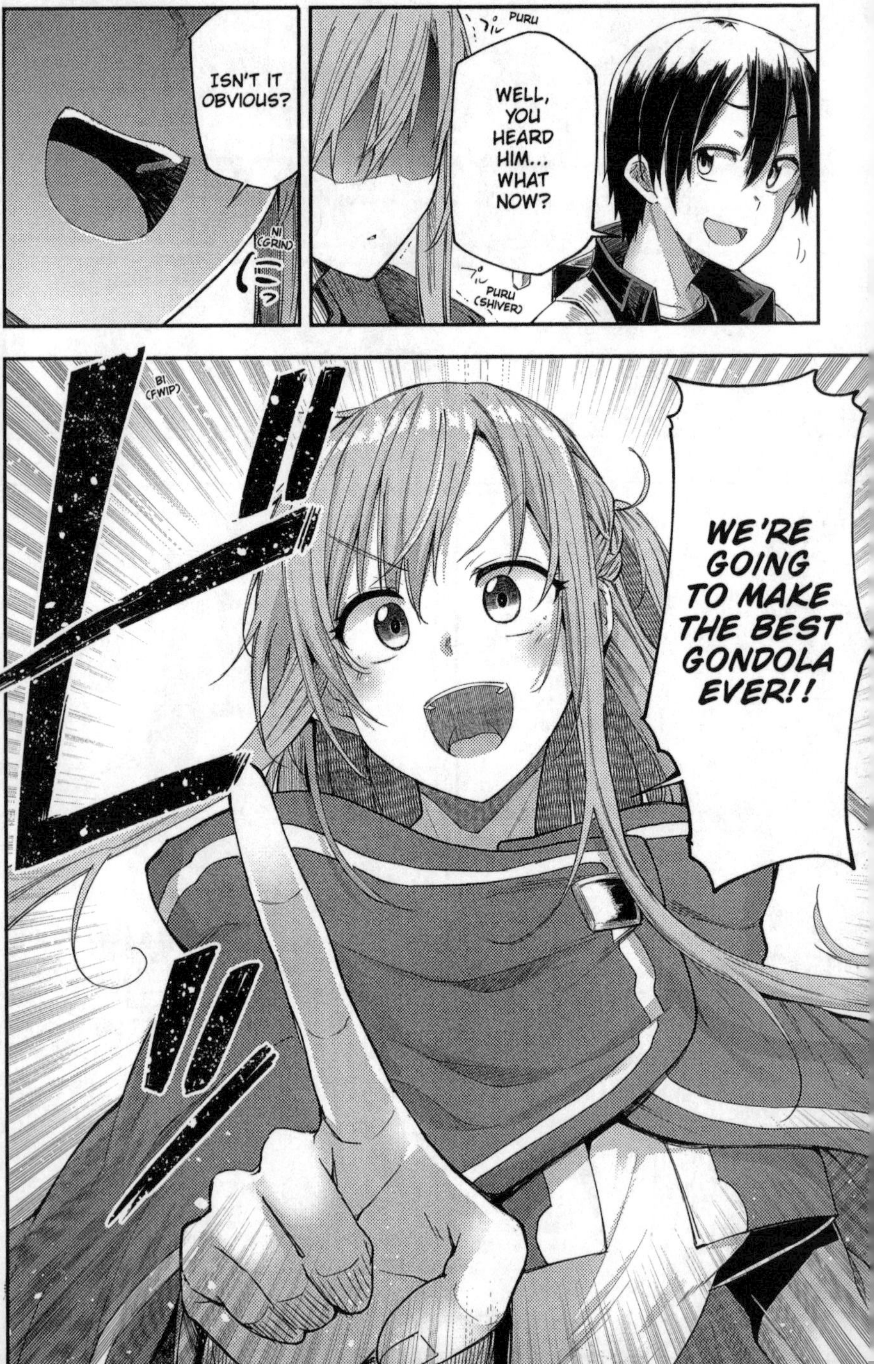
PURU
WELL, YOU HEARD HIM... WHAT NOW?
PURU (SHIVER)
ISN'T IT OBVIOUS?
NI (GRIN)
BI (FWIP)
WE'RE GOING TO MAKE THE BEST GONDOLA EVER!!

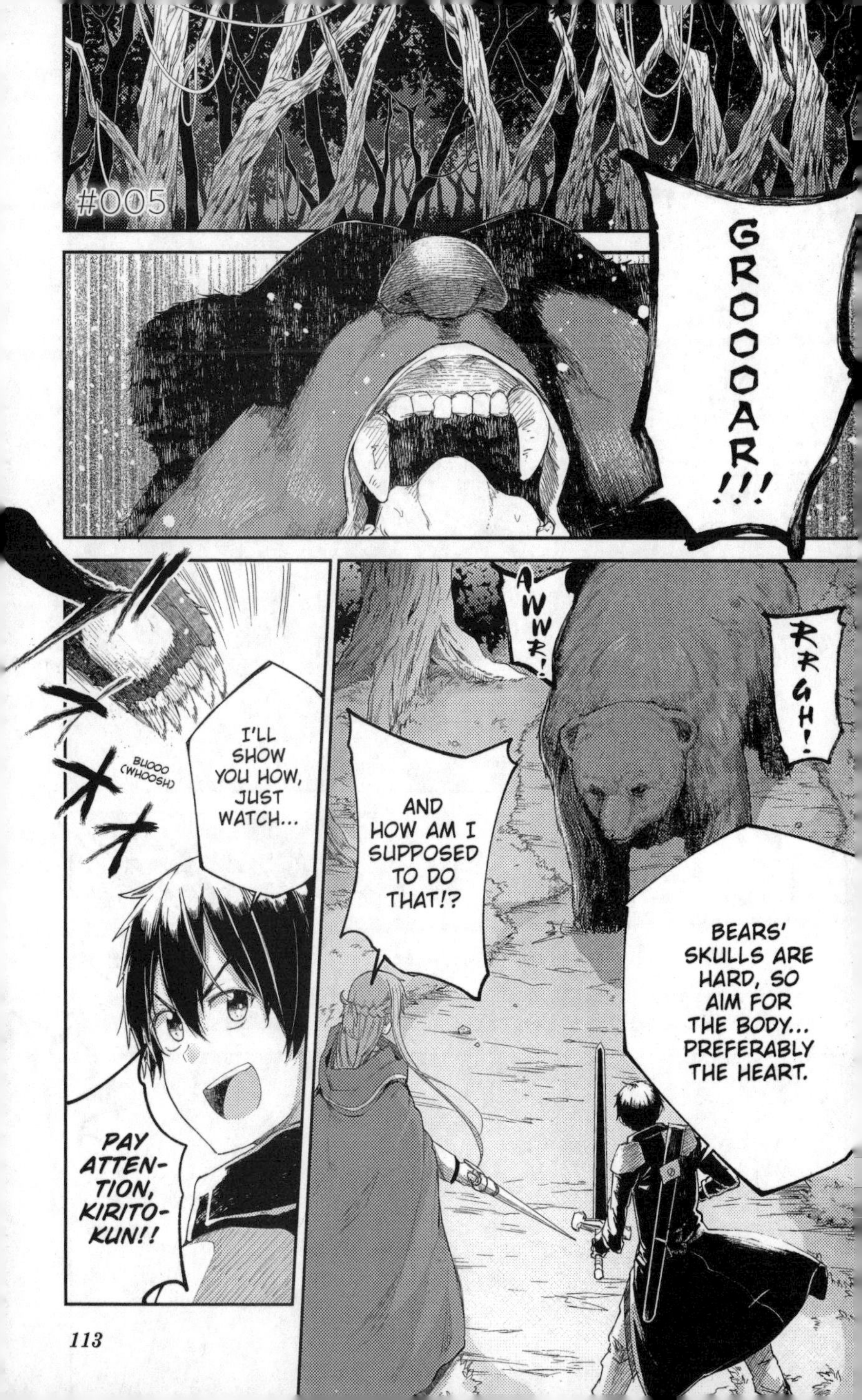
#005
GROOOOAR!!!
RRGH!
AWWR!
BEARS' SKULLS ARE HARD, SO AIM FOR THE BODY... PREFERABLY THE HEART.
AND HOW AM I SUPPOSED TO DO THAT!?
I'LL SHOW YOU HOW, JUST WATCH...
BUOOO (WHOOSH)
PAY ATTENTION, KIRITO-KUN!!

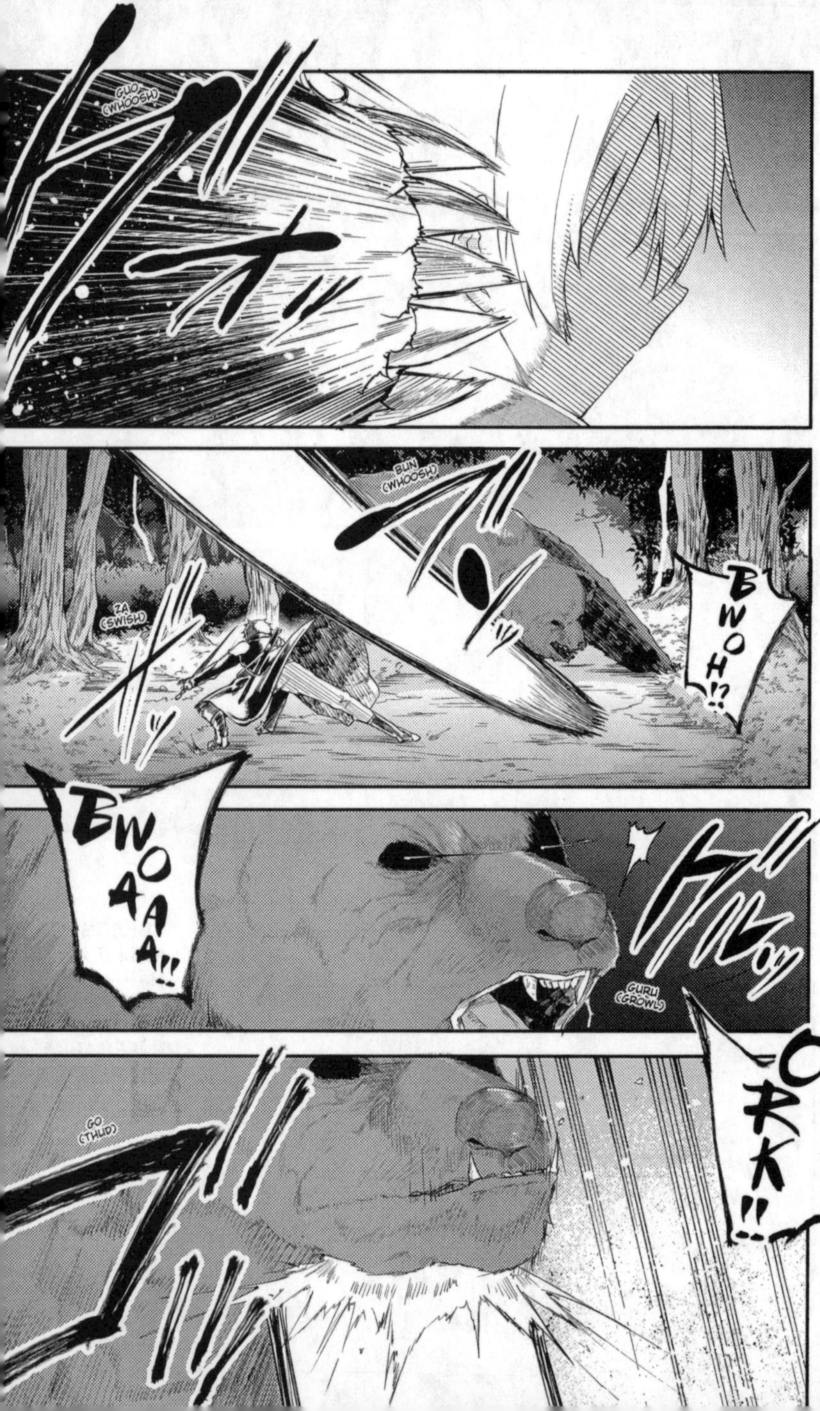
GUO (WHOOSH)
BWOH!?
BUN (WHOOSH)
ZA (SWISH)
GURU (GROWL)
BWOAAAA!!
ORK!!
GO (THUD)

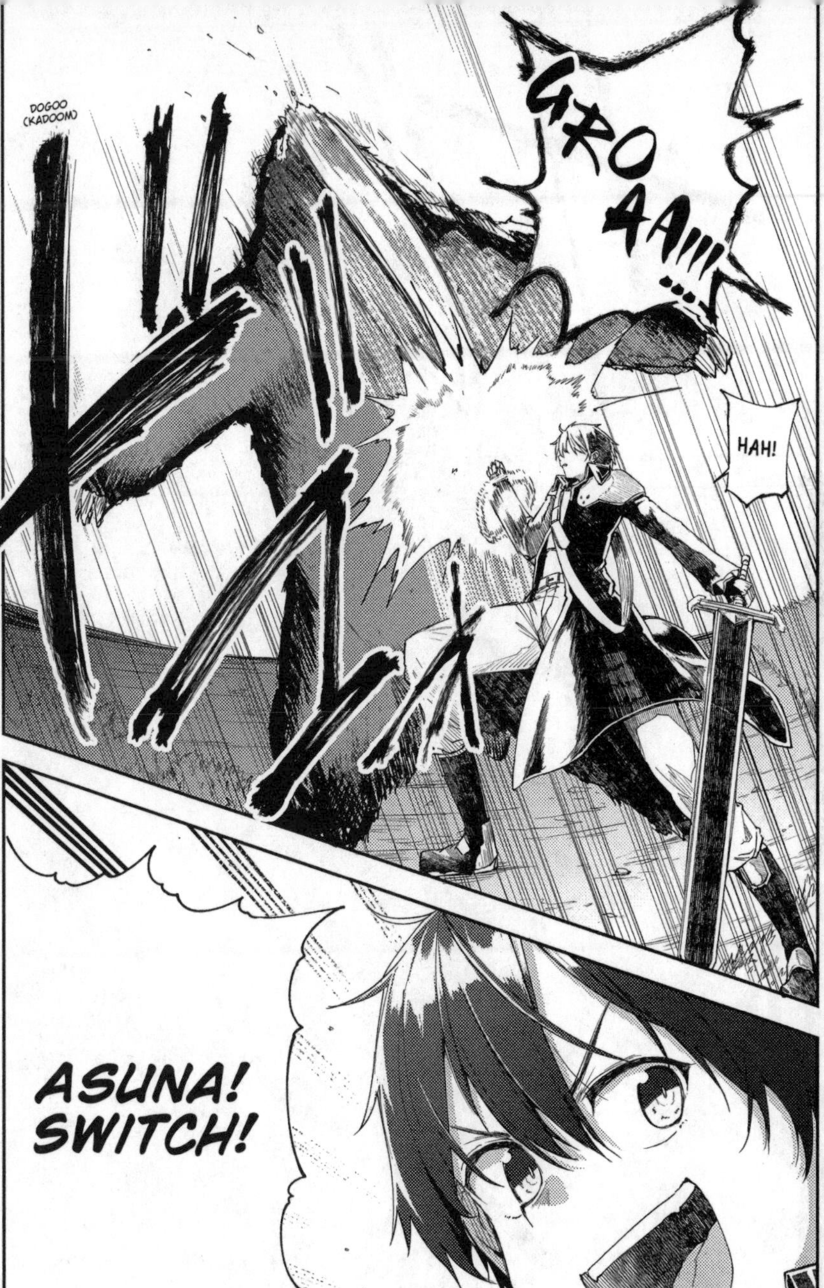
GROAAA!!!...
DOGOO (KADOOM)
HAH!
ASUNA! SWITCH!

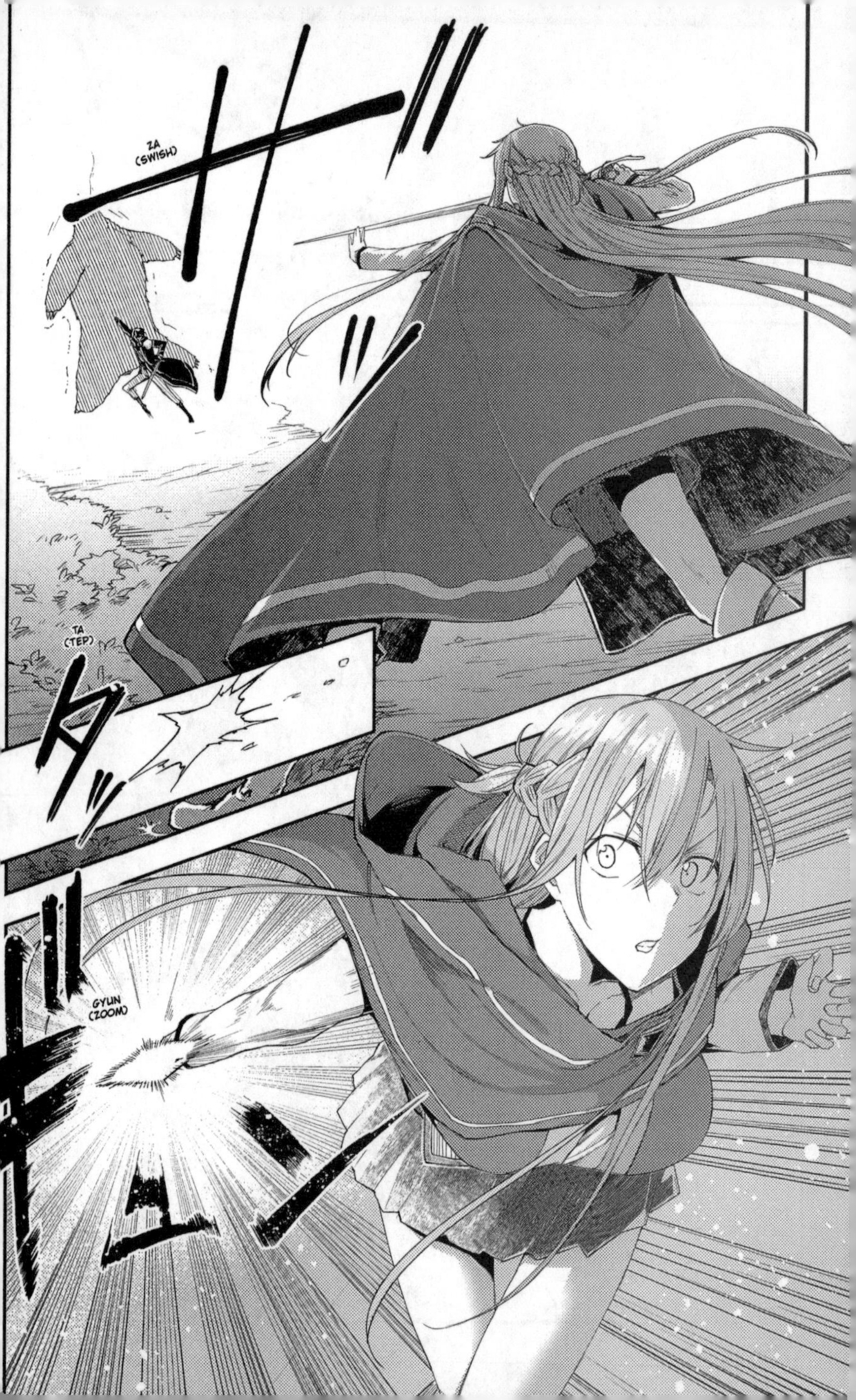
ZA
(SWISH)
TA
(TEP)
GYUN
(ZOOM)

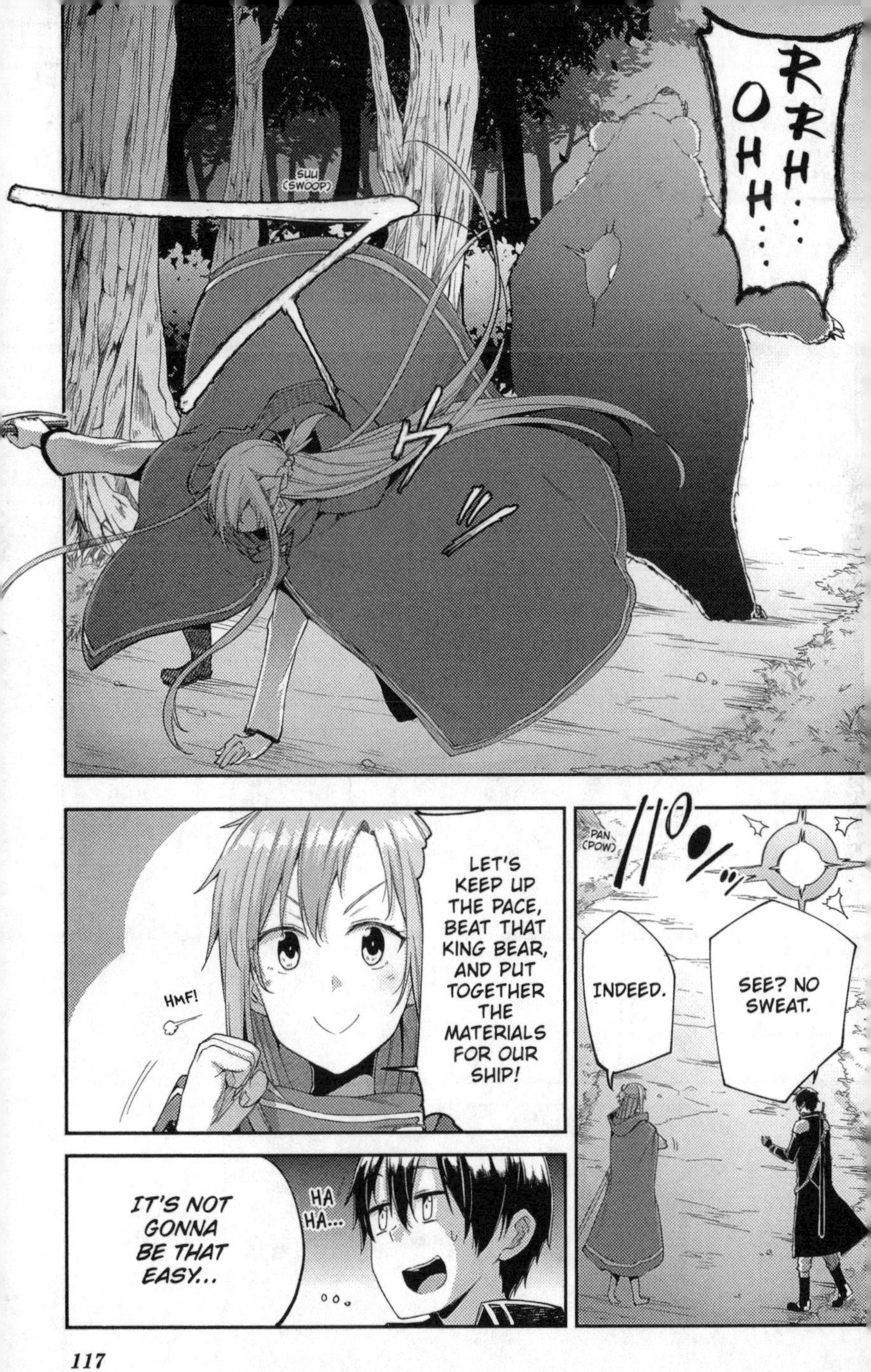
RRH... OHH...
SUU (SWOOP)
PAN (POW)
SEE? NO SWEAT.
INDEED.
LET'S KEEP UP THE PACE, BEAT THAT KING BEAR, AND PUT TOGETHER THE MATERIALS FOR OUR SHIP!
HMF!
HA HA...
IT'S NOT GONNA BE THAT EASY...

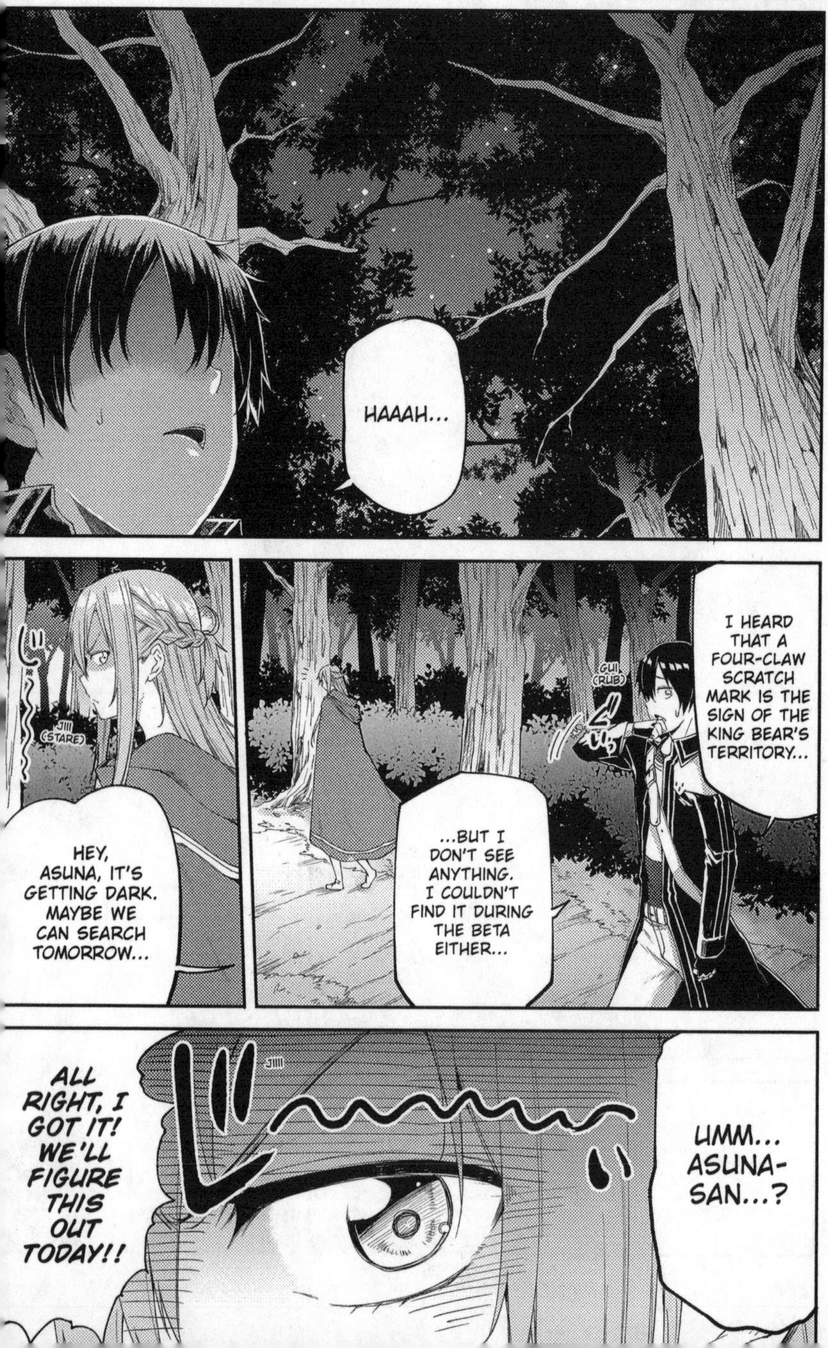
HAAAH...
I HEARD THAT A FOUR-CLAW SCRATCH MARK IS THE SIGN OF THE KING BEAR'S TERRITORY...
GUI (RUB)
...BUT I DON'T SEE ANYTHING. I COULDN'T FIND IT DURING THE BETA EITHER...
JIII (STARE)
HEY, ASUNA, IT'S GETTING DARK. MAYBE WE CAN SEARCH TOMORROW...
UMM... ASUNA-SAN...?
JIIII
ALL RIGHT, I GOT IT! WE'LL FIGURE THIS OUT TODAY!!

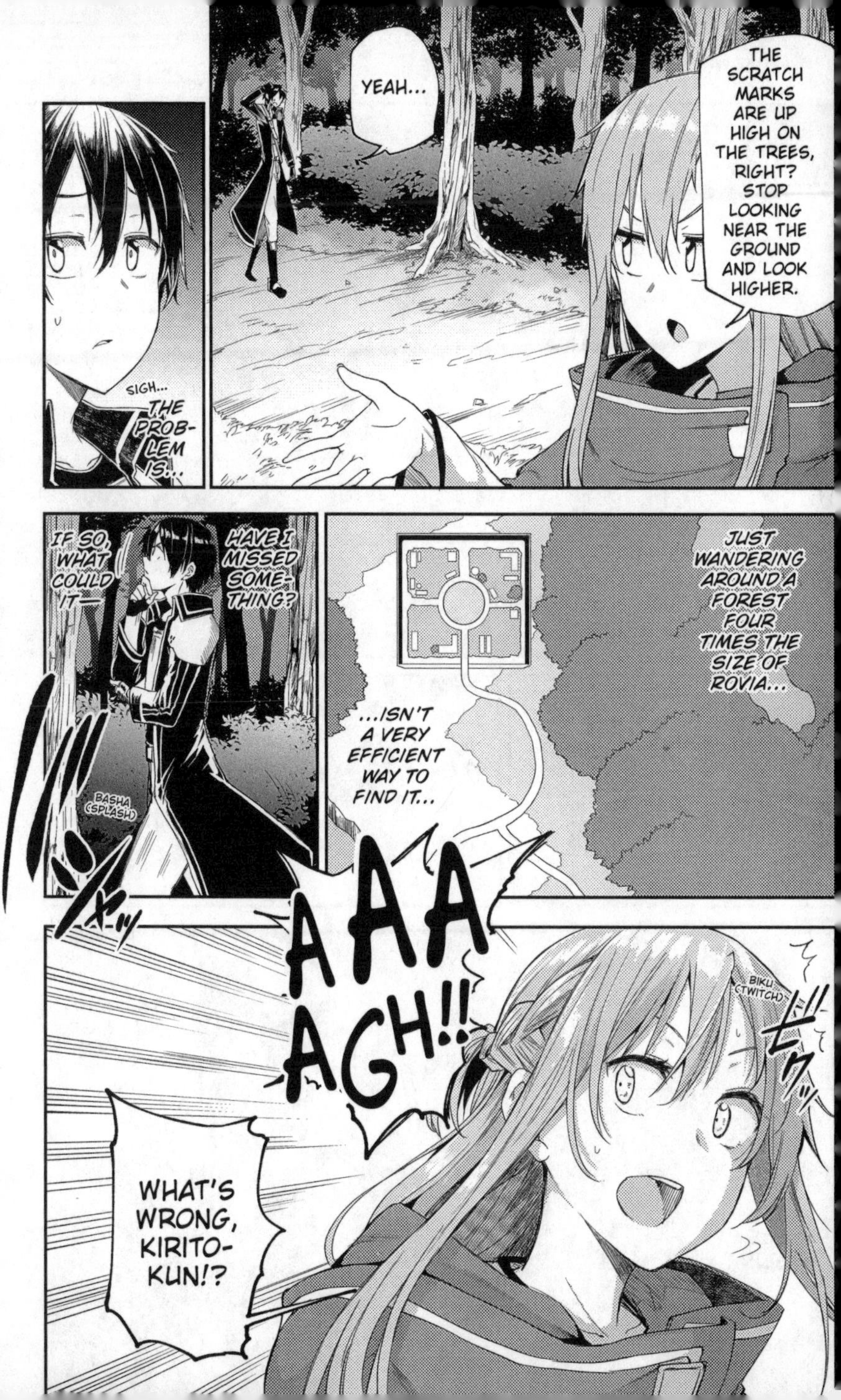
THE SCRATCH MARKS ARE UP HIGH ON THE TREES, RIGHT? STOP LOOKING NEAR THE GROUND AND LOOK HIGHER.
YEAH...
SIGH...
THE PROB-LEM IS...
JUST WANDERING AROUND A FOREST FOUR TIMES THE SIZE OF ROVIA...
...ISN'T A VERY EFFICIENT WAY TO FIND IT...
HAVE I MISSED SOME-THING?
IF SO, WHAT COULD IT—
BASHA (SPLASH)
AAAAGH!!
BIKU (TWITCH)
WHAT'S WRONG, KIRITO-KUN!?

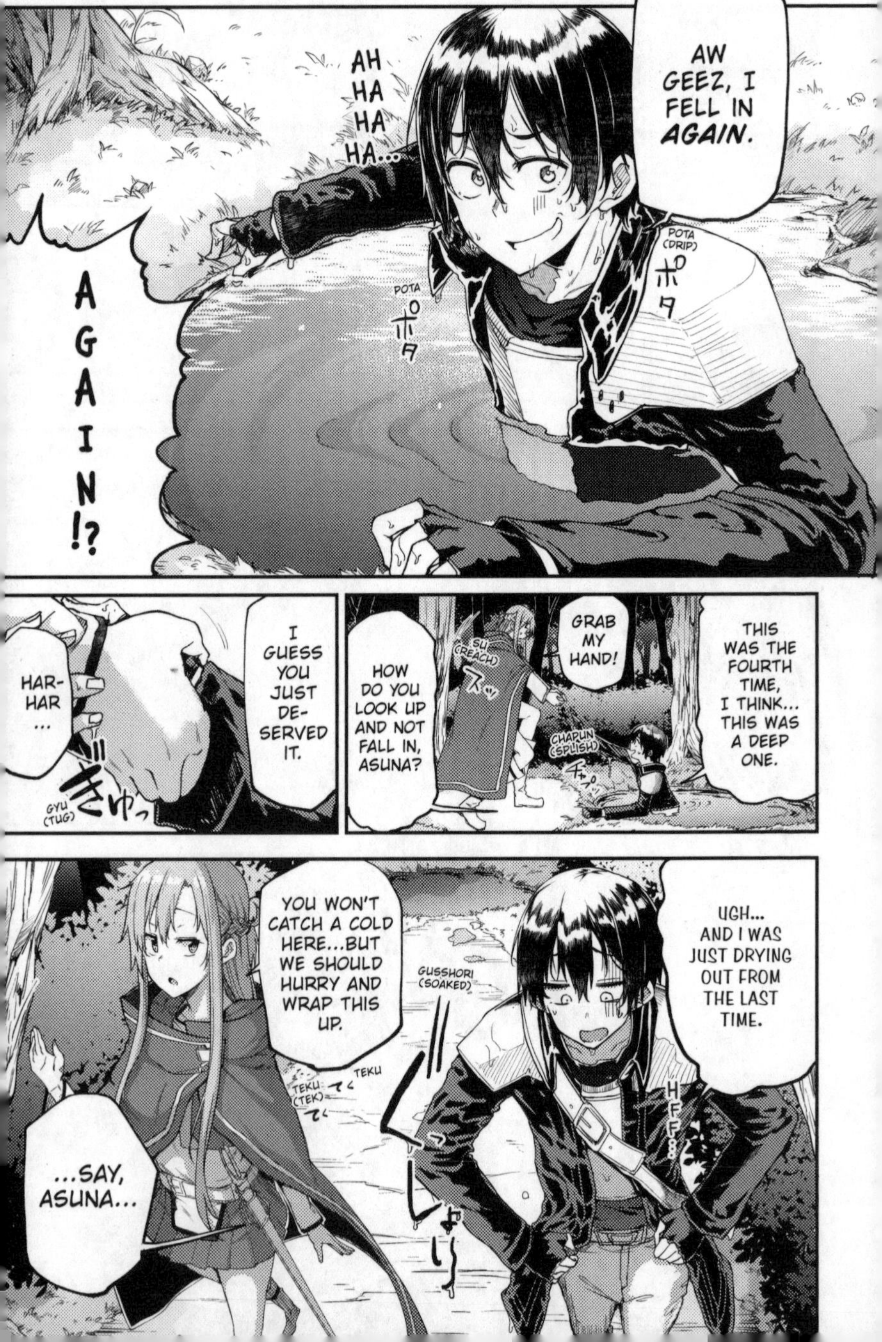
AW GEEZ, I FELL IN AGAIN.
AH HA HA HA...
POTA (DRIP)
ポタ
POTA
ポタ
AGAIN!?
THIS WAS THE FOURTH TIME, I THINK... THIS WAS A DEEP ONE.
GRAB MY HAND!
SU (REACH)
スッ
HOW DO YOU LOOK UP AND NOT FALL IN, ASUNA?
CHAPUN (SPLISH)
チャプッ
I GUESS YOU JUST DE-SERVED IT.
HAR-HAR...
GYU (TUG)
ぎゅっ
UGH... AND I WAS JUST DRYING OUT FROM THE LAST TIME.
HFF...
YOU WON'T CATCH A COLD HERE...BUT WE SHOULD HURRY AND WRAP THIS UP.
GUSSHORI (SOAKED)
TEKU
TEKU (TEK)
てく
てく
...SAY, ASUNA...

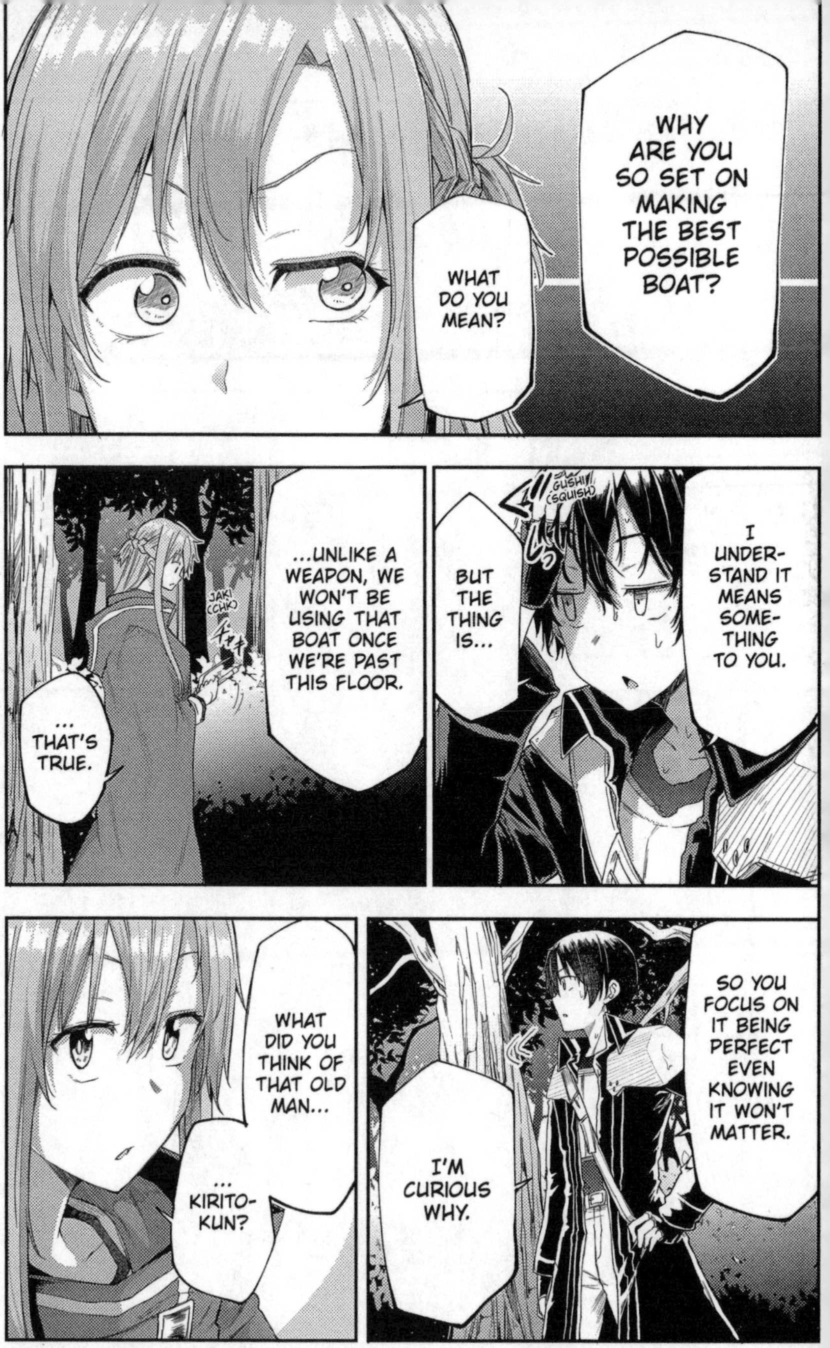
WHY ARE YOU SO SET ON MAKING THE BEST POSSIBLE BOAT?
WHAT DO YOU MEAN?
GUSHI (SQUISH)
I UNDER-STAND IT MEANS SOME-THING TO YOU.
BUT THE THING IS...
...UNLIKE A WEAPON, WE WON'T BE USING THAT BOAT ONCE WE'RE PAST THIS FLOOR.
JAKI (CHK)
...THAT'S TRUE.
SO YOU FOCUS ON IT BEING PERFECT EVEN KNOWING IT WON'T MATTER.
I'M CURIOUS WHY.
WHAT DID YOU THINK OF THAT OLD MAN...
...KIRITO-KUN?

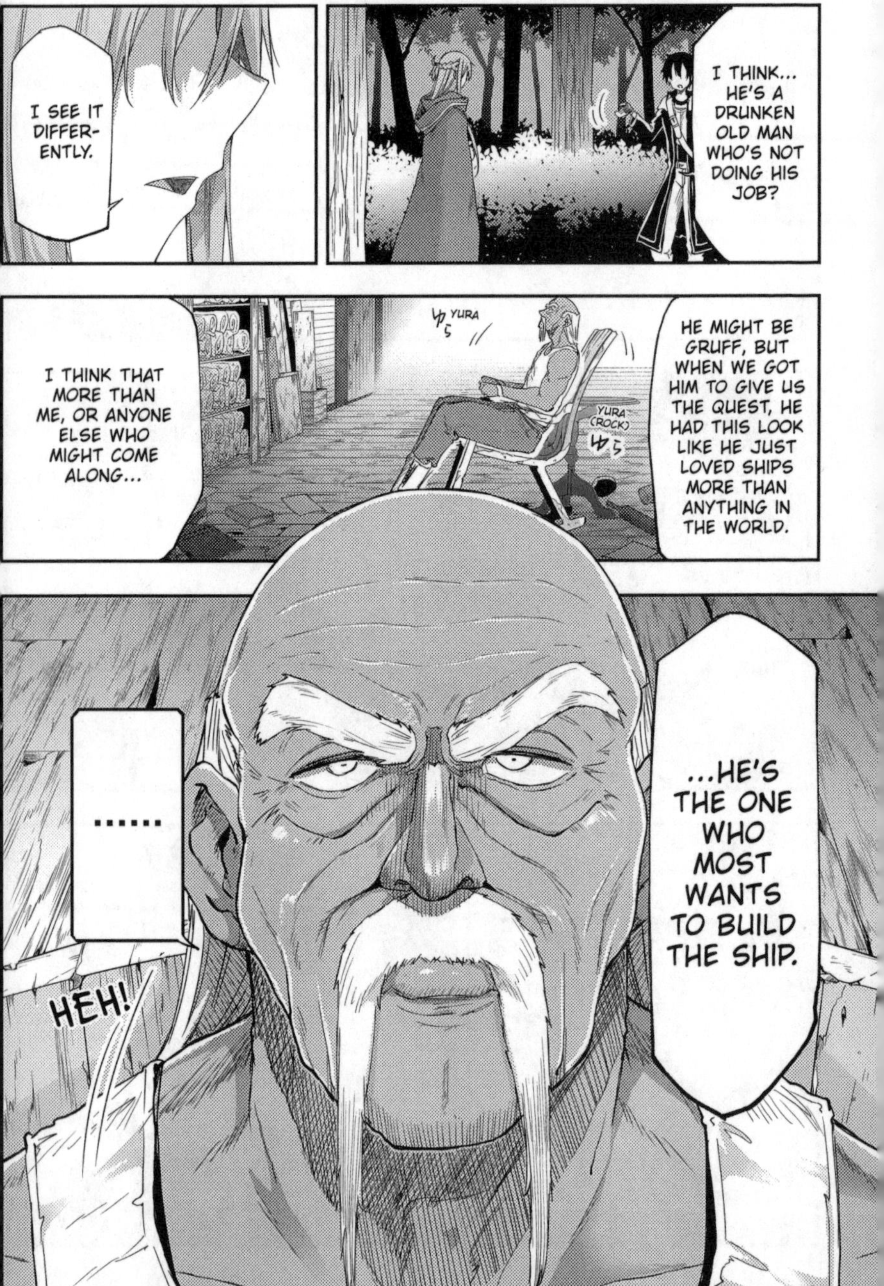
I THINK... HE'S A DRUNKEN OLD MAN WHO'S NOT DOING HIS JOB?
I SEE IT DIFFER-ENTLY.
HE MIGHT BE GRUFF, BUT WHEN WE GOT HIM TO GIVE US THE QUEST, HE HAD THIS LOOK LIKE HE JUST LOVED SHIPS MORE THAN ANYTHING IN THE WORLD.
ゆら YURA
YURA (ROCK) ゆら
I THINK THAT MORE THAN ME, OR ANYONE ELSE WHO MIGHT COME ALONG...
...HE'S THE ONE WHO MOST WANTS TO BUILD THE SHIP.
......
HEH!

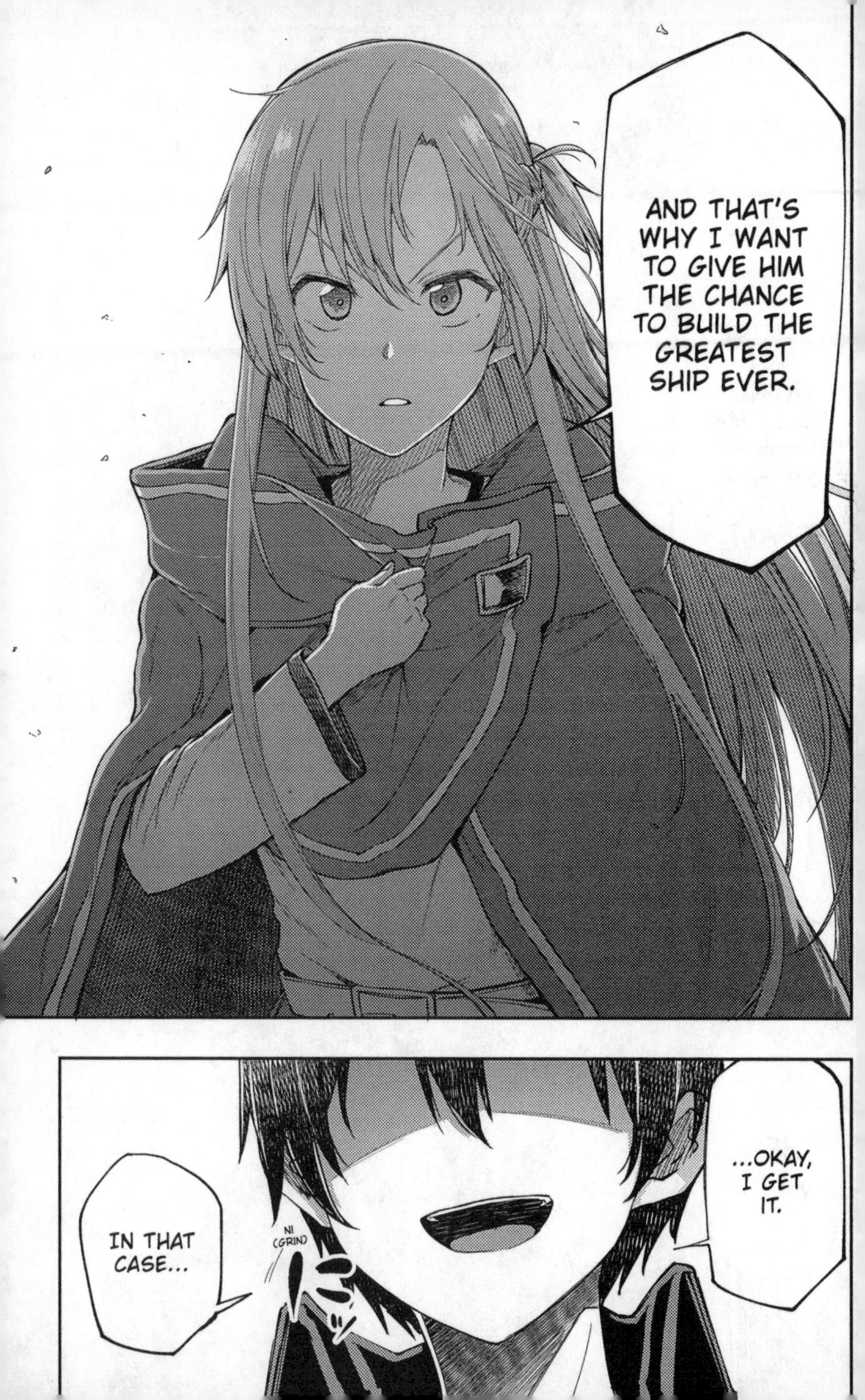
AND THAT'S WHY I WANT TO GIVE HIM THE CHANCE TO BUILD THE GREATEST SHIP EVER.
...OKAY, I GET IT.
NI (GRIN)
IN THAT CASE...

FROM THIS POINT ON...

...WE'RE NOT GOING TO COMPROMISE EVEN A BIT. OKAY?

THAT'S WHAT I'VE BEEN SAYING.

HEE HEE!

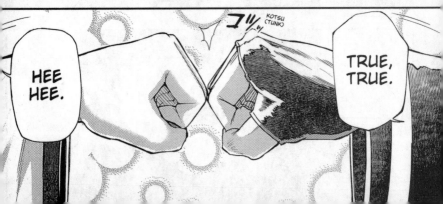

HEE HEE.

コツ
KOTSU (TUNK)

TRUE, TRUE.

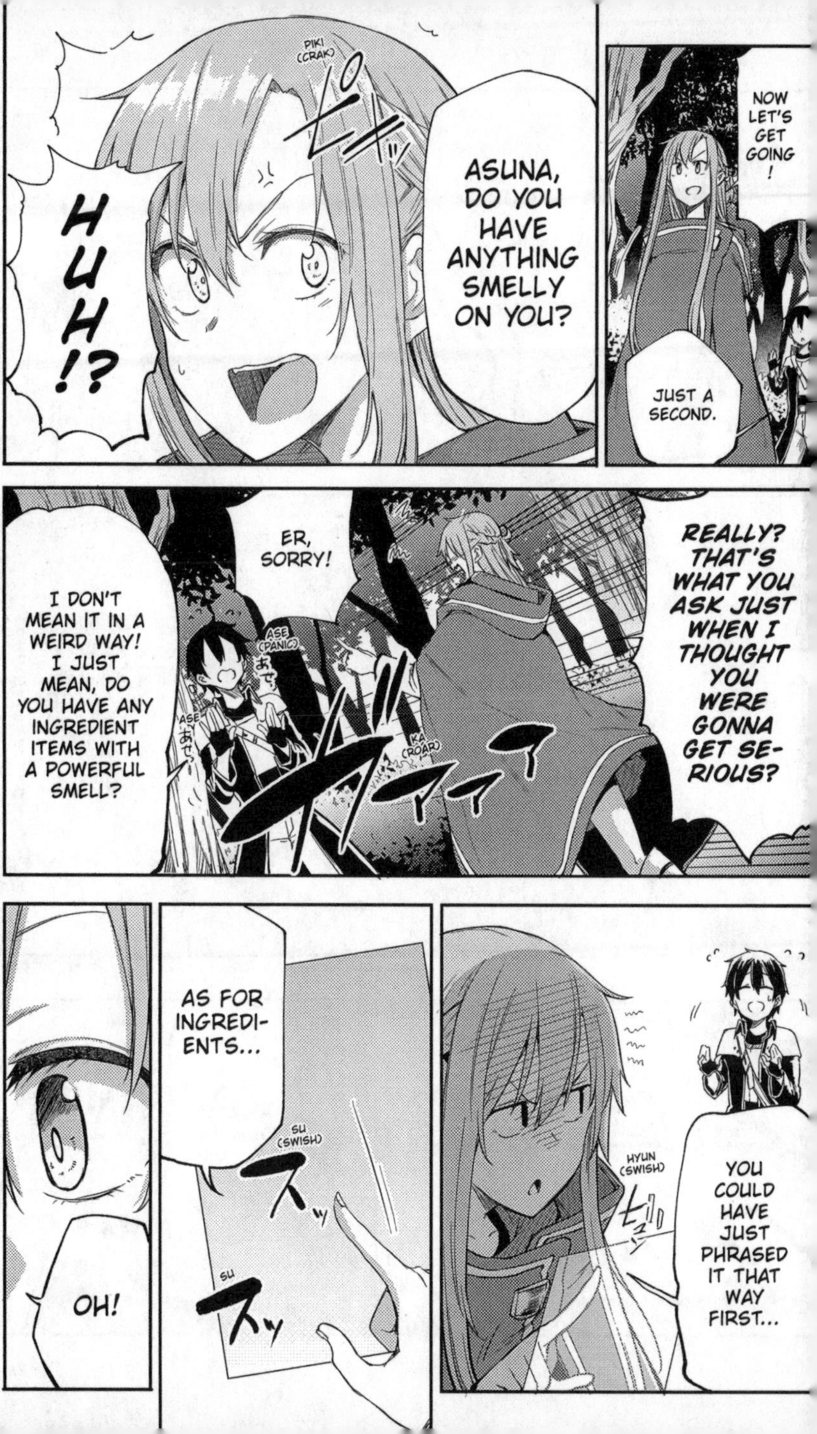
NOW LET'S GET GOING!
JUST A SECOND.
PIKI (CRAK)
ASUNA, DO YOU HAVE ANYTHING SMELLY ON YOU?
HUH!?
REALLY? THAT'S WHAT YOU ASK JUST WHEN I THOUGHT YOU WERE GONNA GET SE-RIOUS?
ER, SORRY!
KA (ROAR)
ASE (PANIC)
I DON'T MEAN IT IN A WEIRD WAY! I JUST MEAN, DO YOU HAVE ANY INGREDIENT ITEMS WITH A POWERFUL SMELL?
ASE
YOU COULD HAVE JUST PHRASED IT THAT WAY FIRST...
HYUN (SWISH)
AS FOR INGREDI-ENTS...
SU (SWISH)
SU
OH!

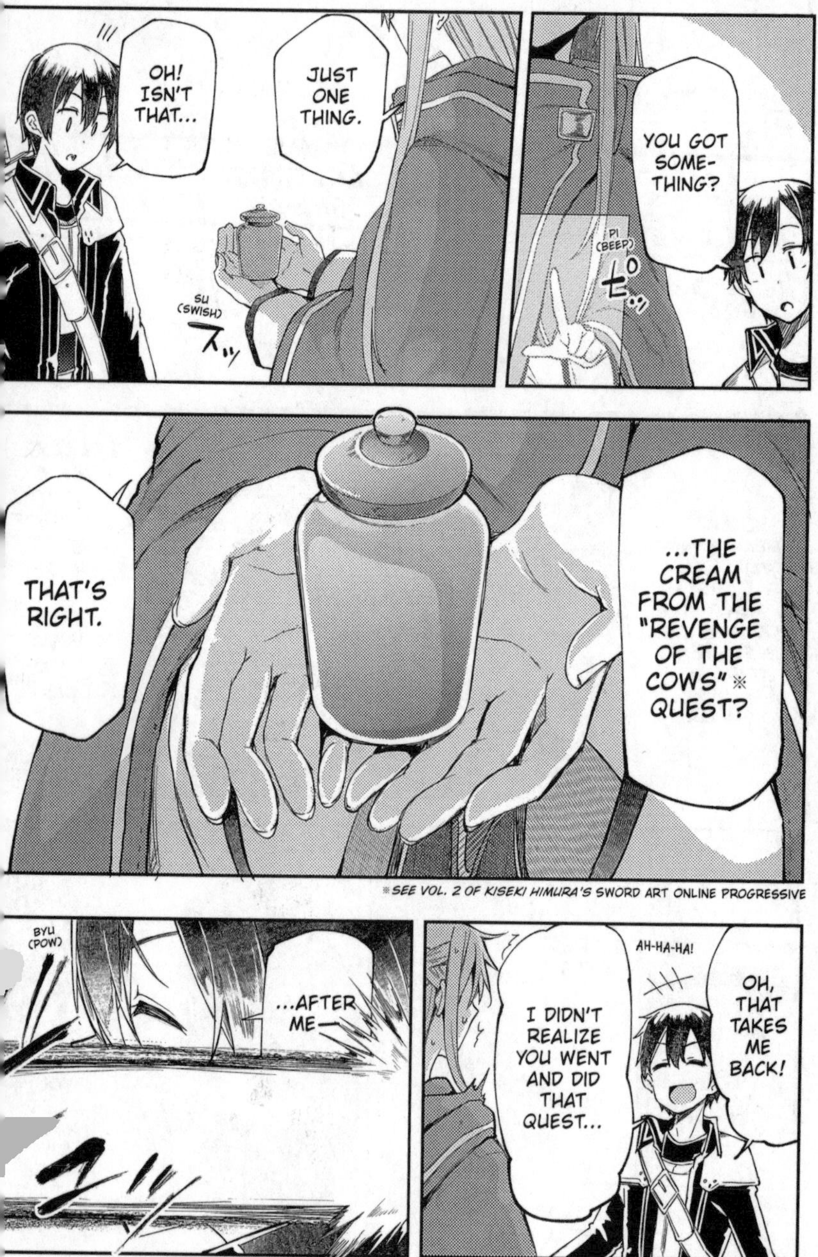
YOU GOT SOME-THING?
PI (BEEP)
ピッ
JUST ONE THING.
OH! ISN'T THAT...
SU (SWISH)
スッ
...THE CREAM FROM THE "REVENGE OF THE COWS" ※ QUEST?
THAT'S RIGHT.
OH, THAT TAKES ME BACK!
AH-HA-HA!
I DIDN'T REALIZE YOU WENT AND DID THAT QUEST...
...AFTER ME—
BYU (POW)

※ SEE VOL. 2 OF KISEKI HIMURA'S SWORD ART ONLINE PROGRESSIVE

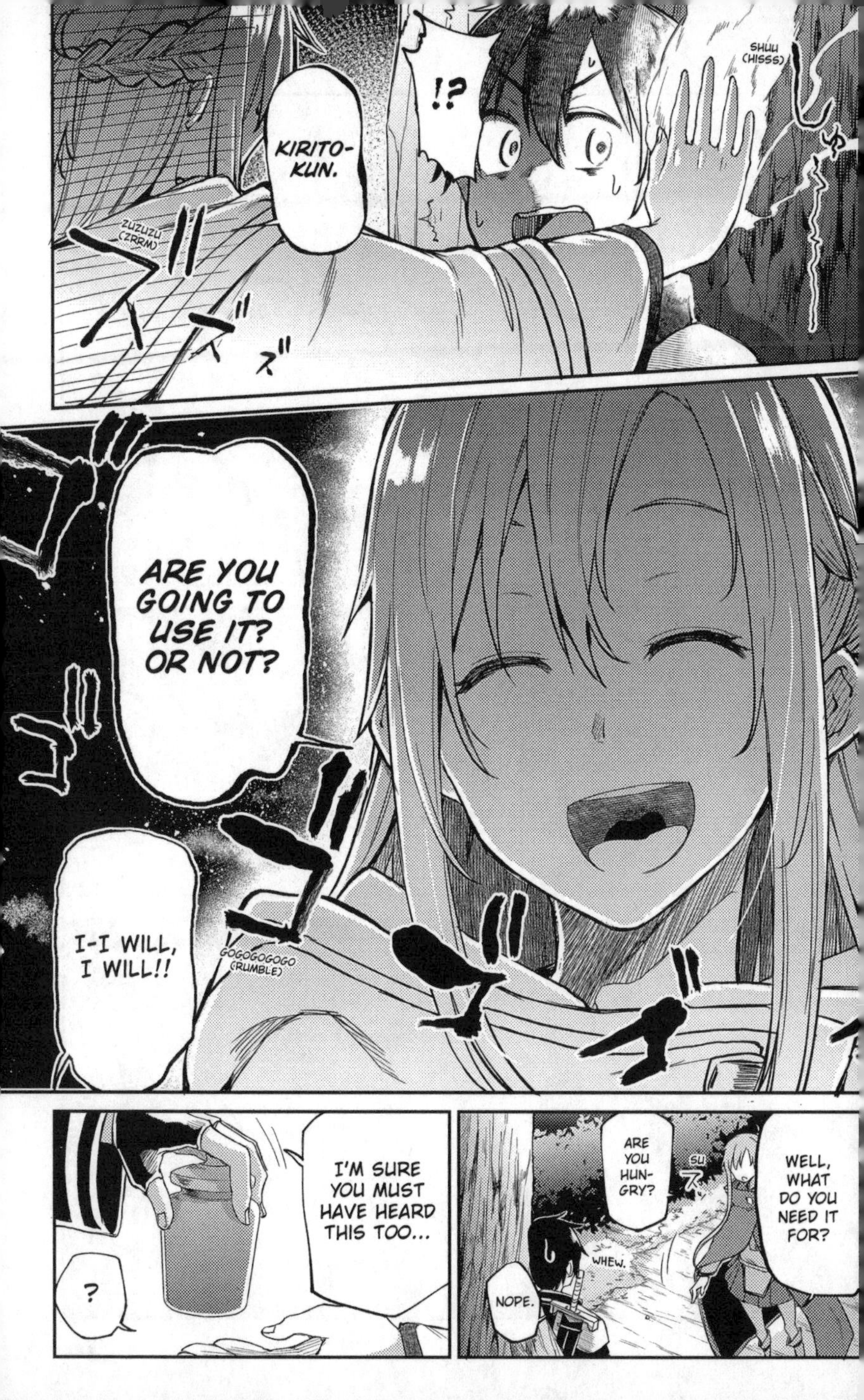
SHUU (HISSS)
!?
KIRITO-KUN.
ZUZUZU (ZRRM)
ARE YOU GOING TO USE IT? OR NOT?
I-I WILL, I WILL!!
GOGOGOGOGO (RUMBLE)
WELL, WHAT DO YOU NEED IT FOR?
SU
ARE YOU HUNGRY?
WHEW.
NOPE.
I'M SURE YOU MUST HAVE HEARD THIS TOO...
?

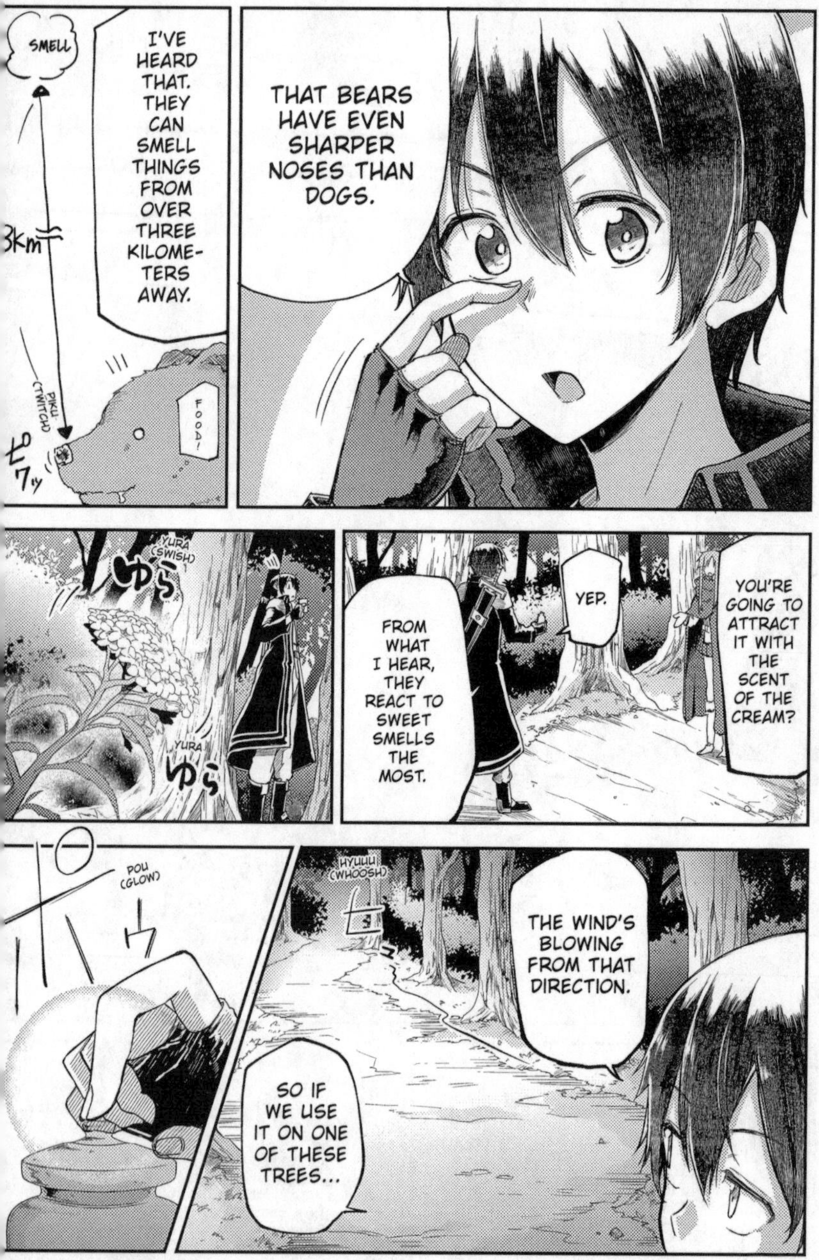
THAT BEARS HAVE EVEN SHARPER NOSES THAN DOGS.
I'VE HEARD THAT. THEY CAN SMELL THINGS FROM OVER THREE KILOMETERS AWAY.
SMELL
3km
PIKU (TWITCH)
FOOD!
YOU'RE GOING TO ATTRACT IT WITH THE SCENT OF THE CREAM?
YEP.
FROM WHAT I HEAR, THEY REACT TO SWEET SMELLS THE MOST.
YURA (SWISH)
YURA
HYUUU (WHOOSH)
THE WIND'S BLOWING FROM THAT DIRECTION.
SO IF WE USE IT ON ONE OF THESE TREES...
POU (GLOW)

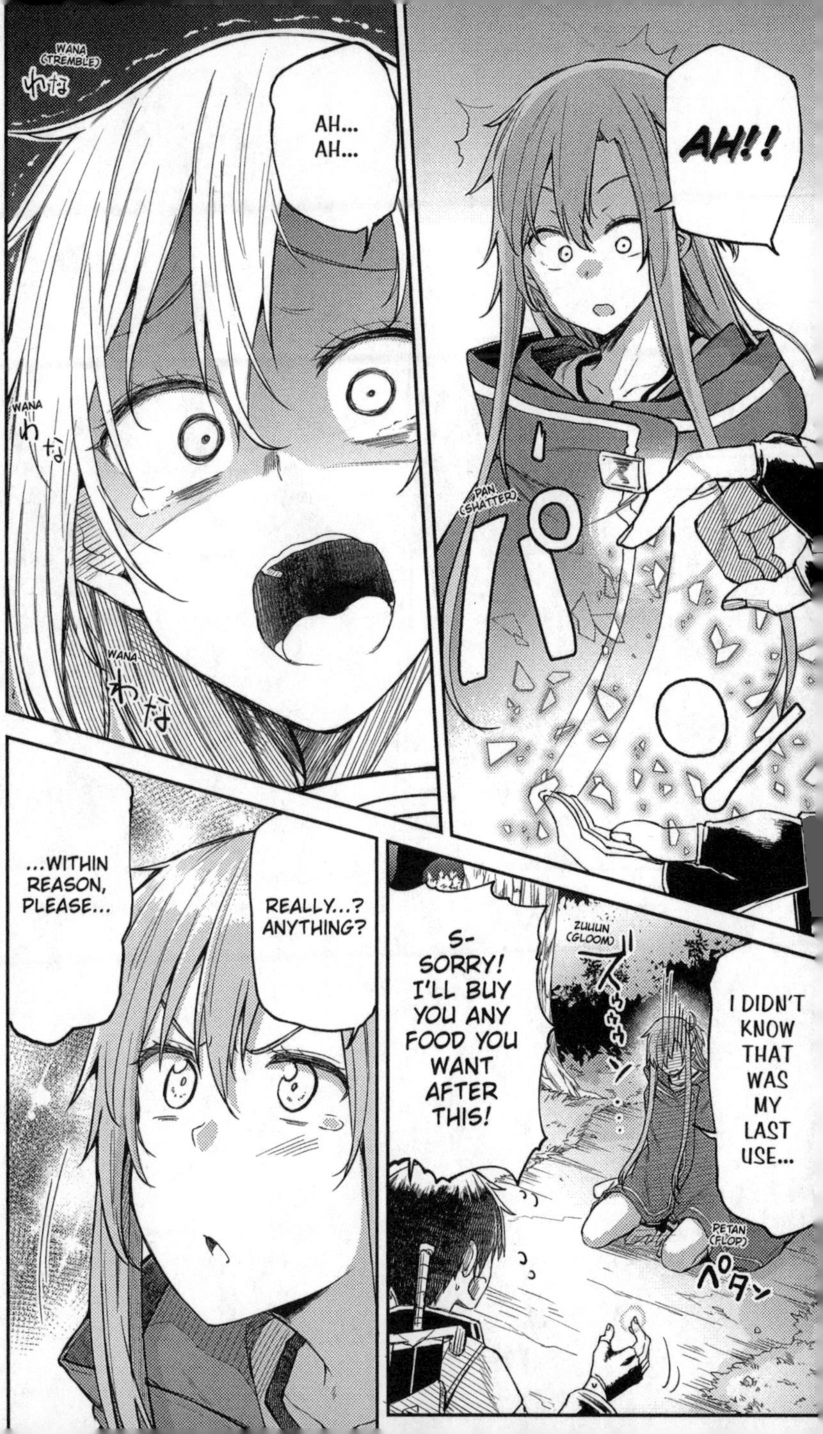
AH!!
PAN (SHATTER)
WANA (TREMBLE)
わな
AH... AH...
WANA
わな
WANA
わな
I DIDN'T KNOW THAT WAS MY LAST USE...
ZUUUN (GLOOM)
S-SORRY! I'LL BUY YOU ANY FOOD YOU WANT AFTER THIS!
PETAN (FLOP)
ペタン
REALLY...? ANYTHING?
...WITHIN REASON, PLEASE...

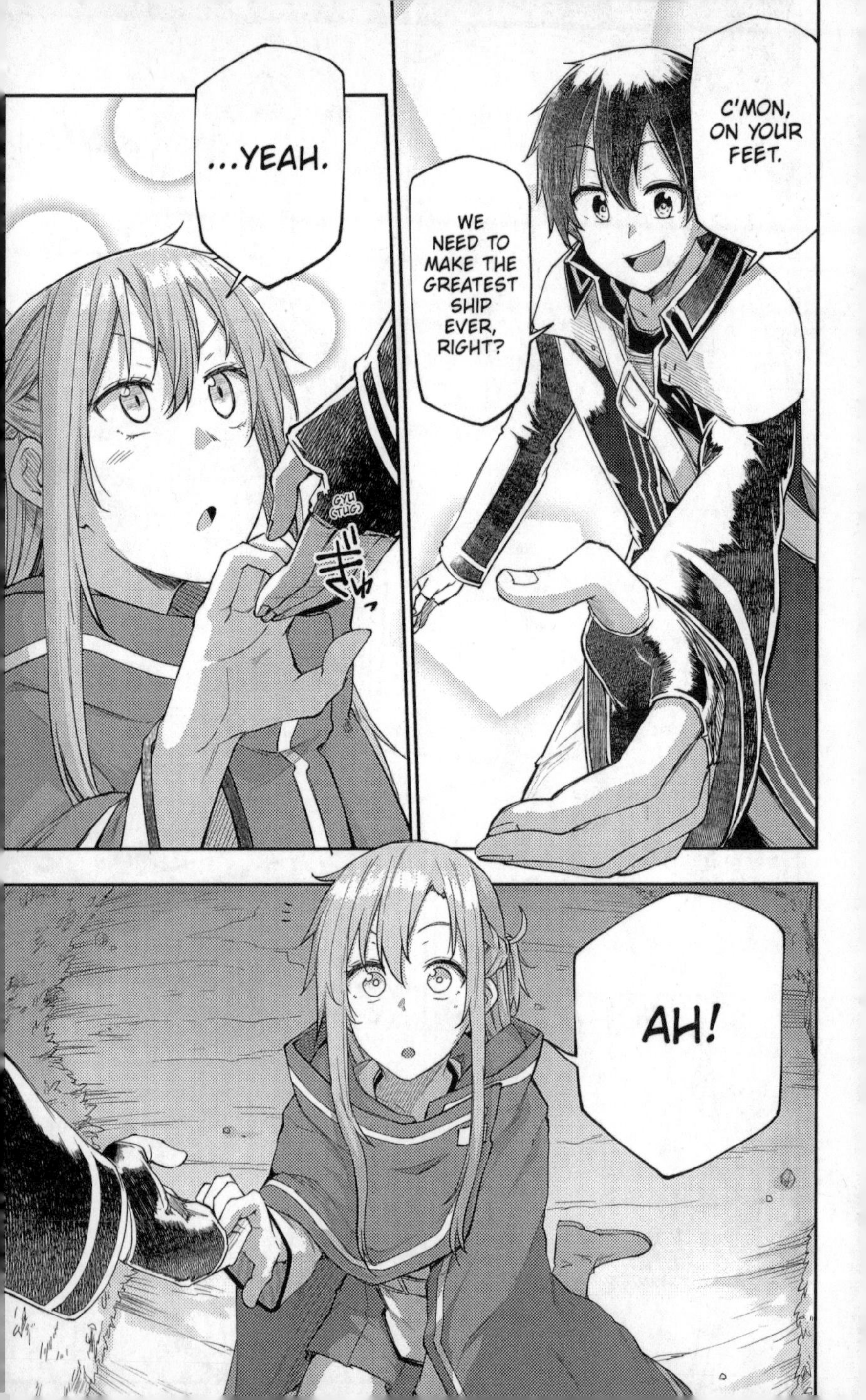
C'MON, ON YOUR FEET.
WE NEED TO MAKE THE GREATEST SHIP EVER, RIGHT?
...YEAH.
GYU (TUG)
ぎゅっ
AH!

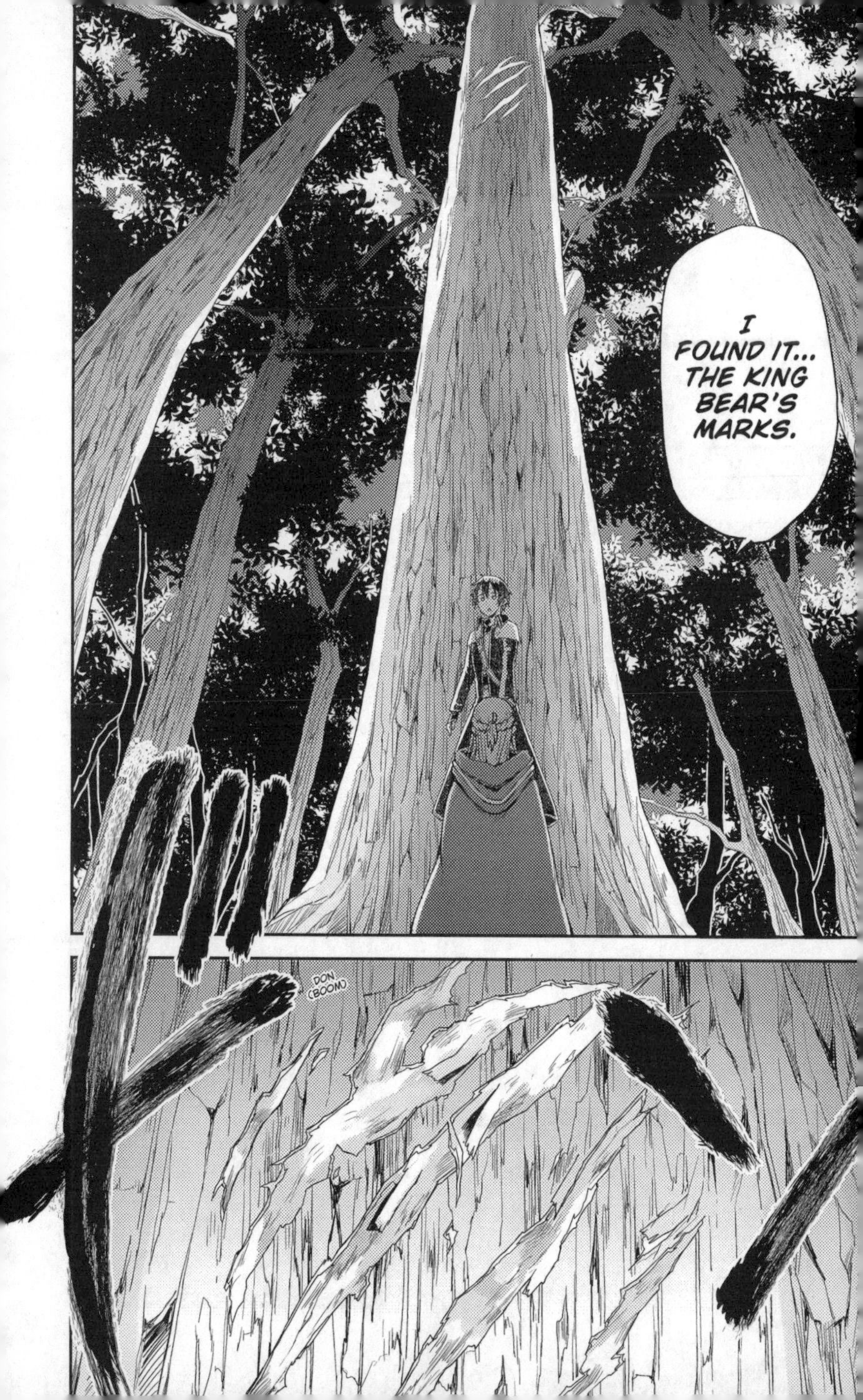
I FOUND IT... THE KING BEAR'S MARKS.
DON (BOOM)

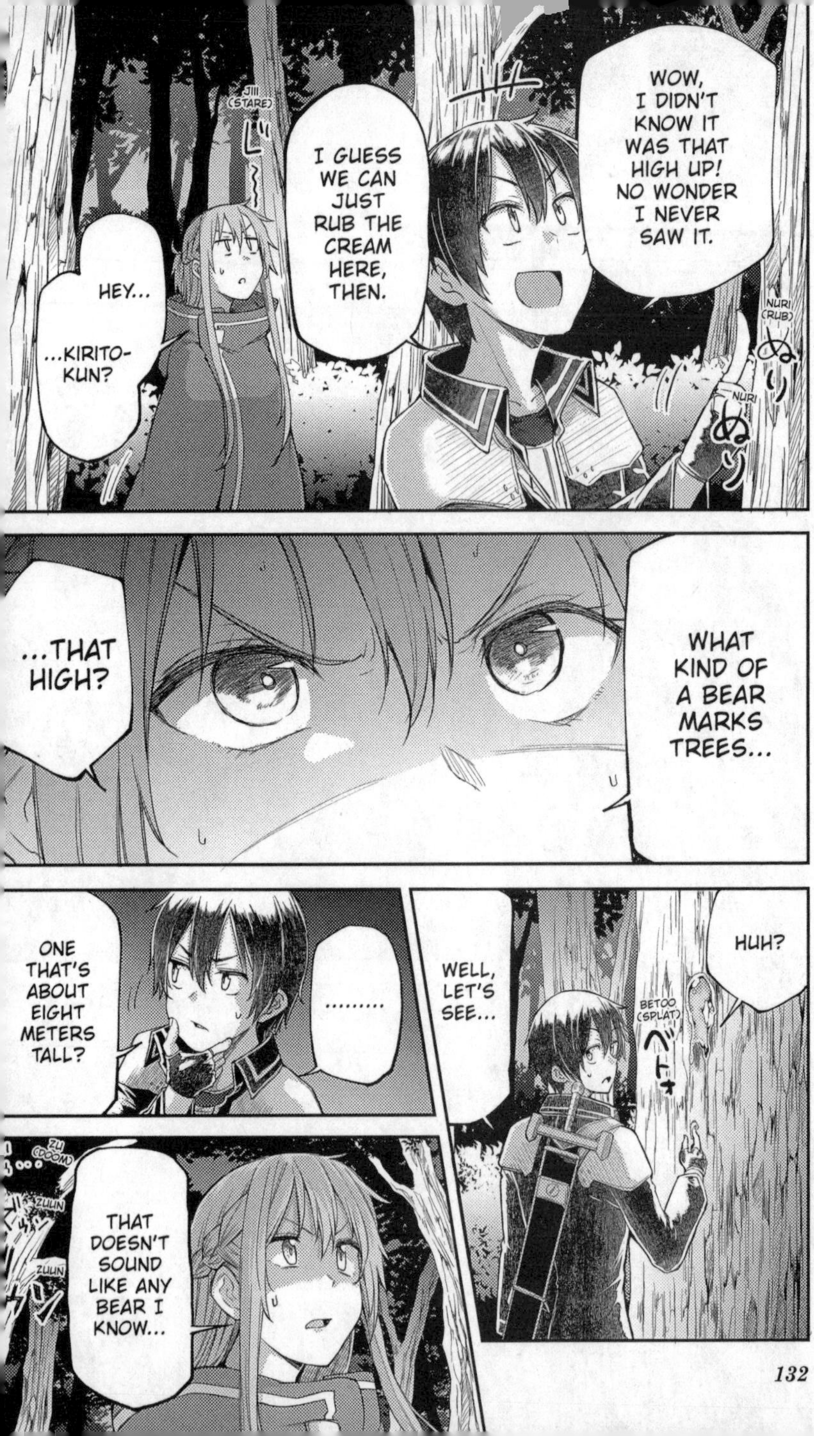
WOW, I DIDN'T KNOW IT WAS THAT HIGH UP! NO WONDER I NEVER SAW IT.
NURI (RUB)
ぬり
NURI
ぬり
I GUESS WE CAN JUST RUB THE CREAM HERE, THEN.
JIII (STARE)
じぃ~
HEY...
...KIRITO-KUN?
WHAT KIND OF A BEAR MARKS TREES...
...THAT HIGH?
HUH?
WELL, LET'S SEE...
BETOO (SPLAT)
ベトォ
....
ONE THAT'S ABOUT EIGHT METERS TALL?
ZU (DOOM)
ZUUN
ZUUN
THAT DOESN'T SOUND LIKE ANY BEAR I KNOW...

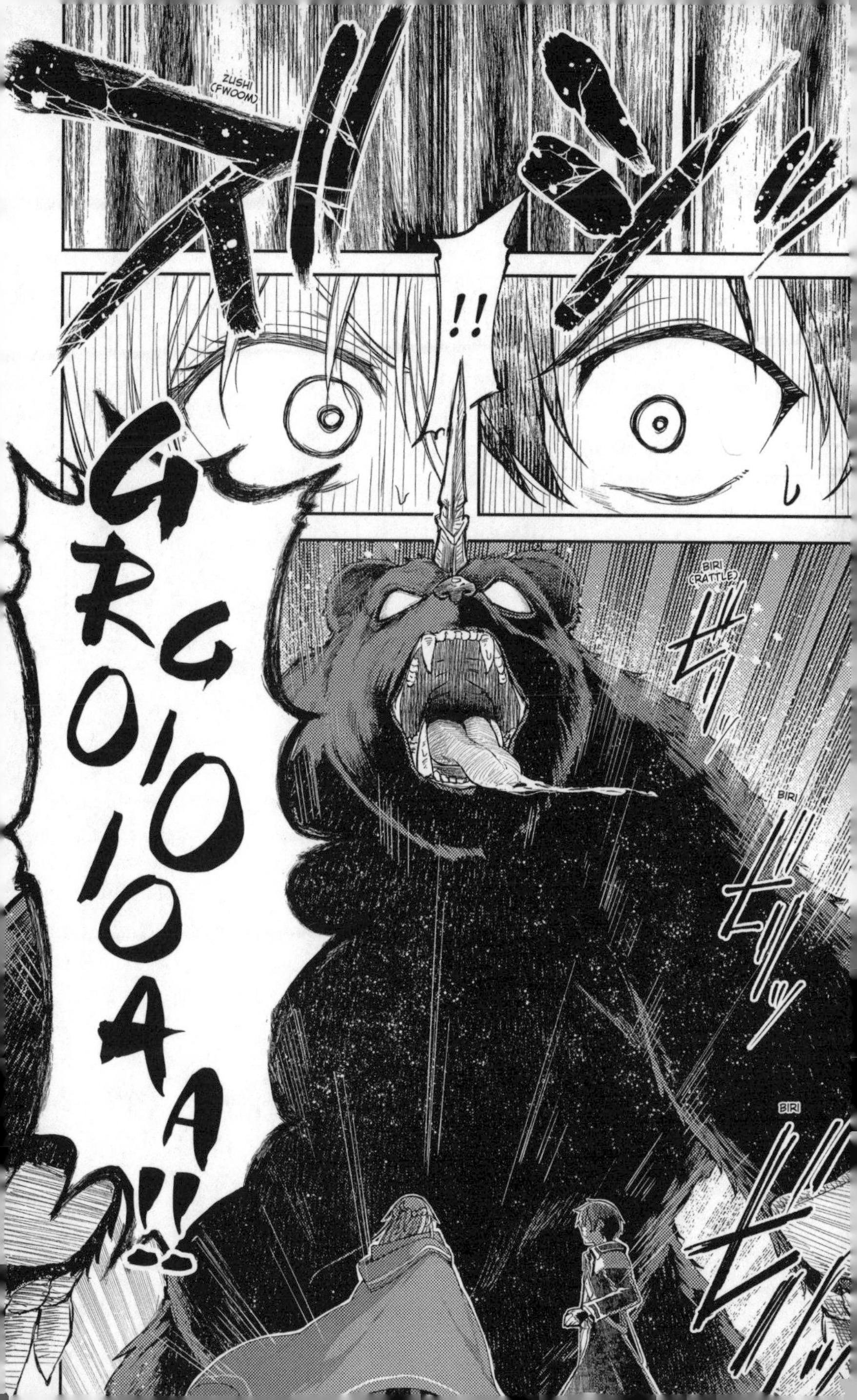
ZUSHI (FWOOM)
!!
BIRI (RATTLE)
BIRI
BIRI
GRGOOOOAAA!!

SWORD
ART
ONLINE
PROGRESSIVE
BARCAROLLE OF FROTH

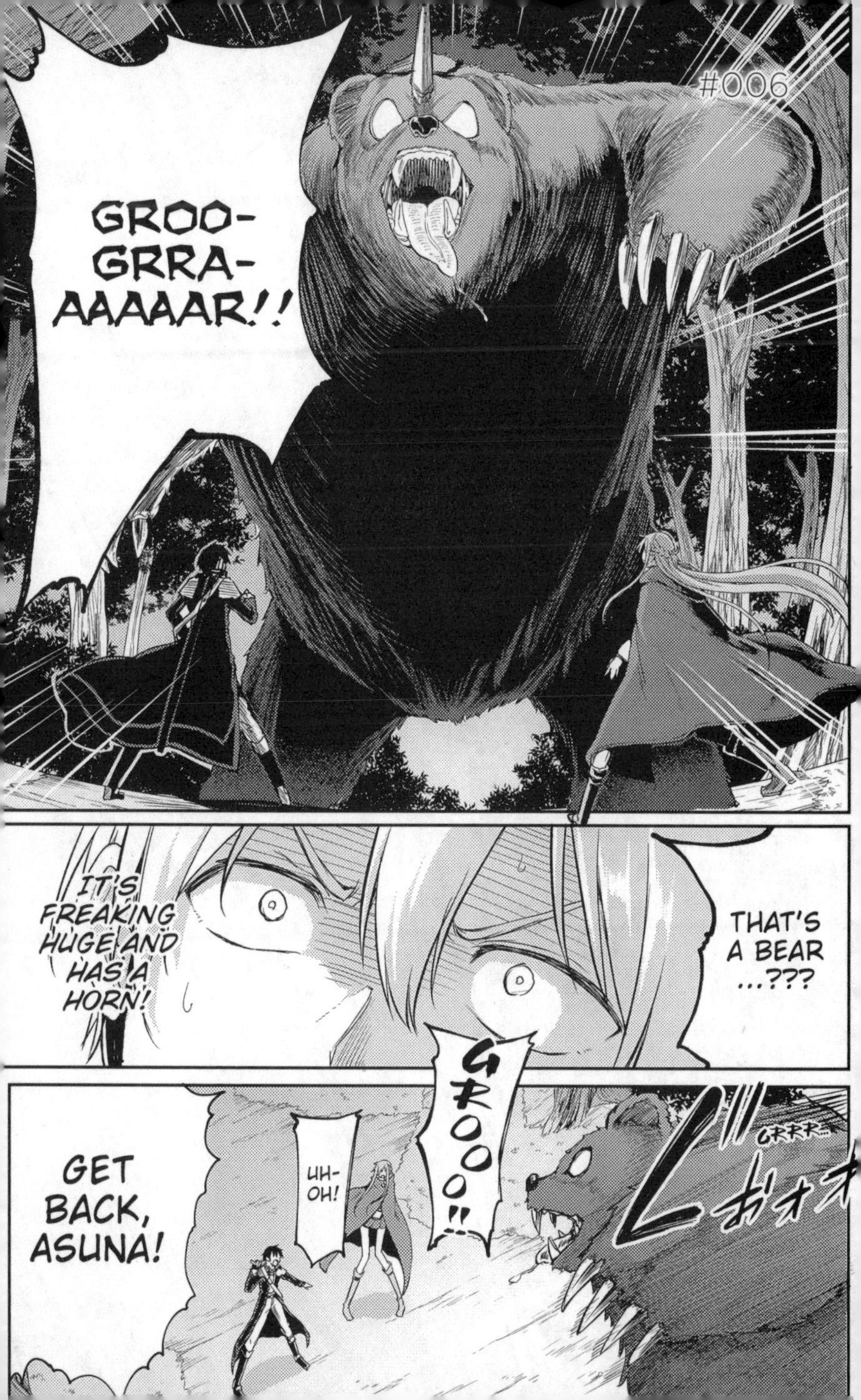
#006
GROO-GRRA-AAAAAR!!
THAT'S A BEAR ...???
IT'S FREAKING HUGE AND HAS A HORN!
GRRR...
GROOOO!!
UH-OH!
GET BACK, ASUNA!

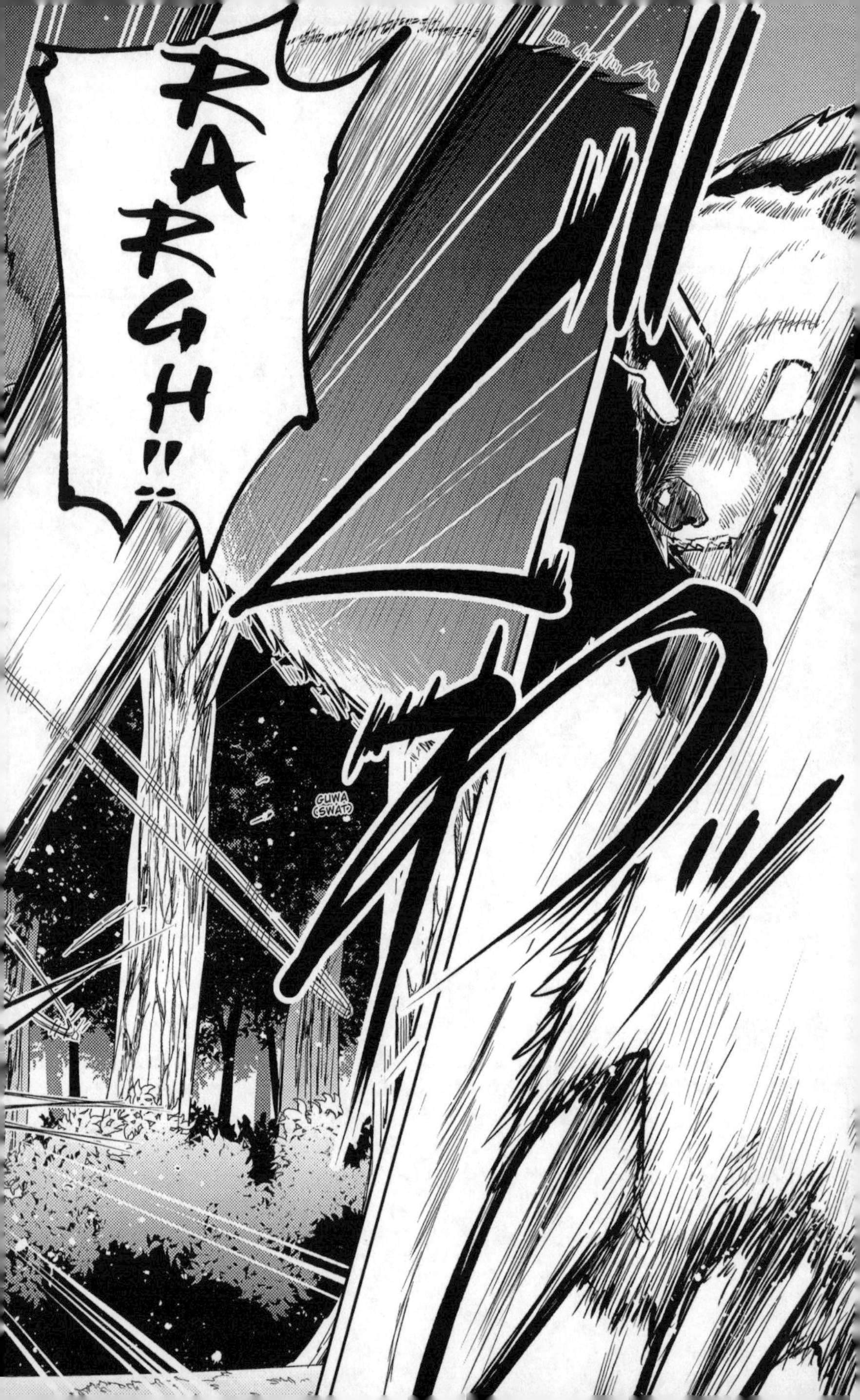
RARGH!!
GUWA (SWAT)

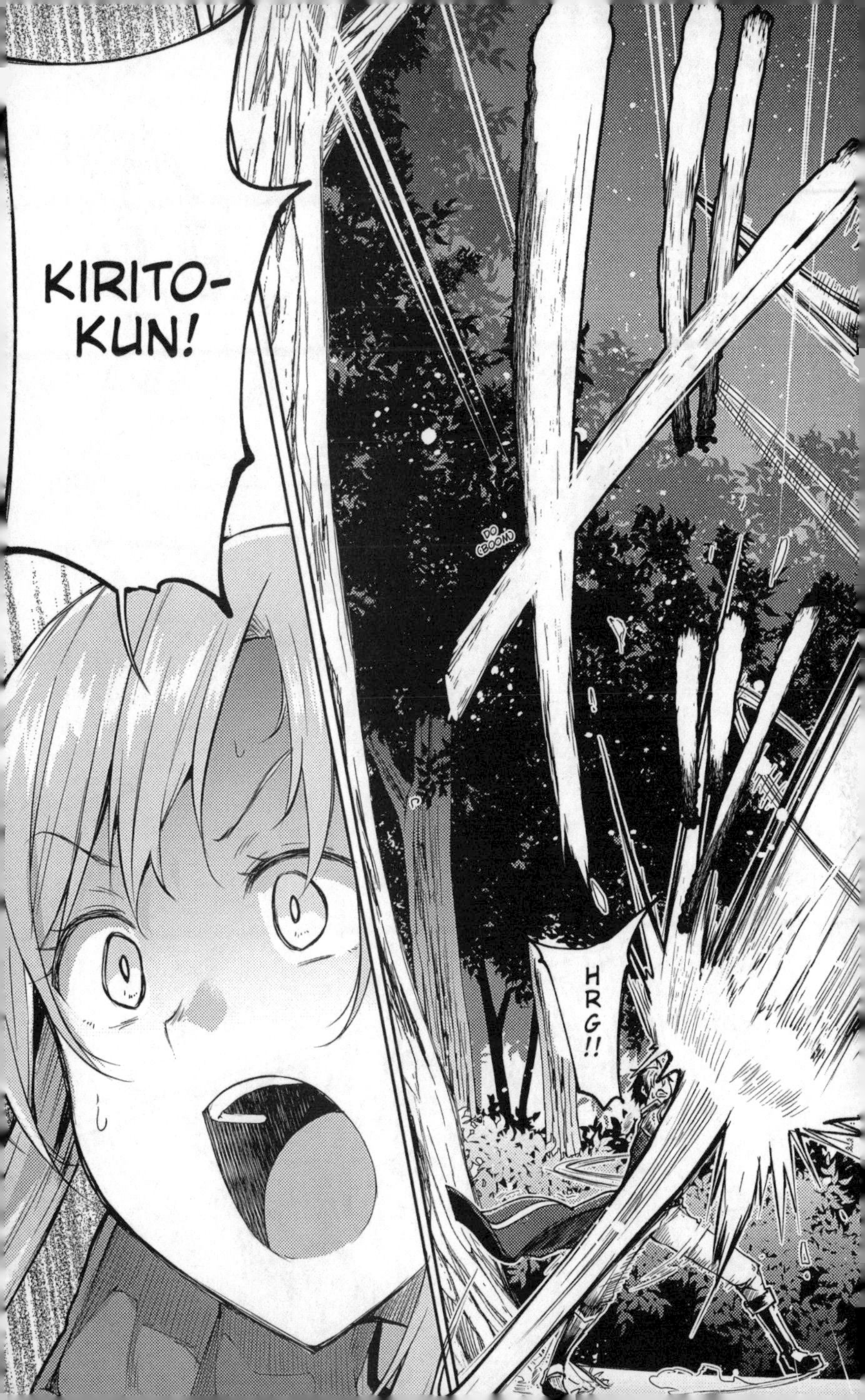
KIRITO-KUN!
DO (BOOM)
HRG!!

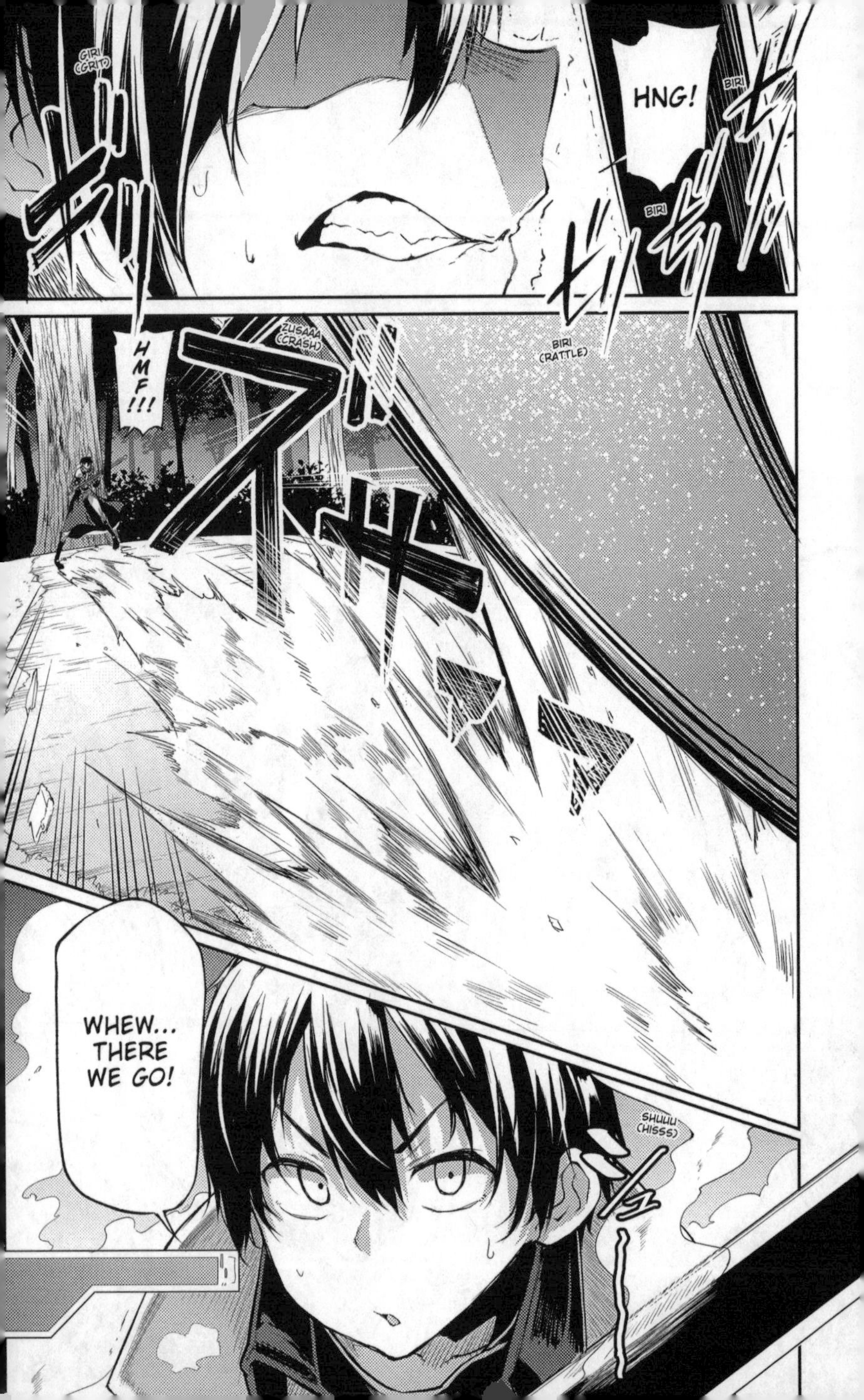
BIRI
HNG!
BIRI
GIRI (GRIT)
BIRI (RATTLE)
ZUSAAA (CRASH)
HMF!!!
SHUUU (HISSS)
WHEW... THERE WE GO!

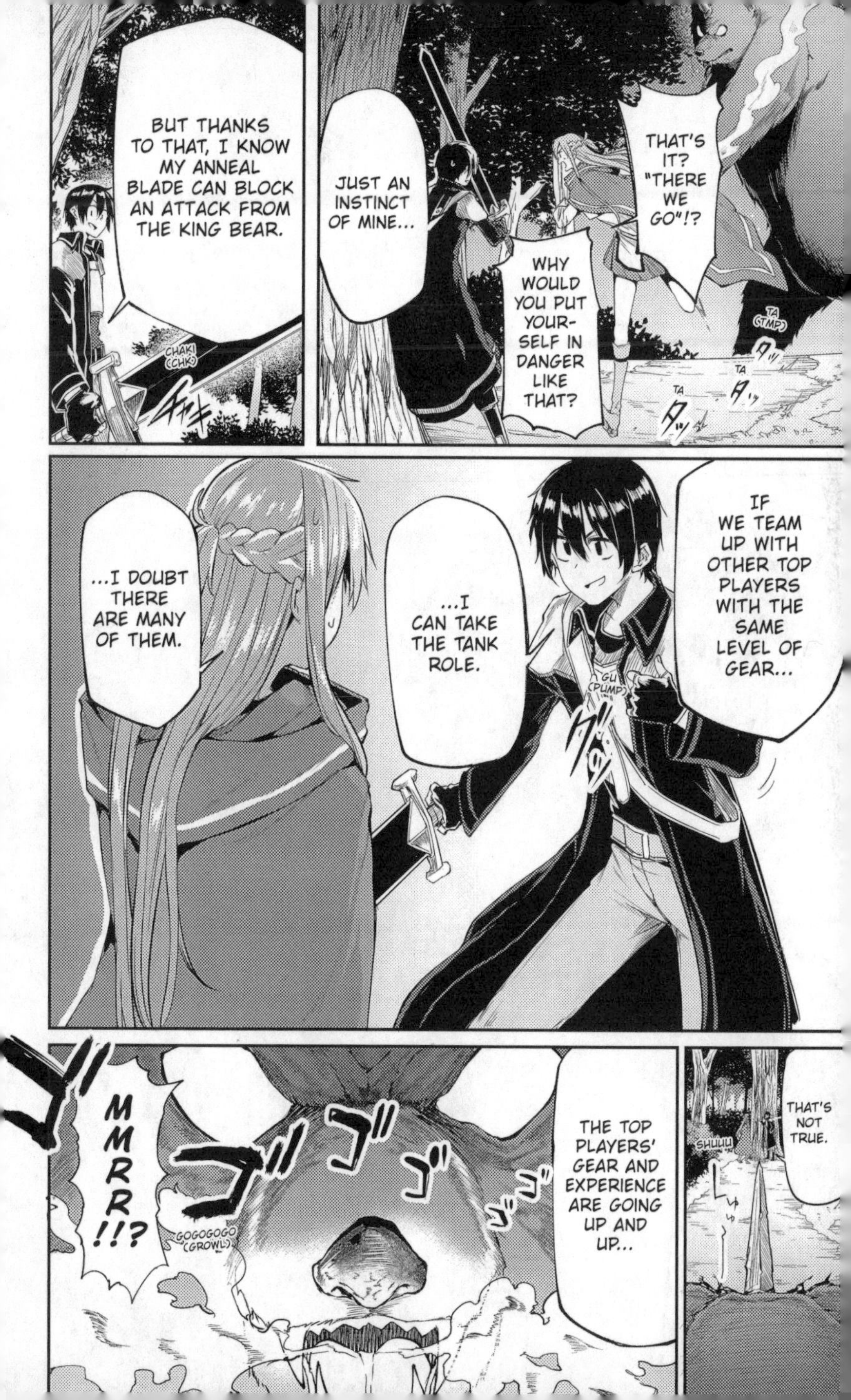
THAT'S IT? "THERE WE GO"!?
WHY WOULD YOU PUT YOURSELF IN DANGER LIKE THAT?
JUST AN INSTINCT OF MINE...
TA (TMP)
TA
TA
BUT THANKS TO THAT, I KNOW MY ANNEAL BLADE CAN BLOCK AN ATTACK FROM THE KING BEAR.
CHAKI (CHK)
IF WE TEAM UP WITH OTHER TOP PLAYERS WITH THE SAME LEVEL OF GEAR...
...I CAN TAKE THE TANK ROLE.
GU (PUMP)
...I DOUBT THERE ARE MANY OF THEM.
THAT'S NOT TRUE.
SHUUU
THE TOP PLAYERS' GEAR AND EXPERIENCE ARE GOING UP AND UP...
GOGOGOGO (GROWL)
MMRR!!?

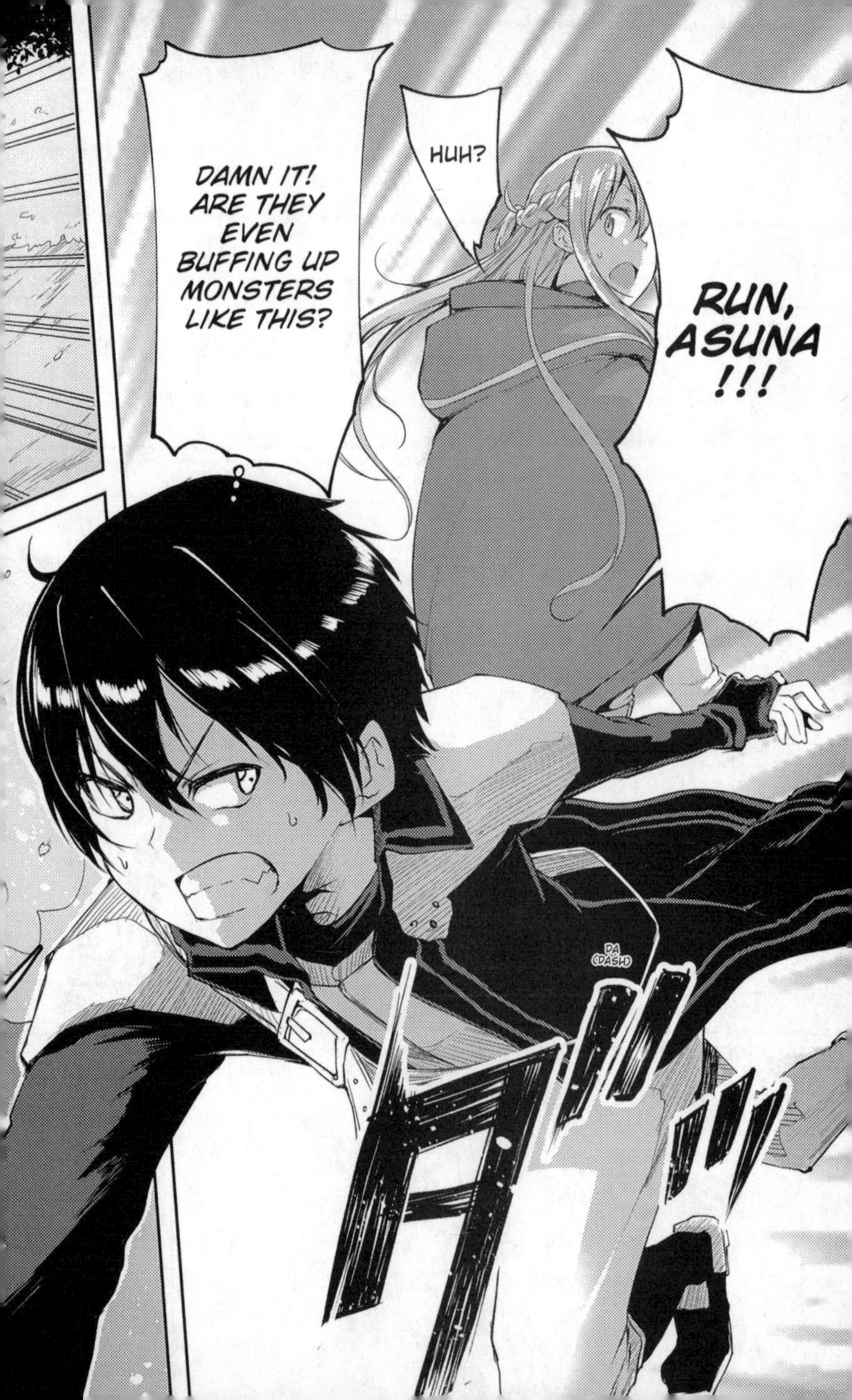
RUN, ASUNA!!!
HUH?
DAMN IT! ARE THEY EVEN BUFFING UP MONSTERS LIKE THIS?
DA (DASH)

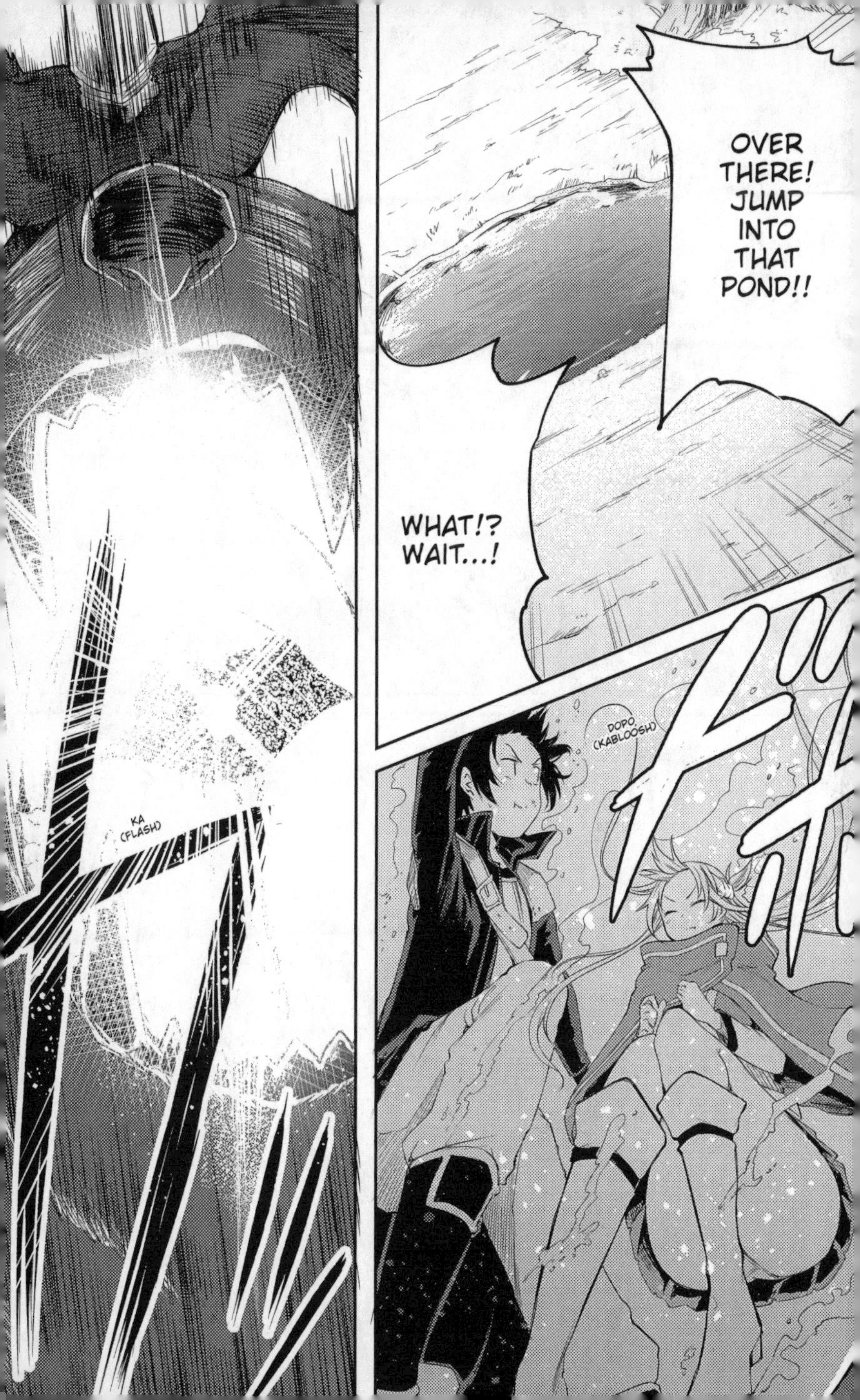
OVER THERE! JUMP INTO THAT POND!!
WHAT!? WAIT...!
DOPO (KABLOOSH)
KA (FLASH)

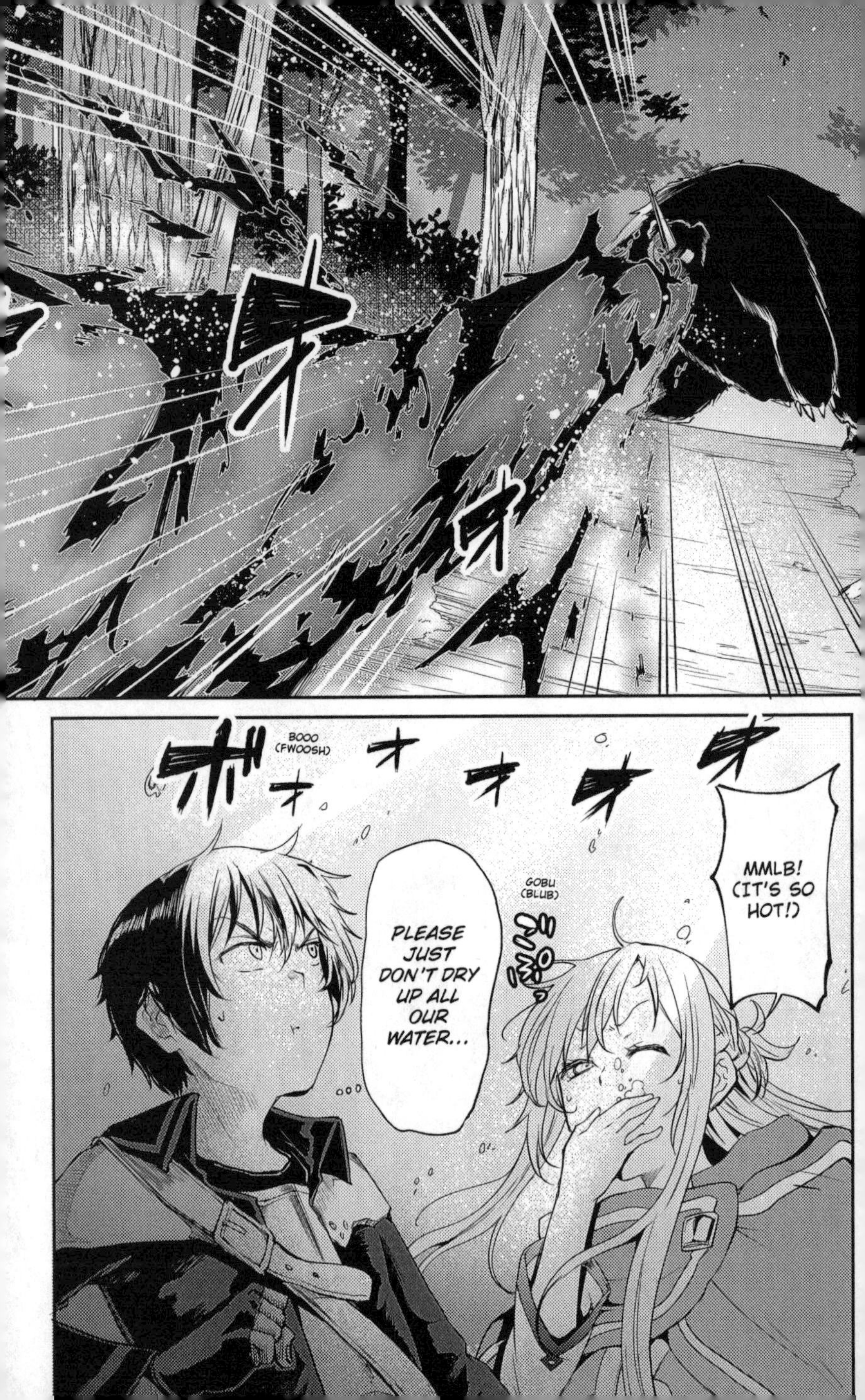
BOOO
(FWOOSH)
MMLB!
(IT'S SO
HOT!)
GOBU
(BLUB)
PLEASE JUST DON'T DRY UP ALL OUR WATER...

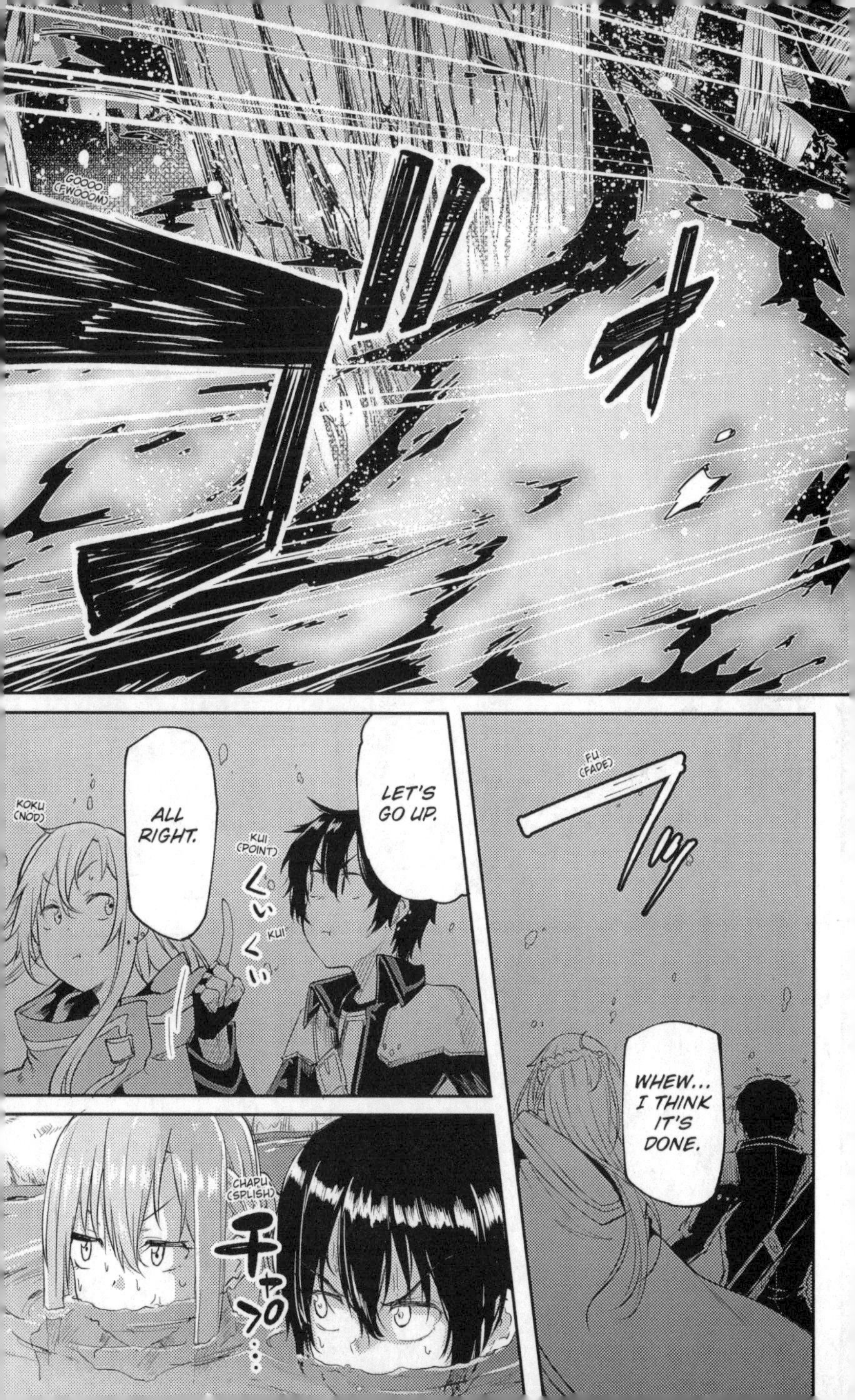
GOOOO (FWOOOM)
FU (FADE)
WHEW... I THINK IT'S DONE.
LET'S GO UP.
ALL RIGHT.
KUI (POINT)
くいくい
KUI
KOKU (NOD)
CHAPU (SPLISH)

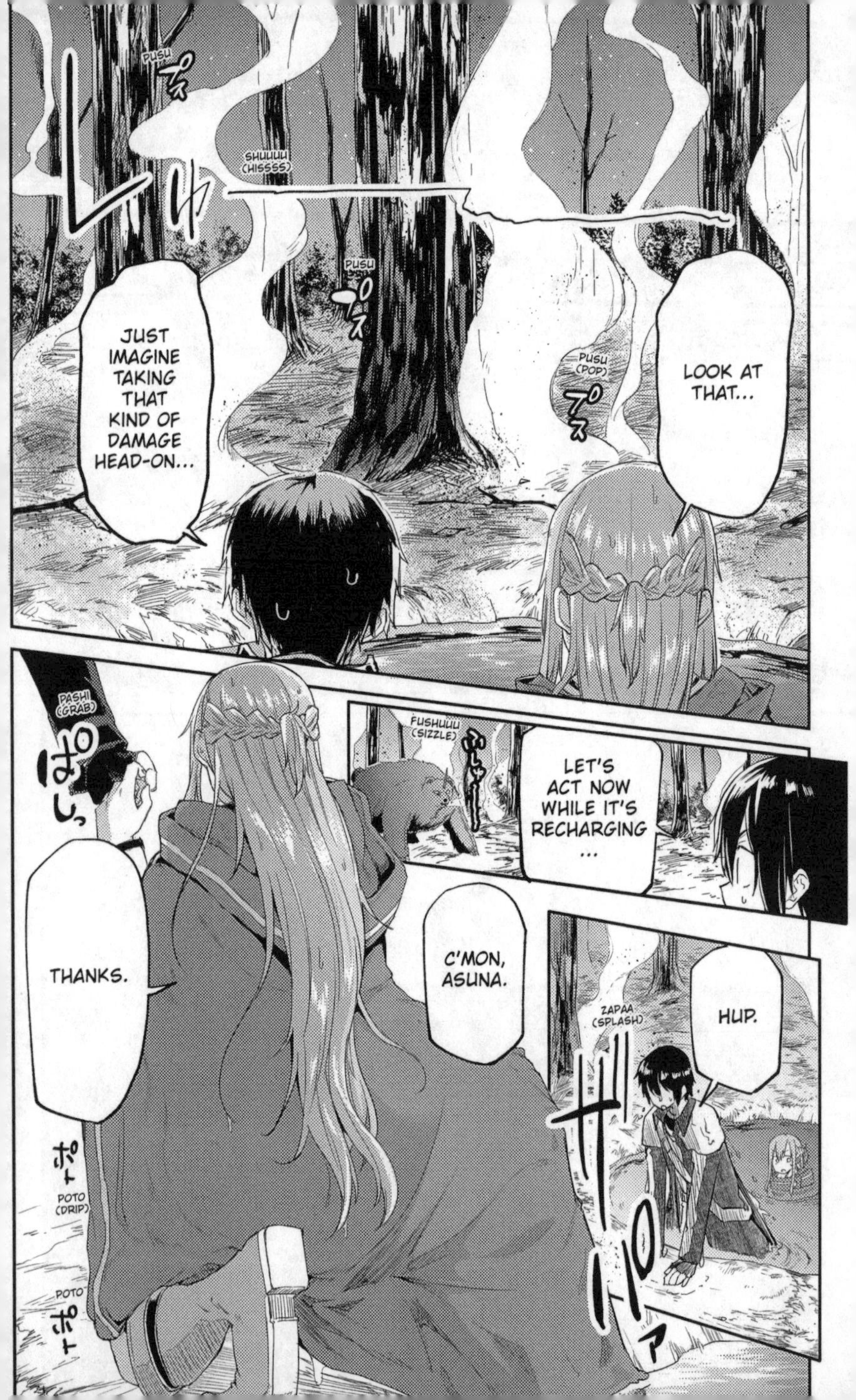
PUSU
SHUUUU (HISSSS)
LOOK AT THAT...
PUSU (POP)
PUSU
JUST IMAGINE TAKING THAT KIND OF DAMAGE HEAD-ON...
LET'S ACT NOW WHILE IT'S RECHARGING ...
FUSHUUU (SIZZLE)
HUP.
ZAPAA (SPLASH)
C'MON, ASUNA.
PASHI (GRAB)
THANKS.
POTO (DRIP)
POTO

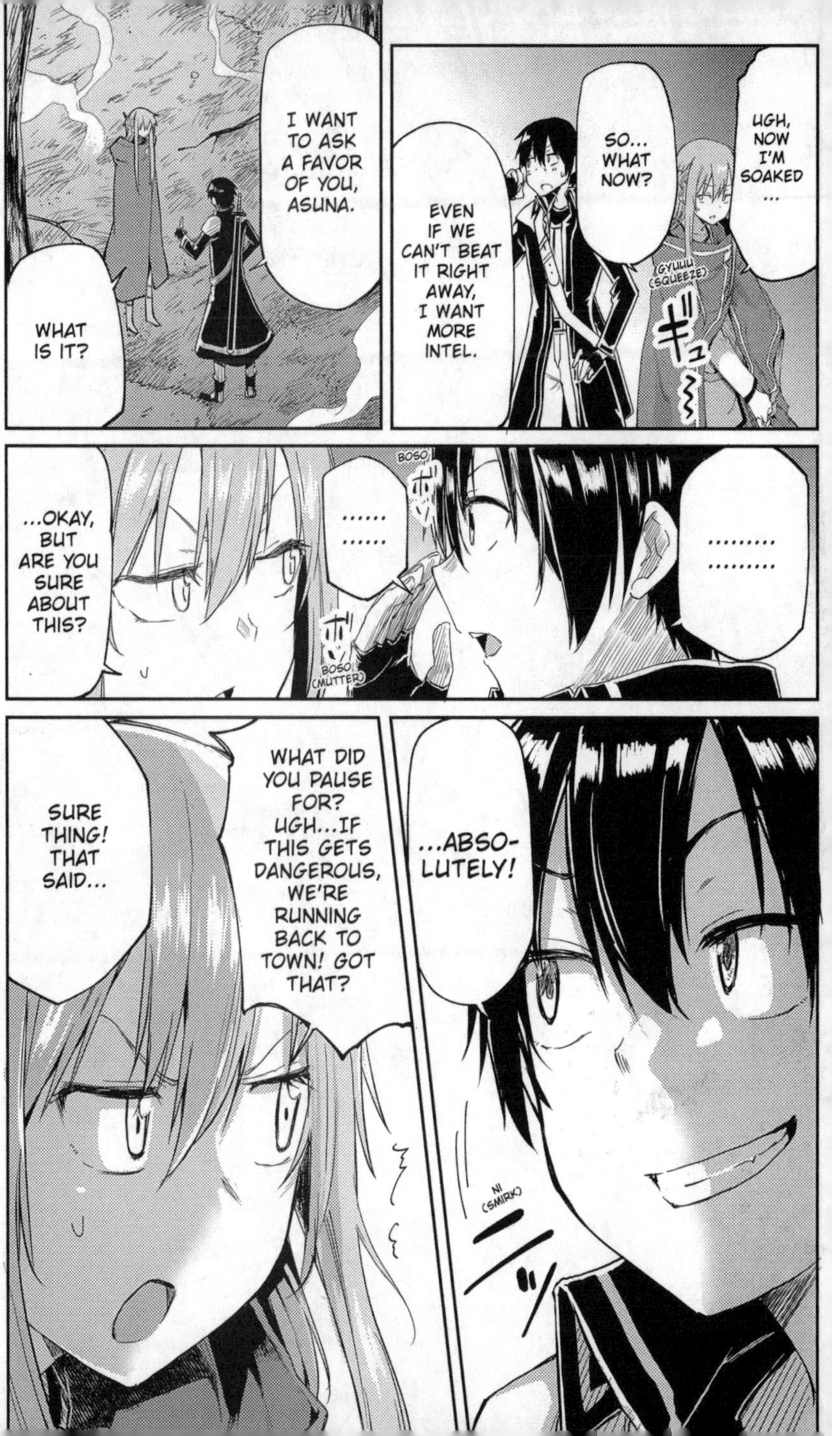
UGH, NOW I'M SOAKED...
GYUUU (SQUEEZE)
ギュ~
SO... WHAT NOW?
EVEN IF WE CAN'T BEAT IT RIGHT AWAY, I WANT MORE INTEL.
I WANT TO ASK A FAVOR OF YOU, ASUNA.
WHAT IS IT?
....
....
BOSO
ボソ
......
......
ボソ
BOSO (MUTTER)
...OKAY, BUT ARE YOU SURE ABOUT THIS?
...ABSO-LUTELY!
NI (SMIRK)
WHAT DID YOU PAUSE FOR? UGH...IF THIS GETS DANGEROUS, WE'RE RUNNING BACK TO TOWN! GOT THAT?
SURE THING! THAT SAID...

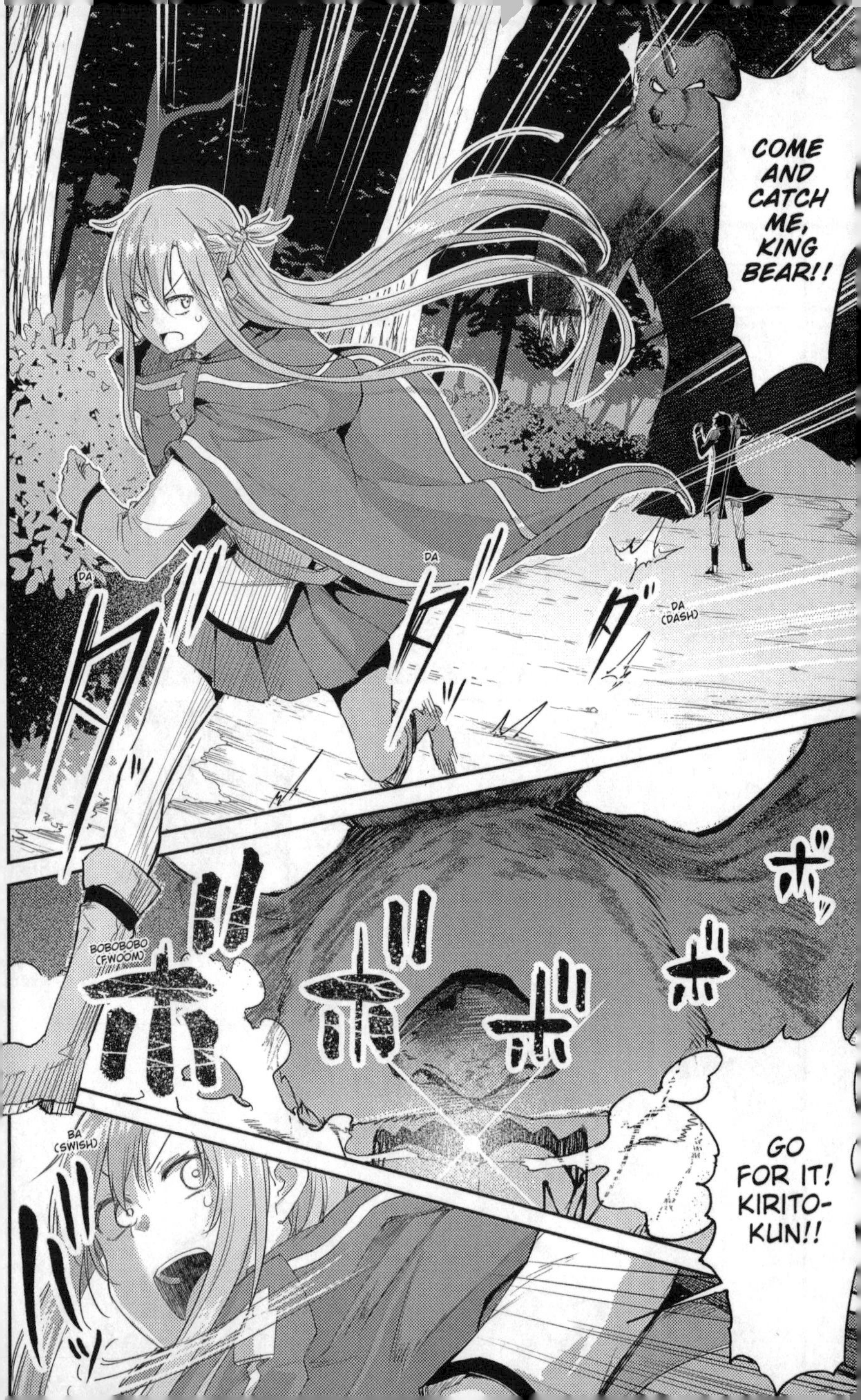
COME AND CATCH ME, KING BEAR!!
DA (DASH)
DA
DA
BOBOBOBO (FWOOM)
GO FOR IT! KIRITO-KUN!!
BA (SWISH)

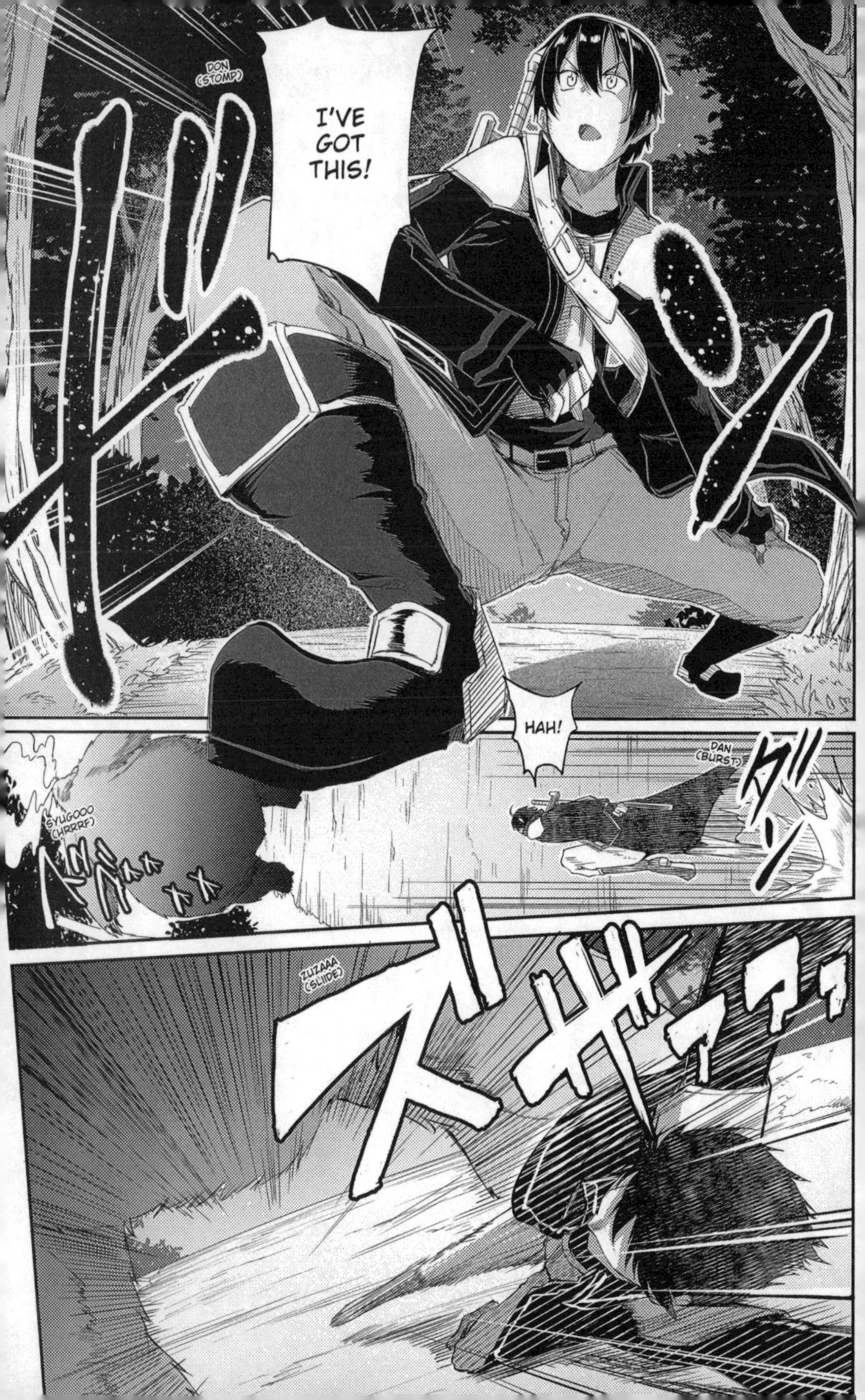
I'VE GOT THIS!
DON (STOMP)
DAN (BURST)
HAH!
SYUGOOO (HRRRF)
ZUZAAA (SLIIDE)

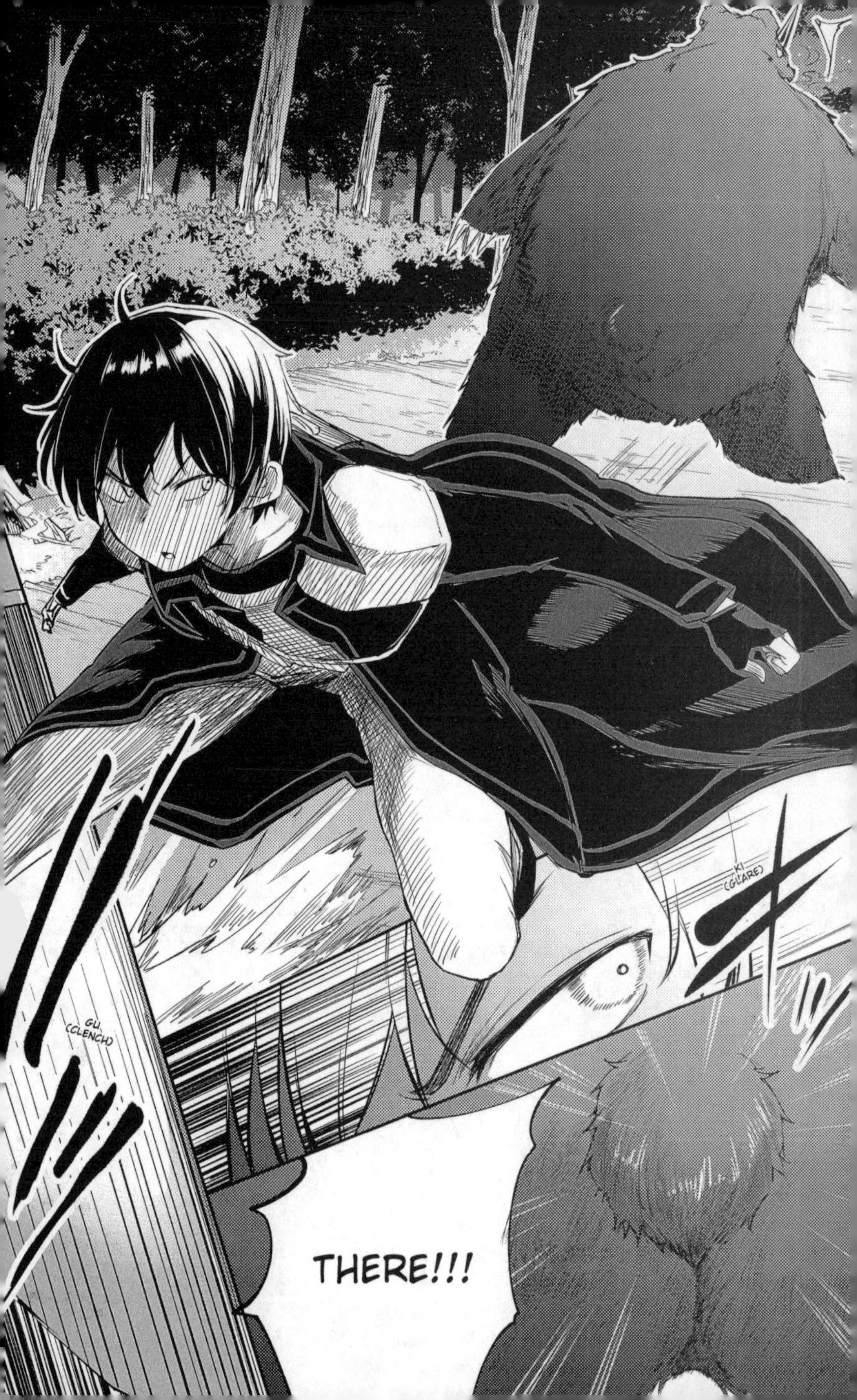
KI (GLARE)
GU (CLENCH)
THERE!!!

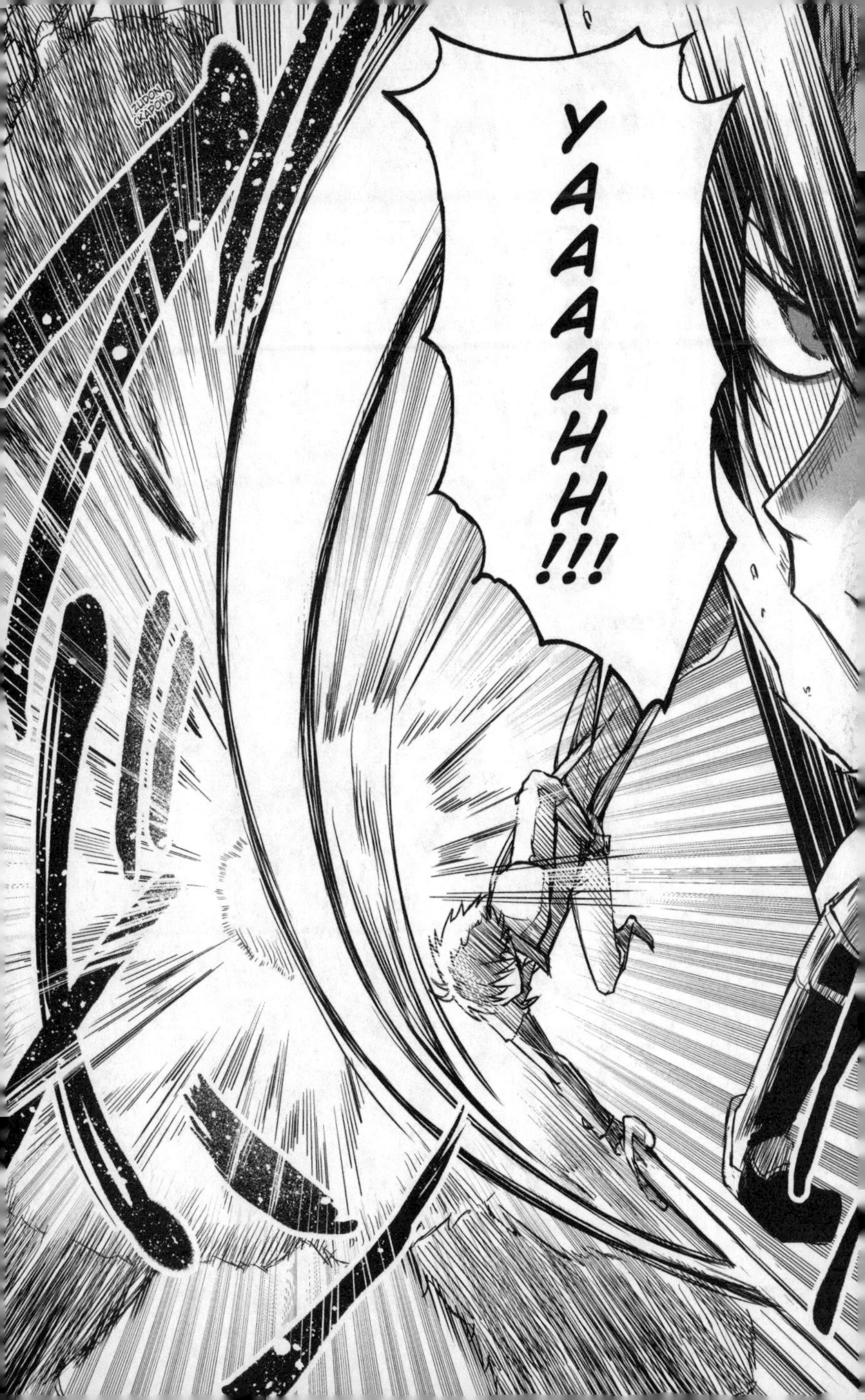
YAAAAHH!!!
ZUDON (KAPOW)

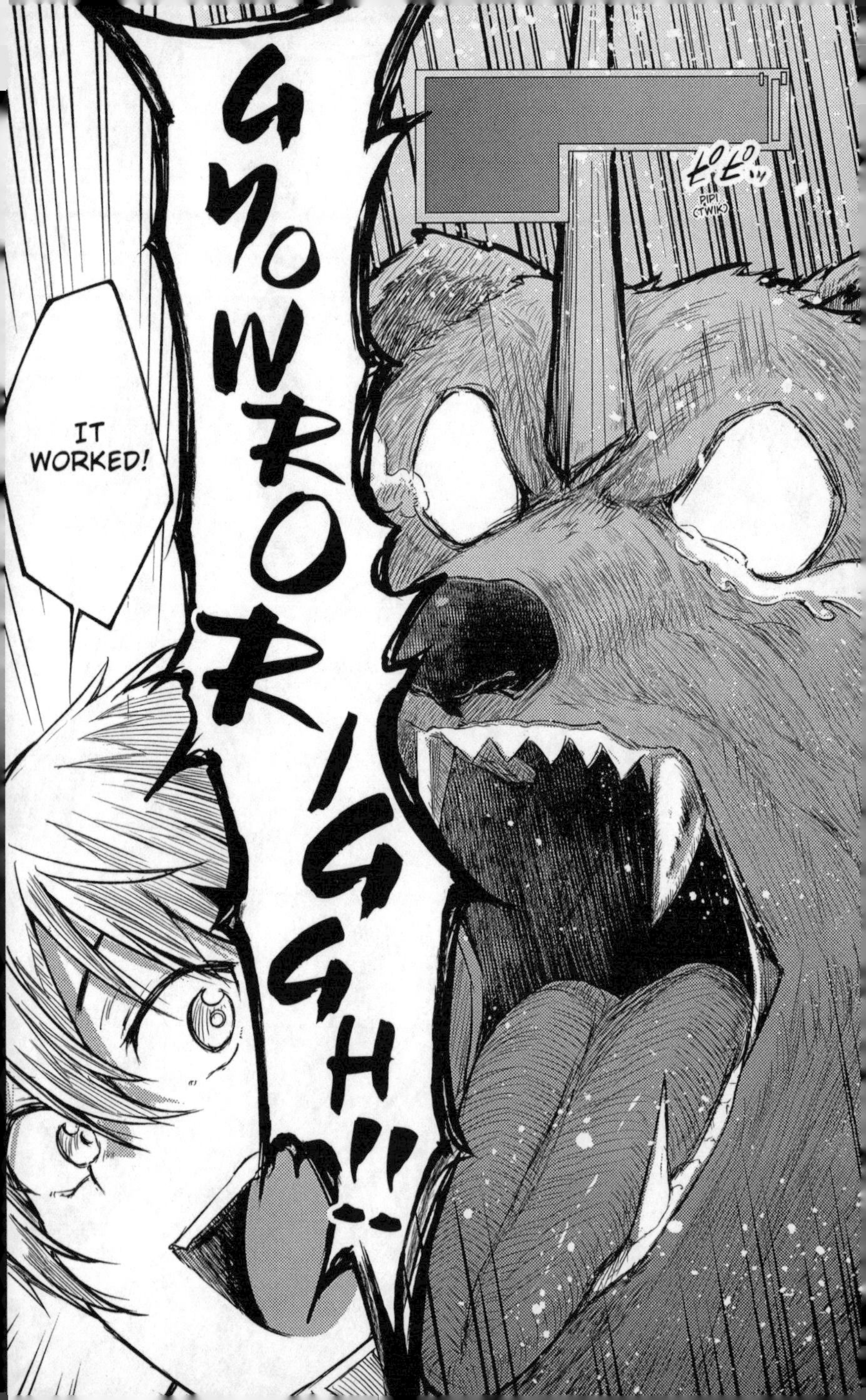
PIPI (TWIK)
GROWRORGGH!!
IT WORKED!

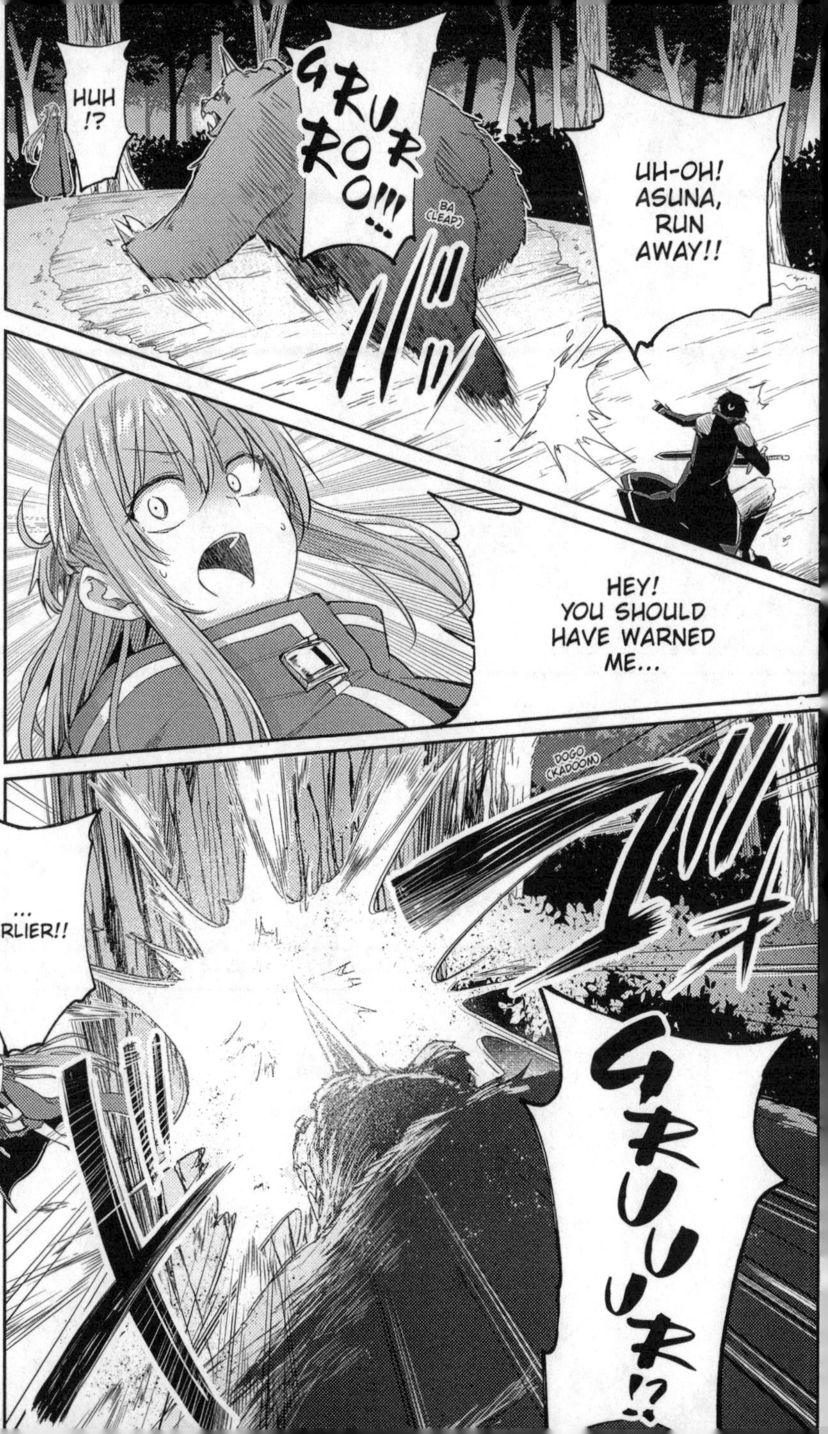
UH-OH! ASUNA, RUN AWAY!!
GRURORO!!!...
BA (LEAP)
HUH!?
HEY! YOU SHOULD HAVE WARNED ME...
DOGO (KADOOM)
GRUUUR!?
... EARLIER!!

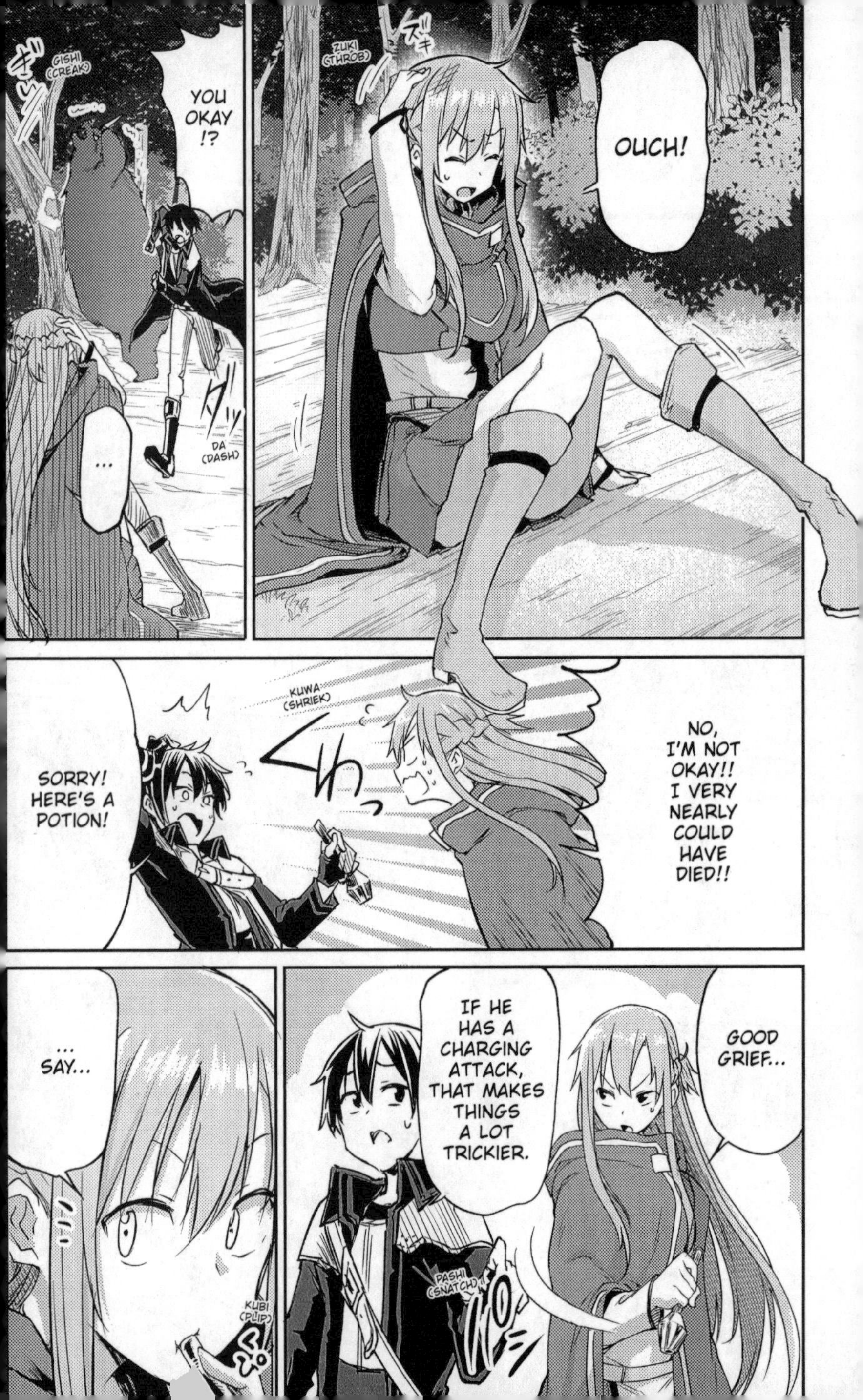
ZUKI (THROB)
OUCH!
GISHI (CREAK)
YOU OKAY !?
...
DA (DASH)
NO, I'M NOT OKAY!! I VERY NEARLY COULD HAVE DIED!!
KUWA (SHRIEK)
SORRY! HERE'S A POTION!
GOOD GRIEF...
IF HE HAS A CHARGING ATTACK, THAT MAKES THINGS A LOT TRICKIER.
PASHI (SNATCH)
... SAY...
KUBI (PLIP)

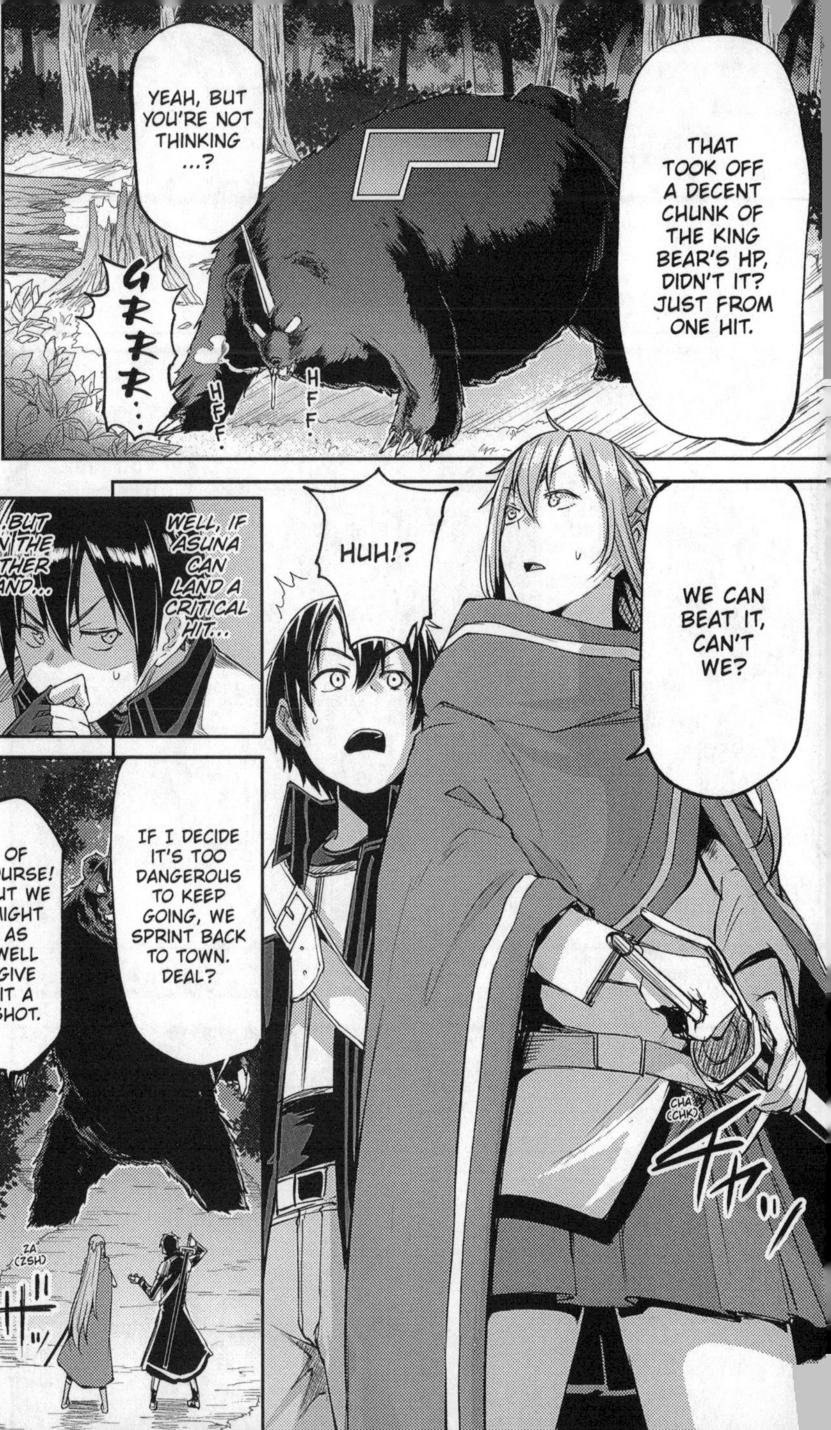
THAT TOOK OFF A DECENT CHUNK OF THE KING BEAR'S HP, DIDN'T IT? JUST FROM ONE HIT.
YEAH, BUT YOU'RE NOT THINKING ...?
GRRRR...
HFF
HFF.
WE CAN BEAT IT, CAN'T WE?
HUH!?
CHA (CHK)
WELL, IF ASUNA CAN LAND A CRITICAL HIT...
...BUT ON THE OTHER HAND...
IF I DECIDE IT'S TOO DANGEROUS TO KEEP GOING, WE SPRINT BACK TO TOWN. DEAL?
OF COURSE! BUT WE MIGHT AS WELL GIVE IT A SHOT.
ZA (ZSH)

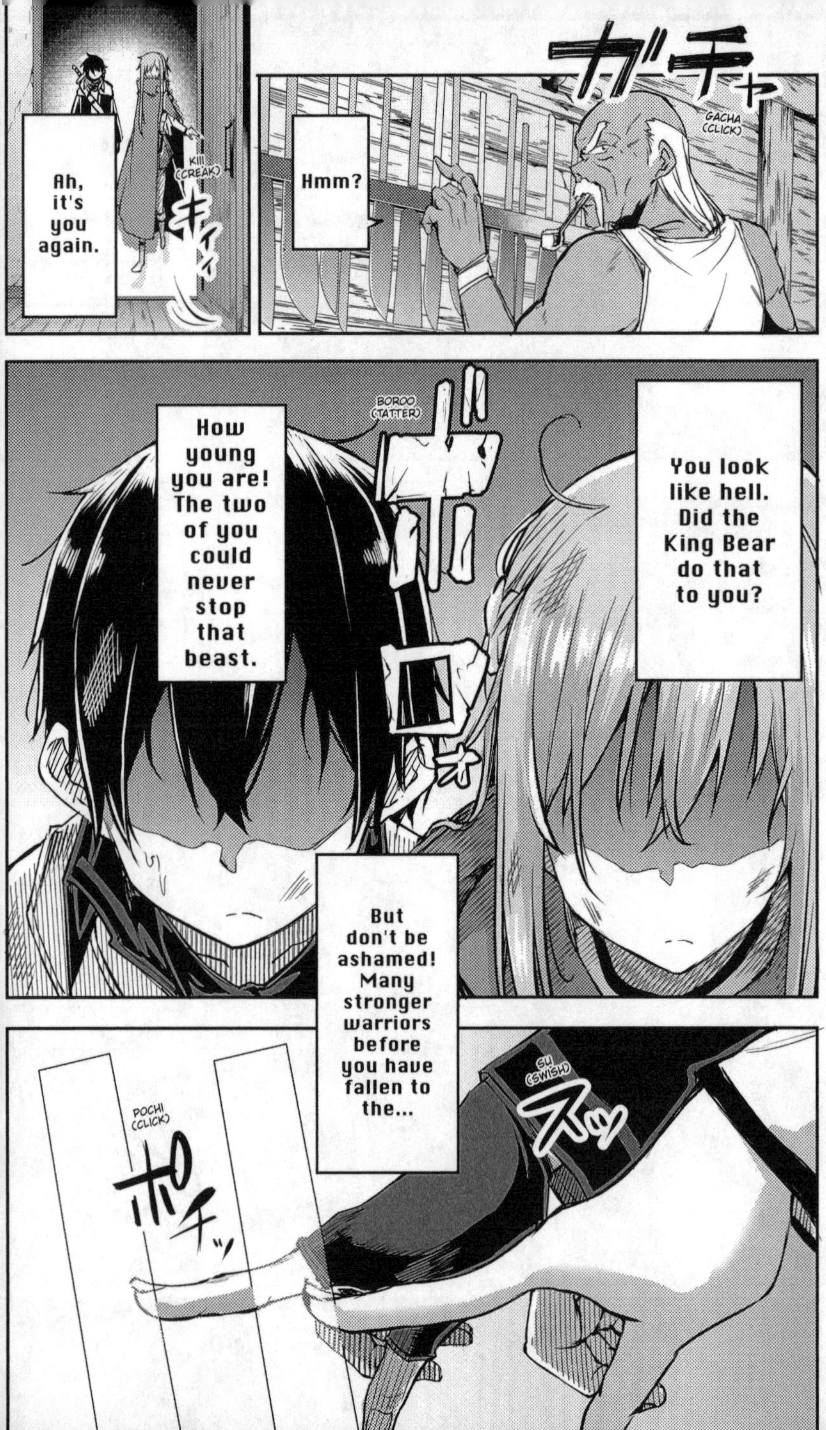

GACHA (CLICK)
Hmm?
KIII (CREAK)
Ah, it's you again.
You look like hell. Did the King Bear do that to you?
BOROO (TATTER)
How young you are! The two of you could never stop that beast.
But don't be ashamed! Many stronger warriors before you have fallen to the...
SU (SWISH)
POCHI (CLICK)

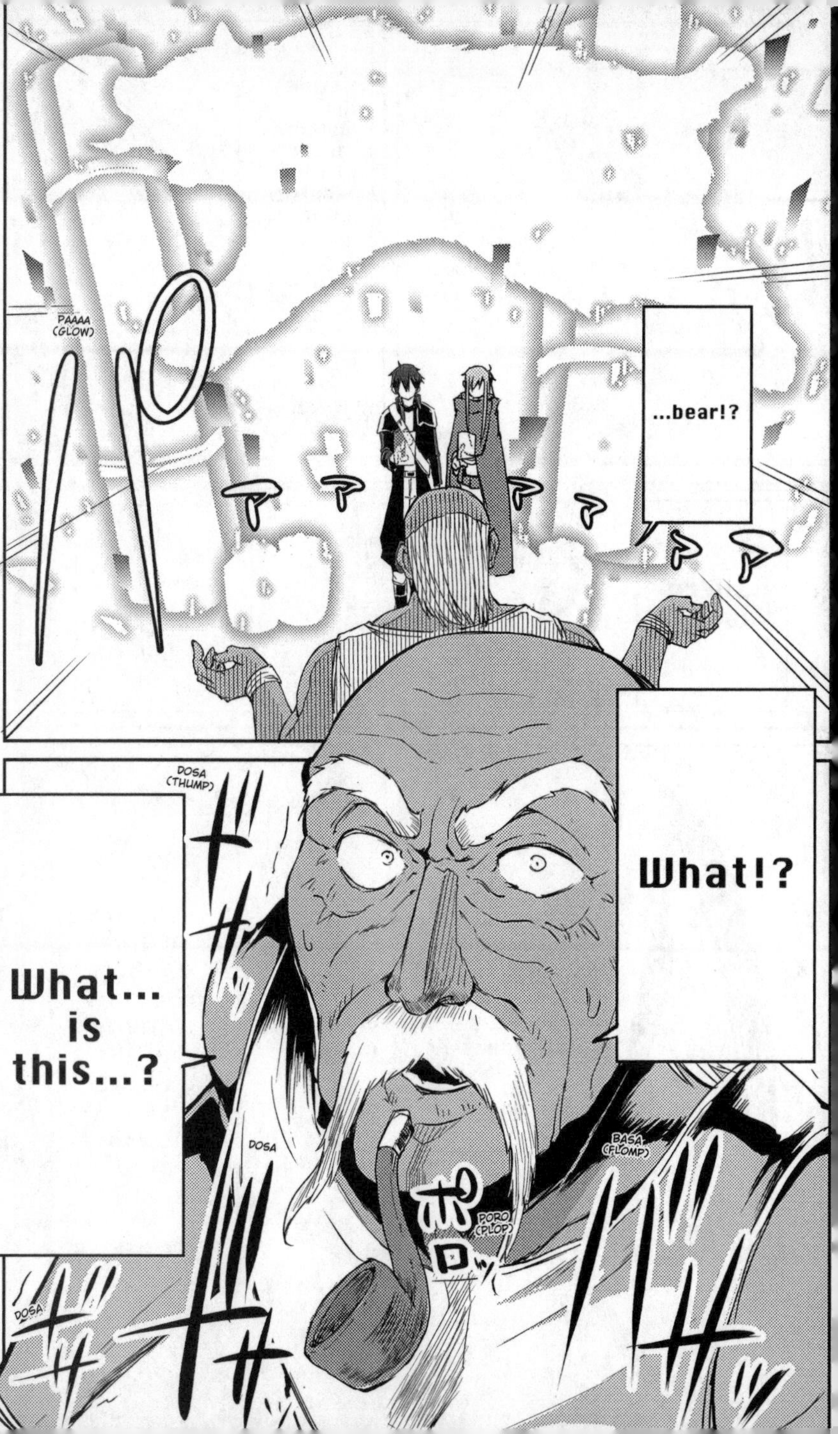
...bear!?
PAAAA (GLOW)
What!?
DOSA (THUMP)
What... is this...?
BASA (FLOMP)
DOSA
PORO (PLOP)
DOSA

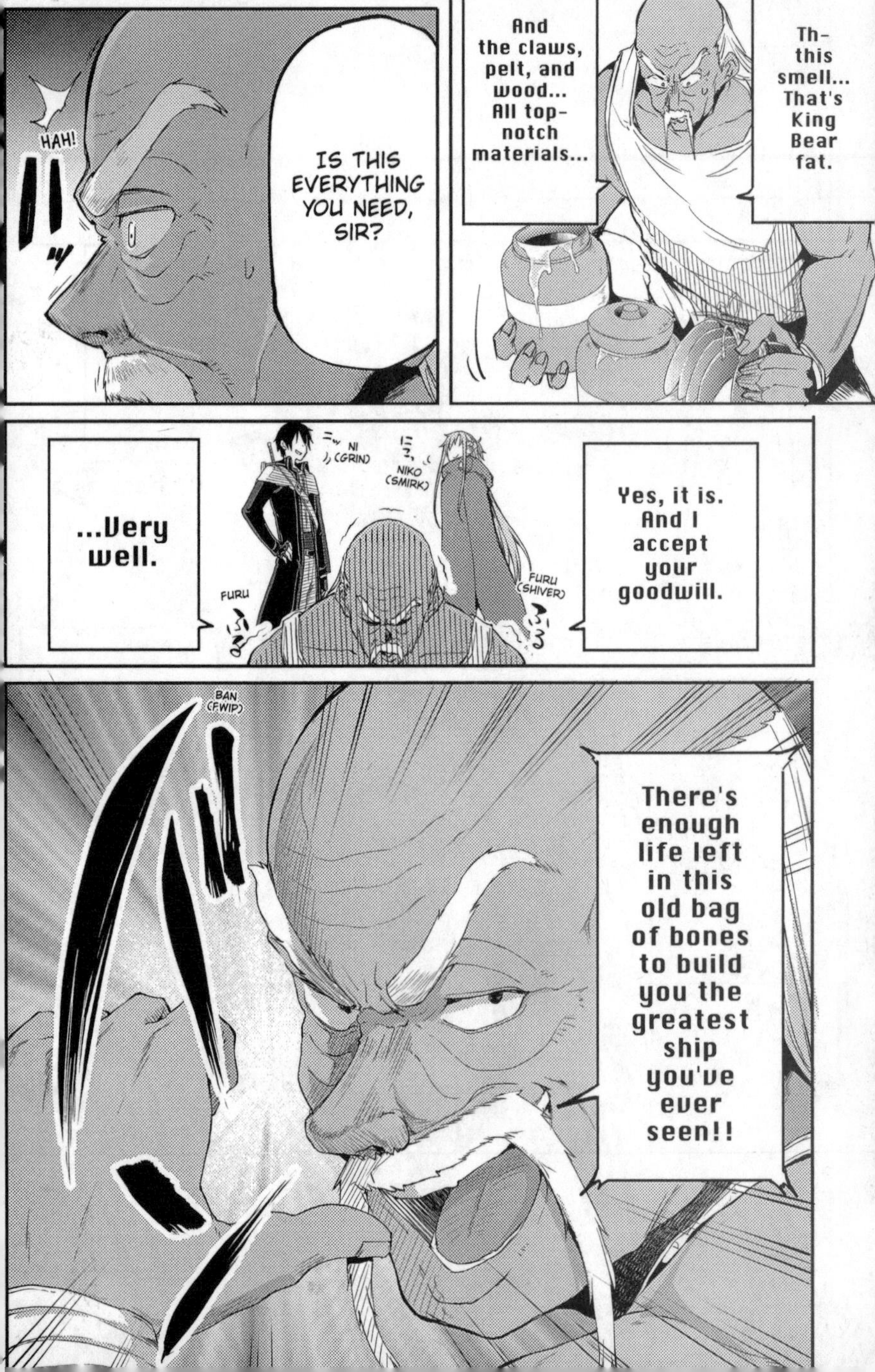
Th- this smell... That's King Bear fat.
And the claws, pelt, and wood... All top-notch materials...
IS THIS EVERYTHING YOU NEED, SIR?
HAH!
Yes, it is. And I accept your goodwill.
FURU (SHIVER)
NIKO (SMIRK)
NI (GRIN)
FURU
...Very well.
There's enough life left in this old bag of bones to build you the greatest ship you've ever seen!!
BAN (F.WIP)

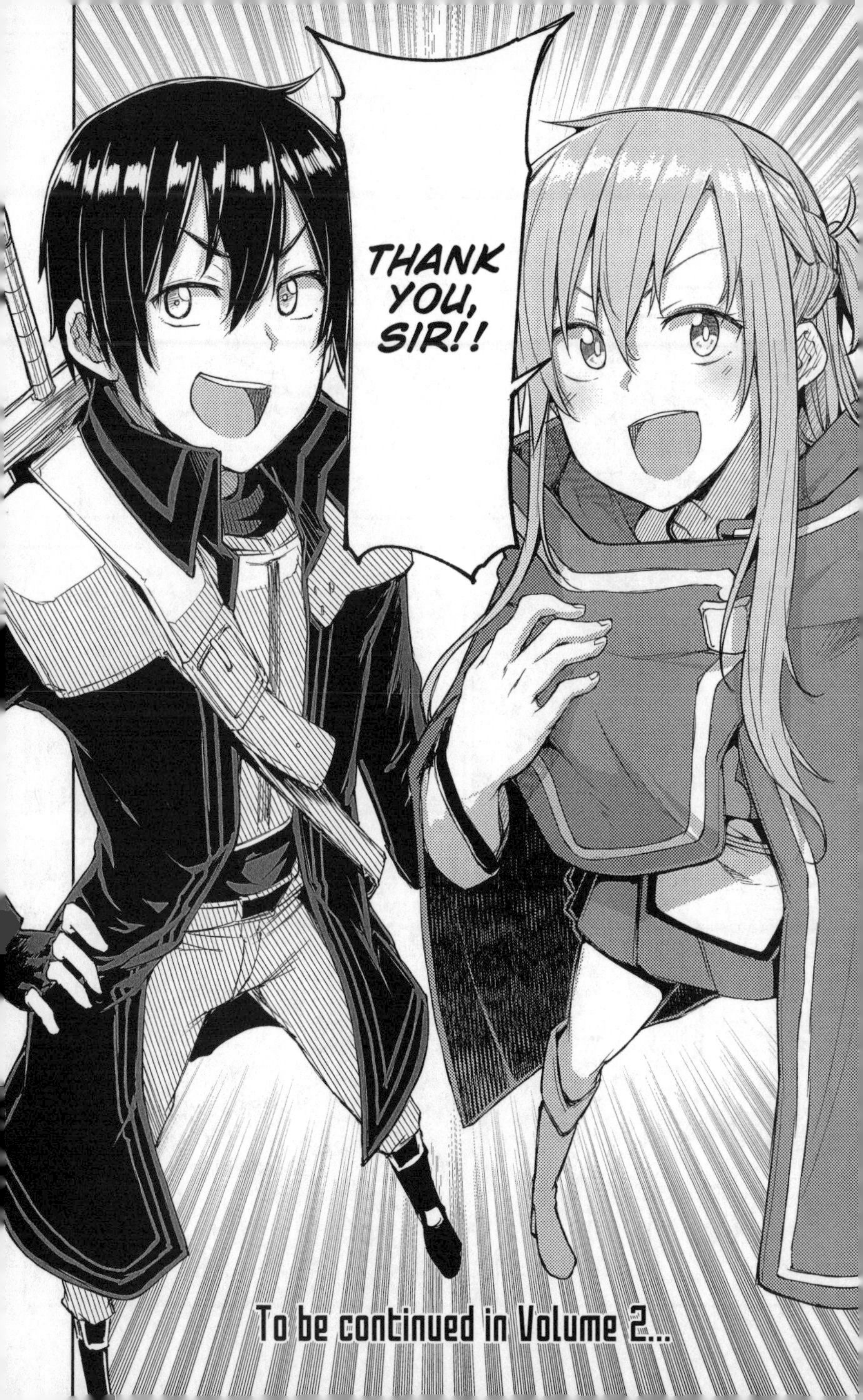
THANK YOU, SIR!!
To be continued in Volume 2...

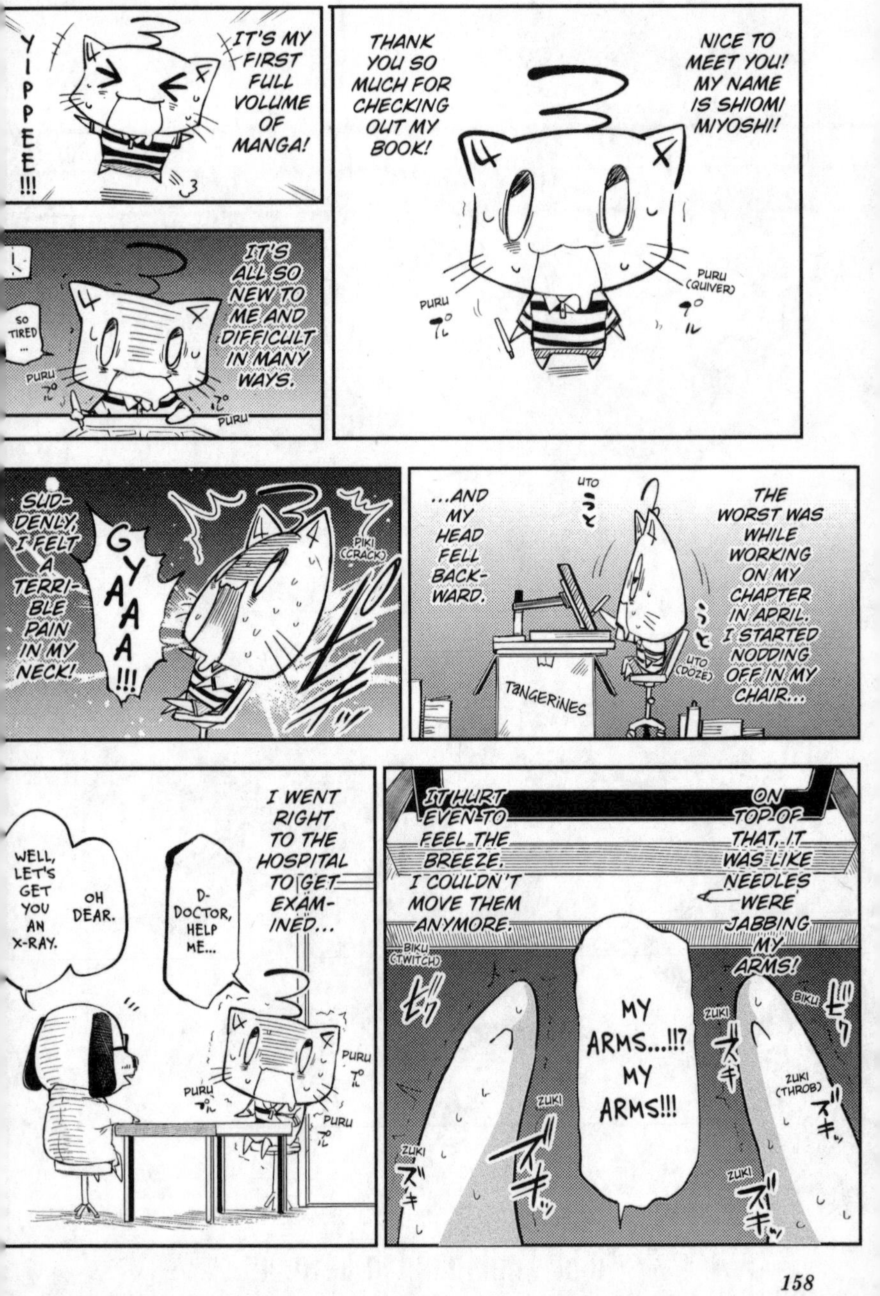
NICE TO MEET YOU! MY NAME IS SHIOMI MIYOSHI!
THANK YOU SO MUCH FOR CHECKING OUT MY BOOK!
PURU (QUIVER)
PURU
IT'S MY FIRST FULL VOLUME OF MANGA!
YIPPEE!!!
IT'S ALL SO NEW TO ME AND DIFFICULT IN MANY WAYS.
SO TIRED...
PURU
PURU
THE WORST WAS WHILE WORKING ON MY CHAPTER IN APRIL. I STARTED NODDING OFF IN MY CHAIR...
UTO
...AND MY HEAD FELL BACKWARD.
UTO (DOZE)
TANGERINES
SUDDENLY, I FELT A TERRIBLE PAIN IN MY NECK!
PIKI (CRACK)
GYAAAA!!!
ON TOP OF THAT, IT WAS LIKE NEEDLES WERE JABBING MY ARMS!
IT HURT EVEN TO FEEL THE BREEZE. I COULDN'T MOVE THEM ANYMORE.
BIKU
BIKU (TWITCH)
MY ARMS...!!? MY ARMS!!!
ZUKI
ZUKI (THROB)
ZUKI
ZUKI
ZUKI
I WENT RIGHT TO THE HOSPITAL TO GET EXAMINED...
D-DOCTOR, HELP ME...
OH DEAR.
WELL, LET'S GET YOU AN X-RAY.
PURU
PURU
PURU

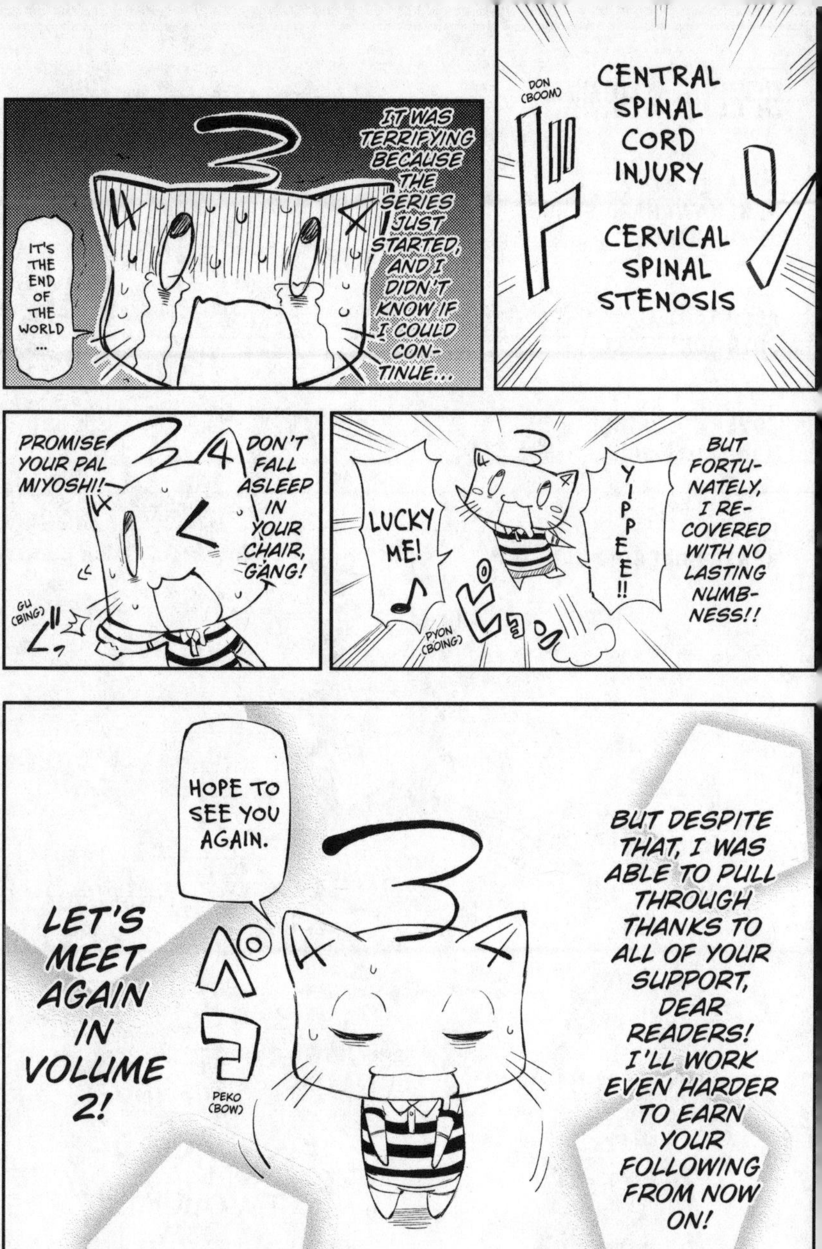
DON (BOOM)
CENTRAL SPINAL CORD INJURY
CERVICAL SPINAL STENOSIS
IT WAS TERRIFYING BECAUSE THE SERIES JUST STARTED, AND I DIDN'T KNOW IF I COULD CON-TINUE...
IT'S THE END OF THE WORLD...
BUT FORTU-NATELY, I RE-COVERED WITH NO LASTING NUMB-NESS!!
YIPPEE!!
LUCKY ME!
PYON (BOING)
DON'T FALL ASLEEP IN YOUR CHAIR, GANG!
PROMISE YOUR PAL MIYOSHI!
GU (BING)
BUT DESPITE THAT, I WAS ABLE TO PULL THROUGH THANKS TO ALL OF YOUR SUPPORT, DEAR READERS! I'LL WORK EVEN HARDER TO EARN YOUR FOLLOWING FROM NOW ON!
HOPE TO SEE YOU AGAIN.
PEKO (BOW)
LET'S MEET AGAIN IN VOLUME 2!

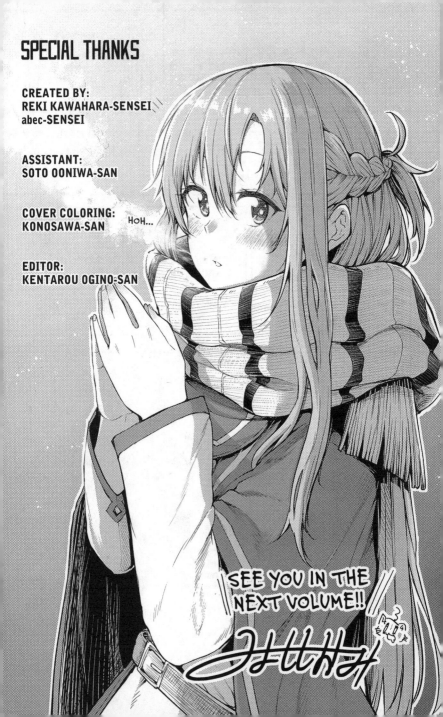

SPECIAL THANKS

CREATED BY:
REKI KAWAHARA-SENSEI
abec-SENSEI

ASSISTANT:
SOTO OONIWA-SAN

COVER COLORING:
KONOSAWA-SAN

EDITOR:
KENTAROU OGINO-SAN

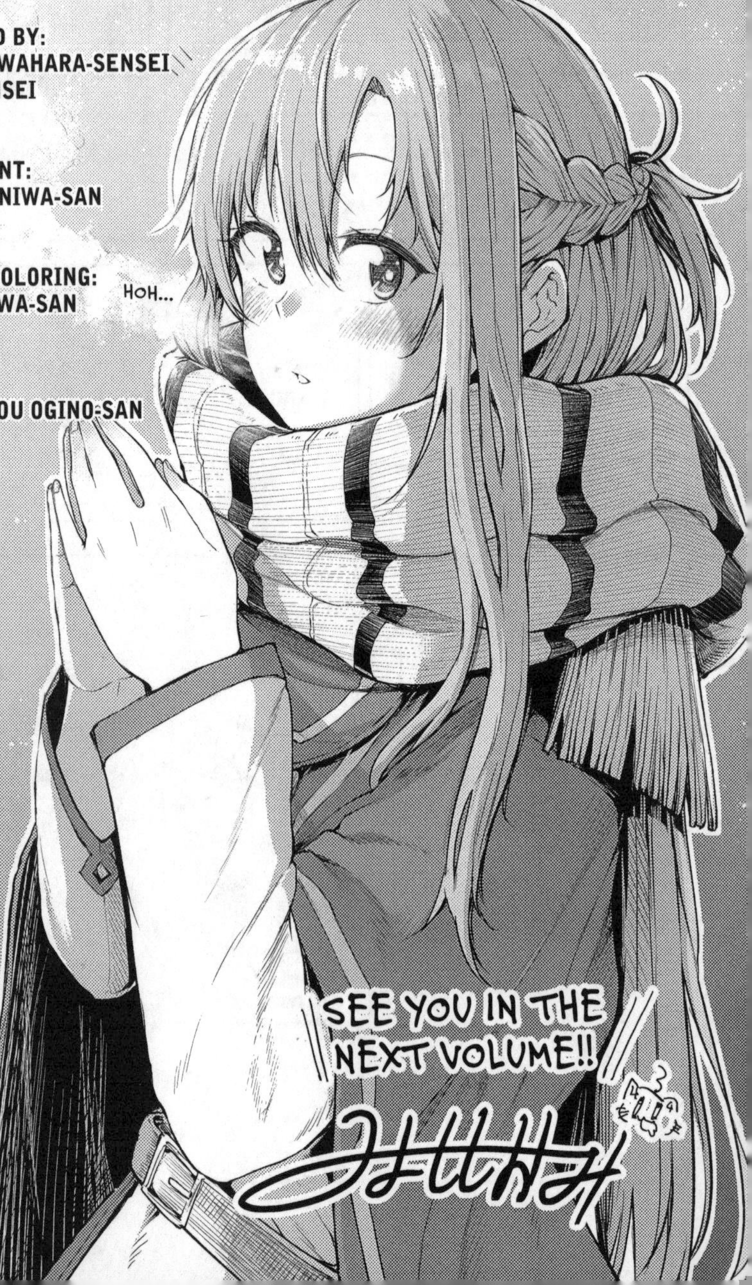
HOH...
SEE YOU IN THE NEXT VOLUME!!